D0969987

SPARKNOTES
101

Philosophy

SPARK PUBLISHING

SPARKNOTES is a registered trademark of SparkNotes LLC

Spark Educational Publishing
A Division of Barnes & Noble Publishing
120 Fifth Avenue
New York, NY 10011
www.sparknotes.com

ISBN-13: 978-1-4114-0029-0
ISBN-10: 1-4114-0029-1

Please submit changes or report errors to
www.sparknotes.com/errors

Printed and bound in the United States.

Library of Congress Cataloging-in-Publication Data

SparkNotes 101 philosophy.
    p. cm.
  Includes bibliographical references and index.
  ISBN 1-4114-0029-1
  1. Philosophy--Textbooks. I. Title: SparkNotes one hundred one philosophy. II. Title: SparkNotes one hundred and one philosophy. III. Title: One hundred one philosophy. IV. Title: One hundred and one philosophy.
  B74.S63 2005
  100--dc22

Contents

A Note from SparkNotes

Welcome to the *SparkNotes 101* series! This book will help you succeed in your introductory college course in Philosophy. We cover the nineteen major philosophers who have had the greatest impact on Western thought and who are studied most often in Philosophy courses.

Every component of this study guide has been designed to help you process the material more quickly and score higher on your exams. Here are some quick tips and explanations to help you get the most out of this book:

Introduction: Before moving on to the chapters on each philosopher, you may want to get a broader view of the field of philosophy. The Introduction discusses five major areas of philosophical study and the major questions and concepts that come up.

Chapters 1–19: Each chapter provides a complete overview of a philosopher's major works, as well as a concise overview of the philosopher's life and career. The key features of each chapter are:

- **Themes, Arguments & Ideas:** An explanation of the key concepts that run throughout each philosopher's work.

- **Summary & Analysis of Major Works:** A concise overview of each of the philosophers' major works, followed by a critical discussion of each work's significance.

- **A+ Student Essay:** It's the real thing. These essays will show you how to pull together the facts from the chapter and use them in a compelling argument. At the same time, these essays delve more deeply into particular topics in philosophy, enriching the content of each chapter.

Index: Use the index at the back of the book to make navigation easier or to look up specific works, ideas, arguments, etc.

We hope *SparkNotes 101: Philosophy* helps you, comforts you, and occasionally saves your butt! Your input makes us better. Let us know what you think or how we can improve this book at ***www.sparknotes.com/comments***.

Introduction

Philosophy is the systematic study of ideas, especially those that are considered to be basic or fundamental. Philosophy is both a tool for uncovering knowledge and a body of knowledge itself—a tradition of learning and study stretching from Plato's Academy to the modern university.

At an early stage in the history of Western philosophy, the word *philosophy* was synonymous with learning and referred to any systematic study. The earliest Greek philosophers were also the first mathematicians, physicists, biologists, astronomers, psychologists, and political theorists. Today, philosophy refers more specifically to the critical study of five major topics:

- Epistemology
- Metaphysics
- Ethics
- Political Philosophy
- Logic

Within each of these areas there are typically many schools of thought, some rooted in the ancient world, others of more modern origin. In addition, there is a major divide today between Analytic philosophy—the primary methodology in the United States and Britain—and Continental philosophy—primarily studied, as the name suggests, in Continental Europe.

Epistemology

Epistemology is the study of knowledge—of what knowledge is, what we can know, and how we can know it. Epistemologists examine whether knowledge is absolute and objective, meaning there is one truth, or relative and subjective, meaning the truth depends on one's perspective. They also question how we can separate truth from falsity, and whether it is ever possible to obtain certain knowledge. If certainty is possible, what can we be certain about? If certainty is not possible, what sense can we make of the world?

Skepticism takes as its starting point the counterintuitive notion that we cannot be certain of the world outside our mind or of the existence of other minds, and attempts to build our knowledge up from basic foundations. *Idealism* rejects this project and claims that our thoughts themselves actually constitute all that is real. Epistemologists also distinguish different types of knowledge, such as knowledge gained from our senses as opposed to knowledge of abstract ideas. *Empiricists* believe the former type should form the basis of all knowledge, and *rationalists* believe the latter type of knowledge to be more secure.

Metaphysics

Metaphysics is the branch of philosophy that asks fundamental questions about the nature of existence and reality. The discipline traces it roots back to the works of Aristotle, who first questioned what we could know about being and the concepts we use in scientific inquiry.

Ontology is the part of metaphysics that examines being and existence. One of the main questions for ontologists is what it means for something to be a physical object. For example, are objects completely defined by the properties they have, such as their color or size, or are those properties merely attached to some sort of prior substance? This question is known as the *problem of substance.* The *problem of universals* poses the challenge of how we understand properties such as color and size, to the extent that it is possible to consider these properties separately from specific objects. The *problem of identity* asks how an object can change in some respects but still remain the same thing.

Metaphysics also examines the nature of the mind as opposed to physical substance, and in particular whether the mind is essentially physical. *Monism* is the school of thought that the mind is not separate from physical reality, while *Dualism* refers to the belief that mind and body are qualitatively different things. Finally, metaphysics is also concerned with the question of whether God exists, as well as questions about the nature of space and time.

Ethics

Ethics is the branch of philosophy concerned with morality and how we should act. *Meta-ethics* is the study of the nature of moral concepts and ethical statements. Meta-ethics addresses such questions as whether ethical statements can be true or false, and whether moral codes ought to be absolute or relative to a culture or individual. *Normative ethics* is concerned with uncovering general ethical rules. Some philosophers, such as Hume and Rousseau, have focused on the role of passion and feeling in this pursuit, while others, such as Kant, have focused on the role of reason. Normative ethicists disagree on which such rules should take into account.

Deontology is the view that ethics should address whether particular actions are good or bad in and of themselves, regardless of the consequences that result from these actions. *Consequentialism*, a contrasting school, holds that the consequences of an action should factor into whether the action ought to be carried out. *Utilitarianism*, the view that the most moral action is the one that produces the greatest good for the greatest number of people, is an example of a consequentialist theory. Modern philosophy is increasingly concerned with *applied ethics*, in which general ethical theories are applied to specific disciplines, such as law and medicine.

Political Philosophy

Political philosophy is the branch of philosophy concerned with different systems of political organization, relationships between the people, state and government, and the nature and legitimacy of political authority. Much modern political philosophy springs from the work of a few Enlightenment philosophers: Hobbes, Locke, and Rousseau. These thinkers held very different beliefs about the nature of human beings considered apart from society, but all of them believed that the legitimacy of government authority ultimately rested on a *social contract* between the ruled and ruler. Hobbes believed that this contract was necessary to protect men from others' darker tendencies; Locke to protect *natural rights* such as life, liberty, and property; and Rousseau to ensure as much freedom as possible so that people could live closer to their natural state. Other philosophers, such as Plato and More, have argued for certain systems of government by describing *utopias*, or societies under ideal governments.

Logic

Logic is the branch of philosophy that examines how we expand our knowledge by building rationally upon what we already know. Logic attempts to clarify and systematize principles or patterns of reasoning, argument, and inference so that we can expand our knowledge without introducing any false beliefs. The syllogism, first pointed out by Aristotle, provides a good example of one of these valid patterns:

All men are mortal.

Socrates is a man.

Therefore, Socrates is mortal.

This is an example of a *deductive* argument, one of the two main types of arguments that logicians study. This argument is deductive because the truth of its premises or assumptions (the first two lines above) guarantees the truth of its conclusion. *Inductive* arguments, on the other hand, do not have this property. Instead, they are generalizations from particular instances to broad rules. For example, an inductive argument might conclude that all men are mortal because all men observed in the world thus far have died. As logic has progressed, logicians have come up with more elaborate systems for representing knowledge and reasoning, often employing symbols rather than natural language. Careful examination of these systems and their properties comprises much of the logical work being done today.

Plato

(c.427–c.347 B.C.)

THEMES, ARGUMENTS & IDEAS
- Dialogue and Dialectic
- Combating the Relativism of the Sophists
- The Theory of Forms
- The Theory of the Tripartite Soul
- The Importance of Education

SUMMARY & ANALYSIS OF MAJOR WORKS
- *Apology*
- *Meno*
- *Phaedo*
- *Symposium*
- *Republic*

Plato was born around 427 B.C. into one of the most prominent families in Athens. As a youth, he found himself drawn to the enigmatic figure of Socrates, an ugly man of no particular wealth or prominence who wandered about the open places of Athens, engaging his fellow citizens in debate. Plato was enraptured by this peculiar man's ability to reduce the most pompous and self-confident aristocrats to a state of bewilderment, and he became Socrates' student.

Plato's family and friends expected him to pursue a political career, but a combination of events turned him decisively away from politics and into philosophy. He came of age during the Peloponnesian War between Athens and Sparta, the two superpowers of the ancient Greek world. The war ended in total defeat for Athens in 404 B.C. Sparta imposed a dictatorship of thirty tyrants, some of whom were Plato's relatives and Socrates' fellow students. The tyrants proved to be a corrupt lot and were soon removed, and Athenian democracy was restored. The new democratic government of Athens tried Socrates on charges of impiety and corrupting the youth of Athens, and they executed him in 399 B.C. Prompted by the failure of his own relatives to govern Athens properly, as well as by the failure of Athenian democracy as evidenced by its persecution of Socrates, the young Plato turned his back on the public life that awaited him.

Inspired by Socrates' example, Plato turned to philosophy. In honor of his beloved teacher, Plato wrote dialogues, recording the kinds of conversations Socrates had in public with his fellow Athenians. Around 388, Plato traveled to Syracuse in Sicily, where he studied Pythagorean philosophy. Soon after his return to Athens, he founded the Academy, where he and like-minded thinkers discussed philosophy and mathematics. Aristotle was among the young students who came to learn from Plato. The Academy lasted in one form or another until A.D. 527 and has served as the prototype of the Western university system.

Plato spent the rest of his life at the Academy, except for two more visits to Syracuse in a failed attempt to mold that city's young tyrant into an ideal philosopher-king. The dialogues he wrote as a mature philosopher still mostly feature Socrates as the protagonist, but it may well be the case that many of the views discussed in these dialogues belong to Plato and not to the historical Socrates. Plato died in Athens at the age of eighty, duly recognized as one of the world's great philosophers.

Plato lived in a transitional period, both for Athens and for Greek civilization generally. As literacy became widespread among the educated classes, a new kind of thinking evolved. The Greeks started recording their history and philosophy, which allowed them to think critically about their past and their inherited wisdom. Religious rituals and myths about gods and titans seemed less convincing in this new worldview, and so a whole set of traditional values fell into doubt. Itinerant sophists traveled from city to city, preaching that morals are relative and offering to instruct young statesmen in the art of rhetoric and debate for a fee. Meanwhile, philosophers, no longer satisfied by the traditional explanations offered by myths, began searching for rational explanations of the world and our place in it. This search gave birth to the Western study of mathematics, science, psychology, and ethics, among other subjects.

Themes, Arguments & Ideas

DIALOGUE AND DIALECTIC

The dialogue form in which Plato writes is more than a mere literary device; it is an expression of Plato's understanding of the purpose and nature of philosophy. For Plato, philosophy is a process of constant questioning, and questioning necessarily takes the form of dialogue. Near the end of the *Phaedrus*, Socrates expresses his reservations about written texts, worrying that people will cease to think for themselves when they have someone else's thoughts written out in front of them. Plato took it upon himself to write his thoughts down anyway, but he was careful not to write them in such a way that we could easily assimilate his thoughts rather than thinking for ourselves. Many of the dialogues reach no definite conclusions, and those that do generally approach those conclusions by casting doubts and examining possible counterarguments. Plato cannot be there in person to share his thoughts with us, but he wants to ensure that we think them through ourselves.

In keeping with this emphasis on dialogue form, Plato develops an increasingly complex conception of dialectic, or logical argument, as the engine that drives philosophical investigations. In the early dialogues, dialectic consists of Socrates cross-examining and refuting his interlocutors until he brings them to a state of perplexity, or *aporia*. Beginning with the *Meno*, Plato recognizes that dialectic can lead people not only to recognize their errors but also to make positive discoveries, as Socrates does with the slave boy in the *Meno*. Plato is sufficiently impressed with the possibilities of the dialectic that, in the *Republic*, he makes it the highest achievement of his rigorous education program. The *Phaedrus* introduces a more systematic version of the dialectic, seeing it as a matter of "division and generalization," whereby we analyze concepts so as to understand the precise relations between them. This process of division and generalization becomes increasingly sophisticated throughout Plato's works, and we witness advanced versions of it in the *Parmenides* and the *Sophist*.

COMBATING THE RELATIVISM OF THE SOPHISTS

Plato considers the sophists to be one of the primary enemies of virtue, and he is merciless in his attacks on them. The sophists, who were relatively new in Plato's day, were a class of itinerant teachers who instructed young statesmen in the arts of rhetoric and debate for a fee. They taught that values are relative, so that the only measure of who is right is who comes out on top. Their teachings capitalized on a void left by the ancient myths and religion, which were falling out of fashion as Greek civilization moved toward a more rational worldview. The old values were losing their relevance, and there were no new values to replace them. Plato could see the danger this moral relativism posed for the state and for the people who lived in it, and his attacks on the sophists show up their hollow bravado that so many took for wisdom. Plato's Theory of Forms, and the whole enterprise of the *Republic*, can be read as an attempt to find a solid grounding for moral values in rational principles.

THE THEORY OF FORMS

The Theory of Forms maintains that two distinct levels of reality exist: the visible world of sights and sounds that we inhabit and the intelligible world of Forms that stands above the visible world and gives it being. For example, Plato maintains that in addition to being able to identify a beautiful person or a beautiful painting, we also have a general conception of Beauty itself, and we are able to identify the beauty in a person or a painting only because we have this conception of Beauty in the abstract. In other words, the beautiful things we can see are beautiful only because they participate in the more general Form of Beauty. This Form of Beauty is itself invisible, eternal, and unchanging, unlike the things in the visible world that can grow old and lose their beauty. The Theory of Forms envisions an entire world of such Forms, a world that exists outside of time and space, where Beauty, Justice, Courage, Temperance, and the like exist untarnished by the changes and imperfections of the visible world.

Plato's conception of Forms actually differs from dialogue to dialogue, and in certain respects it is never fully explained, so many aspects of the theory are open to interpretation. Forms are first introduced in the *Phaedo*, but in that dialogue the concept is simply referred to as something the participants are already familiar with, and the theory itself is not developed. Similarly, in the *Republic*, Plato relies on the concept of Forms as the basis of many of his arguments but feels no need to argue for the validity of the theory itself or to explain precisely what Forms are.

Commentators have been left with the task of explaining what Forms are and how visible objects participate in them, and there has been no shortage of disagreement. Some scholars advance the view that Forms are paradigms, perfect examples on which the imperfect world is modeled. Others interpret Forms as universals, so that the Form of Beauty, for example, is that quality that all beautiful things share. Yet others interpret Forms as "stuffs," the conglomeration of all instances of a quality in the visible world. Under this interpretation, we could say there is a little beauty in one person, a little beauty in another—all the beauty in the world put together is the Form of Beauty. Plato himself was aware of the ambiguities and inconsistencies in his Theory of Forms, as is evident from the incisive criticism he makes of his own theory in the *Parmenides*.

In essence, the Theory of Forms represents Plato's attempt to cultivate our capacity for abstract thought. Philosophy was a relatively new invention in Plato's day, and it competed with mythology, tragedy, and epic poetry as the primary means by which people could make sense of their place in the world. Like philosophy, art and mythology provide concepts that help us to understand ourselves, but art and mythology do so by appealing to our emotions and desires. Philosophy appeals to the intellect. The Theory of Forms differentiates theabstract world of thought from the world of the senses, where art and mythology operate Plato also argued that abstract thought is superior to the world of the senses. By investigating the world of Forms, Plato hopes to attain a greater knowledge.

THE THEORY OF THE TRIPARTITE SOUL

In the *Republic* and the *Phaedrus*, Plato describes the soul as divided into three parts, labeled *appetitive*, *spirited*, and *rational*. He offers this division partly as a way of explaining our psychological complexity and partly to provide a justification for philosophy as the highest of all pursuits, because it corresponds to the highest part of the soul—the rational part. We might feel the pull of these three parts when presented with a bowl of ice cream, a roast we accidentally overcooked ourselves, and a healthy salad. The appetitive part of our soul will crave the sensual pleasures it will derive from the ice cream, the spirited part of our soul will want to eat the charred roast out of a sense of pride in our own work, and the rational part of our soul will want to eat the salad as the healthiest of the three options. In proposing a tripartite soul, Plato acknowledges and seeks to explain the fact that we all experience inner conflict from time to time. We would be justified in seeing this theory as the starting point for psychology. However, Plato's theory seeks not only to explain inner conflict but also to present the rational part of the soul as superior. Philosophy is essentially the practice of refining and foregrounding our rationality.

THE IMPORTANCE OF EDUCATION FOR THE HEALTH OF THE STATE

In both the *Republic* and the *Laws,* Plato identifies education as one of the most important aspects of a healthy state. He lays out detailed education programs that start with exercises pregnant women should perform to ensure the health of the fetus, and he goes on to explain not only what children should study but also what values they should be exposed to and what kinds of art and physical exercise they should engage in. Plato apparently considered most of his fellow Athenians to be hopelessly corrupt, easily inflamed by hollow rhetoric, and seduced by easy pleasures. One can achieve only so much by arguing with a corrupt soul that a virtuous life is better. Instead, Plato recognizes the need to teach children from a young age to live virtuous lives and to seek wisdom. Plato thinks that a child's education is the last thing that should be left to chance or parental whim, since the young mind is so easily molded.

Summary & Analysis

APOLOGY

Summary

Socrates is brought to trial before the citizens of Athens, accused of failing to recognize the gods that are recognized by the state, inventing new deities, and corrupting the youth of Athens. He apologizes that his defense speech will be plain and straightforward, as he hasn't mastered the art of rhetoric employed by so many politicians. A defense speech in Greek is an *apologia*, which gives this dialogue its title.

Socrates first denies previous complaints against him: that he gives physical explanations of divine matters and that he charges a fee for teaching rhetoric. He challenges anyone to testify that he has ever made any positive claims about the heavens or earth or that he has charged a fee for his teaching.

Socrates surmises that his reputation may have come from a prophecy by the Oracle at Delphi, which proclaimed he was the wisest of all men. Socrates has always admitted he knows nothing, so he was puzzled by this prophecy. To test it, he first examined the supposedly wise politicians of Athens and, by questioning them, discovered that they were full of hot air and in fact knew nothing. Next he questioned the poets, only to find that they were less able than others to explain their own works, leading Socrates to infer that it is not wisdom but divine inspiration that guides their writing. Then he questioned the craftsmen, who are very skillful but similar to the politicians in thinking they know all sorts of things they don't know. Through all this questioning, Socrates earned many enemies but also concluded that he is wiser than everyone else because at least he knows that he knows nothing. He takes the Oracle as a command from Apollo to question men who think they are wise to show them that they are not.

Socrates calls forth Meletus, his chief accuser, and questions him about the charges he has laid. Socrates uses a fair bit of bullying and baiting and suggests that Meletus is confused about the teaching of virtue and that he contradicts himself in accusing Socrates both of atheism and of inventing new gods.

Socrates persists in his practice, even though his life is in danger, because he feels he has a duty to Apollo. If he fears death, he would be presuming to know what happens after death. Since he cannot know, it is foolish to fear it, and he shouldn't avoid acting justly because he's afraid of dying. The people of Athens, not Socrates, should fear a death sentence, since they'll be giving up Socrates' valuable service. Socrates compares himself to a gadfly, who stings the lazy horse that is Athens, provoking it into action. Socrates has stayed away from politics at the warning of an inner voice that keeps him from heading into danger, a voice he calls a "supernatural sign." A man like himself would never have lasted in politics, so he would have been prevented from offering his services to Athens.

In closing, Socrates points out that the youth he has supposedly corrupted, including Plato, are upright men who still stand by him. Not even the parents or family of these people claim Socrates is a corrupting influence.

The jury finds him guilty by a vote of 280 to 221, and Socrates is surprised only that the vote is so close. When asked to suggest a penalty for himself, Socrates first claims that if the punishment were just, he would be celebrated as a hero. More soberly, he rejects prison or exile, preferring death. He refuses to give up philosophizing, saying that the unexamined life is not worth living. Socrates is quite poor, but with the help of some of his richer friends, including Plato, he offers to pay a small fine.

The jury sentences Socrates to death, and he warns them they are mistaken in thinking that they can silence true and just criticism. They should try to live better, not kill off their critics.

Turning to his friends, Socrates points out that his "supernatural sign" did not warn him against any of his actions on this day, so perhaps his death is not such a bad thing. He concludes that a good man should fear neither life nor death. He asks his friends to take care of his three sons and bravely heads off to prison.

Analysis

The *Apology* is one of the most eloquent and enduring defenses of the philosophical life. The Greek word *apologia* literally means "a speech made by a defendant in court," but Socrates turns his *apologia* into a defense not just against the crimes of which he has been accused but of his entire way of living. Early in the speech, Socrates contrasts himself with politicians, poets, and craftsmen, as well as with the sophists and the generations of philosophers who have preceded him. By contrasting himself with these other figures—and, importantly, distancing himself from the sophists and earlier philosophers—Socrates stakes a unique claim for what philosophy is or should be. For him, philosophy is not about building up knowledge but rather questioning and clarifying knowledge. While the role of philosophy has changed over the millennia, the task of philosophy is still a central concern. While physicists or economists may study facts and explore new knowledge, philosophers are concerned primarily with understanding what our claims to knowledge amount to and what we ought to do with what we know.

For Socrates, philosophy is not an occupation or a hobby but rather a way of life. His goal, and the goal of any philosopher who follows him, is to seek truth and live justly. This conception of the philosophical life is perhaps best expressed in the phrase "the unexamined life is not worth living." Our duty as humans is to use our rationality to question ourselves and others in order to live more justly and truthfully. In this regard, it is worth noting that outside the Oracle at Delphi, which proclaimed Socrates the wisest of all men, stands the motto "Know Thyself." Socrates is like a gadfly both because he jolts people into vigilant self-examination and because the complacent majority never welcome this jolting. Most of us find it easier to live in ignorance than to acknowledge our shortcomings. Ultimately, the citizens of Athens choose to execute Socrates rather than accept the challenge of self-scrutiny that Socrates offers them.

Though the comparison has its limitations, many parallels exist between Socrates and Jesus. Both were simple men from humble backgrounds who taught anyone who would listen about the importance of self-examination and honest living. Neither of them wrote anything themselves, but both had admiring disciples who recorded their words and deeds. Furthermore, both of them were executed not for any real crimes but for the danger their subversive teachings posed to the state. Socrates' teachings are entirely secular, which might explain why he is the founder of a philosophical tradition rather than a religious one. However, Socrates does claim his own kind of divine inspiration in his "supernatural voice," which warns him against heading into danger. Essentially, this voice keeps Socrates in the path of true justice and wisdom. Socrates does not boast supernatural wisdom himself but rather credits the guidance of the gods. Unlike Jesus, Socrates has no claim to understanding the will or design of divinity, but like Jesus, he does claim to be guided by a supernatural force.

MENO

Summary

In conversation with Socrates, Meno asks whether virtue can be taught. Socrates suggests that if the two of them are to determine whether virtue can be taught, they must first define clearly what virtue is.

Meno first suggests that different kinds of virtue exist for different kinds of people. Socrates replies that Meno's definition is like a swarm of bees: each kind of virtue, like each bee, is different, but Socrates is interested in that quality they all share. Meno next suggests that virtue is being able to rule over people, but Socrates dismisses this suggestion on two grounds: first, it is not virtuous for slaves or children to rule over people, and second, ruling is virtuous only if it is done justly. This response prompts Meno to define virtue as justice. But he then concedes to Socrates that justice is a form of virtue but not virtue itself.

Struggling with Socrates' demands for a definition, Meno asks him to give an example of definitions of *shape* and *color*. Socrates first gives a straightforward definition of shape ("the limit of a solid") and then an elaborate definition of color in the style of the sophists, which shows up their empty pretentiousness.

Meno attempts to define virtue again, suggesting that it involves desiring good things and having the power to secure them, but only if one does so justly. However, this definition again encounters the problem of using "justice" in a definition of virtue: we cannot define something by using an instance of what it is we are defining.

Meno compares Socrates to a torpedo fish, which numbs anything it touches. Socrates has struck Meno dumb, and Meno no longer knows what to say. If they don't even know what virtue is, he asks, how are they to know what to look for?

Socrates responds that learning is not a matter of discovering something new but rather of recollecting something the soul knew before birth but has since forgotten. To show what he means, he calls over one of Meno's slave boys, draws a square with sides of two feet, and asks the boy to calculate how long the side of a square would be if it had twice the area of the one he just drew. The boy suggests four feet and then three feet, and Socrates proves him wrong both times. Socrates then helps the boy recognize that a square of twice the area would have sides with a length equal to the diagonal of the present square—but Socrates leads the boy to this point without actually explaining anything, instead forcing the boy to think the problem through himself. Since the boy reached this conclusion (more or less) on his own without any direct teaching, he must have been recollecting something he already knew.

Meno wants to return to the original question—whether virtue can be taught—and Socrates proposes two hypotheses to lead them on their way. First, if virtue is a kind of knowledge, then it can be taught, and second, if there is anything good that is not knowledge, then it is possible that virtue is not a kind of knowledge. Adding that nothing is good unless it is accompanied by wisdom, Socrates concludes that virtue is wisdom, in whole or in part, so it can't be something we're born with.

Meno is ready to conclude that virtue can be taught, but Socrates is hesitant. If virtue can be taught, where are the teachers? When questioning Anytus, a prominent Athenian, Socrates proposes that the sophists teach virtue. Anytus is outraged because he considers the sophists to be a source of corruption. He suggests instead that any Athenian gentleman is a teacher of virtue, but Socrates points out that many Athenian gentlemen have had dissolute sons to whom they clearly failed to teach virtue. Not even the great poet Theognis seems to have known whether virtue could be taught, leading Socrates to conclude that maybe it isn't a kind of knowledge even though it is a kind of wisdom.

Socrates suggests that virtue is perhaps not a result of knowledge but of true belief. Knowledge is a matter of being able to give an account of what we know, as the slave boy does with the mathematical proof, while we can hold true beliefs without being able to justify them.

The final conclusion, then, is that virtue neither is something innate nor can be taught. Socrates muses that perhaps it is simply a "gift from the gods" that we receive without understanding.

Analysis

Many scholars view the *Meno* as a transitional work between Plato's early and middle periods because it combines features typical of the early Socratic dialogues with the beginnings of more refined theories. We have one of the more worked-out examples of the Socratic *elenchus*, in which Socrates uses questioning to draw out an admission of ignorance from the person with whom he is arguing, and the dialogue ends in *aporia*, the state of inconclusive perplexity. These features are typical of other early works. On the other hand, we find what may be a prototypical Theory of Forms in Socrates' insistence that we find what all instances of virtue share. The theory that knowledge is recollection draws on a desire to see knowledge as grounded not in the vagaries of everyday life but in some form that would cement true knowledge as unchanging and eternal. Such positive steps are absent in Plato's other early works and are typical of so-called middle period dialogues, such as the *Phaedo* and the *Republic*.

Plato takes a few significant steps beyond the typical reach of a Socratic dialogue when he describes Socrates questioning the slave boy, since this type of dialogue usually includes only a pattern of arguments and refutations. The questioning begins in a manner typical of Socrates' *elenchus*. He asks the slave boy whether he knows the length of the side of a square with twice the area of the square he has drawn and then uses questions and counterarguments to bring the boy to a position of acknowledging that he doesn't know. In compressed form, this is how a typical early dialogue unfolds. By means of questioning, Socrates takes someone who is confident in his knowledge and brings him to a place of recognizing his own ignorance. However, once Socrates has brought the slave boy to this state of perplexity, he leads him back out. The slave boy emerges from their exchange with a positive knowledge of mathematics, which he did not have coming in. Furthermore, Socrates claims that the slave boy's knowledge is a consequence of recollecting something he always knew. In other words, their dialogue-within-a-dialogue does not end only with a positive conclusion. It also ends with a positive theory from Socrates to explain this positive conclusion.

When Socrates claims that knowledge is recollection, he is not only explaining what form our knowledge takes but also redefining what qualifies as knowledge at all. Clearly, the definition does not apply to everything we normally consider knowledge. When we find out in the newspaper what happened the previous day, we are not discovering things we've always known but forgotten. We get a hint about what counts as knowledge in the distinction Socrates draws toward the end of the dialogue between knowledge and true belief. This distinction, which plays an important role in the *Republic*, implies that we can be confident in knowing something only if we can give an account of, or justify, our knowledge. The slave boy may have guessed the answer to the mathematical problem at the outset, but he can be sure he knows the answer only because he went through the problem step by step, ensuring that he made no mistakes. This sort of rigorous justification applies only to subjects that consist of unchanging, abstract entities that are not subject to the errors and vagaries of everyday experience, such as mathematics. What we learn from the newspaper can never amount to more than true belief.

The argument that knowledge is recollection is bold and challenging, but it contains a number of problems. Foremost is the controversial question of whether the slave boy does in fact arrive at his own conclusions. Strictly speaking, Socrates only prompts the slave boy with questions, but he often makes statements couched in the form of questions, in which he arguably tells the boy the right answer rather than allow him to figure it out for himself. Even if we do accept that the boy reaches the right answer on his own, it takes another leap to trust that he does so only by recollecting knowledge that he already possessed—let alone knowledge that he possessed before he was even born, as Socrates actually asserts. We could object first that the boy is not activating latent knowledge so much as latent ability. By claiming that the boy's knowledge must be recollection, Socrates assumes that he is passively absorbing a set of facts rather than actively learning how to think mathematically. Second, we could object that the doctrine of knowledge as recollection does not explain how we first come to know things. Even if we believe that all the knowledge we possess came to us before we were born, such as in a previous life, we would still face the question of how we gained that knowledge in the first place.

PHAEDO

Summary

Echecrates presses Phaedo of Elis to give his account of Socrates' death. Socrates had been condemned to commit suicide by drinking the poison hemlock, and a number of his friends and fellow philosophers had gathered to spend his last hours with him. Phaedo explains that among those present with him were Crito and two Pythagorean philosophers, Simmias and Cebes.

In Phaedo's account, Socrates explains to his friends that a true philosopher should look forward to death. The purpose of the philosophical life is to free the soul from the needs of the body. Since the moment of death is the final separation of soul and body, a philosopher should see it as the realization of his aim. Unlike the body, the soul is immortal, so it will survive death.

Socrates provides four arguments for believing the soul is immortal. He bases the first, known as the Argument from Opposites, on the observation that everything comes to be from out of its opposite. For example, a tall man can become tall only if he was short previously. Since life and death are opposites, we can reason analogously that, just as the living become dead, so the dead must become living. Life and death are in a perpetual cycle such that death cannot be a permanent end.

The second argument, known as the Theory of Recollection, asserts that learning is essentially an act of recollecting things we knew before we were born but then forgot. True knowledge, argues Socrates, is knowledge of the eternal and unchanging Forms that underlie perceptible reality. For example, we are able to perceive that two sticks are equal in length but unequal in width only because we have an innate understanding of the Form of Equality—that is, we have an innate understanding of what it means for two things to be equal even though no two things we encounter in experience are themselves perfectly equal. Since we can grasp this Form of Equality even though we never encounter it in experience, our grasping of it must be a recollection of immortal knowledge we had and forgot prior to birth. This argument implies that the soul must have existed prior to birth, which in turn implies that the soul's life extends beyond that of the body's.

The third argument, known as the Argument from Affinity, distinguishes between those things that are immaterial, invisible, and immortal, and those things that are material, visible, and perishable. The soul belongs to the former category and the body to the latter. The soul, then, is immortal, although this immortality may take very different forms. A soul that is not properly detached from the body will become a ghost that will long to return to the flesh, while the philosopher's detached soul will dwell free in the heavens.

Both Simmias and Cebes raise objections to these arguments. Simmias suggests that the soul may be immaterial and invisible in the same way as the attunement of an instrument. The attunement of the instrument can exist only as long as the instrument itself does. Cebes accepts that the soul may survive death, but he suggests that Socrates has proved only that the soul lives longer than the body, not that it is immortal.

Socrates responds to Simmias first, pointing out that his objection conflicts with the Theory of Recollection. The soul is not like the attunement of an instrument because the soul existed before the body did.

His answer to Cebes involves a lengthy discussion that culminates in his fourth argument, based on the Theory of Forms. A Form, unlike qualities in this world, is perfectly itself and does not admit its opposite. For example, the Form of Beauty does not possess any ugliness at all. In contrast, a beautiful person might be beautiful compared to other people but would not seem beautiful compared to a god and thus is not perfectly beautiful. The Form of Beauty, on the other hand, is always and absolutely beautiful.

The soul is what animates us: we are alive because we have a soul. That concept suggests that the soul is intimately connected to the Form of Life. Since the Form of Life does not in any way include its opposite—death—the soul cannot in any way be tainted by death. Thus, Socrates concludes, the soul must be immortal.

Socrates illustrates his conception of the soul by means of a compelling myth that describes the earth we know as a poor shadow of the "true earth" above us in the heavens. Then he has a bath, says his last goodbyes, drinks the poisonous hemlock, and dies peacefully.

Analysis

The Theory of Forms is the most important philosophical aspect of the *Phaedo* and central to Plato's thought in general. Inspired perhaps by the perfect clarity and permanence of mathematics, Plato doubts that the world of our experience, where nothing is perfect or permanent, can really be all there is. Even though all the instances we find of justice and beauty in this world are flawed in some way, we still instinctively have a sense of what true justice and true beauty are. Plato's theory explains that above the unsatisfying world of our experience there is a world that contains the Form of Justice, the Form of Beauty, and other Forms that similarly embody the perfect expression of these ideals. Any beauty or justice we find in this world has beauty or justice only to the extent that it partakes in these Forms. The beauty and justice we find in this world are like shadows cast from above that give us some indication of the nature of the more real world of Forms.

When Socrates first introduces the notion of Forms, the people he's talking to accept the existence of Forms without further debate, leaving us to ponder on our own why we should accept them. Further, we get no clear sense of how many kinds of Forms there are or how exactly they interact with their manifestations in the world of experience. Discussions of Forms in Plato's other dialogues normally focus on abstract ideals such as the Form of Beauty or the Form of Justice. In the *Phaedo*, however, Socrates mentions a Form of Duality, a Form of Equality, and even, under certain interpretations, a Form of Fire and a Form of Snow. Not only do these examples leave us with no defined limit of what kinds of Forms there are, but they also raise a series of problems that do not arise with abstract ideals. We might ask, for example, how the Form of Equality can itself be a perfect paradigm of everything that is equal when equality is a relative term, meaning that nothing can be equal in and of itself but can only be equal in relation to other things.

Each of the four arguments for the immortality of the soul does different work in the dialogue, even if they all aim at proving the same thing. The Argument from Opposites absorbs a line of thinking that was popular among earlier philosophers such as Heraclitus and Pythagoras. By following their lead in seeing the world as being divided into opposites, Plato presents an initial argument that would be sympathetic to his contemporaries. The Theory of Recollection introduces the idea of Forms and, in associating knowledge with the immortal soul, suggests that the soul that survives death is not just an empty life force but includes the intellect. The Argument from Affinity makes explicit the distinction between the soul and the body. By asserting that different fates await different souls depending on how purified the souls are of the needs of the body, Plato endorses the philosophical life. The final argument based on Forms is the only one Plato deems truly definitive, refuting the doubts of Simmias and Cebes.

The distinction Plato draws between the body and the soul was revolutionary in his day and is one of the earliest forms of what we now refer to as "mind–body dualism." Dualism is the idea that mind (or soul) and body are distinct substances with distinctive natures. Plato goes so far as to suggest that they are opposites, placing the soul and body in two opposing categories in the Argument from Affinity. He identifies the self with the soul, suggesting that we have no reason to fear death since it is only our body and not our self that will perish. This identification of self with soul raises some question as to what counts as our "self." Our thinking is largely informed and inspired by what we see, hear, and sense, and our senses are a part of our body that will not survive death. We might doubt whether we can shed the body, and all the influences we draw from it, and become a soul of pure intellect that we can readily identify with the "self" that we think we have.

SYMPOSIUM

Summary

Apollodorus relates to an unnamed companion a story he heard from Aristodemus about a symposium, or dinner party, held in honor of the playwright Agathon. Besides Aristodemus and Agathon, the guests include Agathon's lover Pausanias, the doctor Eryximachus, the great comic poet Aristophanes, and the young Phaedrus. Socrates arrives late, having been lost in thought on a neighboring porch. Once they have finished eating, Eryximachus proposes that, instead of the usual entertainments, the guests should take turns giving speeches in praise of the god of Love.

Phaedrus speaks first, praising Love as the oldest of all the gods and the one that does the most to promote virtue in people. Pausanias speaks next, distinguishing the base desires involved in Common Love from the purity of Heavenly Love, which only ever exists between a man and a boy. In exchange for sexual gratification from the boy, the man acts as a mentor, teaching him wisdom and virtue. Eryximachus, the third speaker, argues that Love promotes order and moderation, not only in people but also in all things. Thus, Love can exist in such fields as music and medicine.

Aristophanes is the next to speak, and he presents his conception of Love in the form of a myth. Humans once had four legs, four arms, two heads, and so on, he says. Some were male, with two sets of male sexual organs; some were females; and some were hermaphrodites, with one set each of male and female sexual organs. We were twice the people we are now, and the gods were jealous, afraid we would overthrow them. Zeus decided to cut us in half to reduce our power, and ever since we have been running all over the earth trying to rejoin with our other half. When we do, we cling to that other half with all our might, and we call this Love.

Agathon speaks next, giving an elaborate and flowery speech about Love, which he describes as young, sensitive, beautiful, and wise. All our virtues are gifts that we receive from this god. Socrates questions Agathon, doubting his speech and suggesting that Agathon has described the object of Love, not Love itself.

To correct him, Socrates explains he once held the same beliefs until he met Diotima of Mantinea, a wise woman who taught him everything he knows about Love. According to Diotima, Love is neither a god nor a mortal but rather a spirit born of a coupling between Resource and Poverty. Love itself is not wise or beautiful and does not have any of the other attributes Agathon ascribed to it. Rather, it is the desire for all these things. As such, Love wishes to give birth to Beauty, so Diotima associates Love with pregnancy and reproduction. Some seek to reproduce sexually, while other seek to give birth to ideas, the children of their minds. We first learn about Beauty by seeing and desiring beautiful people or objects, but our desire for Beauty can be gradually refined until ultimately we love Beauty itself, which is the highest love there is.

As Socrates concludes his speech, the famous politician Alcibiades bursts in completely drunk. He complains that he has consistently tried to seduce Socrates in order to glean wisdom from him but that Socrates resists any kind of sexual advances. Shortly thereafter, more revelers arrive and the party descends into drunken chaos. When Aristodemus wakes up the next morning, he sees Socrates, Agathon, and Aristophanes still engaged in sober conversation. Eventually, Agathon and Aristophanes fall asleep, and Socrates leaves and goes about his daily business.

Analysis

In the *Symposium*, Plato presents the love of wisdom as the highest form of love and philosophy as a refinement of our sexual urges that leads us to desire wisdom over sex. That is, we do not seek wisdom by first suppressing sexual desire and other distractions but rather by refining that desire and training it on a higher purpose. Plato sets his dialogue at a symposium, which was one of the highlights of Athenian social life, and amidst a discussion about Love to show us that philosophy is not removed from the business of everyday life. On the contrary, philosophy is the highest expression of the loves and desires that motivate us in everyday activities. If we could see things clearly, Plato suggests, we would see that our attraction to beautiful people or good music or exciting movies is really an attraction to Beauty itself and that philosophy is the most direct route to getting at what we most desire.

Diotima describes love as the pursuit of beauty in a gradual ascent from the particular to the general, culminating in an understanding of the Form of Beauty. Even the most ignorant soul is drawn to beauty on some level. What most of us don't realize, she suggests, is that what attracts us to a beautiful person, for instance, is that we perceive in that person an idea of the greater Form of Beauty. That is, we are attracted not to the person but to the beauty in the person. If our love is keen enough, we will not be satisfied by beautiful people but will seek out beauty in more generalized forms: in minds, in the structure of a well-ordered state, and ultimately in the Form of Beauty itself, the most generalized form that beauty takes. Once we have come to grasp the Form of Beauty, we will have grasped the fundamental truth that the reality of our experience is just a shadow world compared with the ideal, eternal, and unchanging world of Forms. This Theory of Forms is presented in greater detail in the *Phaedo* and the *Republic.* Here, we get the hint that the way to an understanding of Forms is through a love of beauty.

The dialogue's structure mirrors the progression Diotima describes of pursuing beauty in increasingly refined and generalized forms. Each speech in the dialogue takes us a step closer to understanding the true nature of love. Phaedrus gives us a simple enthusiasm for the value of love; Pausanias distinguishes between good and bad forms of love; Eryximachus expands the definition to cover other fields of inquiry; Aristophanes gives us a delightful account of the urgency of love; and Agathon applies the refined art of rhetoric to understanding love. Only by first considering and seeing the limitations in these earlier speeches can we then appreciate the importance of Socrates' speech. We should also note that, in Eryximachus, Aristophanes, and Agathon, we have representatives of medicine, comedy, and tragedy, all three of which are important components of a healthy life. By having Socrates trump these other three, Plato is suggesting that philosophy is more important to our well-being than these other disciplines.

The original Greek text contains a number of untranslatable puns that enhance our understanding of the relationship between love, desire, and philosophy. The Greek word *eros*, translated as "love," is also the root of our word *erotic* and can be used in Greek to describe sexual desire. Socrates is thus being coy when he explains that Diotima taught him everything he knows about *eros*, a coyness that is enhanced when we discover that Diotima of Mantinea was the name of a well-known temple prostitute in ancient Greece. The implication is that Socrates came to Diotima seeking sex, but she instead taught him about beauty and wisdom. This implication further reinforces the suggestion that the desire for wisdom is a refinement, and not a denial, of our desire for sex. In the dialogue, Diotima becomes the model of Beauty, which every lover seeks, while Socrates becomes the model of Love, being himself neither beautiful nor satisfied but constantly seeking more. This picture of Socrates the lover further plays on the word *philosopher*, which literally means "lover of wisdom."

While the *Symposium* contains a great deal of explicit homoerotic content, it would be a distortion to label characters in the dialogue as homosexual or bisexual. These sorts of categories are modern inventions that do not just denote a person's sexual preference but also define a person according to his or her sexual preference. Greek society, for the most part, didn't consider sexual preference as a defining personality trait, so labeling Greeks as homosexual or heterosexual would be as odd to them as defining modern students as "white sock wearers" or "colored sock wearers." Almost all Greek men married women and had children (Plato is a rare exception), while many Greek men also pursued less permanent sexual relations with other men. The activities thought most to display virtue and glory, such as athletics, warfare, and politics, were exclusively the realm of men, so two men could share in this virtue and glory in a way that a man and a woman could not. Consequently, male–male relationships were often romanticized, whereas male–female relationships were viewed as purely practical affairs, which united families and produced children. These two different kinds of relationships existed alongside one another, and both were considered healthy and natural.

REPUBLIC

Summary

On his return from a religious festival, Socrates encounters Polemarchus and returns with him to the house of his father, Cephalus, where the three men discuss justice. Both Cephalus and Polemarchus give traditional accounts of what justice is, which Socrates shows to be incomplete. Thrasymachus enters the debate, answering that the very conception of justice is a sham meant to keep the strong at bay. True justice, he contends, is the advantage of the stronger. Socrates tries to rebut Thrasymachus's claim, but Thrasymachus remains unconvinced. Book I ends at this point, and the remaining nine books consist of Socrates working out, in dialogue with Glaucon and Adeimantus, a more robust definition of justice.

Glaucon and Adeimantus urge Socrates to prove that justice is good in itself and not only for its consequences. People act justly mostly out of fear of punishment, so if justice is not good in itself, and if they thought they could get away with it, people would have no reason not to act unjustly. Rather than answer their question directly, Socrates proposes to sketch out an ideal republic so they can determine what role justice plays in this republic.

Socrates proposes a principle of specialization, according to which each citizen has a particular role to play. A city needs producers, who produce food and shelter, as well as a class of guardians who protect the state's interests. These guardians are raised according to a rigorous program of education that emphasizes physical fitness, honor, and wisdom. So that they don't become brutish or soft, they are shielded from bad influences, such as myths that portray the gods as possessing vices. The best among the guardians are selected as rulers (also referred to as "guardians"), while the others become "auxiliaries," who act as soldiers. To maintain this strict class structure of producers, auxiliaries, and guardians, Socrates invents a state-sanctioned mythology that discourages people from aspiring to a different class. Class mobility is only possible when a youth in one class is identified with abilities that clearly suit him for a different class.

Socrates identifies the four primary virtues in the different aspects of this republic: the guardians possess wisdom, the auxiliaries possess courage, and the whole possesses justice and moderation. Thus, the justice of an ideal republic does not reside in any particular part of the republic but rather in the structure of the republic as a whole.

Like the just city, the soul of a just person is divided into three parts, and the soul's justice resides in the proper structuring of these parts. The soul has an appetitive part that desires money and other earthly goods, such as the producers; a spirited part that desires honor, such as the auxiliaries; and a rational part that desires truth, such as the guardians. The rational part rules in a just soul, ensuring the health of the whole.

The guardian class lives austerely, having no money or material possessions. They live communally, choose sexual partners by lot, and are separated from their children at birth so as to prevent family ties from overriding loyalty to the state. In a move that is revolutionary for its time, Socrates sees no reason why women should not have status equal to men.

The guardians are philosopher-kings, not to be confused with contemporary philosophers, who are more accurately called "lovers of sights and sounds." These lovers of sights and sounds are drawn only to the appearance of things, whereas true philosophers have knowledge of the unchanging, eternal Forms that lie behind appearance. The world of sights and sounds consists of objects that both are and are not—for example, a beautiful woman is both beautiful and, in comparison to a goddess, not beautiful. Therefore, the things we see and hear are objects of opinion or belief; maybe they're beautiful, maybe not. The world of Forms, such as the Form of Beauty, however, has being in an absolute sense, and these Forms are the objects of knowledge.

The highest knowledge to which the philosopher-kings aspire is knowledge of the Form of the Good. Socrates cannot articulate directly what this is but rather explains it by offering three analogies: the sun, the line, and the cave. Socrates invites us to imagine prisoners chained to a bench in a cave. All they can see are the shadows moving on the wall in front of them, which are cast by statues being moved above and behind, where the prisoners cannot see. Not knowing any better, these prisoners think of the shadows as real, like a person seduced by the imaginative world of stories, unable to recognize a higher reality. If the prisoners were released, they could turn around and see that the shadows they thought were real were only projections of the statues behind them. They would then think of these statues as real, like a person who thinks the world of sights and sounds is the most real thing there is. The prisoners might then wander out of the cave and into the outside world. At first, they would be blinded by the light, but they would eventually come to see all the objects of the world around them. They would think of these objects as real, like a person who can grasp by means of thought the Forms that underlie everyday existence. Finally, these prisoners might be able to look at the sun itself and recognize it as the source of all light and all life. The sun is like the Form of the Good: just as the sun is the source of everything in the visible world, the Form of the Good is the source of everything in the intelligible world.

Socrates invites his friends to imagine a line divided first in two and then in four. The lower part represents the visible realm and the upper part represents the intelligible realm. The visible realm is divided into imagination and belief, belief being better than imagination, just as seeing the statues is better than seeing the shadows. The intelligible realm is divided into thought and understanding, where thought hypothesizes the existence of Forms based on the visible world and understanding grasps the Form of the Good as a first principle from which everything else follows. The divided line is diagrammed in the following figure. The corresponding stages in the prisoner's escape from the cave are on the right.

Understanding	Looking at the sun, the Form of Good
INTELLIGIBLE REALM	
Thought	Looking at the objects in the world outside the cave
Belief	Looking at the statues inside the cave
VISIBLE REALM	
Imagination	Looking at the shadows on the wall of the cave

The education of the philosopher-kings is like the progress of a prisoner from out of the cave. In youth, they study mathematics to give them an intimation of an abstract world behind the visible. After rigorous physical training, they study philosophy and then dialectics. At thirty-five, they spend the next fifteen years running affairs of state before finally achieving the rank of philosopher-king at fifty. These philosopher-kings are like the prisoners who can see the sun, and contemplation of the Form of the Good will be their highest aim. However, they must also take care of the republic and train the next generation, just as freed prisoners must return to the cave to help their comrades.

Because the guardians will inevitably make some errors in judgment, this ideal republic will gradually decline through four stages of progressively worse government: timocracy, oligarchy, democracy, and tyranny. Similarly, a just man can slide into four kinds of degeneracy, tyranny being the worst. People who take whatever they can to please themselves live like tyrants, so people who follow Thrasymachus's "advantage of the stronger" are worst off of all people. Only philosophers live just lives because only they have the ability to recognize the true pleasure to be found in the love of truth. All other pleasures are really just the cessation of pain.

Poets are banished from Socrates' republic because they portray falsehoods and appeal to our emotions and baser instincts in a way that corrupts us. Socrates regrets this necessity and invites others to persuade him not to banish poets.

The last book of the *Republic* contains an argument for the soul's immortality, claiming that injustice if anything would destroy a soul, and yet the soul seems to survive the tyranny of unjust men. Plato concludes with the myth of Er, a slain soldier who discovers that after death, good people spend one thousand years in heaven while bad people spend one thousand years in hell before selecting a new life for themselves.

Analysis

The *Republic* is not so much a practical guide to future policy as it is a set of bold provocations. It is possibly the single most important philosophical work in the Western tradition, and the number of unconventional and bizarre views it contains is surprising. The ideas that men and women should be treated as equals and that justice is to be found within the structure of a state rather than in its actions were revolutionary in Plato's day. Even two and a half millennia after its composition, no state has attempted the fifty-year educational process recommended for the guardians or the communal living that does away with the family and private property. By presenting these radical ideas within the framework of the ideal state, Plato challenges us to find reasons for faulting them. If we want to contradict these unconventional proposals, we will have to think as creatively as Plato has in formulating them.

The *Republic* contains less dialogue than Plato's early work because it deals with such counterintuitive ideas. In dialogues such as the *Euthyphro*, we see Socrates discussing virtue and dismantling the various commonsense definitions of holiness, friendship, courage, and the like. The first book of the *Republic* works along similar lines, with Socrates dismantling the commonsense conceptions of justice held by Cephalus and Polemarchus. Things take a turn, however, when Thrasymachus dismisses justice as a whole, claiming that our very idea of justice has been imposed upon us by rulers who want to keep us in our place. The rest of the *Republic* can be read as a response to Thrasymachus's challenge. Common sense cannot be a guide in responding to Thrasymachus because Thrasymachus has implied that what our common sense tells us about justice is a lie our oppressors manufacture. The Socratic *elenchus* proceeds by teasing out the contradictions in commonsense ideas, so it is of no use to us here. Instead, Plato has Socrates launch into extended speeches, pausing only for the occasional response from Glaucon or Adeimantus, so that Socrates can explore ideas that are far removed from the commonsense notions debated in the earlier dialogues.

Plato's Theory of Forms is the most important bulwark against relativists such as Thrasymachus. Thrasymachus essentially argues for a "might makes right" position, such that truth and justice are nothing more than what the strongest people say they are. Plato responds that Thrasymachus and his like see everything as relative only because they are stuck in the "world of sights and sounds" that makes up our sensory experience. This world is not the real world but rather a shadow of the truly real world of Forms in which nothing changes, nothing passes away, and nothing is imperfect. Instances of justice in the visible world may be relative, and what seems just to one person may seem unjust to another, but the Form of Justice itself is absolute and incontrovertible. Thrasymachus's relativism, then, is simply a consequence of not seeing the whole picture, like someone fix-ated on a rotten banana insisting that all bananas are brown.

The distinction Plato draws between the visible world and the intelligible world claims a separate and superior domain for abstract thought above concrete thought. Everything we can see and hear, he suggests, isn't what is most real. What is most real is what we can grasp by means of the intellect. This includes not only mathematics but also the Forms that lie behind the visible world. Our knowledge of the visible world is imperfect and changing, so it amounts at best to true belief. The abstract principles that govern the intelligible world, how-ever, are perfect and unchanging, so they represent a higher form of knowledge than true belief. The metaphor of the line and especially of the cave are ingenious means of prompting his audience to consider that there is more to the world than mere appearance. Both metaphors suggest that we have an incomplete understanding of the world if we accept only what we see before us. Only a rational, searching mind can uncover the true nature of reality.

The Theory of Forms is perhaps not really a "theory," since we find only compelling metaphors, not arguments, to persuade us of it. When Socrates first introduces the idea that behind the world of appearances are immaterial, eternal, and unchanging Forms, Glaucon and Adeimantus agree without further discussion. The most we get are the related metaphors of the sun, the line, and the cave, which combine to give a compelling account of why we ought to believe Forms exist. Considering that the Theory of Forms is central to the argu-ment of the *Republic*, the fact that Plato feels no need to argue for it suggests intellectual laziness. However, we may be mis-guided in viewing the discussion of Forms as a theory that needs to be argued for. Plato uses metaphors rather than argu-ments in support of Forms, which suggests he is not trying to persuade us of a particular point so much as trying to shift our way of looking at things.

In the *Republic*, the existence of Forms is not a conclusion we must reach but a premise we must start from. Plato never defines the Form of the Good, calling it instead an "unhypo-thetical first principle." A "first principle" is the place at which a chain of reasoning begins. For example, if I reason, "there's no car in the driveway, so my parents must be out, so the house must be locked, so I'd better look under the mat for the key," the observation, "there's no car in the driveway" is the first principle. If I were to say, "I'd better look under the mat for the key," someone could ask "why?" and I could reply, "because the house is locked," and someone could again ask, "why?" and I could reply "because my parents are out," and so on. "There's no car in the driveway" is a "hypothetical" first principle, because we are making a hypothesis in assuming that it's true.

If we are feeling philosophical, we can question this hypothesis by questioning whether our eyes tell us what's real. Plato claims that answering this question leads us to posit the Forms that exist behind appearances, and positing these Forms will ultimately lead us to the Form of the Good. The Form of the Good itself is an unhypothetical first principle because it is not justified by any further facts or evidence. It is the one thing that is true and real in and of itself. As such, the existence of the Form of the Good, and Forms generally, is not something to be argued for. Rather, according to Plato, only by virtue of the Form of the Good can arguments hold ground at all. Without the Form of the Good, there would be nothing to justify any of our reasoning, so to demand reasons for why we should believe in the Form of the Good puts the cart before the horse.

The idea of a tripartite soul explains both the fact of inner conflict and the necessity for honing our reason. The idea that the soul is not simple but rather made up of three distinct parts is an ingenious solution to the problematic fact that we experience inner conflict: we can fight urges, want to want things, surrender ashamedly to temptation, and so on. This fact suggests that we have more than one set of drives working within us. Indeed, Plato's theory of a tripartite soul is the first in a long string of psychological theories that lead down to Freud and beyond. By dividing the soul into a rational part, a spirited part, and an appetitive part, Plato also argues that our shameful or vicious actions are a consequence of giving into our baser desires. A virtuous person always follows the lead of reason, with spirit and appetite on a tight leash.

The *Republic* makes a number of recommendations in favor of authoritarian or even totalitarian government, and commentators have been sharply divided over how to interpret it on this score. Socrates' ideal republic allows for limited personal freedoms and social mobility, is staunchly antidemocratic, and uses strict censorship and propaganda, to the extent of banishing all poets from the city. The philosopher Karl Popper has gone so far as to accuse the *Republic* as being the seminal influence behind the twentieth-century totalitarian regimes of Stalin and Hitler. Others have rightly pointed out that the *Republic* is the first sustained and rigorous examination of political philosophy in the Western tradition and that modern liberal democracy owes Plato a great intellectual debt. No simple answer exists to the question of whether the *Republic*'s political philosophy is benign or dangerous because the *Republic* itself is no simple book. We must recall that at least one purpose of the *Republic* is to provoke intense thought and discussion, so if we find passages shocking, we can assume this is what Plato would have wanted.

The ideal society that Plato describes in the *Republic* is radically different from any actual society in human history, including our own. Are the values reflected in the *Republic* similar to or different from our own?

In both its structure and its basic philosophical under-pinnings, Plato's ideal republic seems far removed from the society we live in today. Contemporary readers may find themselves balking at the republic's strict regimentation, its distrust of the arts, and its staunchly antidemocratic slant. However, Plato's philosophy has taken root in Western culture in ways that we often do not recognize. The strange story of the cave, for example, continues to resonate with modern readers. Although our visual culture is millennia removed from Plato's, we share with him a profound distrust of the representational image. Nowhere is this better epitomized than in our conflicted feelings about the role of television in modern society. Plato could never have imagined this strange invention, but if he had, he would probably have reacted to it much as we do today.

When people talk about being captive to the boob tube or being seduced by the idiot box, they are, consciously or otherwise, alluding to Plato's narrative. Plato's cave dwellers delight in their shadow images, believing them to be reality. Philosophers are the only people who can grasp the reality of the situation and the only ones who take more delight in the real world than in the images. The metaphor of the cave bears a striking resemblance to the modern movie theater, where a collective audience sits in the dark and watches a projection on a wall. The metaphor holds, however, for any situation involving representational imagery, whether film, photography, or television. The philosophical parallels are most prominent when it comes to television, however, since that particular medium lies at the heart of an ongoing debate about the pernicious effects of modern visual culture.

It's become common for people to note that, with the advent of globalization, the Internet, and the explosion of television options, we are more inundated with images than we have ever been before. The world has grown too large for people to experience directly, so to learn what's happening across the world, across the

Student Essay

country, or even in our own halls of government, we have to rely on television and other related media. For most of us, foreign wars and inter-national disasters are something we only experience as a series of news reports, photographs, and video clips. In a way, this situation is inevitable, since it would be physically impossible for any individual to travel to all these places. The danger, however, lies in the potential for viewers to mentally collapse this distance and fool themselves into thinking that televised reports can somehow accurately portray the reality of any situation. If television can convince viewers that what they see is somehow real, then television is a liar. The overwhelming speed and quantity of televised images we receive daily heighten the problem. Complexity is often sacrificed in favor of digestibility, and separating reality from representation becomes increasingly difficult.

Critics often decry the amount of sex and violence on television today, and in this they also repeat Plato's rejections of representational art. Plato outlawed dramatic art in his ideal republic because he believed most people were either unable or unwilling to separate representation from reality. Drama requires conflict, villains, and distasteful situations, and Plato believed that viewers would replicate these things in their own lives. While we might scoff at the idea that watching a performance of *Medea* (in which a mother murders her own children) might lead a person to mimic Medea's crime, we rely on similar rhetoric when we argue that violent television shows and video games increase the occurrence of violence in society at large.

Plato's theory and current debates that reproduce his arguments don't leave much agency for the individual viewer. We could easily argue that contemporary viewers are more discriminating consumers of televisual imagery than they were a generation ago. Most of us are keenly aware of the essential unreality of reality television and that so-called objective media outlets can, in fact, be highly biased. The ability to access multiple, potentially conflicting news sources means that we are far less likely to accept any given representation as the whole truth. We may still face the cave's back wall, but we aren't necessarily chained to that viewing position.

Aristotle

(384–322 B.C.)

THEMES, ARGUMENTS & IDEAS

- The Teleology of Nature
- The Primacy of Substance
- The Rejection of Plato's Theory of Forms
- Biology as a Paradigm
- The Vagueness of the Practical Sciences
- The Unmoved Mover as First Cause

SUMMARY & ANALYSIS OF MAJOR WORKS

- *Organon*
- *Physics*
- *Metaphysics*
- *Nicomachean Ethics*
- *Politics*
- *Poetics*

2

Aristotle was born in Stagira in northern Greece in 384 B.C. His father was a doctor at the court of Amyntas III of Macedon, father of Philip II of Macedon and grandfather of Alexander the Great. In 367, Aristotle moved to Athens to study at Plato's Academy, where he stayed for twenty years. Aristotle left the Academy in 347, the year Plato died, and some have speculated that he felt snubbed that Plato did not choose him as his successor. The more likely explanation, however, is that anti-Macedonian sentiment was on the rise in Athens, causing Aristotle to fear being persecuted for his associations with King Philip's court.

Over the next four years, Aristotle traveled about the eastern Aegean, studying and teaching. During this time, he conducted a remarkable array of experiments and observations in the biological sciences. In 343, he was summoned back north to Macedonia to be the personal tutor to King Philip's son, the young Alexander the Great. We do not know the precise relationship between Aristotle and Alexander, though their relationship has been the subject of much speculation and mythmaking over the centuries.

As the Macedonians came to dominate Greece, Aristotle returned to Athens and set up his own philosophical school at the Lyceum, where he taught from 335 until 323. What we have of Aristotle's writings are mostly lectures he gave at the Lyceum in these years. Their dry style and uneven structure is due partly to the fact that they were lecture notes never intended for publication and partly to the fact that they were patched together into their present form by editors many centuries after Aristotle's death. Aristotle published many popular works admired for their lively style, but none of these have survived.

Historically, Aristotle lived in the twilight years of the Greek city-state. Ancient Greece consisted of a number of independent city-states, of which Athens was the most significant. Though the city-states relied on slave labor and did not allow women to vote, the male citizens established one of the earliest forms of democracy, and in the span of less than two hundred years they managed to establish what the Western world still looks to as the basis of its political institutions, philosophy, mathematics, drama, art, and architecture. Because slaves and noncitizen workers performed the bulk of the city's labor, male citizens enjoyed a great deal of leisure time. This leisure provided the opportunity for open inquiry into the nature of the world, and teachers like Aristotle were not uncommon.

Aristotle's writings show that he was well versed in Platonic philosophy. The centerpiece of Plato's philosophy is his Theory of Forms, according to which the objects of experience are just shadows of a higher world of Forms that lie beyond sensory experience. For example, the various things we see in this world that we call beautiful have beauty because they participate in the Form of Beauty, which is itself immaterial and eternal. In Plato's view, the purpose of philosophy is to train the intellect to see beyond appearances and to grasp the higher world of Forms.

Counterbalancing the idealism of Plato's philosophy is Aristotle's background as the son of a doctor. Aristotle was probably brought up to pursue a medical career, and his writings on biology show a sharp understanding of anatomy. Throughout his writings, Aristotle refers to biology as a paradigm for making sense of the world, much as Plato refers to mathematics. This emphasis on biology leads Aristotle to favor close observation of natural phenomena and careful classification as the keys to making sense of things. As a result, his philosophy is much more empirically oriented than Plato's, and Aristotle rejects the idea that we can only make sense of this world by appealing to invisible entities beyond it.

Aristotle's influence on subsequent generations is immense. Only Plato can compare in importance. Though Aristotle's works were lost to the West for many centuries, they were preserved by Arab scholars and transmitted back to Europe in the Middle Ages. Thanks mostly to the work of St. Thomas Aquinas, Aristotle's writings carried an authority in the late Middle Ages that was second only to the Bible. His work in logic and biology was not significantly improved upon until the nineteenth century. Though modern science and philosophy found their legs by rejecting or disproving many of Aristotle's results, his methods continue to have a deep influence on philosophical and scientific thought.

Aristotle's published writings were all lost or destroyed in the centuries after his death, and what we have are lectures, or notes on lectures, that Aristotle gave at the Lyceum. These works were first collected two centuries after Aristotle's death by Andronicus of Rhodes. As a result, not only do we not know the chronology of Aristotle's writings, but we are also unsure whether Andronicus arranged them in the order that Aristotle had intended, or even whether all the works collected by Andronicus were written by Aristotle. We can also be quite confident that what Andronicus collected constitutes less than one-third of all of Aristotle's writings. Even this small portion is impressive: Aristotle's works are as vast as they are challenging.

Themes, Arguments & Ideas

THE TELEOLOGY OF NATURE

Teleology is the study of the ends or purposes that things serve, and Aristotle's emphasis on teleology has repercussions through-out his philosophy. Aristotle believed that the best way to under-stand why things are the way they are is to understand what purpose they were designed to serve. For example, we can dissect an animal to see how its anatomical organs look and what they're made of, but we only understand each organ when we perceive what it's supposed to do. Aristotle's emphasis on teleol-ogy implies that there is a reason for everything. Just as Aristotle sees purpose in anatomical and biological systems, he sees human life as organized and directed toward a final end as well. Because we are essentially rational, Aristotle argues that rational-ity is our final cause and that our highest aim is to fulfill our rationality. This argument has a deep impact both on Aristotle's ethics and on his politics. The good life, for which all our virtue and wisdom prepares us, consists primarily of rational contem-plation, and the purpose of the city-state is to arrange matters in such a way as to maximize the opportunities for its citizens to pursue this good life.

THE PRIMACY OF SUBSTANCE

The term *substance* designates those things that are most funda-mental to existence. However, since there is no clear or definite answer as to what those things are, *substance* is effectively a meta-physical placeholder, a word that refers to a problem rather than a definable thing. Aristotle points out that some things do seem to be more fundamental than others. For example, colors can only exist if there are physical objects that are colored, though it seems conceivable that physical objects could potentially exist in a world devoid of color. If there is a hierarchy to being, such that some things are more fundamental than others, there must be a most fundamental thing on which everything else depends. Aris-totle thinks that he can approach this most fundamental thing by examining definition. Properly speaking, a definition should list just those items without which the thing defined could not exist as it is. For instance, the definition of a toe should mention a foot, because without feet, toes could not exist. Since we cannot define toes without making mention of feet, we can infer that feet are more fundamental than toes. A substance, then, is something whose definition does not rely on the existence of other things besides it.

Aristotle's insistence on the primacy of substance reflects his view that there is no single category of being. We can talk about existence in connection with all sorts of things. Colors exist, ideas exist, places exist, times exist, movements exist, and so on. Part of Aristotle's insight is that these things do not all exist in the same way. That is, there is not some one thing called "existence" in which colors and places partake in markedly different ways. Rather, there are different categories of existence that apply to different categories of things. Colors and places have two entirely different kinds of existences. However, if different sorts of things exist in different ways, how is it that there seems to be a single cosmos in which color, place, time, and all the rest, seem to exist together? The fact that color and substance have two different kinds of existence does not prevent substances from being colored. For the cosmos to be unified, there must be a base unit of existence on which all other kinds of existence depend. Aristotle's argument for the primacy of substance, then, is his way of saying that it is substance, and not time or location, that binds the cosmos together.

THE REJECTION OF PLATO'S THEORY OF FORMS

By rejecting Plato's Theory of Forms, Aristotle clears the way for his empirical approach, which emphasizes observation first and abstract reasoning second. Aristotle received his philosophical education at Plato's Academy, so it is natural that he would feel obliged to justify at length why he departs from the doctrines of his teacher. He provides detailed arguments against many of Plato's doctrines in almost all of his major works, focusing in particular on the Theory of Forms. In Aristotle's view, this theory is essentially an assertion of the superiority of universals over particulars. Plato argues that particular instances of, say, beauty or justice exist only because they participate in the universal Form of Beauty or Justice. On the contrary, Aristotle argues that universal concepts of beauty and justice derive from the instances of beauty and justice in this world. We only arrive at a conception of beauty by observing particular instances of beauty, and the universal quality of beauty has no existence beyond this conception that we build from particular instances. By saying that the particulars come first and the universals come after, Aristotle places emphasis on the importance of observing the details of this world, which stands as one of the important steps in the development of the scientific method.

BIOLOGY AS A PARADIGM

Aristotle's methods in biology reveal a great deal about his general methods in philosophy. He was the son of a doctor, and his work shows a particular aptitude for biology. We might contrast this fact with Plato's aptitude for mathematics. Throughout Plato's work, we see a continual reference to the forms of reasoning involved in mathematics as the paradigmatic example of what reasoning ought to be. By contrast, we find Aristotle applying the lessons he draws from his biological studies to philosophical questions far removed from biology. Two pertinent examples are Aristotle's emphases on teleology and classification. Aristotle finds it useful when studying living organisms always to ask what function an organ or a process serves, and from this practical method he infers in general that all things serve a purpose and that we can best understand the workings of things by asking what ends they serve. Similarly, Aristotle develops an ingenious system of classifying the various kinds of living organisms according to species and genus, among other things, and proceeds to find systems for classifying everything from the forms of poetry to the categories of being. Most important, perhaps, is that Aristotle draws from his biological research a keen eye for detail and an emphasis on observation as the key to knowledge.

THE VAGUENESS OF THE PRACTICAL SCIENCES

Aristotle rarely sets down hard and fast rules in the practical sciences because those fields are naturally inclined to a degree of vagueness. Aristotle is generally credited with being the first thinker to recognize that knowledge is compartmentalized. For example, he recognizes that the practical sciences, such as ethics or politics, are far less precise in their methods and procedures than, say, logic. This is not a failure of ethics and politics to live up to some ideal, but rather just the nature of the beast. Ethics and politics deal with people, and people are quite variable in their behavior. In the *Politics,* Aristotle seems to waver in determining what kind of constitution is best, but this is not so much ambiguity on his part as a recognition that there is no single best constitution. A thriving democracy relies on an educated and unselfish population, and failing that, another form of government might be preferable. Similarly, in the *Nicomachean Ethics,* Aristotle does not lay down any hard and fast rules regarding virtue, because different behaviors are virtuous in different situations. The vagueness of Aristotle's recommendations regarding the practical sciences are then part and parcel of his general view that different forms of study require different approaches.

THE UNMOVED MOVER AS FIRST CAUSE

Aristotle's theology is based on his perception that there must be something above and beyond the chains of cause and effect for those chains to exist at all. Aristotle perceives change and motion as deep mysteries. Everything is subject to change and motion, but nothing changes or moves without cause. Tracing how things cause one another to change and move is the source of many of Aristotle's most fundamental insights. He believes that all causes must themselves be caused and all motion must be caused by something that is already in motion. The trouble with this belief is that it leads to an infinite regress: if all causes have antecedent causes, there is no first cause that causes motion and change to exist in the first place. Why is there change and motion rather than stillness? Aristotle answers that there must be a first cause, an unmoved mover, that is the source of all change and motion while being itself unchanging and unmoving. To motivate the heavens to move, this unmoved mover must be perfect, so Aristotle comes to associate it with God.

Summary & Analysis

ORGANON (ARISTOTLE'S LOGICAL TREATISES)

Aristotle wrote six works that were later grouped together as the *Organon*, which means "instrument." These works are the *Prior Analytics, Posterior Analytics, On Interpretation, Topics, Sophistical Refutations,* and *Categories.* These texts are considered the body of Aristotle's work on logic, though there is a great deal in the *Organon* that we would not consider logic, and many of Aristotle's other works, most notably the *Metaphysics,* deal to some extent with logic. These six works of the *Organon* have a common interest not primarily in saying what is true but in investigating the structure of truth and the structure of the things that we can say such that they can be true. Broadly speaking, the *Organon* provides a series of guidelines on how to make sense of things.

Our discussion of the *Organon* is divided into two parts. The first discusses the syllogism, the main weapon in Aristotle's logical arsenal, which he treats primarily in *Prior Analytics* and *On Interpretation.* The second discusses Aristotle's more general remarks on the structure of being, knowledge, and argument, covered primarily in the four other works that constitute the *Organon.*

Summary: The Syllogism

Aristotle's most famous contribution to logic is the syllogism, which he discusses primarily in the *Prior Analytics.* A syllogism is a three-step argument containing three different terms. A simple example is "All men are mortal; Socrates is a man; therefore, Socrates is mortal." This three-step argument contains three assertions consisting of the three terms *Socrates, man,* and *mortal.* The first two assertions are called *premises* and the last assertion is called the *conclusion*; in a logically valid syllogism, such as the one just presented, the conclusion follows necessarily from the premises. That is, if you know that both of the premises are true, you know that the conclusion must also be true.

Aristotle uses the following terminology to label the different parts of the syllogism: the premise whose subject features in the conclusion is called the *minor premise* and the premise whose predicate features in the conclusion is called the *major premise.* In the example, "All men are mortal" is the major premise, and since "mortal" is also the predicate of the conclusion, it is called the *major term*. "Socrates" is called the *minor term* because it is the subject of both the minor premise and the conclusion, and *man*, which features in both premises but not in the conclusion, is called the *middle term*.

In analyzing the syllogism, Aristotle registers the important distinction between particulars and universals. "Socrates" is a particular term, meaning that the word "Socrates" names a particular person. By contrast, "man" and "mortal" are universal terms, meaning that they name general categories or qualities that might be true of many particulars. "Socrates" is one of billions of particular terms that falls under the universal "man." Universals can be either the subject or the predicate of a sentence, whereas particulars can only be subjects.

Aristotle identifies four kinds of "categorical sentences" that can be constructed from sentences that have universals for their subjects. When universals are subjects, they must be preceded by *every*, *some*, or *no*. To return to the example of a syllogism, the first of the three terms was not just "men are mortal," but rather "all men are mortal." The contrary of "all men are mortal" is "some men are not mortal," because one and only one of these claims is true: they cannot both be true or both be false. Similarly, the contrary of "no men are mortal" is "some men are mortal.".

Aristotle identifies sentences of these four forms—"All X is Y," "Some X is not Y," "No X is Y," and "Some X is Y"—as the four categorical sentences and claims that all assertions can be analyzed into categorical sentences. That means that all assertions we make can be reinterpreted as categorical sentences and so can be fit into syllogisms. If all our assertions can be read as premises or conclusions to various syllogisms, it follows that the syllogism is the framework of all reasoning. Any valid argument must take the form of a syllogism, so Aristotle's work in analyzing syllogisms provides a basis for analyzing all arguments. Aristotle analyzes all forty-eight possible kinds of syllogisms that can be constructed from categorical sentences and shows that fourteen of them are valid.

In *On Interpretation,* Aristotle extends his analysis of the syllogism to examine modal logic, that is, sentences containing the words *possibly* or *necessarily*. He is not as successful in his analysis, but the analysis does bring to light at least one important problem. It would seem that all past events necessarily either happened or did not happen, meaning that there are no events in the past that possibly happened and possibly did not happen. By contrast, we tend to think of many future events as possible and not necessary. But if someone had made a prediction yesterday about what would happen tomorrow, that prediction, because it is in the past, must already be necessarily true or necessarily false, meaning that what will happen tomorrow is already fixed by necessity and not just possibility. Aristotle's answer to this problem is unclear, but he seems to reject the fatalist idea that the future is already fixed, suggesting instead that statements about the future cannot be either true or false.

Analysis

Aristotle's logic is one of the most mind-boggling achievements of the human intellect, especially when we bear in mind that he invented the entire field of logic from scratch. His work was not significantly improved upon until the invention of modern mathematical logic in the late nineteenth century. Obviously, Aristotle is not the first person to make use of a syllogism in an argument, and he is not even the first person to reason abstractly about how arguments are put together. However, he is the first person to make a systematic attempt to sort out what kinds of arguments can be made, what their structure is, and how we can prove rigorously whether they are true or false, valid or invalid. His analysis of the syllogism lays bare the mechanics of rational argumentation so that we can see the truth plainly through the many layers of rhetoric, ambiguity, and obscurity. With the proper analysis, Aristotle tells us, any argument can be laid out as a series of simple and straightforward statements, and its validity or invalidity will be obvious.

Aristotle's logic rests on two central assumptions: the fundamental analysis of a sentence divides it into a subject and a predicate, and every sentence can be analyzed into one or more categorical sentences. Aristotle identifies four kinds of categorical sentences and distinguishes each by the way the subject relates to the predicate. In other words, the way in which subject and predicate are connected is what allows us to distinguish one kind of sentence from another. Furthermore, Aristotle argues that, at heart, there are only four kinds of sentences. Every variation that we see in ordinary human speech is just one categorical sentence, or a combination of several, with window dressing to make it look less plain. With these twin assumptions, Aristotle can show that there are only forty-eight possible kinds of arguments that can be made—fourteen of them are valid and thirty-four of them are invalid. In theory, he has given us a foolproof map: with suffi-cient analytical skill, we can reduce any argument to a series of simple subject–predicate sentences of four different kinds and then quickly determine whether the combination of these sen-tences produces a valid or an invalid inference.

Modern mathematical logic departs from Aristotle primarily by recognizing that the subject–predicate form of grammar is not the fundamental unit of logical analysis. Bertrand Russell famously uses the example of the sentence, "the present king of America is bald" to show that, on Aristotle's logic, we are com-mitted to accepting that the phrase "the present king of America" has a clear meaning, which leads to all sorts of difficulties. A modern logician would analyze that same sentence as being a combination of three smaller sentences: "there is a person who is the present king of America," "there is only one person who is the present king of America," and "that person is bald." We know that there is no king of America, so we can immediately see that the first of these three sentences is false and don't need to worry about the complications of accepting "the present king of America" as a subject in a syllogism.

The fundamental insight that there is more to logic than subject–predicate analysis opens the way for several other important blows to Aristotle's logic, primarily that the categorical sentence is not the only kind of sentence and that the syllogism is not the only form of argument. There are a number of kinds of sentence that cannot be analyzed into one or more categorical sentences, most notably sentences that contain other sentences ("If you are over forty or have false teeth then you will not enjoy candy as much as a ten-year-old unless you have recently undergone sur-gery"), sentences that express relations ("My left foot is bigger than my right foot"), and sentences that involve more than one quantifier ("No people love all people who hate some people"). These sentences can be easily analyzed with the technical machinery of modern logic but only by accepting that they can fit into nonsyllogistic arguments. The first and the third examples of noncategorical sentences just given contain more than two terms and so cannot fit into a syllogism. Logical deductions can be made from them in combination with other premises, but the conclusion may take many more than two steps to reach.

Summary: The Structure of Knowledge

The *Categories,* traditionally interpreted as an introduction to Aristotle's logical work, divides all of being into ten categories. These ten categories are as follows:

- Substance, which in this context means what something is essentially (e.g., human, rock)
- Quantity (e.g., ten feet, five liters)
- Quality (e.g., blue, obvious)
- Relation (e.g., double, to the right of)
- Location (e.g., New York, home plate)
- Time (e.g., yesterday, four o'clock)
- Position (e.g., sitting, standing)
- Possession (e.g., wearing shoes, has a blue coat)
- Doing (e.g., running, smiling)
- Undergoing (e.g., being run into, being smiled at)

Of the ten, Aristotle considers substance to be primary, because we can conceive of a substance without, for example, any given qualities but we cannot conceive of a quality except as it pertains to a particular substance. One important conclusion from this division into categories is that we can make no general statements about being as a whole because there are ten very different ways in which something can have being. There is no common ground between the kind of being that a rock has and the kind of being that the color blue has.

Aristotle's emphasis on the syllogism leads him to conceive of knowledge as hierarchically structured, a claim that he fleshes out in the *Posterior Analytics*. To have knowledge of a fact, it is not enough simply to be able to repeat the fact. We must also be able to give the reasons why that fact is true, a process that Aristotle calls *demonstration*. Demonstration is essentially a matter of showing that the fact in question is the conclusion to a valid syllogism. If some truths are premises that can be used to prove other truths, those first truths are logically prior to the truths that follow from them. Ultimately, there must be one or several "first principles" from which all other truths follow and which do not themselves follow from anything. However, if these first principles do not follow from anything, they cannot count as knowledge because there are no reasons or premises we can give to prove that they are true. Aristotle suggests that these first principles are a kind of intuition of the universals we recognize in experience.

Aristotle believes that the objects of knowledge are also structured hierarchically and conceives of definition as largely a process of division. For example, suppose we want to define *human*. First, we note that humans are animals, which is the genus to which they belong. We can then take note of various differentia that distinguish humans from other animals. For example, humans walk on two legs, unlike tigers, and they lack feathers, unlike birds. Given any term, if we can identify its genus and then identify the differentia that distinguish it from other things within its genus, we have given a definition of that term, which amounts to giving an account of its nature, or essence. Ultimately, Aristotle identifies five kinds of relationships a predicate can have with its subject: a genus relationship ("humans are animals"); a differentia relationship ("humans have two legs"); a unique property relationship ("humans are the only animals that can cry"); a definition, which is a unique property that explains the nature or essence of the subject; and an accident relationship, such as "some humans have blue eyes," where the relationship does not hold necessarily.

While all true knowledge descends from knowledge of first principles, actual argument and debate is much less pristine. When two people argue, they need not go back to first principles to ground every claim but must simply find premises they both agree on. The trick to debate is to find premises your opponent will agree to and then show that conclusions contrary to your opponent's position follow necessarily from these premises. The *Topics* devotes a great deal of attention to classifying the kinds of conclusions that can be drawn from different kinds of premises, whereas the *Sophistical Refutations* explores various logical tricks used to deceive people into accepting a faulty line of reasoning.

Analysis

Aristotle's treatment of logical categories commits him to asserting a strong link between language and reality. To take a salient point, it is not clear whether his ten categories are meant to denote the ten kinds of being that exist or the ten kinds of predicates we can use in language. It seems most likely that he is suggesting both. That is, there are ten kinds of predicates we can use in language, and these ten predicates denote the ten kinds of being that exist. In other words, the structure of language mirrors the structure of the world. This is not a ridiculous assumption to make, but neither is it an obvious one. There has been much philosophical debate in the twentieth century as to the degree to which ordinary language reveals the structure of the world to us and the degree to which it obscures the structure of the world from us. As we see in the *Metaphysics,* Aristotle's ten categories, his conception of definition, his five "predicables," and his conception of first principles all loom large not just as means of making sense of the world but also as the fundamental struts on which reality itself is built.

When Aristotle talks about knowledge as requiring demonstration, he is using the word *knowledge* in a much narrower sense than what we usually think of when we use the word. This term is a rough translation of the Greek term *epistêmê*, which specifically denotes knowledge of a scientific or rigorously proven kind. In saying that such knowledge requires demonstration, Aristotle is showing the influence of his teacher, Plato, who insists on distinguishing knowledge, which must be justified, from mere true belief. Demonstration establishes that we not only know a certain fact but can show why it must necessarily be so and why it could not be otherwise. This conception of scientific knowledge is quite a step away from our current conception of science, which relies fundamentally on hypothesis and experiment rather than on logically rigorous demonstration. As a means of showing that something is necessarily as it is and could not possibly be otherwise, demonstration is closely linked with Aristotle's conception of definition. Both of these terms intend to get to the heart of a matter, to show what it really is rather than what it appears to be on the surface.

Aristotle's claim that substance is the primary category figures prominently in his *Metaphysics,* but the claim itself is far from certain. On the surface, it makes intuitive sense. We are inclined to think that rocks and trees and pigeons are more real somehow than the colors or qualities or numbers that we might associate with them. However, it is very difficult to show exactly how and why substances are primary. Aristotle argues that substance can exist without quality or any of the other categories, but none of those categories can exist without substance. Certainly, it is hard to imagine any of those other categories in a universe without substance, but it is equally difficult to imagine a substance that has no qualities, or no location, or that sits outside of time. In the *Metaphysics,* Aristotle reconsiders his conception of substance, so that species, and not individual particulars, become the fundamental substances that make up reality, but this does not help to resolve the difficulty of showing why substance should be prior to the other categories in the first place.

PHYSICS

The *Physics* takes its title from the Greek word *phusis,* which translates more accurately as "the order of nature." The first two books of the *Physics* are Aristotle's general introduction to the study of nature. The remaining six books treat physics itself at a very theoretical, generalized level, culminating in a discussion of God, the First Cause.

Summary: Books I to IV

The *Physics* opens with an investigation into the principles of nature. At root, there must be a certain number of basic principles at work in nature, according to which all natural processes can be explained. All change or process involves something coming to be from out of its opposite. Something comes to be what it is by acquiring its distinctive form—for example, a baby becomes an adult, a seed becomes a mature plant, and so on. Since this the baby or the seed were working toward this form all along, the form itself (the idea or pattern of the mature specimen) must have existed before the baby or seed actually matured. Thus, the form must be one of the principles of nature.

Another principle of nature must be the privation or absence of this form, the opposite out of which the form came into being. Besides form and privation, there must be a third principle, matter, which remains constant throughout the process of change. If nothing remains unchanged when something undergoes a change, then there would be no "thing" that we could say underwent the change. So there are three basic principles of nature: matter, form, and privation. For example, a person's education involves the form of being educated, the privation of being ignorant, and the underlying matter of the person who makes the change from ignorance to education. This view of the principles of nature resolves many of the problems of earlier philosophers and suggests that matter is conserved: though its form may change, the underlying matter involved in changes remains constant.

Change takes place according to four different kinds of cause. These causes are closer to what we might call "explanations": they explain in different ways why the change came to pass. The four causes are:

1. Material cause, which explains what something is made of
2. Formal cause, which explains the form or pattern to which a thing corresponds
3. Efficient cause, which is what we ordinarily mean by "cause," the original source of the change
4. Final cause, which is the intended purpose of the change

For example, in the making of a house, the material cause is the materials the house is made of, the formal cause is the architect's plan, the efficient cause is the process of building it, and the final cause is to provide shelter and comfort. Natural objects, such as plants and animals, differ from artificial objects in that they have an internal source of change. All the causes of change in artificial objects are found outside the objects themselves, but natural objects can cause change from within.

Aristotle rejects the idea that chance constitutes a fifth cause, similar in nature to the other four. We normally talk about chance in reference to coincidences, where two separate events, which had their own causes, coincide in a way that is not explained by either set of causes. For instance, two people might both have their own reasons for being in a certain place at a certain time, but neither of these sets of reasons explains the coincidence of both people being there at the same time.

Final causes apply to nature as much as to art, so everything in nature serves a useful purpose. Aristotle argues against the views both of Democritus, who thinks that necessity in nature has no useful purpose, and of Empedocles, who holds an evolutionary view according to which only those combinations of living parts that are useful have managed to survive and reproduce themselves. If Democritus were right, there would be as many useless aspects of nature as there are useful, while Empedocles' theory does not explain how random combinations of parts could come together in the first place.

Books III and IV examine some fundamental concepts of nature, starting with change, and then treating infinity, place, void, and time. Aristotle defines change as "the actuality of that which exists potentially, in so far as it is potentially this actuality." That is, change rests in the potential of one thing to become another. In all cases, change comes to pass through contact between an agent and a patient, where the agent imparts its form to the patient and the change itself takes place in the patient.

Either affirming or denying the existence of infinity leads to certain contradictions and paradoxes, and Aristotle finds an ingenious solution by distinguishing between potential and actual infinities. He argues that there is no such thing as an actual infinity: infinity is not a substance in its own right, and there are neither infinitely large objects nor an infinite number of objects. However, there are potential infinities in the sense that, for example, an immortal could theoretically sit down and count up to an infinitely large number but that this is impossible in practice. Time, for example, is a potential infinity because it potentially extends forever, but no one who is counting time will ever count an infinite number of minutes or days.

Aristotle asserts that place has a being independent of the objects that occupy it and denies the existence of empty space, or void. Place must be independent of objects because otherwise it would make no sense to say that different objects can be in the same place at different times. Aristotle defines place as the limits of what contains an object and determines that the place of the earth is "at the center" and the place of the heavens as "at the periphery."

Aristotle's arguments against the void make a number of fundamental errors. For example, he assumes that heavier objects fall faster than lighter ones. From this assumption, he argues that the speed of a falling object is directly proportional to an object's weight and inversely proportional to the density of the medium it travels through. Since the void is a medium of zero density, that would mean that an object would fall infinitely fast through a void, which is an absurdity, so Aristotle concludes that there cannot be such a thing as a void.

Aristotle closely identifies time with change. We register that time has passed only by registering that something has changed. In other words, time is a measure of change just as space is a measure of distance. Just as Aristotle denies the possibility of empty space, or void, Aristotle denies the possibility of empty time, as in time that passes without anything happening.

Analysis

Aristotle's conception of the natural world is based fundamentally on change. Rather than simply accept the fact that things change, Aristotle marvels at this fact and puzzles over how the world must be if change is possible. What change is and how it comes to pass sit at the heart of Aristotle's scientific investigations. He investigates the fundamental principles of nature by asking what takes place in a process of change. He outlines four causes that explain change. He treats time as a measure of change. Later in the *Physics*, he expends a great deal of ingenuity on refuting paradoxes that suggest that change does not exist. This fascination with change allows Aristotle to look more deeply into the workings of nature than most of us would think to. By the end of book I, he claims to have discovered the three basic principles of nature without which change would be impossible. That is, by asking how it is that change might be possible, he develops a basic sense of how the universe must be arranged.

Aristotle's investigation of the principles of matter leads him to draw the important distinction between form and matter. A classic example that illustrates this distinction is that of a bronze statue: the bronze is the matter, while the figure of the statue is the form. Neither matter nor form can exist independently. Even a lump of bronze would have some form, though the form would be less distinctive than that of a statue. Similarly, it would be impossible for a form to exist without some matter to take on that form. The statue need not be made of bronze to have its form, but it must be made of something. The form–matter distinction does a great deal of work for Aristotle, especially in the *Physics* and the *Metaphysics,* as it allows him to explain how something can both change and remain the same. If the bronze statue were melted down, for instance, the form would have changed but the matter would remain the same. If there were no unchanging matter, we would have no grounds for saying that the lump of bronze was in some way the same bronze as that which made up the statue.

Aristotle's conception of change as being a process of something coming to be out of its opposite is troubling and does not sit well with his conception of the four causes. The idea gains strength from instances of change between binary opposites. For example, for something to become hot, it must have been colder before, so we can say that heat comes to be from out of its opposite, cold. However, there are many examples of change that do not mediate between binary opposites. In the summary just presented, we used the example of building a house when discussing the four causes. Aristotle might argue that the house comes to be from out of its opposite, which is "not a house," but this is unconvincing. A house comes to be from out of a pile of bricks, wood, and mortar, and it seems far-fetched to argue that a pile of bricks, wood, and mortar are the opposite of a house. That same pile of bricks, wood, and mortar could be used to build many different kinds of structure, so Aristotle would have to say that the same pile of bricks, wood, and mortar is the opposite of an infinite number of possible buildings.

In his treatment of final causes, Aristotle boldly asserts that all of nature is teleological, meaning that it is organized toward a final end. In other words, he believes that all natural things have not only form and matter but also purpose. This belief in teleology informs all of Aristotle's work, from his scientific writings to his ethics. This belief also clashes sharply with modern conceptions of science, which explicitly does not try to identify purpose in the processes it observes.

Aristotle's conception of teleology in nature comes primarily from his impression of biological organisms, all of which are complex and highly efficient. Such organisms could not possibly come into being at random, he reasons, and so must all be designed with a particular purpose. It is interesting to note that, in arguing for this conclusion, Aristotle rejects an evolutionary conception of nature as advanced by Empedocles. Empedocles did not have the understanding of genetics or speciation that make modern evolutionary biology coherent, so Aristotle's attack on Empedocles is valid. This fact may lead us to wonder, however, whether we might have developed modern evolutionary biology sooner than the nineteenth century had Aristotle not convinced his peers that Empedocles' views were mistaken.

Summary: Books V to VIII

There are three kinds of change: generation, in which something comes into being; destruction, in which something is destroyed; and variation, in which some attribute of a thing is changed while the thing itself remains constant. Of the ten categories Aristotle describes in the *Categories* (see previous summary of the *Organon*), change can take place only in respect of quality, quantity, or location. Change itself is not a substance and so it cannot itself have any properties. Among other things, this means that changes themselves cannot change. Aristotle discusses the ways in which two changes may be the same or different and argues also that no two changes are opposites, but rather that rest is the opposite of change.

Time, space, and movement are all continuous, and there are no fundamental units beyond which they cannot be divided. Aristotle reasons that movement must be continuous because the alternative—that objects make infinitesimally small jumps from one place to another without occupying the intermediate space—is absurd and counterintuitive. If an object moves from point A to point B, there must be a time at which it is moving from point A to point B. If it is simply at point A at one instant and point B at the next, it cannot properly be said to have moved from the one to the other. If movement is continuous, then time and space must also be continuous, because continuous movement would not be possible if time and space consisted of discrete, indivisible atoms.

Among the connected discussions of change, rest, and continuity, Aristotle considers Zeno's four famous paradoxes. The first is the dichotomy paradox: to get to any point, we must first travel halfway, and to get to that halfway point, we must travel half of that halfway, and to get to half of that halfway, we must first travel a half of the half of that halfway, and so on infinitely, so that, for any given distance, there is always a smaller distance to be covered first, and so we can never start moving at all. Aristotle answers that time can be divided just as infinitely as space, so that it would take infinitely little time to cover the infinitely little space needed to get started.

The second paradox is called the Achilles paradox: supposing Achilles is racing a tortoise and gives the tortoise a head start. Then by the time Achilles reaches the point the tortoise started from, the tortoise will have advanced a certain distance, and by the point Achilles advances that certain distance, the tortoise will have advanced a bit farther, and so on, so that it seems Achilles will never be able to catch up with, let alone pass, the tortoise. Aristotle responds that the paradox assumes the existence of an actual infinity of points between Achilles and the tortoise. If there were an actual infinity—that is, if Achilles had to take account of all the infinite points he passed in catching up with the tortoise—it would indeed take an infinite amount of time for Achilles to pass the tortoise. However, there is only a potential infinity of points between Achilles and the tortoise, meaning that Achilles can cover the infinitely many points between him and the tortoise in a finite amount of time so long as he does not take account of each point along the way.

The third and fourth paradoxes, called the arrow paradox and the stadium paradox, respectively, are more obscure, but they seem to aim at proving that time and space cannot be divided into atoms.

This is a position that Aristotle already agrees with, so he takes less trouble over these paradoxes.

Aristotle argues that change is eternal because there cannot be a first cause of change without assuming that that cause was itself uncaused. Living things can cause change without something external acting on them, but the source of this change is internal thoughts and desires, and these thoughts and desires are provoked by external stimuli. Arguing that time is infinite, Aristotle reasons that there cannot be a last cause, since time cannot exist without change. Next, Aristotle argues that everything that changes is changed by something external to itself. Even changes within a single animal consist of one part of the animal changing another part.

Aristotle's reflections on cause and change lead him ultimately to posit the existence of a divine unmoved mover. If we were to follow a series of causes to its source, we would find a first cause that is either an unchanged changer or a self-changing changer. Animals are the best examples of self-changers, but they constantly come into being and pass away. If there is an eternal succession of causes, there needs to be a first cause that is also eternal, so it cannot be a self-changing animal. Since change is eternal, there must be a single cause of change that is itself eternal and continuous. The primary kind of change is movement and the primary kind of movement is circular, so this first cause must cause circular movement. This circular movement is the movement of the heavens, and it is caused by some first cause of infinite power that is above the material world. The circular movement of the heavens is then in turn the cause of all other change in the sublunary world.

Analysis

The problems associated with time, change, continuity, and infinity are all related. If space and time are continuous, that implies that there are an infinite number of points in space or moments in time between any two given points or moments. As Zeno's paradoxes illustrate, assuming continuity in space and time then raises the problem of how we can ever cross an infinite number of points in space or pass an infinite number of moments in time. If they are infinite, by definition they have no end. How we make sense of the concepts of infinity and continuity, then, are not simply mathematical questions but questions that have real bearing on how the world is put together. One solution, proposed by philosohers known as the Atomists, is that time and space are not continuous but consist rather of very small, indivisible units. Aristotle rejects this position on the grounds that it makes nonsense of the idea of change: something can only be in a state of change if it makes a continuous transition from one state to another. Aristotle wants to hold on to change, but to do so, he must also uphold the continuity of time and space, which puts him into trouble with Zeno's paradoxes.

Aristotle's distinction between potential and actual infinities is an ingenious means of maintaining the continuity of space and time without falling victim to Zeno's paradoxes. Denying out of principle the very idea of infinity would raise all sorts of complicated mathematical problems, so Aristotle does not want to rule infinity out entirely. However, he is steadfast in denying the actuality of infinity: he says that the universe is not infinitely large, that there is not an infinite amount of matter in it, and so on. However, he grants, it is in theory possible that we could count up to infinity or measure an infinite number of points on a ruler, and so on. Because we could potentially divide up time or space infinitely, we can accept the continuity of space and time as well as the existence of a state of change. However, because neither space nor time can ever *actually* be divided up infinitely, Zeno's paradoxes do not hold muster.

Aristotle's distinction between actual and potential infinities has been the topic of a great deal of debate and has ultimately been proved false. In the nineteenth century, mathematicians developed a rigorous means of expressing concepts such as continuity and infinity that renders Aristotle's distinction between two kinds of infinity unnecessary. It turns out Zeno was right, at least in a limited sense: though change is possible, there is no such thing as a state of change. We can accept that space is continuous and accept that an object moving through space passes through an infinite number of points so long as we do not insist that it is in a continuous state of change. For example, we can easily show how Achilles overtakes the tortoise by showing in a table the relative positions of Achilles and the tortoise at different moments in time. This table will show position and time but will say nothing about the motion of the two bodies. Motion is something we can infer from the fact that Achilles is at one place at one moment and at another the next, but Achilles is not in a "state of motion" at any of those given moments. Not all mathematicians would agree to the solution outlined here, and Zeno's paradoxes remain a subject of debate even now.

Aristotle returns to his idea of an unmoved mover in greater detail in the *Metaphysics,* but it is worth noting here the role this divine figure plays relative to the rest of the cosmos. Aristotle places the Earth at the center of the cosmos, orbited by a number of concentric spheres holding the sun, the moon, the planets, and ultimately the stars. The movement of all heavenly bodies, then, is circular, and the Earth itself is a sphere at the center of other spheres. Aristotle explains that all these spheres are in motion because of a divine figure beyond the outer sphere of stars. This unmoved mover can himself only move the sphere of the stars, and the movement of the stars in turn influences the movement of all the other spheres and hence of life on Earth. We can see in this conception of the cosmos why astrology has had such a grip on the Western mind: everything that happens on the Earth in Aristotle's conception is ultimately a reaction to the movement of the heavens.

METAPHYSICS

Aristotle's *Metaphysics* is divided into fourteen books, which are usually named after the first thirteen letters of the Greek alphabet. The books, in order, are Alpha, Alpha the Lesser, Beta, Gamma, Delta, Epsilon, Zeta, Eta, Theta, Iota, Kappa, Lambda, Mu, and Nu. Though all fourteen books treat certain common themes, many of them are independent of all the others. Scholars believe that the *Metaphysics* is really a compilation of a number of Aristotle's writings that later editors grouped together. Some of the material in the *Metaphysics* repeats that covered in the *Physics*.

Summary: Books Alpha to Epsilon

Knowledge consists of particular truths that we learn through experience and the general truths of art and science. Wisdom consists of understanding the most general truths of all, which are the fundamental principles and causes that govern everything. Philosophy provides the deepest understanding of the world and of divinity by pursuing the sense of wonder we feel toward reality.

There are four kinds of cause, or rather kinds of explanation, for how things are:

1. Material cause, which explains what a thing is made of

2. Formal cause, which explains the form a thing assumes

3. Efficient cause, which explains the process by which it came into being

4. Final cause, which explains the end or purpose it serves

The explanations of earlier philosophers have conformed to these four causes but not as coherently and systematically as Aristotle's formulation. Aristotle acknowledges that Plato's Theory of Forms gives a strong account of the formal cause, but it fails to prove that Forms exist and to explain how objects in the physical world participate in Forms.

Book Alpha the Lesser addresses some questions of method. Though we all have a natural aptitude for thinking philosophically, it is very difficult to philosophize well. The particular method of study depends on the subject being studied and the inclinations of the students. The important thing is to have a firm grasp of method before proceeding, whatever the method. The best method is that of mathematics, but this method is not suitable for subjects in which the objects of study are prone to change, as in science. Most reasoning involves causal chains, in which we investigate a phenomenon by studying its causes, and then the cause of those causes, and so on. This method would be unworkable if there were infinitely long causal chains, but all causal chains are finite, meaning that there must be an uncaused first cause to every chain.

Book Beta consists of a series of fifteen metaphysical puzzles on the nature of first principles, substance, and other fundamental concepts. In each case, Aristotle presents a thesis and a contradicting antithesis, both of which could be taken as answers to the puzzle. Aristotle himself provides no answers to the puzzles but rather takes them as examples of extreme positions between which he will try to mediate throughout the rest of the *Metaphysics*.

Book Gamma asserts that philosophy, especially metaphysics, is the study of being *qua* being. That is, while other sciences investigate limited aspects of being, metaphysics investigates being itself. The study of being *qua* being amounts to the search into first principles and causes. Being itself is primarily identified with the idea of substance but also with unity, plurality, and a variety of other concepts.

Philosophy is also concerned with logic and the principles of demonstration, which are supremely general, and hence concerned with being itself. The most fundamental principle is the principle of noncontradiction: nothing can both be something and not be that same something. Aristotle defends this principle by arguing that it is impossible to contradict it coherently. Connected to the principle of non-contradiction is the principle of the excluded middle, which states that there is no middle position between two contradictory positions. That is, a thing is either *x* or not-*x*, and there is no third possibility. Book Gamma concludes with an attack on several general claims of earlier philosophers: that everything is true, that everything is false, that everything is at rest, and that everything is in motion.

Book Delta consists of the definitions of about forty terms, some of which feature prominently in the rest of the *Metaphysics,* such as principle, cause, nature, being, and substance. The definitions specify precisely how Aristotle uses these terms and often distinguish between different uses or categories of the terms.

Book Epsilon opens by distinguishing philosophy from the sciences, not just on the basis of its generality but also because philosophy, unlike the sciences, takes itself as a subject of inquiry. The sciences can be divided into practical, productive, and theoretical. The theoretical sciences can be divided further into physics, mathematics, and theology, or first philosophy, which studies first principles and causes.

We can look at being in four different ways: accidental being, being as truth, the category of being, and being in actuality and potentiality. Aristotle considers the first two in book Epsilon; examines the category of being, or substance, in books Zeta and

Eta; and investigates being in actuality and potentiality in book Theta. Accidental being covers the kinds of properties that are not essential to a thing described. For example, if a man is musical, his musicality is accidental since being musical does not define him as a man and he would still be a man even if he were not musical. Accidental being must have a kind of accidental causation, which we might associate with chance. That is, there is no necessary reason why a musical man is musical; rather, it just so happens by chance that he is musical. Being as truth covers judgments that a given proposition is true. These sorts of judgments involve mental acts, so being as truth is an affection of the mind and not a kind of being in the world. Because accidental being is random and being as truth is only mental, they fall outside the realm of philosophy, which deals with more fundamental kinds of being.

Analysis

The first five books of the *Metaphysics* jump around a great deal, and what ultimately emerges is a hodgepodge preparation for the investigation of substance that follows in books Zeta and Eta. Aristotle himself never uses the word *metaphysics* to describe his enterprise (the word was invented by a later editor and literally signifies nothing more than the books "after the Physics"), and it is not likely that he arranged for the various books of the *Metaphysics* to be grouped together. We should not be surprised, then, to find, for example, a series of unresolved puzzles in book Beta, only some of which are addressed later in the *Metaphysics,* or a set of definitions in book Delta, only some of which are used later in the *Metaphysics.* At some points, Aristotle seems to claim that his primary interest is "first principles," at others he seems fundamentally interested in logic, and at one point he equates metaphysics with theology. All six books, however, set out to find the best approach to the truly fundamental questions of philosophy. Without these preliminary attempts, the stage would not properly be set for the investigation of substance that follows.

Metaphysics is not unique in that it studies being—after all, almost every field of study is interested in things that exist—but rather that it studies being *qua* being. The word *qua* is a Latin term often used by philosophers, and it means something like "in its capacity as." For example, there are many different ways we could study humans. Biologists study humans in their capacity as living organisms, psychologists study humans in their capacity as beings with minds and consciousness, and anthropologists study humans in their capacity as social beings. A metaphysician, by contrast, would study humans in their capacity as beings that exist. That is, metaphysics is not so much interested in the different facts about existent entities as it is in the fact that these entities exist at all. What is it, metaphysics asks, that characterizes being itself? Aristotle says that this investigation is a search into first principles and causes. That is, metaphysics investigates the reason that there should be being at all, whereas the other sciences study the reasons behind various manifestations of being.

Aristotle often refers to metaphysics as "first philosophy," and though he doesn't specify in what sense metaphysics is "first," we can see that there is a sort of primacy to the investigation of being *qua* being. We can say all sorts of things about humans—they have consciousness, they have language, they have opposable thumbs—but all of these things can only be true of humans so long as they exist. We might say that metaphysics is a "first philosophy" because it approaches those things that must hold if any further science or philosophy is to have a purpose. We might go so far as to say that we must understand metaphysics before we can properly understand the rest of science and philosophy. Talking about how humans think or behave is only so much talk unless we know what it means for humans to exist in the first place. On the other hand, we cannot start studying metaphysics before we have some grasp of less fundamental topics. Just as it makes no sense to study auto mechanics if one has never seen a car, it also makes no sense to study being itself if one has no experience of the various manifestations of being.

Summary: Books Zeta and Eta

Referring back to his logical work in the *Categories,* Aristotle opens book Zeta by asserting that substance is the primary category of being. Rather than consider what being is, we can consider what substance is.

Aristotle first rejects the idea that substance is the ultimate substrate of a thing, that which remains when all its accidental properties are stripped away. For example, a dog is more fundamental than the color brown or the property of hairiness that are associated with it. However, if we strip away all the properties that a dog possesses, we wind up with a substrate with no properties of its own. Since this substrate has no properties, we can say nothing about it, so this substrate cannot be substance.

Instead, Aristotle suggests that we consider substance as essence and concludes that substances are species. The essence of a thing is that which makes it that thing. For example, being rational is an essential property of being human, because a human without rationality ceases to be human. But being musical is not an essential property of being human, because a human without musical skill is still human. Individual people, or dogs, or tables, contain a mixture of essential and inessential properties. Species, on the other hand—for instance, people in general, dogs in general, or tables in general—contain only essential properties.

A substance can be given a definition that does not presuppose the existence of anything else. A snub, for example, is not a substance, because we would define a snub as "a concave nose," so our definition of snub presupposes the existence of noses. A proper definition of a thing lists only its essential properties, and Aristotle asserts that only substances have essential properties or definitions. A snub nose, by contrast, has only accidental properties—properties like redness or largeness that may hold of some snubs but not of all—and *per se* properties—properties like concavity, which necessarily holds of all snubs but is not essential.

Physical objects are composites of form and matter, and Aristotle identifies substance with form. The matter of an object is the stuff that makes it up, whereas the form is the shape that stuff takes. For example, the matter in a bronze sphere is the bronze itself, and the form is the spherical shape. Aristotle argues that form is primary because form is what gives each thing its distinctive nature.

Aristotle argues that the definitions of substances cannot presuppose the existence of anything else, which raises the question of how there can be a definition that does not presuppose the existence of anything else. Presumably, a definition divides a whole into its constituent parts—for example, a human is defined as a rational animal—which suggests that a substance must in some way presuppose the existence of its constituent parts. Aristotle distinguishes between those cases in which the parts of an object or definition are prior to the whole and those cases in which the whole is prior to the parts. For example, we cannot understand the parts of a circle without first understanding the concept of circle as a whole; on the other hand, we cannot understand the whole of a syllable before we understand the letters that constitute its parts.

Aristotle argues that, in the case of substance, the whole is prior to the parts. He has earlier associated substance with form and suggests that we cannot make sense of matter before we can conceive of its form. To say a substance can be divided by its definition is like saying a physical object can be divided into form and matter: this conceptual distinction is possible, but form and matter constitute an indivisible whole, and neither can exist without the other. Similarly, the parts of a definition of a substance are conceptually distinct, but they can only exist when they are joined in a substance.

Having identified substance with essence, Aristotle attacks the view that substances are universals. This attack becomes effectively an attack on Plato's Theory of Forms, and Aristotle argues forcefully that universal Forms can neither exist prior to the individual instances of them nor be properly defined. Therefore, universal forms cannot play *any* role in science, let alone a fundamental role. He also argues against the suggestion that substances can be genus categories, like "animal" or "plant." Humans and horses, unlike animals, have the property of "thisness": the words *human* and *horse* pick out a particular kind of thing, whereas nothing particular is picked out by *animal*. Genuses are therefore not specific enough to qualify as substances.

Book Eta contains a number of loosely connected points elaborating Aristotle's views on substance. Aristotle associates an object's matter with its potentiality and its form with its actuality. That is, matter is potentially a certain kind of substance and becomes that substance in actuality when it takes on the form of that substance. By associating substance with form and actuality, Aristotle infers a further connection between substance and differentia: differentia are those qualities that distinguish one species in a genus from another. Book Eta also contains reflections on the nature of names, matter, number, and definition.

Analysis

This section of Aristotle's *Metaphysics* is one of the most difficult and controversial texts in the history of philosophy. The problems are many-layered. First, there is the difficulty of the subject matter, which is fundamental and very abstract. Second, there is the difficulty of translation, as Aristotle uses many technical coinages that read oddly in Greek and are difficult to render clearly in English. Third, there is the difficulty of consistency, as Aristotle does not seem to reach any settled conclusions and does not have a clear central thrust to his argument. This third difficulty is related to a fourth: it seems the various chapters were written at different times and may have been roughly patched together by a later editor. For all these reasons, commentators are divided not only over how to interpret these passages of the *Metaphysics* but also over what they mean.

Aristotle's metaphysics has been called a "metaphysics of substance" because he takes the fundamental questions of being to be equivalent to asking what substance is. In his *Categories* (see the *Organon*, page 44), Aristotle distinguishes ten fundamental categories of being: substance, quantity, quality, relation, location, time, position, possession, doing, and undergoing. One of the consequences of dividing being into these ten categories is that there is no overarching concept of "being" that applies to all things. Animals have a categorically different kind of being than colors, and though we can say that both exist, they have totally different kinds of existence. Since Aristotle has stated that the *Metaphysics* studies being *qua* being, that is, that it looks at what it means to say something exists at all, this division of being into ten categories would seem to complicate matters a bit. However, Aristotle argues both here and in the *Categories* that substance is the most fundamental kind of being, so the study of being is at heart the study of substance. The tricky part, it turns out, is sorting out what sorts of things qualify as substances.

Defining substances as species is a brilliant compromise between particularity and generality. Problems arise when we try to identify substances with individual entities (such as Joe or my pet rock Tony), but problems also arise when we try to identify substances with genus categories (such as animal or mineral), or universals (such as justice or beauty). The problem posed by particular entities is that they have nonessential properties. Let's imagine our friend Joe, who is clean-shaven. Joe can grow a beard and still be Joe, so the property of beardlessness that holds of Joe is accidental, not essential. If we were to give a definition of "Joe," we would not mention that he has no beard. On the other hand, if we were to give a description of Joe, we would have to mention that he has no beard if we wanted people to be able to distinguish Joe from his cousin Adam, who looks just like Joe but has a beard. So our description of Joe would make mention of properties that are not a part of his essence. In other words, to distinguish Joe from other people, we have to presuppose the existence of things, like beards, that are not essential to Joe. If substances are the fundamental building blocks of reality, their existence should not presuppose the existence of anything else. Since we cannot distinguish Joe without presupposing the existence of beards, Joe cannot be a substance. More generally, individual entities cannot be substances because they have nonessential properties that presuppose the existence of other things beyond themselves.

The trouble with genus categories and universals is that they do not have the property that Aristotle calls *thisness*. By thisness, he means a thing's ability to be distinguished from among others of its kind. Joe has thisness because we can distinguish him from among other people, and humans as a species have thisness because they can be distinguished from among other animals. However, animals themselves are a general category, and we tend not to need to distinguish animals from other categories of anything. We can appreciate the importance of thisness by understanding Aristotle's conception of definition. A definition consists of a genus term and differentia. For example, humans belong to the genus animal and can be differentiated from other animals by virtue of being rational. Humans, then, have thisness because they have differentia: they can be distinguished from others of their genus. A genus, on the other hand, has no differentia and thus cannot be distinguished as clearly from other things. If substances are fundamental, then we must come to know all other things through our knowledge of substance. Knowledge would be impossible if we were unable to distinguish between the objects of our knowledge, so the fundamental objects of knowledge must have differentia, or thisness. Therefore, genus categories and universals cannot be substances.

Species are the best candidates for substancehood because they have no nonessential properties but they also have thisness. While Joe and Adam have particular quirks that are true of only them, the species of human in general has no particular quirks outside the definition that holds of all humans. The essential properties of being human, like rationality, do not presuppose the existence of anything else, because rationality is a part of what it is to be human. These essential properties also make humans distinguishable from ducks or rocks or trees. Hence, Aristotle reaches the remarkable conclusion that humans and ducks and rocks and trees are the most fundamental building blocks of reality. We can imagine particular humans or ducks or rocks or trees only because these species exist, and we can only infer general categories such as animal or mineral or plant from the existence of species that fit within these categories.

Summary: Books Theta to Nu

Book Theta discusses potentiality and actuality, considering these concepts first in regard to process or change. When one thing, F, changes into another, G, we can say that F is G in potentiality, while G is G in actuality. F changes into G only if some other agent, H, acts on it. We say that H has active potentiality and F has passive potentiality. Potentiality can be either rational or irrational, depending on whether the change is effected by a rational agent or happens naturally. Aristotle distinguishes rational potentiality from irrational potentiality, saying that rational potentiality can produce opposites. For example, the rational potentiality of medicine can produce either health or sickness, whereas the irrational potentiality of heating can produce only heat and not cold. All potentialities must eventually be realized: if a potentiality never becomes an actuality, then we do not call it a potentiality but an impossibility. A potentiality is also determinate, meaning that it is the potential for a particular actuality and cannot realize some other actuality. While irrational potentialities are automatically triggered when active and passive potentialities come together, this is not the case with rational potentialities, as a rational agent can choose to withhold the realization of the potentiality even though it can be realized.

CHAPTER 2
ARISTOTLE

Aristotle identifies actuality with form, and hence substance, while identifying matter with potentiality. An uncarved piece of wood, for example, is a potential statue, and it becomes an actual statue when it is carved and thus acquires the form of a statue. Action is an actuality, but there are such things as incomplete actions, which are also the potentiality for further actions. Aristotle distinguishes between incomplete and complete actions by saying that incomplete actions do not contain their purpose within them, while the latter do. For example, dancing is a complete action because it is an end in itself, whereas fetching wood for a fire is an incomplete action because the end of fetching wood is to create a fire. If one thing can turn into another, that first thing is always potentially the other. That means that anything is potentially something else and that it was something else in the past with the potential to become what it is now. Aristotle speculates about the existence of an ultimate matter, which is potentially anything.

Aristotle argues that actuality is more fundamental than potentiality for three reasons. First, we cannot think of something as a potentiality without also thinking of the actuality it can potentially become, but we can think of an actuality without thinking of its potentiality. Second, for something to be potentially something else, that something else must already exist in actuality or there would be nothing for that potentiality to become. Third, Aristotle identifies actuality with form, which is in turn related to substance, which is the most fundamental thing that there is.

Book Iota treats the topic of unity, which is important to Aristotle because he has argued in book Zeta that both a substance and its definition are unities. Unity itself, however, is not a substance for two reasons. First, unity is a universal, not a species. Second, unity is always a property of something else: there is one table, one person, one chair, but never the number one by itself.

The discussion of unity leads into a discussion of contrariety, which Aristotle defines as a maximum of difference. Contrariety can thus hold only between two extremes. Two species of the same genus differ from one another in having contrariety in their forms. For example, one animal that has wings and one that does not have wings are different species within the genus animal. On the other hand, men and women are not of different species because the contrariety that exists between them is on the level of matter, not form.

Book Kappa, which some scholars doubt was even written by Aristotle, consists mostly of repeating doctrines already enunciated in the *Physics* or in earlier books of the *Metaphysics.*

Book Lambda begins with an overview of philosophy that stands somewhat independent of the rest of the *Metaphysics.* Aristotle re-emphasizes the primacy of substance and explains that there are three kinds of substance: two kinds of perceptible substances, perishable or imperishable, which are the subject of natural science, and substance that is immune to change, which is the subject of logic and mathematics.

Theology investigates the question of whether there is some common source to all substance—a common source that Aristotle identifies as a divine "prime mover." There must be some kind of eternal, unchanging substance because the Earth and time are not perishable, so there must be some substance within them that is also imperishable. This eternal substance has no potentiality but only actuality, and its perpetual actuality makes the world eternal as well. This eternal substance must also be the prime mover, the source of all movement and change in the cosmos. To be the prime mover, this substance must itself be unmoving. The prime mover is an object of desire for the heavenly bodies, causing them to move. The prime mover is an object of desire only because it is supremely desirable, so it must enjoy the best possible life. Aristotle hence identifies this prime mover with a benign God, who spends his time in contemplation of contemplation itself.

Aristotle wavers between saying there is a single prime mover or multiple prime movers. If there are many, their number, based on astronomical calculations, is either 47 or 55. The prime mover contemplates contemplation because anything lower would be unworthy of it and anything higher would imply that there is something more desirable than the existence of the prime mover himself. Because the prime mover is good, this means the universe as a whole is good.

Books Mu and Nu consider the metaphysical status of mathematics, and in them Aristotle concludes that mathematical entities are not substances. Aristotle attacks in particular Plato's view that each number corresponds to a Form, primarily because this view obscures the relationships between numbers and fails to explain the relationship between numbers and sensible particulars. Aristotle suggests instead that numbers are physical objects considered in abstraction from their physical and accidental properties. For example, the number five is the same thing as five cats once we factor out everything that makes the cats cats instead of something else. Aristotle concludes by rejecting the idea that numbers can play a causal role in nature, reaffirming his view that substance is at the foundation of nature.

Analysis

In arguing that actuality is more fundamental than potentiality, Aristotle effectively argues that the chicken comes before the egg, as one commentator puts it. He is telling us that an object can only be a potential something if there is already an actual something for that object to become. This claim has the paradoxical result that, for instance, the chicken must already exist for the egg to be a potential chicken. Of course, it is obviously false that individual chickens precede individual eggs: every chicken that now exists must have been an egg at some point. However, according to book Zeta, individual chickens are not substances. The species of chicken is a substance, and there can be no chicken eggs until there is a species called "chicken" for those eggs to become. After all, we cannot point to an object and say, "that is a chicken egg" if there is no such thing as a chicken. Substance is the most fundamental thing there is, so substance must be an actuality. Since, as Aristotle has argued earlier, nothing can exist unless substance exists, that means that potentialities cannot exist unless their actualities as substances already exist.

Aristotle's discussion of actuality and potentiality in book Theta provides an important link between the discussion of substance in books Zeta and Eta and the discussion of theology in book Lambda. In book Zeta, Aristotle tells us that species are substances, so the universe is fundamentally made up of the sorts of things we find in the world around us. In book Theta, he explains that substances are fundamental because they have actuality: they are what other things are trying to become. With actuality added as a new and important criterion for substancehood, we can infer that the most fundamental substances are completely actual, with no potentiality. Substances such as humans and chickens have potentiality in the form of fetuses and eggs, so they are not completely actual. In book Lambda, Aristotle suggests that there are also eternal substances and that these are more important and more fundamental than the species of the world around us because they are only actuality, with no potentiality. The concept of actuality, then, points to a way in which the material substances discussed in book Zeta fall a bit short of the fundamental role Aristotle wants them to play, and the theological discussion of book Lambda must make up for this shortfall.

When Aristotle talks about a prime mover or a first cause, he means that this mover or cause comes first conceptually rather than chronologically. That is, we should not imagine a universe at rest however many billions of years ago that is then set in motion by the prime movers: they do not come first in the sense that they are what first set everything in motion. On the contrary, Aristotle argues at a number of points in the *Physics* and *Metaphysics* that time is eternal, so that there is no beginning to time. Rather, we should think of the prime movers as first conceptually. For example, we could ask why the soccer ball is rolling and say that Ronaldo kicked it. We could then ask why Ronaldo moved his leg and say that he felt a certain desire. We could then explain the desire by appealing to certain causes in Ronaldo's life, and so on. So the movement of the soccer ball could be explained by the movement of Ronaldo's leg, by Ronaldo's desire, by Ronaldo's life story, and so on. The deepest explanation of any movement, says Aristotle, are these prime movers. They are not first in time so much as they are the ultimate explanation to which one can appeal in explaining any movement.

The seemingly bizarre conclusions that the prime movers are objects of desire for the heavens and that they occupy themselves by contemplating contemplation are consequences of Aristotle's claim that prime movers themselves are unmoved. Aristotle wants the prime movers to be unmoved for fear of an infinite regress: if they are moved, we can ask what moves them, and then ask what moves their movers, and so on. However, according to Aristotle's theory of causation, something cannot cause another thing to move unless it imparts movement to that other thing. A person cannot move a box without pushing or pulling on it. The only cause of motion that seems not to require movement is desire. If the prime movers were to push the heavens in their circular movements, they would themselves be moving. But if the heavens move in a circular pattern out of a desire for the perfection of the prime movers, this does not call for any movement on the part of the prime movers. This, of course, raises the question of what makes the prime movers so perfect that the heavens should move for them. For reasons previously outlined, Aristotle concludes that they engage in the perfect activity of contemplating contemplation.

NICOMACHEAN ETHICS

Scholars disagree about the source of the name for the _Nicomachean Ethics_. Both Aristotle's father and Aristotle's son were named Nicomachus, so it is possible that the book is dedicated to either one. Other scholars suggest that Aristotle's son may have edited the book after Aristotle died, so that the title "Nicomachean" may refer to this particular edition of Aristotle's ethical works.

Summary: Books I to IV

Happiness is the highest good and the end at which all our activities ultimately aim. All our activities aim at some end, though most of these ends are means toward other ends. For example, we go grocery shopping to buy food, but buying food is itself a means toward the end of eating well and thriftily. Eating well and thriftily is also not an end in itself but a means to other ends. Only happiness is an end in itself, so it is the ultimate end at which all our activities aim. As such, it is the supreme good. The difficulty is that people don't agree on what makes for a happy or good life, so the purpose of the _Ethics_ is to find an answer to this question. By its nature, the investigation is imprecise because there are so many variables involved when considering a person's life as a whole.

Aristotle defines the supreme good as an activity of the rational soul in accordance with virtue. Virtue for the Greeks is equivalent to excellence. A man has virtue as a flautist, for instance, if he plays the flute well, since playing the flute is the distinctive activity of a flautist. A virtuous person is someone who performs the distinctive activity of being human well. Rationality is our distinctive activity, that is, the activity that distinguishes us from plants and animals. All living things have a nutritive soul, which governs growth and nutrition. Humans and animals are distinct from plants in having a sensitive soul, which governs locomotion and instinct. Humans are distinct above all for having also a rational soul, which governs thought. Since our rationality is our distinctive activity, its exercise is the supreme good.

Aristotle defines moral virtue as a disposition to behave in the right manner and as a mean between extremes of deficiency and excess, which are vices. We learn moral virtue primarily through habit and practice rather than through reasoning and instruction. Virtue is a matter of having the appropriate attitude toward pain and pleasure. For example, a coward will suffer undue fear in the face of danger, whereas a rash person will not suffer sufficient fear. Aristotle lists the principal virtues along with their corresponding vices, as represented in the following table. A virtuous person exhibits all of the virtues: they do not properly exist as distinct qualities but rather as different aspects of a virtuous life.

Sphere of action or feeling	Excess (vice)	Mean (virtue)	Deficiency (vice)
Fear and confidence	Rashness	Courage	Cowardice
Pleasure and pain	Licentiousness	Temperance	Insensibility
Getting and spending (minor)	Prodigality	Liberality	Illiberality
Getting and spending (major)	Vulgarity	Magnificence	Pettiness
Honor and dishonor (major)	Vanity	Magnanimity	Pusillanimity
Honor and dishonor (minor)	Ambition	Proper ambition	Unambitiousness
Anger	Irascibility	Patience	Lack of spirit
Self-expression	Boastfulness	Truthfulness	Understatement
Conversation	Buffoonery	Wittiness	Boorishness
Social conduct	Obsequiousness or flattery	Friendliness	Cantankerousness
Shame	Shyness	Modesty	Shamelessness
Indignation	Envy	Righteous indignation	Malicious enjoyment

We can only be held responsible for actions we perform voluntarily, not for cases involving physical compulsion or unavoidable ignorance. The best measure of moral judgment is choice, since choices are always made voluntarily by means of rational deliberation. We always choose to aim at the good, but people are often ignorant of what is good and therefore aim at some *apparent* good instead, which is in fact a vice.

Analysis

The *Nicomachean Ethics* advances an understanding of ethics known as *virtue ethics* because of its heavy reliance on the concept of virtue. The word we translate as *virtue* is *aretê*, and it could equally be translated as "excellence." Something has *aretê* if it performs its function well. A good horseman, for example, has the *aretê* of being good at handling horses, and a good knife has the *aretê* of sharpness. For the ancient Greeks, moral virtue was not essentially different from these other kinds of excellence. The Greeks did not have a distinctive concept of morality like we do, which carries associations of sanctity or duty. Moral virtue for them was simply a matter of performing well in the function of being human. For the ancient Greeks, the motivation for being good was not based in a divine legislator or a set of moral dos and don'ts but rather in the same kind of striving after excellence that might make an athlete train hard. The Greek word *ethos,* from which we derive the word *ethics*, literally means "character," and Aristotle's goal is to describe which qualities constitute an excellent character.

The important lesson to draw from Aristotle's Doctrine of the Mean is that virtue consists of finding an appropriate middle ground between two extremes. As such, each virtue has not one opposite but two. The opposite of courage is both cowardice and rashness, for example. This idea that there are two opposites for every virtue goes against much of the received wisdom of Aristotle's time, including Plato's writings on virtue. It also emphasizes the importance of moderation: we achieve virtue by finding a middle ground, not by aiming for an extreme. Where exactly this middle ground lies, however, is less obvious. Aristotle repeats a number of times that his table presents only a rough approximation and that virtues lie closer to one vice than another to different extents for different people. The Table of Virtues just presented is not intended as a set of exact rules. On the contrary,

Aristotle argues that a truly virtuous person will naturally be inclined to behave appropriately and will have no need of rules.

Aristotle is clear that we arrive at moral virtue primarily through practice and that the value of studying ethical texts such as the one he has written is limited. This view makes sense when we consider that moral virtue is not essentially different from other forms of excellence as far as the Greeks are concerned. If we want to achieve excellence in rock climbing, for instance, it helps to study texts that show us how to improve our technique, but we can't make any significant improvements except by getting on a rock wall and practicing. Analogously, though it helps to read texts like the *Nicomachean Ethics* to get a clearer understanding of moral virtue, the only way to become more virtuous is through practice. We can only become more courageous by making a point of facing down our fears, and we can only become more patient by making a habit of controlling our anger. Since practice, not study, is the key to becoming virtuous, Aristotle takes a strong interest in the education of the young. He perceives that there is only so much we can do to improve a nasty adult, whereas we can more easily mold virtuous youths by instilling the proper habits in them from a young age.

Aristotle calls happiness an "activity," which distinguishes his conception of happiness both from our modern conception of happiness and from virtue, which Aristotle calls a "disposition." We tend to think of happiness as an emotional state and hence as something we *are,* rather than as something we *do.* The Greek word generally translated as "happiness" is *eudaimonia,* and it can equally be rendered as "success" or "flourishing." People who are *eudaimon* are not in a particular emotional state so much as they are living successfully. While happiness is the activity of living well, virtue represents the potential to live well. Excelling in all the moral virtues is fine and good, but it doesn't ensure our happiness unless we exercise those virtues. Courageous people who never test their courage by facing down fear have virtue but are not happy. Aristotle illustrates this distinction between happiness and virtue by saying that the best athletes only win at the Olympic Games if they compete. A virtuous person who does not exercise virtue is like an athlete who sits on the sideline and watches. Aristotle has a proactive conception of the good life: happiness waits only for those who go out and seize it.

Summary: Books V to X

The term *justice* can apply both to a general disposition in a person and to questions concerning exchanges and illegal infractions. Justice is a distinct kind of virtue because it encompasses all the other virtues and because it treats the interactions between people rather than simply the dispositions of an individual person. Aristotle distinguishes between distributive justice, which deals with the distribution of goods among members of a community, and rectificatory justice, which deals with unjust gains or losses between two people, through trade, theft, or assault. Distributive justice accords goods and honor proportionately, giving most to those who deserve most, whereas rectificatory justice aims to restore imbalances. No one willingly suffers an injustice, and it is not possible to treat oneself unjustly. While the laws are a good guideline, they do not cover every particular case. On occasion, agreed-upon equity must settle cases that the laws do not.

Acting morally requires not only that we have all the moral virtues but also that we have the intellectual virtue of prudence, or practical reason. Prudence is one of five intellectual virtues, the other four of which are scientific knowledge, intuition, wisdom, and art or technical skill. Prudence is the kind of intelligence that helps us reason properly about practical matters. Having the right motives is a matter of having all of the moral virtues, but choosing the right course of action is a matter of prudence.

As well as plain, unthinking brutishness and vice, which are the opposite of virtue, people may also do wrong through incontinence, or a lack of self-control. Incontinence is not as bad as vice, since it is partially involuntary, but it is also harder to remedy, since it is unreasoned. Though we are led into incontinence from an excessive desire for pleasure, pleasure is generally a good thing. Our pursuit of the good life is itself the pursuit of pleasure, and pleasure only leads us astray when we have a defective character.

Friendship is an essential component of the good life. The best kind of friendship is one in which two people are attracted to each other because they admire each other's virtue and in which each friend takes more interest in giving love than in receiving. Inferior kinds of friendship are based on utility or pleasure. Our attitude toward ourselves reflects our attitude toward our friends:

people who love and respect themselves are likely to treat their friends well. Self-love is more important than friendship, and people only look down on it because people who love themselves imperfectly seek honor or pleasure for themselves rather than goodness. Since friendship is essential to the good life, not even wholly self-sufficient people can be truly happy without friends.

Friendship is closely tied to justice, since both have to do with how we treat others. Aristotle's discussion of friendship thus reaches outward to encompass other forms of human interaction such as family relationships and government. The three good kinds of government are monarchy, aristocracy, and timocracy, which is a kind of democracy with a basic property requirement for voting rights. They are analogous, respectively, to a father–son relationship, a husband–wife relationship, and a brother–brother relationship. Corrupted monarchy becomes tyranny, corrupted aristocracy becomes oligarchy, and corrupted timocracy becomes democracy, by which Aristotle means a kind of mob rule.

The highest goal of all is rational contemplation, and the good life consists of pursuing this activity above all others. No one can live a life of pure contemplation, but we should aim to approximate this ideal as best as possible. Pleasure accompanies and perfects our activities, and a good person will feel the highest pleasure in this activity of rational contemplation. The practical sciences of ethics and politics are guides for dealing with our everyday lives and arranging things so that we can find the surest path to the good life.

Analysis

Aristotle's discussion of incontinence refines Socrates' famous claim that no one ever knowingly does wrong. According to Socrates, ignorance is the source of all wrongdoing, so perfect wisdom is the best guard against vice. The idea of incontinence— a rough translation of the Greek word *akrasia,* which more accurately translates as "lacking self-control"—raises a problem for this view because some people clearly do wrong knowingly. A person addicted to cigarettes might light up, saying, "I know this stuff is bad for me and I know I should quit, but I just can't help it." This person does not smoke because she is ignorant of the ill effects of smoking but because she lacks the self-control to do what she knows is right. Earlier in the *Ethics,* Aristotle suggests that virtue is, above all, a matter of habit, and someone raised with the wrong habits will inevitably fall into vice. Virtue, for Aristotle, is a matter of practice. For this reason, he differs from Socrates and Plato by saying that an intellectual understanding of virtue is not enough to guarantee virtue. We can do wrong knowingly if we have been raised without the strength of character not to want to do wrong.

Aristotle's emphasis on self-love makes more sense when we understand it in the context of the Greek city-state. His argument that self-love is more important than friendship positions him as one of the early proponents of *ethical egoism,* the view that if we all took proper care to become good people ourselves, the world would work out for the best, and there would be no need for selflessness. This view may seem callous in the modern world of capitalist individualism, in which looking out for number one often comes at the expense of others, but it is less so in the context of Aristotle's Greece. The Greek city-states were tightly knit communities where citizens would identify themselves with their city to the extent that exile was considered a fate worse than death. In such a world, one's own well-being was largely determined by the well-being of one's city, so it would be in the self-interest of every citizen to look out for the welfare of the city-state and its citizenry. Aristotle's conception of self-love, then, is much more community-oriented than the self-love espoused by modern pseudophilosophers such as Ayn Rand.

Aristotle's ultimate conclusion that rational contemplation is the highest good is based on a teleological conception of human nature. According to Aristotle, everything in nature has a *telos,* or end goal. The *telos* of a knife, for instance, is to cut, and the *telos* of a shoe is to protect and cushion the foot. In each case, we can see that the *telos* of an object consists of its distinctive activity. According to Aristotle, the distinctive activity of humans is our capacity for rational thought. For that reason, the exercise of our rational powers is our *telos,* the highest good we can achieve. Aristotle lists five intellectual virtues with which we can exercise our rational powers. Prudence and art are both practical virtues and hence means to other ends. Of the other three, scientific knowledge and intuition both contribute to gaining a broad understanding of things, while wisdom rests in the contemplation we are capable of when we achieve this understanding. As such, the exercise of wisdom in rational contemplation seems to be the highest achievement of the intellectual virtues.

The conclusion that the *telos*, or end goal of being human, is rational contemplation may seem strange to modern readers, who have grown up in a world that does not see nature in such teleological terms. We might agree that knives and shoes have distinctive activities, but only because they were created by humans to serve very specific purposes. The analogy of "distinctive activities" itself is at best tenuous, first because, unlike knives and shoes, we were not created for a specific purpose (so far as we know), and second because, depending on our point of view, we could identify all sorts of activities as distinctive to humans, from using tools to playing golf. Aristotle would argue that only our rationality is an essential feature of our humanity: we could be human even if we didn't use tools or play golf, whereas we couldn't be human without being rational. However, even if we accept this argument, we do not have to accept that we should concentrate our energies on rational contemplation simply because that is the "most human" use of our energies.

POLITICS

Summary

All associations are formed with the aim of achieving some good. The Greek city-state, or *polis,* is the most general association in the Greek world, containing all other associations, such as families and trade associations. As such, the city-state must aim at achieving the highest good. Aristotle concludes that "man is a political animal": we can only achieve the good life by living as citizens in a state. In discussing the economic relations that hold within a city-state, Aristotle defends the institution of private property, condemns excessive capitalism, and notoriously defends the institution of slavery. Before presenting his own views, Aristotle discusses various theoretical and actual models current at his time. In particular, he launches lengthy attacks on Plato's *Republic* and *Laws,* which most commentators find unsatisfying and off the mark, and also criticizes other contemporary philosophers and the constitutions of Sparta, Crete, and Carthage.

Aristotle identifies citizenship with the holding of public office and administration of justice and claims that the identity of a city rests in its constitution. In the case of a revolution, in which the citizenship and constitution change, a city's identity changes, so it cannot be held responsible for its actions before the revolution.

Roughly speaking, there are six kinds of constitution, three just and three unjust. A constitution is just when it benefits everyone in the city and unjust when it benefits only those in power. When a single person rules, a constitution is a monarchy if the ruler is good and a tyranny if the ruler is bad. When a small elite rules, a constitution is an aristocracy if the rulers are good and an oligarchy if the rulers are bad. When the masses rule, a constitution is a polity if they rule well and a democracy if they rule badly. Aristotle acknowledges that giving full sovereignty to either the governing body or the laws might make room for abuses of power and suggests that a polity is probably least susceptible to corruption, especially when the laws are given higher authority than the governing body. He proposes a principle of distributive justice, saying that benefits should be conferred upon different citizens differently, depending on the contribution they make to the well-being of the state.

In books IV to VI, Aristotle turns from his theoretical speculations to a practical examination of political institutions as they exist in the Greek world. He observes that the needs of city-states vary greatly depending on their wealth, population, class distribution, and so on. He examines the different varieties of states and constitutions and makes a number of general recommendations. The greatest tension in any state is the mutual resentment between the rich and the poor. Consequently, a strong middle class keeps a state in balance and guards against corruption and oppression.

The three branches of civic government are the deliberative, which makes the major political decisions of the state; the executive, which runs the day-to-day business of the state; and the judicial, which oversees the legal affairs of the state. Though it is not necessary to give everyone equal access to public office, it is never wise to exclude entirely any group from power. Constitutions are usually changed by a large, dissatisfied faction that rises up against the people in power. To preserve a constitution, Aristotle recommends moderation, education, and inclusiveness. The interests of the rich minority and poor majority can be balanced by allowing both factions a roughly equal amount of power. In such an arrangement, each individual rich person would have more political power than each individual poor person, but the poor and the rich as groups would be balanced against each other.

Books VII and VIII return to the question of what the ideal state would be like. The good life consists primarily of rational contemplation, so even though political action is admirable and necessary, it is only a means to the end of securing the ultimate happiness of rational contemplation. An ideal city-state should be arranged to maximize the happiness of its citizens. Such a city would be large enough for self-sufficiency but small enough to ensure fellow feeling. It should be located by the water to allow for easy sea commerce. Young citizens serve in the military, middle-aged citizens govern, and older citizens take care of religious affairs while noncitizen laborers take care of farming and crafts. Education is important to ensuring the well-being of the city, and Aristotle prefers a public program of education to private tutoring. He recommends that care be taken to breed the right habits in children from the time they are in the womb, so that when they mature they learn to hone their reason. His recommended curriculum consists of reading and writing, physical education, music, and drawing. This education will help citizens make the most of both work and play, as well as the leisure time in which to pursue the good life.

Analysis

Aristotle's discussion of politics is firmly grounded in the world of the Greek city-state, or *polis*. He assumes that any state will consist of the same basic elements of a Greek city-state: male citizens who administer the state, and then women, slaves, foreigners, and noncitizen laborers who perform the necessary menial tasks to keep the city running. Citizenship in the Greek world was a much more involved responsibility than it is in modern representative democracies. All citizens in a Greek city-state took part in government and held various public offices, which is why Aristotle takes public office as a defining feature of citizenship. Because citizenship involves an active role in running the state, a citizen identifies strongly with the city-state to which he belongs, to the point that the Greeks considered exile to be a fate worse than death. The tight bond between citizen and city-state also explains why Aristotle considers active citizenship a necessary feature of the good life. He insists that we can only fully realize our rationality and humanity as citizens of a city-state, and so he concludes that fully realized humans are, by necessity, political animals.

Aristotle's *Politics* is sometimes classified as "communitarian" because it places the well-being of the community as a whole above the well-being of the individual. Aristotle calls humans "political animals" because we cannot be fully human without active participation in a city-state. Thus, his recommendations regarding justice and education bear in mind only what will make for the strongest state. Absent entirely is the concern of modern liberalism with individual freedoms and the protection of a citizen's private life from the public eye. Aristotle does not fail to discuss the tension between individual liberty and the demands of the state so much as he does not live in a world where this tension exists. The idea of a private life would seem absurd in a Greek city-state. All the highest aims in life, from political debate to physical exercise, take place in the public sphere, and there is no conception of a "private persona" different from the face that different people present in public. Consequently, the interests of the individual and the interests of the state are equivalent in Aristotle's view. His prioritizing of the community above the individual, as well as his warnings about the dangers of unrestrained capitalism, had a strong influence on the work of Karl Marx.

Although Aristotle's conception of distributive justice gives a clear indication of his own aristocratic leanings, much of Aristotle's discussion of justice remains relevant to this day. Distributive justice is the idea that honors and wealth should be distributed according to merit, so that the best people get the highest rewards. Though Aristotle insists that "best" is a matter of merit, he seems unconcerned that the rich have much greater opportunities for achieving merit and that noncitizens, women, and slaves have no opportunity at all. Effectively, he condemns them to the lowest rung of the social ladder by insisting that benefits be accorded to those with merit and defining merit in terms of qualities that their low status bars them from. Despite these aristocratic leanings, however, Aristotle has a keen sense of the dangers of power abused. In book III, he discusses at length the difficulties of ensuring that all citizens are accountable.

He is not the first to recommend that the written law have greater authority than the ruling class, but he makes the argument forcefully, and it is largely thanks to his influence that we take the primacy of the law as a given in the modern world.

One of the less attractive features of the *Politics* is Aristotle's endorsement of slavery, which, not surprisingly, rings hollow. His argument rests on the claim that everyone needs to be ruled and that those who lack the rationality to rule themselves need to be ruled by others. Aristotle opposes the enslavement of other Greeks because he believes that all Greeks are at least somewhat rational beings, so their enslavement would be unjust. However, in typical Greek fashion, Aristotle regards all non-Greeks as inferior barbarians, many of whom can only live productively in a state of slavery. However, he also argues that slaves need sufficient rationality to understand and carry out the orders of their masters. This argument contradicts the argument that slaves deserve their lot because they lack rationality entirely. If we follow Aristotle's reasoning to its logical conclusion, we can argue that slavery is always wrong because those who make capable slaves necessarily have a level of rationality that renders their enslavement unjust. Unfortunately, Aristotle himself seems too caught up in the prejudices of his time to recognize that his argument refutes itself.

POETICS

Summary

Aristotle proposes to study poetry by analyzing its constitutive parts and then drawing general conclusions. The portion of the *Poetics* that survives discusses mainly tragedy and epic poetry. We know that Aristotle also wrote a treatise on comedy that has been lost. He defines poetry as the mimetic, or imitative, use of language, rhythm, and harmony, separately or in combination. Poetry is mimetic in that it creates a representation of objects and events in the world, unlike philosophy, for example, which presents ideas. Humans are naturally drawn to imitation, so poetry has a strong pull on us. It can also be an excellent learning device, since we can coolly observe imitations of things like dead bodies and disgusting animals when the real thing would disturb us.

Aristotle identifies tragedy as the most refined version of poetry dealing with lofty matters and comedy as the most refined version of poetry dealing with base matters. He traces a brief and speculative history of tragedy as it evolved from dithyrambic hymns in praise of the god Dionysus. Dithyrambs were sung by a large choir, sometimes featuring a narrator. Aeschylus invented tragedy by bringing a second actor into dialogue with the narrator. Sophocles innovated further by introducing a third actor, and gradually tragedy shifted to its contemporary dramatic form.

Aristotle defines tragedy according to seven characteristics:

1. It is mimetic.
2. It is serious.
3. It tells a full story of an appropriate length.
4. It contains rhythm and harmony.
5. Rhythm and harmony occur in different combinations in different parts of the tragedy.
6. It is performed rather than narrated.
7. It arouses feelings of pity and fear and then purges these feelings through catharsis.

A tragedy consists of six component parts, which are listed here in order from most important to least important: plot, character, thought, diction, melody, and spectacle.

A well-formed plot must have a beginning, which is not a necessary consequence of any previous action; a middle, which follows logically from the beginning; and an end, which follows logically from the middle and from which no further action necessarily follows. The plot should be unified, meaning that every element of the plot should tie in to the rest of the plot, leaving no loose ends. This kind of unity allows tragedy to express universal themes powerfully, which makes it superior to history, which can only talk about particular events. Episodic plots are bad because there is no necessity to the sequence of events. The best kind of plot contains surprises—surprises that, in retrospect, fit logically into the sequence of events. The best kinds of surprises are brought about by *peripeteia,* or reversal of fortune, and *anagnorisis,* or discovery. A good plot progresses like a knot that is tied up with increasingly greater complexity until the moment of *peripeteia,* at which point the knot is gradually untied until it reaches a completely unknotted conclusion.

For a tragedy to arouse pity and fear, we must observe a hero who is relatively noble going from happiness to misery as a result of error on the part of the hero. Our pity and fear is aroused most when it is family members who harm one another rather than enemies or strangers. In the best kind of plot, one character narrowly avoids killing a family member unwittingly thanks to an *anagnorisis* that reveals the family connection. The hero must have good qualities appropriate to his or her station and should be portrayed realistically and consistently. Since both the character of the hero and the plot must have logical consistency, Aristotle concludes that the untying of the plot must follow as a necessary consequence of the plot and not from stage artifice, like a deus ex machina (a machine used in some plays, in which an actor playing one of the gods was lowered onto the stage at the end).

Aristotle discusses thought and diction and then moves on to address epic poetry. Whereas tragedy consists of actions presented in a dramatic form, epic poetry consists of verse presented in a narrative form. Tragedy and epic poetry have many common qualities, most notably the unity of plot and similar subject matter. However, epic poetry can be longer than tragedy, and because it is not performed, it can deal with more fantastic action with a much wider scope. By contrast, tragedy can be more focused and can take advantage of the devices of music and spectacle. Epic poetry and tragedy are also written in different meters. After defending poetry against charges that it deals with improbable or impossible events, Aristotle concludes by weighing tragedy against epic poetry and determining that tragedy is, on the whole, superior.

Analysis

Aristotle takes a scientific approach to poetry, which bears as many disadvantages as advantages. He studies poetry as he would a natural phenomenon, observing and analyzing first and only afterward making tentative hypotheses and recommendations. The scientific approach works best at identifying the objective, lawlike behavior that underlies the phenomena being observed. To this end, Aristotle draws some important general conclusions about the nature of poetry and the ways in which it achieves its effects. However, in assuming that there are objective laws underlying poetry, Aristotle fails to appreciate the fact that art often progresses precisely by overturning the assumed laws of a previous generation. If every play were written in strict accordance with a given set of laws for a long enough time, a revolutionary playwright would be able to achieve powerful effects by consciously violating these laws. In point of fact, Euripides, the last of the three great tragic poets of Ancient Greece, wrote many plays that violated the logical and structured principles of Aristotle's *Poetics* in a conscious effort to depict a world that he saw as neither logical nor structured. Aristotle himself gives mixed reviews to Euripides' troubling plays, but they are still performed two and a half millennia after they were written.

Aristotle's concept of mimesis helps him to explain what is distinctive about our experience of art. Poetry is mimetic, meaning that it invites us to imagine its subject matter as real while acknowledging that it is in fact fictional. When Aristotle contrasts poetry with philosophy, his point is not so much that poetry is mimetic because it portrays what is real whereas philosophy is nonmimetic because it portrays only ideas. Rather, the point is that the ideas discussed in philosophical texts are as real as any ideas ever are. When we see an actor playing Oedipus, this actor is clearly a substitute through whom we can imagine what a real Oedipus might be like. When we read Aristotle's ideas on art, we are in direct contact with the ideas, and there is nothing more real to imagine. Art presents reality at one level of remove, allowing us a certain detachment. We do not call the police when we see Hamlet kill Polonius because we know that we are not seeing a real event but only two actors imitating real-world possibilities. Because we are conscious of the mimesis involved in art, we are detached enough that we can reflect on what we are experiencing and so learn from it. Witnessing a murder in real life is emotionally scarring; witnessing a murder onstage gives us a chance to reflect on the nature and causes of human violence so that we can lead a more reflective and sensitive life.

Aristotle identifies catharsis as the distinctive experience of art, though it is not clear whether he means that catharsis is the purpose of art or simply an effect. The Greek word *katharsis* originally means purging or purification and refers also to the inducement of vomiting by a doctor to rid the body of impurities. Aristotle uses the term metaphorically to refer to the release of the emotions of pity and fear built up in a dramatic performance. Because dramatic performances end, whereas life goes on, we can let go of the tension that builds during a dramatic performance in a way that we often cannot let go of the tension that builds up over the course of our lives. Because we can let go of it, the emotional intensity of art deepens us, whereas emotional intensity in life often just hardens us. However, if this process of catharsis that allows us to experience powerful emotions and then let them go is the ultimate purpose of art, then art becomes the equivalent of therapy. If we define catharsis as the purpose of art, we have failed to define art in a way that explains why it is still necessary in an era of psychiatry. A more generous reading of Aristotle might interpret catharsis as a means to a less easily defined end, which involves a deeper capacity for feeling and compassion, a deeper awareness of what our humanity entails.

Aristotle insists on the primacy of plot because the plot is ultimately what we can learn from in a piece of art. The word we translate as "plot" is the Greek word *muthos,* which is the root for *myth*. *Muthos* is a more general term than *plot*, as it can apply to any art form, including music or sculpture. The *muthos* of a piece of art is its general structure and organization, the form according to which the themes and ideas in the piece of art make themselves apparent. The plot of a story, as the term is used in the *Poetics,* is not the sequence of events so much as the logical relationships that exist among events. For Aristotle, the tighter the logical relationships among events, the better the plot. *Oedipus Rex* is a powerful tragedy precisely because we can see the logical inevitability with which the events in the story fall together. The logical relationships among events in a story help us to perceive logical relationships among the events in our own lives. In essence, tragedy shows us patterns in human experience that we can then use to make sense of our own experience.

Throughout history, there have been stories of feral children, or human children who have been raised by animals in the wild. The most famous fictional examples are Tarzan, King of the Apes, and Mowgli of *The Jungle Book*, but there have been documented real-life cases as well. Imagine such a child is found and brought into human society. Would Aristotle consider this child capable of experiencing happiness?

Today, we use the word *happiness* to refer to a broad category of emotion, mood, or pleasurable sensation. According to our understanding of the term, dogs can feel happiness, as can infants and the mentally disabled. But when Aristotle discussed happiness in the *Nicomachean Ethics*, he was actually talking about something much more specific, something that only a minority of human beings is truly capable of achieving. The Greek word that Aristotle used is *eudaimonia*, and while this is generally translated as "happiness," it refers more specifically to the ultimate expression of human virtue. As defined by Aristotle, *eudaimonia* involves much more than feelings of pleasure or contentment. Only rationally competent, virtuous adults can experience *eudaimonia*, because *eudaimonia* is the state that results from a human being fully understanding and achieving everything that human beings were intended to do.

A feral child, discovered and brought into human society, might be perfectly pleased to have left the wild. A warm bed, regular meals, and safety from predators might make the child happy. But, as Aristotle might say, there is happiness and then there is *proper* happiness. According to his conception of *telos*, the ultimate goal of human beings must be that thing which ultimately distinguishes humans from other living creatures. Wolves and apes can experience feelings of contentment, sensations of physical pleasure, and brief moments of satisfaction. Therefore, these kinds of happiness cannot represent humankind's essential *telos* (the end or purpose for which human beings were made). The capacity of rational thought separates humans from animals, and therefore the exercise of rational thought represents the supreme good.

Student Essay

Virtuous humans know that true happiness is that happiness that only humans can achieve, which involves the application of rational thought to a sense of moral virtue. When a person can apply reason to his or her own actions, and do it consistently, he or she has achieved *eudaimonia*. According to Aristotle, we are not born with an innate sense of moral virtue. Rather, virtue should be understood as a series of habits we have acquired. A feral child could be docile, sweet-natured, and well behaved, but that wouldn't automatically make the child virtuous. True virtue has an element of consciousness: one needs to be fully aware that he or she is acting for the sake of virtuousness. The moral ignorance of a child raised by animals, without the socialization afforded by human company, would render that child fundamentally incapable of virtuous action. The child's total isolation does relieve him from the burden of responsibility, since he remains innocent for his state of ignorance. However, by the same token, the child cannot achieve *eudaimonia*. From Aristotle's point of view, Jean- Jacques Rousseau's noble savage—the solitary, precivilized human who lives a moral life untainted by human society—would be a patently ridiculous figure and could hardly be considered a true human being.

There remains hope for the feral child, however. Crucially, *eudaimonia* is something we *do*, not something we *are*. Virtue and vice are both latent dispositions and only gain meaning when they are performed or activated. A physically agile person who never competes in sporting games is worthless as an athlete; similarly, a virtuous person who does not exercise virtuous action can never be *eudaimon*. If the feral child can be taught virtue and can be trained to exercise it, then the child can certainly attain *eudaimonia*. It would be a hard task, as Aristotle knew. Proper moral education was crucial, he felt, because virtue and vice were learned habits. Once a person got into the habit of acting virtuously—or viciously—the cycle proved extremely hard to break. Joining human society, though, is an important first step for the feral child. In *Politics*, Aristotle claimed that one cannot realize one's true human nature outside the bounds of society. By leaving the wild and joining civilization, the child has the potential to learn his true *telos* and become a fully ethical, moral agent.

Saint Augustine

(A.D. 354–430)

THEMES, ARGUMENTS & IDEAS

- The Problem of Evil
- Free Will and Responsibility
- The Importance of the Body and the Soul
- The Possibility of Certitude

SUMMARY & ANALYSIS OF MAJOR WORKS

- *The Confessions*
- *The City of God*

Saint Augustine of Hippo, whose full name was Aurelius Augustinus, was born in A.D. 354, in the city of Tagaste, in the Roman North African province of Numidia (now Algeria). His moderately well-to-do family was religiously mixed. His father, Patricius, was a pagan who still adhered to the old gods of Rome, and his mother, Monica, was a devout Christian. Such families were typical of this era, when paganism was in retreat and Christianity was spreading. Despite his mother's strong influence, Augustine was not baptized a Christian until he was in his early thirties.

Augustine was an intellectually gifted child, and his parents carefully schooled him so he could secure a good position for himself in the Roman civil service. At the age of seventeen, his parents sent him to Carthage to study. There, he quickly discovered the joys of sex and soon fell deeply in love with a woman who became the mother of his son, Adeodatus. Augustine never married this woman, but she remained his mistress for many years—a common arrangement in the fourth century.

Augustine's mother still harbored her ambitions for Augustine and persuaded him to get rid of his mistress and move to Italy, where he could secure a good career for himself—the reason he'd been so carefully schooled. Augustine listened to his mother and headed to Italy with her and his son. The three of them settled in Milan, the administrative capital of the Roman Empire at that time, and Augustine took up teaching. His mother soon had him engaged to a girl half his age who came from a wealthy and well-placed family. Augustine never married this girl and instead took up with another woman.

In A.D. 386, a momentous event occurred in Augustine's life: he heard a voice that told him to read the Bible. When he held the Bible, it fell open to Romans 13:13, a passage in the New Testament, in which he read that drunkenness and sexual indulgence should be abandoned. This passage had a profound effect on him, and there and then he decided to convert. Bishop Ambrose of Milan baptized both Augustine and his son. Not long afterward, Augustine's mother died suddenly, and he went into deep depression. He emerged a changed man and decided to give up sex, leave the woman he was living with, and move back to North Africa with his son, where he would concentrate on being spiritual and contemplative.

Augustine settled near the town of Hippo Regius (now Annaba, Algeria). The townsfolk, liking the idea of having a learned man nearby, suggested to Augustine that he become their bishop, since the seat was currently vacant. Augustine refused. However, tragedy struck again: his son died, and Augustine mourned greatly. The townsfolk once again approached him about becoming the bishop, and this time Augustine accepted, hoping that the rigorous demands of the position might keep him from thinking about his son.

Augustine was ordained as a priest in 391, and in 396 he became the bishop of Hippo, a position he undertook with conviction and held until his death. He ministered to his flock with great dedication, especially in the ensuing years of troubling uncertainty when the Roman Empire crumbled away, one province after another falling to the invading Germanic tribes. One tribe, the Vandals, who were responsible for the sacking of Rome in 410, sailed across the Mediterranean to North Africa and quickly overran it. The story goes that Augustine died in the year 430 in his bed, reading the Psalms, as the Vandals began to attack Hippo. He was buried in the city's cathedral.

Augustine wrote all his life, and his work includes books as well as letters and homilies, all written in Latin. His early works are purely philosophical, whereas his later writings concentrate solely on religious matters. After his conversion in 386, he wrote *Against the Academics*, in which he critiqued skepticism; *On Free*

Choice of the Will, in which he dealt with the existence and problem of evil; *The Catholic and Manichean Ways of Life*, in which he explored the subject of ethics; and *On the Teacher*, in which he examined concepts of knowledge and language. These works formed the basis of his philosophy.

In 401, five years after he became the bishop of Hippo, he published his *Confessions*, which is the first work of autobiography in Western literature. *The Confessions* is an account of his riotous early years of sensual living, but since he wrote the work in his later years, many philosophical passages appear as well. In the year 410, the unthinkable happened: the Vandals, a relatively obscure Germanic tribe, conquered Rome, looting and destroying much of the city and killing or raping many of its inhabitants. This calamitous event shook the entire Roman Empire to its core. In response to the anxiety and uncertainty felt by the Roman Christians, Augustine wrote *The City of God*, in which he reminds Christians that their true city was never Rome. Instead, their city is heaven itself, which alone is eternal. This attempt to understand a traumatic event gave Augustine the opportunity to elaborate his political theory, and *The City of God* became his most influential and widely read work.

Augustine shaped the medieval mind more than any other thinker. He was concerned not only with philosophical inquiry but with the construction of Christian wisdom itself. He stated that it was possible to learn about the good, or God, by way of reason. Augustine established the paradigms for a theology of history, which regarded history in its totality and set forth a new view of human society—one that was harmonious, whole, and in the image of heaven. This first description of utopia would prove to be a rich vein in philosophy, influencing such thinkers as More, Leibniz, Campanella, and Marx.

Themes, Arguments & Ideas

THE PROBLEM OF EVIL

One question preoccupied Augustine from the time he was a student in Carthage: why does evil exist in the world? He returned to this question again and again in his philosophy, a line of inquiry motivated by personal experience. Augustine lived in an era when the pillar of strength and stability, the Roman Empire, was being shattered, and his own life, too, was filled with turmoil and loss. First he lost his mistress, then his mother, and finally his son. To believe in God, he had to find an answer to why, if God is all-powerful and also purely good, he still allows suffering to exist.

Augustine's answers to this question would forever change Western thought. First, he states that evil exists because we have free will. God enables humans to freely choose their actions and deeds, and evil inevitably results from these choices. Even natural evils, such as disease, are indirectly related to human action, since they become evil only when in contact with people. According to this theory, a disease spreads only because men and women put themselves in harm's way. Augustine gave a more theological explanation later in his life: we cannot understand the mind of God, and what appears evil to us may not be evil at all. In other words, we cannot judge God's judgment. The roots of both of these answers stemmed from two philosophies, Manicheanism and Neoplatonism, which shaped Augustine's ideas.

FREE WILL AND RESPONSIBILITY

Before Augustine, Manicheanism was extremely influential among early Christians. Manicheanism was a cult that first arose in Roman North Africa, begun by a Persian named Mani, who died around A.D. 276. This cult combined elements of Christianity with elements of Zoroastrianism, the ancient religion of Persia, or Iran. Mani taught that the universe is a battlefield of two conflicting forces. On one side is God, who represents light and goodness and who seeks to eliminate suffering. Opposing him is Satan, who represents darkness and evil and is the cause of misery and affliction. Human beings find themselves caught in the middle of these two great forces. According to Manicheanism, the human body, like all matter, is the product of Satan and is inherently evil, whereas the soul is made of light. The only escape from evil is to free the soul from the body through the practices of asceticism and meditation. Manicheanism taught that Satan alone is responsible for all the evil in the world and that humankind is free of all responsibility in bringing about evil and misery. Augustine became a follower of Manicheanism during his student days in Carthage but ultimately broke with the Manicheans over the question of responsibility for evil, since he believed that human beings are capable of free will and are among the causes of suffering in the world. This disagreement led him to Neoplatonism, a system of philosophy developed by Plato's follower, Plotinus, that would prove to be the most influential in his life and work.

THE IMPORTANCE OF THE BODY AND THE SOUL

Plato's influence on philosophy was widespread during the later Roman Empire, the time in which Augustine lived. The philosopher Plotinus (A.D. 204–270), in particular, was responsible for redefining and reshaping Platonic philosophy into a cohesive system of thought called Neoplatonism. To explain the presence of evil, Plotinus drew on Plato's distinction between the world of physical, tangible things and a world of intangible ideas or Forms. Plato taught that the physical world is changeable, perishable, and imperfect, in contrast with world of ideas or Forms, which is constant, perfect, and everlasting. Because the physical world is marked by change and corruption, it is impossible to fully know it. True knowledge can be achieved only by thinking about the eternal and perfect forms, of which the tangible world is only a copy, just as a painting is only an imitation of something real.

The Neoplatonists used this distinction between the physical and the ideal to explain the relationship between the body and the soul. They taught that the soul is perfect but trapped in an imperfect body. Because the body belongs in the physical realm, it is the root of evil. Thus, the soul seeks to break free of the body so it can live true to its perfection, in the realm of ideal forms. In Plotinus, Augustine found the important idea that human beings are not a neutral battleground on which either goodness or evil lays claim, as the Manicheans believed. Rather, human beings are the authors of their own suffering. Plotinus carried this line of thought further than Augustine was willing to accept, asserting that the body is unimportant in defining a human being and that true human nature involves only the soul and has nothing to do with the body. Augustine disagreed, maintaining that human beings are both body and soul together. We bring evil on ourselves because we actively choose corruptible elements of the physical world rather than the eternal, perfect forms, which are spiritual. Augustine argues that God does not allow evil to exist so much as we choose it by our actions, deeds, and words. Later, he came to the conclusion that it is impossible for us to understand the mind of God, and therefore we cannot come to a proper comprehension of why suffering exists.

THE POSSIBILITY OF CERTITUDE

A number of philosophers before Augustine had argued that certainty is impossible and that the best the human mind can hope to achieve is the conviction that its conclusions are highly probable. Augustine disagreed with this premise and sought to demonstrate philosophically that certitude is in fact possible. His first argument is that if we accept the possibility of our conclusions being probable, we've already implicitly assumed that certainty exists, because things can only be "probably" true if truth (in other words, certainty) does in fact exist. If there is no truth, there is no probability. Second, happiness is the result of acquired wisdom, which all human beings desire. Thus, to say wisdom cannot be attained is to say that happiness is impossible—an unacceptable conclusion. Third, Augustine takes issue with the idea that the senses cannot be trusted, and he does not agree with his opponents that the mind is entirely dependent on the senses. On the contrary, our senses do seem reliable to a certain extent, and the mind can understand things independently of the senses, so therefore it must be even more reliable than the senses. Finally, Augustine points out that our mental states are beyond doubt. Whatever we may say or not say, we cannot doubt that at this moment we are thinking. We may say that we are being deceived, but this very fact of being deceived proves that we exist. These four reasons support the thesis that certitude is possible.

Summary & Analysis

Summary

The Confessions is the first autobiography in Western literature, but Augustine meant it to be far more than simply an account of his life. He wrote it during the first three years of his tenure as bishop of Hippo. The word *confessions* in the title implies not only that the narrative will reveal intimate facts about the author but also that it will be guided by a spirit of remorse and the praise of God.

In book I, Augustine describes his early years, from his childhood to the age of fifteen. He admits that as a teenager he preferred hedonism to studying. In book II he speaks of his early pursuit of sexual pleasure. Around the age of sixteen, he gave up studying, chased women, and even became a thief. He moves through three years in book III, to the age of nineteen, when he lives in Carthage. Though still chasing women, he has also discovered the Manichean cult. Over the nine years of book IV, he finishes his studies and becomes a published author; one of his publications is a book on Aristotle. In book V, Augustine is twenty-nine years old. He has given up on the Manicheans and his mistress and is in Rome, where he has found friendship with Bishop Ambrose. In books VI and VII, he describes his spiritual journey, during which he seeks personal happiness. He also considers the nature of evil. He understands God but does not understand Jesus Christ.

In book VIII, Augustine describes his conversion to Christianity. By book IX, he is thinking about giving up teaching, and tragedy strikes. Two of his close friends die, and not long after, so does his mother, Monica. In book X, he meditates on what will lead him to God and bring happiness in his life. In book XI, he begins to study the Bible in earnest, which allows him to talk about the nature of time. Book XII contains a detailed examination of the first chapter of the book of Genesis, through which he outlines his view of matter. Finally, in book XIII, he explains the goodness of God when he created all things. Augustine then reads the first chapter of Genesis in an allegorical manner and states that God works to bring happiness to those who are holy.

Analysis

Scholars generally accept that the idea of autobiography begins with the letters of Saint Paul in the New Testament. However, Augustine in his *Confessions* takes this idea and expands it into an entire genre that critically inquires what it means to be a person. In other words, he explores the idea of the self until he discovers personal subjectivity. As Augustine constructs a view of God that would come to dominate Western thinking, he also creates a new concept of individual identity: the idea of the self. This identity is achieved through a twofold process: self-presentation, which leads to self-realization. Augustine creates a literary character out of the self and places it in a narrative text so that it becomes part of the grand allegory of redemption. In *The Confessions*, Augustine plays the lead role in the story of his own life. By telling this tale he transforms himself into a metaphor of the struggle of both body and soul to find happiness, which exists only in God's love. He reads his life as an allegory to arrive at a larger truth.

All autobiography needs an audience, and Augustine's audience is not his readers but God. This results in an interesting and informative outcome: Augustine transforms himself into a literary character to present himself to God. By doing so, Augustine juxtaposes eternity with the transient, the all-powerful with the weak, and the Creator with the created. This union may seem unequal, but Augustine presents it to teach a pertinent lesson: only in the presence of the Omnipotent and the Omniscient can the self attain happiness and completeness. *The Confessions* is thus a work of prayer and repentance as well as praise.

One of the most important and powerful passages of *The Confessions* relates the journey of the self toward wholeness. The scene, which occurs in book VIII, occurs in the garden of Augustine's house in Milan in July 386. Augustine was in poor health and felt that his life was going nowhere. He no longer wanted to teach and wanted to abandon all his worldly ambitions of securing a glorious career. Throughout *The Confessions*, Augustine is torn between two opposing forces, sexual desire and spiritual desire, and he confronts the conflict here one final time. Augustine is writing from a distance of fourteen years, and he clearly casts the struggle in Neoplatonic terms, in which to be truly free one must choose the interior world of the soul and abandon the distractions of the senses. In his Milan garden, Augustine came to a decision that would forever end this struggle.

In his garden, he heard a child's voice saying, in Latin, "*tolle, lege*," which means "take and read." Augustine was reading the letters of Saint Paul, and he let the book fall open on its own. He was astonished to read the thirteenth verse of the thirteenth chapter of the Letter to the Romans, in which Paul exhorts his readers to give up the way of the senses and walk the path of Christ. Augustine chose to heed Paul's advice. He decided he would give up sex (which he began calling a "bitter sweetness"), never marry, and live a spiritual life. To implement these decisions, he decided to become a Christian and receive baptism as well as give up his teaching position. Augustine says he was flooded with peace and a great calm. He had finally learned to make his own life an allegory, in which the lessons taught by the Neoplatonists, of emphasizing the soul over the body, became an actual reality. In his own life, he shows the merging of the pagan past with the Christian present. He chooses the soul over the body, the intellect over desire, faith over questioning, and reason over uncertainty. In *The Confessions*, Augustine single-handedly creates a theology of the self—a total, complete view of the self in relation to God.

THE CITY OF GOD

CHAPTER 3
AUGUSTINE

Summary

In A.D. 410, a pivotal moment in Western history occured when the Vandals, under the command of their king, Alaric, captured the city of Rome. Rome was known as the Eternal City because the Romans thought that it would never fall; the year 410 shook this belief to its foundations and ultimately led to the collapse of the Roman Empire. The world itself seemed to have been destroyed, and everyone sought answers about what to do and what to believe in. Those who adhered to the waning pagan faith were quick to blame the Christians, claiming that the gods had abandoned Rome because many Romans had forsaken them and taken the new faith. These Romans claimed that Christians were unpatriotic because they asked people to serve God rather than the state and because they advocated forgiveness toward enemies. More important, they said the Christian God had failed to protect Rome, as he should have done, since Constantine had declared him to be the one true God. The angry wrangling between the two communities prompted Augustine to begin writing *The City of God* in 413.

The first ten books of *The City of God*, which make up the first part of the work, refute the pagans' charges that Christians brought about the fall of Rome. The first five books deal with the pagan belief that people must worship the old gods to achieve material advantages in this world, including the continuation of the Roman Empire and the supremacy of the city of Rome. In book I, Augustine attacks the pagans, who claimed that Rome fell because the Christian religion had weakened it, and he stresses that misfortune happens to everyone. In book II, he demonstrates that the fall of Rome is not a unique event in human history. The Romans suffered calamities before, even when the old gods were being actively worshipped, and those gods did nothing to prevent those calamities from happening. He suggests that Romans became weak because of these gods, since they gave themselves up to moral and spiritual corruption. In book III, Augustine continues discussing catastrophes that occurred in pagan times to further prove that Christianity did not cause Rome to fall. To drive home his point, he asks again why the old gods failed to defend Rome in the past.

In book IV, Augustine suggests an alternative view. Rome endured for many centuries because it was the will of the true God, and its survival had nothing to do with pagan gods such as Jove, who behaved only in the lowest manner. In book V, Augustine addresses the pagan notion of fate, which many people saw as a viable force that had held the Roman Empire together. Rather, says Augustine, the Romans of ancient times were virtuous, and God rewarded that virtue, even though they did not worship him. When he reaches book VI, Augustine shifts focus and devotes the next five books to refuting those who claimed that people must worship the old gods to gain eternal life. Augustine uses pagan authors to destroy this notion by saying that the gods were never held in high regard and so all the old ways, old myths, and old laws are useless in ensuring eternal happiness. This piecemeal destruction of pagan theology continues through book X.

Book XI begins the second part of *The City of God*, in which Augustine describes the doctrine of the two cities, one earthly and one heavenly. In the next three books, he details how these two cities came about, based on his reading of the Bible. The next four books explain the prehistory of the city of heaven, from Genesis to the age of Solomon, whose story is allegorized as Christ and the church. In book XVIII, Augustine undertakes a similar process of portraying the prehistory of the city of the world, from Abraham to the Old Testament prophets. In book XIX, Augustine focuses on how the two cities will end and, in the process, outlines the nature of the supreme good. He emphasizes the idea that the peace and happiness found in the heavenly city can also be experienced here on earth. Book XX deals with the Last Judgment and the evidence found for it in the Bible. Augustine continues with this theme in book XXI and describes the eternal punishment of the damned, arguing that it is not a myth. The final book, book XXII, tells of the end of the city of God, after which the saved will be given eternal happiness and will become immortal.

Analysis

In *The Confessions*, Augustine created a theology of the self; in *The City of God*, he initiates a theology of history. He uncovers a wide-ranging explanation of history that begins with creation itself, moves through the turmoil and upheaval of manmade states (the City of the World), and continues to the realization of the kingdom of God (the City of God). In effect, *The City of God* is a completion of the project he began in *The Confessions*, in which he traced the progress of the self toward completion in God. Likewise, human society finds completion in the realm of God. Along with a theology of history, Augustine seeks to put together a Christian philosophy of society. In other words, he gives the various areas of philosophical inquiry, such as ethics and politics, a unity in the universality of divine revelation. History completes itself in divine law. The philosophers of the past, such as Plato, had all said that a person does not owe full and absolute loyalty to any earthly society, and Augustine rigorously critiques this concept in the light of Christian doctrine. He states that the Scriptures alone can instruct human beings about the highest good and the highest evil and that without this guidance, human endeavor has no purpose.

Augustine presents the four essential elements of his philosophy in *The City of God*: the church, the state, the City of Heaven, and the City of the World. The church is divinely established and leads humankind to eternal goodness, which is God. The state adheres to the virtues of politics and of the mind, formulating a political community. Both of these societies are visible and seek to do good. Mirroring these are two invisible societies: the City of Heaven, for those predestined for salvation, and the City of the World, for those given eternal damnation. This grand design allows Augustine to elaborate his theory of justice, which he says issues from the proper and just sharing of those things necessary for life, just as God freely distributes air, water, and light. Humankind must therefore pursue the City of Heaven to maintain a proper sense of order, which in turn leads to true peace.

In effect, *The City of God* is a challenge to human society to choose which city it wishes to be a part of, and Augustine sees his task as clearly marking out the parameters of each choice. Augustine concludes that the purpose of history is to show the unfolding of God's plan, which involves fostering the City of Heaven and filling it with worthy citizens. For this purpose, God initiated all of creation itself. In such a grand plan, the fall of Rome is insignificant.

CHAPTER 3
AUGUSTINE

Is St. Augustine's philosophy essentially hopeful or essentially pessimistic?

St. Augustine wrote and preached during a time of intense political and social volatility. In his personal life, he also struggled with his attempts to reconcile his faith, his rationality, and his human appetites. His philosophy concerns itself with how one can make sense of and live within a world that seems so complicated and so dangerous. Fundamentally, I argue that Augustine's work presents an optimistic picture of the world, though perhaps not unqualifiedly so.

Augustine's notion of the eternal city, for example, is an essentially hopeful doctrine, which nevertheless includes certain elements that may be considered distressing or problematic. When Rome, the so-called Eternal City, fell to the Vandals in 410, the faith of the Roman citizens was shaken to its core. If Rome could be destroyed, then it seemed that nothing in the world could be certain, definite, or assured. Anything one deemed precious could eventually be lost. Augustine's theory seeks to soothe an anguished populace but at the same time capitalizes on the moment to redirect the people's attention toward God. Drawing on the Platonic notion of Forms, Augustine argued that the city of Rome was never a truly eternal city. The true eternal city was the kingdom of God, and no earthly city could ever be more than a degraded copy of that best, purest, original city. Thus, the Romans' grief was unfounded, or at the very least misplaced. The idea that a better existence waits beyond our daily, material world recurs frequently in Christian thought. It offers believers hope and gives strength to victims suffering through loss during traumatic times. However, it also raises the question of whether it is possible to find meaning in a world that is, essentially, unreal.

Augustine's moral worldview is similarly characterized by an interplay between the temporal and the eternal and similarly seems to represent both an optimistic and pessimistic perspective. By rejecting Manicheanism, the religion he subscribed to before Christianity, Augustine rejected the idea that evil was a pervasive external force that threatened human existence. He also rejected the idea that materiality was necessarily evil and that the soul should strive to rid itself of the taint of the mortal body. Augustine argued instead that evil results from human choices. Evil is not a thing in and of itself but a matter of turning away from God and rejecting righteous action. Rather than present good and evil as two equal, contending forces, Augustine proposed that good was the only substantive entity and that evil was merely a degradation, a lessening, or a deprivation of the former. The notion that evil is not a metaphysical force battling over our eternal soul is, in its way, comforting, as it lessens the magnitude of the threat. However, positing evil as an entity that exists outside ourselves means we can divest ourselves of responsibility. In the Manichean picture, humans are the victims of evil but not its authors.

The Augustinian philosophy of evil seems deeply distressing, as it intimately involves human beings in the creation and perpetuation of evil. However, the philosophy's fundamental optimism lies in that same fact. If we are responsible for creating evil, then we are capable of eliminating it or at the very least managing it. The paradigm is a daunting one, but it gives human beings a striking amount of empowerment. Augustine was the first to reconcile the notion of free will with the basic Christian ideology of God's all-encompassing power. God has created goodness, and anything that deviates from that goodness is the result of humans turning away from God. The question of Augustine's optimism or pessimism depends, finally, on whether one finds greater comfort in the prospect of being a bystander or in being an active participant.

Saint Thomas Aquinas

(c. 1225–1274)

THEMES, ARGUMENTS & IDEAS

- Theology as Superior to Philosophy
- The Importance of Aristotle's Four Causes
- Existence as Superior to Essence

SUMMARY & ANALYSIS OF MAJOR WORKS

- *Summa Theologica*
  - Structure, Scope, and Purpose
  - Proofs for the Existence of God
  - The Nature and Limits of Human Knowledge
  - The Purpose of Man

An indefatigable student, teacher, and writer, St. Thomas Aquinas was the greatest Christian theologian of the Middle Ages. He was born at Roccasecca, Italy, as the youngest son of Count Landolfo of Aquino and Countess Teodora of Teano. At age five, he began his studies at the Benedictine monastery in Monte Cassino. From there, he went on to study at the University of Naples and, over the objections of his family, became a Dominican friar in 1244. He continued his studies in philosophy and theology at Paris and then, from 1248 to 1252, at Cologne with Albert the Great. After further study and teaching at the University of Paris, he returned to Italy in 1259 and spent nearly ten years teaching and working at Dominican monasteries near Rome.

Back at the University of Paris in 1268, Aquinas became embroiled in arguments with clerics and theologians who opposed his philosophical positions. He returned to Italy in 1272 and taught for one year at the University of Naples before declining health forced him to quit teaching in 1273. In early 1274, while en route to a church council in Lyon, he fell gravely ill and died not far from the town of his birth.

He was declared a saint by Pope John XXII in 1323, pronounced the "Angelic Doctor" by Pope Pius V in 1567, and named Patron of Catholic Schools by Pope Leo XIII in 1879.

Aquinas was a prolific writer. His most extensive work is the *Summa Theologica*, which he probably wrote between 1265 and 1272 but left unfinished. This imposing set of tomes, which comprises thousands of pages of tightly-reasoned responses to an astonishing range of questions about church theology and doctrine, is not only the crown jewel of Scholasticism—that is, of medieval theology and philosophy—but one of the crown jewels of Western culture. His *Summa contra Gentiles* is remarkable as an attempt to demonstrate to nonbelievers the reasonableness of the Christian faith. In addition to these two most famous works, Aquinas also wrote commentaries on numerous treatises by Aristotle; various Bible commentaries; records of theological and philosophical disputes; and sundry treatises, letters, and notes. This prodigious output is especially impressive because Aquinas produced it all within the span of about twenty years.

Aquinas's greatest influence on intellectual history was his shift in attention from the works of Plato to those of Aristotle. Much of the history of Western philosophy involves the elaboration and development of ideas that are either explicit or implicit in the writings of these two great ancient Greek philosophers. Plato was particularly influential among thinkers in the church's early history, and St. Augustine (A.D. 354–430), one of the church fathers, derived many of his views from Plato's writings. Plato had maintained that an unbridgeable divide separates the transient, illusory, material world that we perceive with our senses and the changeless, eternal world of transcendent reality. For Plato, the realm of eternal and perfect Forms is the only proper object of study, containing as it does the only true reality. St. Augustine saw Plato's philosophy as well suited to Christianity in that Plato's concept of two worlds, one eternally perfect and the other inherently imperfect, mirrors Christianity's own postulation of two worlds, earthly and divine.

In contrast, Aristotle had drifted into obscurity, if not outright oblivion, as far as the church was concerned. In fact, it is thanks only to the efforts of Jewish and Arabic scholars that his writings survived at all until Aquinas came along. Thus, the teachings of Plato reigned supreme in church orthodoxy when Aquinas was studying. Aquinas bucked this tradition, recovering Aristotle for the West and virtually single-handedly assimilating him into Catholic orthodoxy.

Aquinas's views are of more than merely philosophical interest, as they are official Catholic doctrine and thus represent a living set of traditions and beliefs. The Roman Catholic Church is one of the world's oldest, most enduring, and most powerful institutions, spanning nearly two thousand years and claiming some one billion adherents all over the globe. In 1879, Pope Leo XIII declared Aquinas's teachings to be official church doctrine, cementing Aquinas's status as one of the most influential philosophers and theologians in history. The question of whether Aquinas's writings represent the achievement of human reason or the products of divine inspiration has been the subject of fierce debate, and one's answer to that question is likely to depend on whether one accepts church teachings in the first place. Within the church, it is safe to say that Aquinas's significance is inescapable.

CHAPTER 4
AQUINAS

Themes, Arguments & Ideas

THEOLOGY AS SUPERIOR TO PHILOSOPHY

As a theologian, Aquinas who employs philosophy in an attempt to provide, insofar as possible, a rational explanation of doctrines that are revealed knowledge, or matters of faith. Although the *Summa Theologica* is in some respects a work of philosophy, its primary purpose is as a work of theology. This distinction was important to Aquinas and his fellow Scholastics, who held that theology and philosophy proceed according to different paths. Theology concerns itself with knowledge that has been revealed by God and that man must accept on faith. Philosophy, at least as defined by Aristotle, is concerned with knowledge that man acquires through sensory experience and the use of reason. In other words, philosophy attempts to arrive at general principles through a consideration of that which is perceived by the senses and then rationally evaluated. Although some subjects, such as knowledge of the existence of God, are common to theology and philosophy, theology also encompasses subjects that reason cannot fathom, such as the mystery of the Holy Trinity.

Following Aristotle's famous dictum that "all men by nature desire to know," Aquinas holds that people naturally seek knowledge of that which is their true goal and happiness—that is, the vision of God. While reason and philosophy have their respective roles in the acquisition of knowledge, they are inherently limited in their ability to apprehend all truths. Rather, philosophical knowledge is a subset of theological knowledge: all theologians are philosophers, but not all philosophers are theologians. The fact that theological knowledge is based on revealed truth and faith rather than on sensory experience and the exercise of reason does not mean that theological knowledge is in any way inferior to philosophical knowledge. On the contrary, theological knowledge is superior to philosophical knowledge not only insofar as it deals with issues of the utmost importance but also insofar as it alone can actually afford us complete knowledge of those issues.

THE IMPORTANCE OF ARISTOTLE'S FOUR CAUSES

Aquinas adopts Aristotle's doctrine of the Four Causes and couches much of his theology and philosophy in its terms. (See Chapter 2, Aristotle, *Physics*, pages 51–60.) The Four Causes are:

1. Material cause

2. Formal cause

3. Efficient cause

4. Final cause

The material cause, as its name implies, pertains to matter or the "stuff" of the world. Matter is potentiality, that is, that which something can become. The formal cause is the form or pattern that governs a particular thing, or the genus to which it belongs. The formal cause can also be called a thing's essence. For example, the formal cause of a particular human being is his or her humanity, the essence of what it means to be human. God is the only creature embodying pure actuality and pure being, and God is thus the only pure formal cause. The efficient cause is what we normally understand by the word *cause* and indicates something that has an effect. The final cause is the goal or purpose toward which a thing is oriented.

Each of these causes is given a special application in Aquinas's thought. The concept of material cause is crucial to his view of how humans gain knowledge of the external world and also appears in his proofs for the existence of God. The concept of formal cause is essential to his theory of knowledge and the nature of man but also defines his conception of God, whom Aquinas sees as complete actuality and thus without potential. The concept of efficient cause predictably appears in his theory of knowledge about the physical world but also explains human action, which is directed by the will. The concept of final cause explains the nature of the will itself, which naturally strives to achieve its goal of beholding the Divine Essence.

EXISTENCE AS SUPERIOR TO ESSENCE

Aquinas revolutionized a thousand years of Christian tradition by rejecting Plato in favor of Aristotle. Plato maintained that ultimate reality consists of essence, whereas Aristotle maintained that existence is primary. For Plato, the world around us that we perceive with our senses contains nothing except impermanent, ever-changing objects. Plato reasoned that for our observations of the world to count as true knowledge and not just as anecdotal evidence, our minds need to make a conceptual leap from individual instances of things to general ideas. He concluded that there must be something permanent that lies behind and unites individual existences, and he referred to this something as "essence." According to Plato, existence, or the everyday world of objects such as tables, chairs, and dogs, is inherently inferior to essence. Early church thinkers saw in Plato's ideas a parallel to their own division of the universe into the inherently imperfect, corrupt world of matter and everyday existence and the perfect and heavenly world of spirit.

Aquinas follows Aristotle in concluding that Plato's theory is deficient, in part because it is unable to account for the origin of existence and in part because it is unacceptably dismissive of existence. Holy Scripture states that after each of the six days of Creation, God saw that the fruit of his day's work was "good" or even "very good." Furthermore, when Moses asks God how he should refer to him, God responds, "I am that I am," thereby equating himself with being. In other words, God is pure existence or Being itself. Aquinas argues that man's purpose consists exactly in developing himself toward Being, not in attempting to escape Being. In the traditional church view prior to Aquinas, the difference between God and his creatures was one of kind, as existence was something that in itself separated us from God. In Aquinas's view, the difference between God and his creatures is one of degree, and we are separate from God insofar as we do not have as much existence as God. Prior to Aquinas, traditional church thought maintained that existence was the chief impediment to the realization of our spiritual destiny. Aquinas held that our spiritual destiny consists precisely of the enhancement of our existence.

Summary & Analysis

SUMMA THEOLOGICA

Summary

THE STRUCTURE, SCOPE, AND PURPOSE OF THE SUMMA The *Summa Theologica* is divided into three parts, and each of these three parts contains numerous subdivisions. Part 1 deals primarily with God and comprises discussions of 119 questions concerning the existence and nature of God, the Creation, angels, the work of the six days of Creation, the essence and nature of man, and divine government. Part 2 deals with man and includes discussions of 303 questions concerning the purpose of man, habits, types of law, vices and virtues, prudence and justice, fortitude and temperance, graces, and the religious versus the secular life. Part 3 deals with Christ and comprises discussions of 90 questions concerning the Incarnation, the Sacraments, and the Resurrection. Some editions of the *Summa Theologica* include a Supplement comprising discussions of an additional 99 questions concerning a wide variety of loosely related issues such as excommunication, indulgences, confession, marriage, purgatory, and the relations of the saints toward the damned. Scholars believe that Rainaldo da Piperno, a friend of Aquinas, probably gathered the material in this supplement from a work that Aquinas had completed before he began working on the *Summa Theologica*.

The *Summa Theologica*, as its title indicates, is a "theological summary." It seeks to describe the relationship between God and man and to explain how man's reconciliation with the Divine is made possible at all through Christ. To this end, Aquinas cites proofs for the existence of God and outlines the activities and nature of God. Approximately one-half of the *Summa Theologica* then examines the nature and purpose of man. Finally, Aquinas devotes his attention to the nature of Christ and the role of the Sacraments in effecting a bridge between God and man. Within these broad topical boundaries, though, Aquinas examines the nature of God and man in exquisite detail. His examination includes questions of how angels act on bodies, the union of body and soul, the cause and remedies of anger, cursing, and the comparison of one sin with another. Aquinas attempts to offer a truly universal and rational view of all existence.

Analysis

Adopting Aristotelian principles and concepts, Aquinas attempts to explain the origin, operation, and purpose of the entire universe and the role that everything in the universe plays in the attainment of that purpose. Aquinas never doubts the truth of the tenets of his faith. Rather, he employs techniques of argument that he learned in the *disputatios* to state, defend, and elaborate those tenets. The grandiose scope of the *Summa Theologica* derives from Aquinas's belief that a significant portion of theology can be expressed and codified in a comprehensive and ratio-nal system.

Aquinas writes not only as a philosopher who is intellectually interested in the pursuit of truth but also as a Catholic who is convinced that the salvation of humanity itself is at stake. This conviction propels him toward a rational exegesis of topics whose truth is ultimately derived and founded on divine revelation. When a specific topic allows, Aquinas uses philosophical concepts and vocabulary to examine that topic. The major topics allowing such philosophical examination are the existence of God, the nature and limits of human knowledge, and the purpose of man. For most other topics, Aquinas articulates a decidedly Catholic position on issues of Christian interest, such as the Holy Trinity, original sin, and the like.

At first glance, it would seem astonishing and even counterintuitive that Aquinas reframes much of Catholic theology in terms of Aristotle's pre-Christian philosophy. The pursuit of philosophy traditionally re-quires one to enter into debates with an open mind and to identify and reexamine one's own core assumptions about a given issue, yet Aquinas enlists Aristotle not for his aid in the unbiased critical examination of the tenets of Catholic belief but rather for the explication and defense of those tenets. At the same time, though, Aquinas's enlistment of Aristotle reveals Aquinas to be a remarkably fair, open-minded, and indeed tolerant medieval thinker. He apparently believes that the fruits of the exercise of reason are not necessarily corrupt if the thinker is a non-Christian. This suggests that Aquinas believes that every human being, regardless of his or her beliefs, shares in humanity through the possession and use of reason. In this, Aquinas again reveals his indebtedness and allegiance to Aristotle, who maintained that reason is the essential quality of humanity: it is that without which man cannot be man.

Summary

PROOFS FOR THE EXISTENCE OF GOD Question 1 of part 1 of the *Summa* considers the nature and extent of "sacred doctrine," or theology. Aquinas concludes that although theology does not require philosophy to promote knowledge of God, philosophy nevertheless can be of service to the aims of theology.

Question 2 of part 1 concerns the existence of God and is subdivided into three Articles. In the First Article, Aquinas maintains that the proposition "God exists" is self-evident in itself, but not to us, and thus requires demonstration. The Second Article concludes that such a demonstration is indeed possible, despite objections to the contrary. The famous Third Article addresses the question of whether God exists, and in this Article, Aquinas offers his Five Ways as proofs for the existence of God.

First, we observe that some things in the world are in motion. Whatever is in motion is put into motion by another object that is in motion. This other object, in turn, was put into motion by still another object preceding it, and so forth. This series cannot go on backward to infinity, though, since there would otherwise be no first mover and thus no subsequent movement. Therefore, we must conclude that there is a first unmoved mover, which we understand to be God.

Second, we observe that everything has an efficient cause and that nothing is or can be the cause of itself. It is impossible, though, that the series of causes should extend back to infinity because every cause is dependent on a prior cause and the ultimate cause is thus dependent on a previous cause. So if there is no first cause, there will be no intermediate causes and no final cause. But the absence of such causes clearly does not square with our observation, and so there must therefore be a first efficient cause, which everyone calls God.

Third, we observe in nature things that are possible to be and not to be, as they come into existence and pass out of existence. Such things could not always exist, though, because something that could possibly not exist at some time actually does not exist at some time. Thus, if it is possible for everything not to exist, then, at some time, nothing did exist. But if nothing ever did exist, then nothing would exist even now, since everything that exists requires for its existence something that already existed. Yet it is absurd to claim that nothing exists even now. Therefore, not all beings are merely possible, but there must be something the existence of which is necessary. Now, every necessary thing has its necessity caused by something else or it does not. Since it is impossible for there to exist an infinite series of causes of necessary things, we must conclude that there is something that is necessary in itself. People speak of this thing as God.

Fourth, beings in the world have characteristics to varying degrees. Some are more or less good, true, noble, and so forth. Such gradations are all measured in relation to a maximum, however. Thus, there must be something best, truest, noblest, and so on. Now, as Aristotle teaches, things that are greatest in truth are also greatest in being. Therefore, there must be something that is the cause of being, goodness, and every other perfection that we find in beings in the world. We call this maximum cause God.

Finally, we observe in nature that inanimate and nonintelligent objects act toward the best possible purpose, even though these objects are not aware of doing so. It is clear that these objects do not achieve their purpose by sheer chance but rather according to a plan. Any inanimate or nonintelligent object that acts toward a purpose, though, must be guided by a being that possesses knowledge and intelligence, just as an arrow is directed by an archer. Therefore, there must be some intelligent being that directs all natural things toward their purpose. We call this being God.

Having presented these proofs for the existence of God, Aquinas goes on to discuss God in terms of his simplicity, perfection, goodness, infinity, knowledge, and other attributes. This discussion leads into a protracted consideration of questions pertaining to the Creation, the nature of angels, demons, and the work done on the individual six days of the Creation, which culminated with the creation of man.

Analysis

The existence of God is the necessary foundation of any theology. Before discussing any other topics, Aquinas needs to establish the crucial fact that God exists, since, without certainty of God's existence, the conclusions of the rest of the *Summa* would be in doubt or even in vain. To this end, he advances five arguments intended to prove the existence of God. Arguments 1, 2, and 5 are based on observation of the natural world, whereas Arguments 3 and 4 are based on rational speculation. In Arguments 1, 2, 4, and 5, Aquinas concludes that only the existence of God can provide a sufficient explanation for the questions raised. In Argument 3, he concludes that God must necessarily exist for his own sake. Thus, Arguments 1, 2, 4, and 5 conclude that God exists because the world requires him as an explanation, and Argument 3 concludes that God could not *not* exist.

Argument 1 considers and attempts to account for the presence of change in the world. Aquinas draws his argument from Aristotelian physics, which was known as "natural philosophy" in Aquinas's day and which studied motion and change in the physical world. Just as everything that exists in the world is generated by something before it, so too must motion be passed from one object to another. Rigidly applying this principle, though, we find ourselves confronted with an infinitely regressive series and thus with the need for a first unmoved mover to set the entire series into motion. Aquinas is saying that an infinitely regressive series is impossible, and from the impossibility of such a series, he concludes that the first unmoved mover can be only God.

Argument 2 marks a transition from argumentation based on physics to argumentation based on metaphysics and considers the existence of the world as a whole. In this argument, Aquinas relies on the "principle of efficient causation," a cardinal assumption of physics that states that every effect must have a cause. Aquinas reasons by analogy that just as no object in the world comes into being from nothing or by itself but every object is caused, so too must the world as a whole come into being through a cause—namely, through God.

Argument 3 carries the premise of Argument 2 into the realm of metaphysics and rational speculation about being itself. Aquinas first defines possible beings as those that can either exist or not exist, thereby implying that necessary beings are those that necessarily must, and thus do, exist. All objects in the world are possible beings and thus can either exist or not exist. Aquinas reasons that, since these objects can, in principle, either exist or not exist at any time, then they did in fact not exist at some time. Yet, Aquinas continues, if they did not exist at some time, then we are at a loss to explain the obvious existence of the world now, since all that exists requires a cause for its existence. Aquinas concludes that there must be an absolutely necessary being, that is, one that

1. Must necessarily exist and

2. Thus owes its existence to no other being.

Argument 4 is unique among the five Arguments in that it considers not the physical or metaphysical but the qualitative. By a leap of abstraction, Aquinas, adopting Aristotle, concludes that there must be something in relation to which all individual qualities, such as good, true, beautiful, and noble, are measured and from which those qualities derive their existence. For example, the existence of something good implies the existence of something best that not only serves as the ultimate benchmark against which the good thing is measured but also even causes the good thing to exist. The idea that ultimate qualities are responsible for the existence of lesser instances of qualities is strongly reminiscent of Plato's idea that Forms (i.e., essences) are the real and true originals of which lesser beings (i.e., existences) are pale and inferior copies. Nevertheless, Aquinas, following Aristotle, invests these ultimate qualities with being—in other words, with existence.

Argument 5 appeals to our wonder in the face of the apparent purposive activity of the animate and inanimate worlds alike. The world, functioning with such smoothness, efficiency, detail, and aim, simply cannot be the product of chance but must be the product of a sort of grand architect, that is, of God. Aquinas is drawing two rather bold conclusions here: there is a designer and that the designer is God.

There are strong conceptual ties between and among the first three Arguments. Arguments 1 and 2 are similar in that both maintain that there cannot be a series of causes stretching back infinitely. The two Arguments are different, though, in that Argument 1 considers the cause of motion in individual objects in the world, whereas Argument 2 considers the cause of the entire world itself. Argument 1 takes the existence of the world for granted and seeks to account for observable change in the physical world. Argument 2, on the other hand, does draw on observation of the world but attempts to account for the existence of the world. Argument 3 considers the concept of being itself and casts its gaze toward theoretical, nonobservable states of the world far beyond our possible experience. Thus, the first three Arguments attempt to force one to accept the proposition that only the existence of God can account for

1. Change in the physical world

2. The existence of the physical world

3. Existence itself

Having established that God exists, Aquinas is free to consider God's nature and works.

Summary

THE NATURE AND LIMITS OF HUMAN KNOWLEDGE In part 1 of the *Summa*, Aquinas begins his examination of the operation and limits of man's intellect after discussing the soul and the union of body and soul. Questions 84, 85, and 86, each of which is subdivided into various Articles, address

1. The question of how the soul, when united with the body, understands corporeal things

2. The mode and order of understanding

3. What our intellect knows in material things

The soul knows bodies through the intellect by a knowledge that is immaterial, universal and necessary, although only God can understand all things. The cognitive soul has the potential to form principles of understanding and principles of sensation. Individual objects of our knowledge are not derived from Platonic forms but rather from the mind of God. Intellectual knowledge is formed by a conjunction of the passive senses and the active intellect. It is impossible for the intellect to understand anything without the mind forming phantasms, that is, mental images.

The intellect understands by abstracting from phantasms and thereby attains some knowledge of immaterial things. Our knowledge of things, though, is not the same as knowledge of our phantasms, for, if the two types of knowledge were the same, then the taste of honey, for example, could be either sweet or bitter, depending on the state of the perceiver. Rather, the phantasms are the means by which we come to understand things. Knowledge of individuals is prior to knowledge of universals.

The intellect is incapable of directly knowing individual things because it perceives them by means of phantasms. On the other hand, the intellect does perceive universals directly by means of abstraction. The intellect is potentially capable of understanding the concept of infinity insofar as it can form the idea of infinite succession, but it is actually incapable of comprehending infinity. Contingent things are known through sense experience and indirectly by the intellect, but necessary principles governing those contingent things are known only by the intellect. Although only God can know how the future will be in itself, we nevertheless can have some knowledge of the future insofar as we have knowledge of causes and effects.

Aquinas then proceeds to discuss additional questions pertaining to the soul, the production of the bodies of the first man and woman, human offspring, and man's natural habitat. The Treatise on Divine Government concludes part 1 of the *Summa*.

Analysis

Aquinas's discussion of man's capacity for knowledge occurs within the context of his discussion of man's soul. This fact is significant, for it indicates that Aquinas believes that the intellect is not a capacity separate from the soul but a component of the soul itself. To have a soul is to have reason and intelligence. Aquinas thus accepts Aristotle's notion that rationality is the essence of man, although Aquinas does not equate man's entire essence with rationality.

Aquinas accepts the proposition that any knowledge that is to count as real knowledge must be universal, but he rejects Plato's view that knowledge derives from a contemplation of ideas that exist latently and innately in the mind. Aquinas insists that the soul, which includes the intellect, would have no use for the body if, as Plato held, all knowledge were derived from the mind alone. Not only does Aquinas thereby affirm the necessity of the body and reject the notion that the body is an impediment to our acquisition of truth, he also rejects the doctrine of innate ideas. In other words, he contradicts Plato in asserting that there is nothing in the mind that was not first in the senses. At the same time, though, he says that the mind contributes to the acquisition of knowledge by forming "phantasms"—that is, mental images—that are ultimately derived from sense experience and by forming universal ideas and principles. Thus, sense experience provides the passive component of knowledge and the mind provides the active component of knowledge.

The mental images that we form are not universal knowledge itself. If we were to equate our mental images with universal knowledge, then we would be confronted with the problem of how to deal with the ideas that confused or even irrational people have. It would be absurd, for example, to say that honey is both sweet and bitter, but if all phantasms were to count as knowledge, we would fall into exactly such a radical subjectivism in which there was no objective standard of truth. Aquinas concludes that phantasms are indeed ultimately derived from individual things but require the abstraction that the intellect provides to rise to the level of being knowledge. This process of abstraction results in the formation of ideas of universals—that is, of ideas that define objects according to their essential qualities.

Aquinas arrives at the surprising notion that, although sense experience of a particular object is necessary to formulate both a mental image of that object and a universal concept that applies to that and all similar objects, knowledge of the particular *material* object, as that object is in itself, is impossible precisely because we have a mental image of it. It is true that we get to know the essence of the object through abstraction. Yet we do not, and indeed cannot, have knowledge of the object as a material object. Aquinas is thus saying that all knowledge worth the name "knowledge" is necessarily abstract.

This process of abstraction makes scientific knowledge—that is, knowledge of causes and effects—possible at all, so we can have some knowledge of the future through scientific prediction. Nevertheless, the intellect has limits even with respect to abstract knowledge. We gain an abstract concept of infinity through the idea of infinitely adding numbers, for example, yet we are unable to comprehend an infinite series of numbers itself.

Summary

THE PURPOSE OF MAN The first section of part 2 of the *Summa*, consisting of 114 questions, offers an extensive discussion of man, who is said to have been made in God's image. The first five questions, each of which is subdivided into various articles, deal with man's last end, the things in which man's happiness consists, what happiness is, the things that are required for happiness, and the attainment of happiness.

First, in contrast to irrational animals, man has the faculty and will of reason. The will, also known as the rational appetite, seeks to achieve both its end and the good. Therefore, all acts, being guided by the will, are for an end.

Second, man's happiness does not consist of wealth, honor, fame, glory, power, the goods of the body, or pleasure. In fact, man's happiness cannot consist of any created good at all, since the ultimate object of man's will, the universal good, cannot be found in any creature but rather only in God, who is the source of all good.

Third, happiness is man's supreme perfection, and each thing is perfect insofar as it is actual. Man's final and complete happiness can consist only in contemplating the Divine Essence, although the possibility of this contemplation remains withheld from us until we are in the world to come. As long as man desires and seeks something, he remains unhappy. The intellect seeks the essence of a thing. For example, knowing an effect, such as a solar eclipse, the intellect is aroused and is unsatisfied until it discovers the cause of the eclipse. Indeed, the intellect desires to understand the essence of the cause. For this reason, the intellect is unsatisfied to know merely *that* the First Cause—that is, God—exists. The intellect seeks to penetrate farther to the very essence of the First Cause itself.

Fourth, the things required for happiness must derive from the way in which man is constituted and designed for a purpose, since happiness consists of man's attainment of that final purpose. Perfect knowledge of the intelligible end, actual attainment of the end, and delight in the presence of the end attained must all coexist in happiness. Happiness in this life, which is necessarily imperfect, requires rectitude of the will, the existence of the body, and certain external goods and consists in the use of the intellect either speculatively or practically (i.e., with respect to morality). Perfect happiness, which is possible only in the life to come, consists of contemplation of the Divine Essence, which is goodness.

Finally, man is capable of attaining happiness—that is, of seeing God—and one person can be happier than another insofar as she is better inclined to enjoy him. Happiness excludes the presence of evil, though, and since evil is present in this world, it is impossible for man to be happy in this life. Furthermore, man cannot attain perfect happiness because he is incapable of seeing God in this life. Imperfect happiness can be lost, but perfect happiness cannot. Neither man nor any creature can attain final happiness through his natural powers. Since happiness is a good surpassing anything that has been created, no creature, even an angel, is capable of making man happy. Happiness is the reward for works of virtue. Some people do not know what happiness consists of and thus do not desire it.

The remaining questions of the first section of part 2 deal with a wide variety of issues related to the will, emotions and passions, virtues, sins, law, and grace. The second section of part 2, consisting of 189 questions, considers the "theological virtues," such as faith, hope, charity, prudence, justice, fortitude, and temperance, and the gifts of grace, such as the power of prophecy, that some people possess. Finally, part 3, consisting of 90 questions, concerns a wide variety of issues related to Christ, such as his nature, his life, the Resurrection, the Sacraments, and penance. A supplemental set of 99 questions concerns a wide variety of loosely related issues such as excommunication, indulgences, confession, marriage, purgatory, and the relations of the saints toward the damned.

Analysis

Happiness is the goal of human life, and every human being is on the path toward the complete actualization of his or her potential. Indeed, humans' actualization and realization of their potential is exactly what constitutes happiness. Humans' potential, or what humans can be, consists of the contemplation of the Divine Essence. Happiness and the contemplation of the Divine Essence are thus identical and inseparable.

The contemplation of the Divine Essence is not only necessary for happiness, it is the only path to happiness. Nothing except the contemplation of the Divine Essence can bring happiness. No worldly or material good—fame, honor, glory, power, health, or even pleasure itself—can bring happiness, as even pleasure is just a component of happiness. A state of happiness can exist only when the will no longer seeks anything. Since the will naturally seeks the Divine Essence, it will continue to seek, and thus to be unhappy, until it finds it.

Aquinas applies Aristotle's notions of efficient and final cause here, whereby human nature (in the form of the will) is the efficient cause, and happiness (or contemplation of the Divine Essence) is the final cause. The will thus inescapably propels every individual to seek happiness. The process of becoming leads naturally to God, who is pure being and actuality. The culmination of this process, though, is possible only in the next life and only works of virtue—that is, performance of the will of God—can lead to this culmination. Thus, the will achieves its goal, which is happiness, only when it is at one with the Divine Will.

The remainder of the *Summa* examines these various works of virtue, as well as sin, and explains the role of Christ, who mediates between God and man. The supplement to the *Summa*, which was added to the *Summa* after Aquinas's death, discusses sundry related issues that Aquinas presumably might have incorporated into his great work had he lived to complete it.

Throughout his career, Thomas Aquinas played two roles—
that of a theologian and that of a philosopher. As a
philosopher, he attempted to establish the existence of
God as a rational certainty rather than a matter of faith.
How effective was this attempt?

A devout Christian, Aquinas argued that both the truths of reason
and the truths of faith were gifts to human beings from God, and
therefore there was no reason that the two should be
contradictory. In his Five Ways, Aquinas tried to prove God's
existence through an appeal to rational principles. However,
Aquinas himself began from the position of already believing in
God, and this fundamental assumption ends up compromising the
validity of his logic.

Aquinas begins each proof with rational arguments, but by the
end of each proof he has leaped to a conclusion based on faith.
Aquinas builds his proofs on a posteriori conclusions, or
observations based on experiences in the sensible, material world.
For example, the First Way observes that objects require a
stimulus to transition from stillness to motion. Aquinas imagines a
chain of stimuli, each being moved in turn by a prior stimulus, like
a series of pool balls ricocheting off one another. This chain cannot
stretch infinitely into the past, Aquinas argues. At some point
there had to be a Prime Mover, which began the whole process of
motion. This Prime Mover, he claims, is God. Neither of these
conclusions, however, is fully self-evident.

Aquinas follows a curiously disjointed logical pattern in these
proofs. He initially posits that all motion must be initiated by some
already moving thing. The Prime Mover, however, is defined by the
fact that it does not require a stimulus or initiator. Thus, the first
conclusion of the First Way violates the First Way's fundamental
premise, but for no good reason. How does this special category of
being come to be exempt from the rule? No one has ever witnessed
the beginning point of an apparently infinitely regressing series.
Thus, Aquinas's assertion that such a thing must exist is
apparently a piece of a priori knowledge, or self-evident
knowledge that exists without reference to experience. Here,
Aquinas makes a leap from rational argument based on

Student Essay

observation into the realm of faith. If no one has actually observed the beginning of an infinitely regressing series, how do we know that a beginning must exist? It's a difficult concept to fathom, but then, God is also supposed to be beyond our ability to truly comprehend. To an agnostic, an infinitely regressing chain of events is just as valid—if just as mind boggling—as the idea of an omnipotent, omniscient being who can create itself ex nihilo, or from nothing.

Even if we accept the notion of the Prime Mover, we don't necessarily have to consent to the assertion that the Prime Mover is, in fact, the Judeo-Christian God. Aquinas presents this second conclusion as a self-evident conclusion, but it is only self-evident to one who already believes in God. We could easily plug in Allah, Sun-Ra, or Brahma for God without disturbing any of Aquinas's logical structure. Perhaps even more threateningly for Christian ideology, we could also replace God with the Big Bang in many of the Five Ways. After all, scientists have proposed that the Big Bang was caused essentially ex nihilo and that it caused motion, life, and change in the universe. We could get increasingly fantastical with our extrapolations and still not contradict any of Aquinas's contentions. Aquinas never explained why there must be a single Prime Mover. There could have been several gods, working in concert, as in the Hindu or ancient Greek systems. Perhaps our world has been created by a single Prime Mover, but Prime Movers might be like car manufacturers. Maybe there are several of them in operation, each one churning out a different product. These situations might seem somewhat absurd, but they remain completely valid in Aquinas's system and still undermine the notion that Aquinas's God is somehow necessary, inevitable, and rationally verifiable.

Thomas More

(1478–1535)

THEMES, ARGUMENTS & IDEAS
- The Limitations of Principles
- The Importance of Social Critique

SUMMARY & ANALYSIS OF MAJOR WORKS
- *Utopia*

Thomas More was born into a prosperous London family in 1478. When More was twelve years old, he began working as a page boy in the household of Cardinal Morton, the Archbishop of Canterbury and a member of King Henry VII's cabinet. He learned about the affairs of church and state, impressed Morton with his intelligence and wit, and went on to study Greek and Latin literature at Oxford. In 1501, he became a lawyer and, in 1504, a member of the English parliament.

While still very young, More befriended the Dutch philosopher Desiderius Erasmus, an important figure in a movement known as Humanism. Humanists championed the revival of Greek and Roman philosophy and literature. Inspired by ancient thinkers such as Plato and Aristotle, Erasmus and other humanists tended to regard tradition with skepticism, arguing that reason and a belief in human dignity should govern human conduct and the reform of political and religious practices. In 1516, filled with these ideas, More wrote his most important work, *Utopia*, a critical examination of contemporary English institutions and customs.

More's life took a dramatic turn when he became an advisor to King Henry VIII, whose ascension to the English throne in 1509 introduced a period of political and religious strife. Early in his reign, Henry began to rely on More's talents, and, in 1521, he enlisted More's help in writing the famous *Defense of the Seven Sacraments*, an attack on the German theologian Martin Luther. Luther had recently begun to criticize the Catholic Church on matters of doctrine and the abuse of church power. A movement was growing around Luther's teachings that would eventually lead to the Reformation, a cataclysmic social upheaval that resulted in the division of the church into Catholicism and Protestantism. More was a devout Catholic and feared that Luther's Reformation would weaken the church.

More defended Catholicism and won Henry's respect and trust, and Henry named him Lord Chancellor. However, Henry's religious allegiances soon shifted when the pope forbade him from divorcing his wife, Katharine of Aragon, thus making it impossible for him to marry his young mistress, Anne Boleyn. Henry married Anne anyway, and the pope promptly excommunicated him from the Church. In response, Henry renounced the pope's authority and appointed himself head of the church in England, although he never ceased denouncing Luther's teachings and continued his persecution of Protestants. The deeply religious More steadfastly opposed the break from Rome and made a point of not attending Anne's coronation. He declined to take the Oath of Succession and Supremacy, which was required of all Henry's subjects as proof of their allegiance to the new queen Anne and her descendents and also to Henry as supreme head of the new Church of England. By refusing to take the oath, More committed treason, a capital offense. In April 1534, he was imprisoned in the Tower of London, and on July 6, 1535, he was beheaded.

Because of More's complex character, scholars are divided as to the true nature of More's outlook on the world. On one hand, More seems to belong to the tradition of Renaissance Humanism, a progressive movement that emphasized the role of individual moral conscience in matters of politics and religion. Scholars regard More's greatest work, *Utopia*, as a brilliant piece of humanist political and social critique. Also, More's resistance to Henry VIII is often cited as one of the great acts of moral courage in history, a view of him encouraged by the popular 1966 film *A Man for All Seasons*. On the other hand, though More had much to say about how the church ought to change, he numbered among the courageous few in England who sided with Rome against the rising tide of Protestantism, an act that 400 years later would earn him sainthood in the Catholic Church. More oversaw the cruel persecution and condemnation of Protestant dissenters in England in the years before Henry VIII himself turned against the Catholic Church, and in this regard, More seems to be a defender of tradition and the status quo.

Themes, Arguments & Ideas

THE LIMITATIONS OF PRINCIPLES

Because of his Humanist studies of classical philosophy, More had an ideal vision of morality that contrasted with the realities of his world, and one of the major goals of the Humanist movement was to integrate those ideals into real life. However, More knew that principles alone don't get anyone very far in politics. More's father was a notable judge and raised him amid politics and politicians, so More had seen how corrupt political life could be. A major theme of an early work, *The History of King Richard III*, was the deception and ruthlessness of rulers. The bloody War of the Roses, a vicious power struggle over the English throne that had thrown the country into chaos for much of the previous century, remained potent in English memory. In book I of *Utopia*, More accuses the character Hythloday of being too "academic" in his attitude toward advising rulers. More seems to be saying that one cannot simply represent ideal principles and then despair that corrupt leaders will never heed them. Instead, to gain influence, a conscientious political advisor must learn to play the game and to accept the realities of a world dominated by power and greed.

THE IMPORTANCE OF SOCIAL CRITIQUE

In *Utopia*, More contends that thorough scrutiny of institutions is valuable and that conceiving of ideal or imaginary alternatives to reality may yield important insights into how institutions can improve. While some scholars have been tempted to read More's *Utopia* as a set of recommendations for the conduct of real-world affairs, an outright critique of contemporary rulers and laws would not have been possible for More, who was a respected statesman and close advisor to Henry VIII. The narrator More criticizes the fantastical accounts of the Utopians, effectively distancing the author More from Hythloday's provocative recommendations, which include the abolition of private property. However, the extent to which the author More favors Utopian practices is unclear. In *Utopia*, More contrasts the problems of the real world, such as poverty, crime, and political corruption, with the harmony, equality, and prosperity of Utopian society, which suggests that More believes that at least some of the principles underlying Utopian practices are noble, even if the practices themselves are far-fetched. In any case, in describing and critiquing Utopian society, More gives new perspectives on the problems and strengths of his own society.

Summary & Analysis

Summary

Concerning the Best State of a Commonwealth and the New Island of Utopia

MORE MEETS HYTHLODAY The narrator, Thomas More, arrives in Bruges, in present-day Belgium, and meets his friend Peter Giles. Giles introduces More to Raphael Hythloday, an explorer who has seen much of the world. More, Giles, and Hythloday go to More's house, and Hythloday describes his travels. Giles asks him why he hasn't offered his services to rulers, who could use his knowledge of diverse customs and practices to improve society. More and Giles explain that a person of learning and experience has an obligation to use his talents to better humanity. Hythloday, unconvinced, attempts to demonstrate why offering one's wisdom to government is not desirable.

Analysis

Hythloday, a fictional character, plays an ambiguous role in *Utopia*. On one hand, Giles describes him as wise and well traveled and therefore qualified to comment on a wide range of issues. Hythloday has traveled with the famed explorer Amerigo Vespucci, but since the author More and many others thought Vespucci was a fraud, it is unclear whether Hythloday's association with Vespucci lends him credibility or suggests that Hythloday is prone to exaggeration. *Hythloday* in Greek means "speaker of nonsense," which may suggest that Hythloday's remarks, despite being blended with factual elements from the author More's life, should be taken with a grain of salt.

More and Hythloday's conversation about placing one's talents at the service of a ruler demonstrates a conflict between two ways of thinking. Hythloday believes in the purity of the ideal of truth, whereas More believes that such purity has no value and that talents must be put to public use, even if the original ideal is compromised by doing so. More is committed to the Humanist ideal of individual conscience and wrestles with the problem of whether one can remain true to one's principles and to truth while in the employment of a ruler. As Hythloday attempts to demonstrate, reality would force a conscientious person to make many concessions to power and corruption. However, More and Giles argue that the wise cannot leave leadership to the corrupt and must attempt to better society when possible.

The author More struggled with the issue of whether to join the service of the king or remain a philosopher, and at the time he wrote *Utopia*, More was on the cusp of joining the king's service. The argument between the narrator More and Hythloday suggests an internal argument between More and himself as he struggled to choose between remaining free to pursue the ideal and compromising that ideal for the sake of social utility. He eventually rose to the position of lord chancellor, the most powerful office in England next to the king himself, but he ultimately abandoned pragmatism for the ultimate ideal of martyrdom.

Summary

HYTHLODAY AT CARDINAL MORTON'S Hythloday describes a dinner he had with Cardinal Morton in England, where he discusses punishment for thieves. A lawyer believes that thieves should be hanged, but Hythloday thinks this punishment is too severe and that one should try to understand the reasons men steal in the first place, such as a lack of jobs. He describes how greedy landlords, pursuing the wool tade, are evicting peasants from their property, rendering them jobless. Cardinal More asks why Hythloday would eliminate the death penalty, and Hythloday says that death is not a deterrent. He describes the ancient Polyerites, who enslaved their thieves and killed them only if they tried to escape. Though the lawyer rejects Hythloday's suggestion that England adopt this policy, Cardinal Morton recommends that it at least be tried for thieves as well as beggars, and others agree. An exchange ensues about what to do with the poor and sick follows, with a jokester suggesting they become brothers and nuns.

Hythloday explains to More that this episode at Cardinal Morton's table shows the futility of counseling political rulers, as the officials who were present mocked his reasonable advice. More cites Plato's argument that philosophers must advise kings whenever possible, and Hythloday cites Plato in return: unless the king is himself a philosopher, he will be unlikely to take philosophers

CHAPTER 5 MORE

seriously. Hythloday proposes a scenario in which he is present at a discussion between the king of France and his advisors, who recommend various ways the king might manipulate treaties and connive diplomatically to increase his power in Italy. In this situation, Hythloday would want to tell the king to worry about the welfare of his own people and leave Italy alone—surely an unwelcome opinion. Hythloday goes on to give further examples of the futility of hoping to change politics.

More concedes that Hythloday's suggestions would not be seriously considered in such scenarios, but he says that a wise statesman must act subtly if he hopes to wield any influence. He must make a dire situation as good as possible, even if the outcome is not wholly to his liking. Hythloday counters that court advisors must approve of the worst things and that, by compromising, they become complicit in corruption. He believes private property to be the source of this corruption and explains that in Utopia all property is communal and that Utopia consequently lacks many of the ills that plague a country such as England. More remains skeptical about the desirability of communal property and argues that in such a society people would have no motivation to work. Hythloday insists that Utopia is a well-ordered society, much older and wiser than European societies. Indeed, Utopia is so ancient and advanced that when a party of Romans were shipwrecked there, the Utopians quickly mastered everything the Romans taught them. More then requests a thorough description of Utopia, and Hythloday begins his lengthy account.

Analysis

The scene at Cardinal Morton's validates some of Hythloday's concerns about putting his wisdom at the service of rulers. The author More had been involved in politics since childhood and was certainly familiar with the various personalities that make up the court. The dismissive lawyer is doubtless reminiscent of many of the unsavory characters More encountered both as page boy in the very same Cardinal Morton household and as a member of parliament and advisor to Henry VIII. However, the fact that Cardinal Morton was himself willing to entertain the idea of implementing Hythloday's proposed policy suggests that hope is not lost. Though More is probably somewhat sympathetic to Hythloday's skeptical attitude, he seems to suggest that a person of conviction and intelligence can, if tactful and persevering, win small battles.

Book I illuminates the author More's perceptions of the social ills of early sixteenth-century England. Many historians believe that the wool trade was partly responsible for the destruction of rural peasant society, and More and many of his contemporaries criticized those who profited from the high price of wool by evicting peasant farmers from the land to turn it over to sheep herding. The resulting mass poverty contrasted sharply with the increasingly opulent lifestyles of the wealthy, and More saw their greed not only as a corrupting influence but also as an offense to Christian piety. Hythloday claims that theft is only a symptom of a larger social issue—a suggestion that in More's time was a novel way of approaching political and social problems. The understanding that social structures such as wealth and power can be the cause of individuals' actions was a remarkable insight, since many of More's contemporaries still believed in the Great Chain of Being, the idea that God determined social and political status.

The vice of greed is a recurring theme throughout *Utopia*. Foreign rulers are interested only in increasing their wealth and care little for the welfare of the people, and Hythloday believes abolishing private property to be the only real solution. The narrator More expresses doubts that this plan would actually work, but his response to Hythloday's provocative reflections occupies an ambiguous middle ground. The author More uses Hythloday to introduce idealistic models; the narrator More, to show how they might play out in practice. In some ways, this two-sidedness is in keeping with the author More's personal attempt to reconcile principle with political reality. More advocates a realistic attitude in contrast to Hythloday, whose idealism has left him cynically inactive. However, More seems also to suggest that some element of truth exists in the ideals Hythloday represents and that those ideals can be realized only if they can be reconciled with the realities of politics and practical life.

Summary

"THE GEOGRAPHY OF UTOPIA" Utopia is a crescent-shaped island country, 500 miles long and 200 miles wide. In the crescent's curve, large underwater rocks protect a harbor from attack. Utopia had once been connected to the mainland, but when a man named

Utopus conquered and civilized the barbarian inhabitants, he made them dig a canal to turn Utopia into an island.

Utopia consists of fifty-four cities, with the capital, Amaurot, in the center. Every year, each city sends three wise old men to Amaurot to discuss matters that affect Utopia. In the country-side, groups called "families" occupy and work the farmland for two-year periods, producing enough food to sustain the entire country. A "family" consists of forty male and female workers, two slaves, and a leader, or phylarch. Twenty people each year return to the cities and are replaced by twenty new people. If a city has a surplus, it shares that surplus with neighboring cities.

"THEIR CITIES, ESPECIALLY AMAUROT" Hythloday says that all the cities of Utopia look about the same, and he describes Amaurot to give a general impression of the others. Amaurot is a walled city of two square miles, surrounded by thorn-filled trenches on three sides and the river Anyder on the fourth. Uniform houses, which citizens trade every ten years, line wide streets. Because private property does not exist, people leave their doors unlocked and roam wherever they wish. All houses have gardens.

Each year, each group of thirty families elects a representative leader called a syphogrant. Groups of ten syphogrants in turn elect a tranibor, and the 200 syphogrants elect the prince. The tranibors, with rotating representatives of the syphogrants, meet secretly with the prince to manage the commonwealth's affairs. To prevent corruption, the council must discuss legislation on at least three separate days, and members are prohibited from discussing political matters outside of the council meeting, penalty of death.

Analysis

The first descriptions of Utopia seem to suggest a cautious reading of Utopian practices. The translation of *Utopia*, a word of Greek origin, suggests both "good place" and "no place," and *Anyder*, the name of the river running through the capital, means "no water." Utopia, in other words, is a fantasy. Many details in Hythloday's account are unrealistic, such as the fact that Utopia could have evolved from barbarism into a perfect civilization virtually overnight. By drawing attention to Utopia's unreality, the author More seems to imply that the seemingly superior elements of this society cannot simply be adopted into actual society. At the same time, he does seem to encourage comparisons between Utopia and the real world. Utopia, despite its many fantastical elements, in many ways resembles More's England. Amaurot, for example, closely follows London in its basic layout. We may be tempted to conclude that More really does believe that Utopia provides a viable model for the real world and that he treats his own ideas as absurdities because they are so radical and subversive of the status quo. On the other hand, More's point may be that Utopia truly is unrealistic and fanciful but that we can gain insight into the real world by comparison.

By describing the agricultural practices and layout of the cities, Hythloday reveals some of the main principles governing Utopian life. Utopia is a cooperative society of shared resources, and citizens work together to better the whole. No private property exists, and Utopians enforce the absence of status differences and materialism through strict uniformity. This vision of equality and communalism foreshadows the socialist and communist visions that would emerge centuries after More—many readers have seen *Utopia* as a precursor to Marx and Engels's *Communist Manifesto*. Modern readers, remembering nightmarish twentieth-century totalitarian regimes, may see an inhuman authoritarianism in the Utopians' insistence on equality through uniformity. However, some of More's contemporaries might have believed just the opposite. For them, outward conformity was liberating, since clothing and lifestyle in sixteenth-century England reflected the rigid class system.

The government and agricultural practices Hythloday describes in these sections are admirable models, but they are far removed from the realities of More's world. The system of government in Utopia is a representative democracy with built-in protections to ensure transparency and the rule of law—a form of government very different from the politics of More's England. English politics, and European politics in general, were rife with corruption and power struggles. Parliaments existed, but the vast majority of the population had no say in government. Not for another 300 years would commoners be allowed to vote on their government. The idea of a communal method of agricultural work is similarly radical. In England and Europe, agricultural work was an occupation for the poor, disdained by those with any wealth or station. In Utopia, those class distinctions blur because working on the land is a necessary part of life. Utopians view the land as something to be worked, not owned.

Summary

THEIR WORK-HABITS All citizens both work on farms and learn a useful trade, such as weaving or carpentry. Boys generally apprentice with their fathers, and women work trades that do not require physical strength. The Utopians punish laziness on the job, but the workday lasts only six hours. Unlike in Europe, all members of Utopian society share the workload equally, and the Utopians are extremely productive. They take good care of the things they create and avoid luxuries. With such a short workday, all Utopians can enjoy activities such as music, sports, and gardening. The only citizens exempted from manual labor are those who show intellectual promise, and they study to become tranibors, ambassadors, and priests.

SOCIAL AND BUSINESS RELATIONS Each city consists of no more than 6,000 households. If a city's population grows too large, some citizens move to another city. If Utopia's population grows too large, some citizens form a colony on the mainland. Households live communally, giving to and taking from large warehouses that hold everything they need. The sick stay in efficient hospitals, food is distributed fairly, and all meals are shared.

TRAVEL AND TRADE Citizens are free to travel throughout Utopia, though they must get the prince's permission. Leaving without permission brings severe punishment. All cities share their surpluses with cities in need, and when all need has been met, they sell their surpluses abroad. Utopians keep a large store of money in the treasury and generally use it in wartime.

THEIR GOLD AND SILVER Utopians have so much gold and silver that they use it to make their bathroom fixtures, and they scorn the metals rather than covet them. This way, if gold and silver are needed, such as to pay soldiers in wartime, citizens do not hesitate to turn them over.

Analysis

Although More argues that Utopian society will never be wealthy because common ownership deprives people of the incentive to work, Hythloday maintains that strategic punishment ensures that all citizens will pull their own weight. Moreover, he agrees that this system of punishment must exist for Utopia's communal society to succeed. Though an individual in a market-based economy who works incredibly long hours to beat out his competition is certainly more productive than the average Utopian worker, Hythloday explains that for every productive person, there are numerous people who make no productive contribution. While no one in Utopia is phenomenally productive, everyone is fairly productive, and laziness on the job is punished. This punishment system admits to the flawed nature of man—Utopia may be perfect, but Utopians are not. The narrator More points out the potential pitfalls of a communal society, but Hythloday maintains that these problems can be overcome by properly structuring society. Utopia is ideal not because its people are perfect but rather because its laws compel citizens to act perfectly despite their inherent human failings.

Summary

"THEIR MORAL PHILOSOPHY" All Utopians are educated, as education is the meaning by which an individual's values and attitudes take shape. Utopians devote much of their free time to learning, and they are advanced in the sciences. They avoid pointless abstractions in philosophy and focus instead on the meaning of life and the nature of happiness—themes that relate to their belief in the afterlife. They distinguish between true pleasure, which arises from care of the mind and body, and false pleasure, which comes from status and appearance.

"THEIR DELIGHT IN LEARNING" Hythloday describes how eager the Utopians were to learn Greek and how happy they were to read the works of Greek grammarians, historians, and philosophers that Hythloday left behind after a journey. The Utopians are fast learners and are always ready to learn skills to make life more agreeable, such as printing and paper-making.

"SLAVES" Utopians do not execute criminals but rather condemn them to slavery. Moreover, they offer asylum to criminals sentenced to death in other countries. The slave class consists not only of domestic and foreign criminals but also of foreign soldiers captured in battle.

"CARE OF THE SICK AND DYING" Utopians properly care for the sick, and priests encourage euthanasia for the terminally ill. Those who refuse euthanasia are still well cared for. Suicide is condemned, however, and the bodies of people who kill themselves without priests' approval are disposed of carelessly.

"MARRIAGE CUSTOMS" Utopians view marriage as a sacred institution. Premarital intercourse is prohibited and severely punished, but the bride and the groom view each other naked before the wedding day to avoid unwanted surprises. The Utopians permit divorce in cases of abuse or adultery, and they sentence the adulterer to slavery.

"PUNISHMENTS" Utopia has no lawyers. Politicians are respected but not venerated, and since there is no money or property, bribery is unknown.

"FOREIGN RELATIONS" Utopians avoid the dishonesty and ruthlessness characteristic of Europeans. They do not believe in treaties because treaties imply conflict and deceit among the parties.

"WARFARE" The Utopians maintain a skilled army for self-defense and for humanitarian interventions. When possible, they hire mercenaries to fight in their place. They send supplies to allies under attack, and if the situation is especially dire, they send soldiers. To avoid war, they carry out covert propaganda campaigns in enemy territory in an effort to cause political turmoil, such as by offering rewards for the assassination of the enemy leader. Utopia has no forced military service unless the country is invaded, in which case men are sent into battle with their wives and children so that they are inspired to fight bravely.

"RELIGIONS" Utopians consider atheism immoral but tolerate other forms of religious expression. Many worship planets, animals, or an ancient virtuous hero, but the majority believe in one mysterious and all-powerful God. Many Utopians were baptized after Hythloday and the other travelers taught them about Christ. All worship together at the same ceremony. Priests, both male and female, conduct the service, educate the children, and act as moral and spiritual guides.

CONCLUSION Hythloday concludes his description of Utopia by extolling its virtues and superiority. He believes that their contempt for money is the reason for their happiness. Pride prevents rich men in other countries from changing. More disagrees with many of the Utopians' choices but still hopes to institute some of their practices in actual cities.

Analysis

The Utopian belief in education as a right and a necessity was revolutionary. In More's Europe, only the rich and powerful could hope to get an education. The proliferation of learning during the Renaissance applied only to the nobility and wealthy upper classes, and most Europeans remained illiterate. In Utopia, on the other hand, all people can share in an intellectual life. Utopian education is systematized and uniform, unlike the European system, which often involved independent private tutors and differed from school to school. Through their rational education system, Utopians feel they can shape the morality and values of their children and give them the ability to be good citizens. Education in Utopia is not just a means of intellectual enlightenment but a program of moral and cultural development designed to ensure that Utopia will always replenish itself through its children.

Although Utopia is a fantasy, Hythloday's descriptions reveal a great deal about sixteenth-century Europe, and many of Utopia's most provocative elements are meant to encourage reflection on the true nature of European society. For example, slavery in Utopia is premised not on race, ethnicity, or belief but rather on moral behavior: only criminals can become slaves. However, the fact that slavery could be conceived as existing even within this ideal society suggests that ideal societies themselves are products of their times, subject to the beliefs and prejudices of the world from which they spring.

The Utopian system of medical care, too, reveals a great deal about the state of medicine in the early sixteenth century. Utopians not only allow but encourage euthanasia—an idea at odds with religious doctrine of the time, which contended that suicide of any kind was a sin that damned its perpetrator to hell. Utopian attitudes toward marriage and war, though fanciful and highly impractical in many respects, are deliberately provocative, and More may have included them to give new perspectives on the actual customs of his day.

CHAPTER 5 MORE

Given the absence of private property in Utopian society, do you think More was in favor of abolishing private property in real life?

Thomas More's exact motivations for writing *Utopia* remain unclear. In describing the fantastic practices of Utopian society in such rich detail, More may have been presenting a detailed blueprint for a wholesale renovation of society. Yet despite the narrator Hythloday's praise of the numerous benefits of Utopian life, it is unlikely that More would genuinely advocate the establishment of a socialist system in England.

If we take the conclusion of *Utopia* as a guide, then we can claim fairly assertively that More would be an unlikely proponent of abolishing private property. After Hythloday finishes his narrative on Utopia, More (as a character in the narrative) disparages many aspects of Utopian life as absurd, from the methods of warfare to the relaxed views on religion. But it is the doctrine of communal property that he finds especially nonsensical. As More sees it, the desire for material gain is the origin of all the ultimate glories of European society. The character More admits that certain elements of Utopian governance are appealing, though he doubts they will or could ever be enacted in England.

The historical More would also be an unlikely supporter of Utopian-style communalism. When he wrote *Utopia*, More was emerging as one of King Henry VIII's most trustworthy counselors, and he would not have been in a position to openly advocate any of more radical Utopian practices championed by Hythloday, least of all the abolition of private property. The most likely conclusion is that More recognized that a comparison to Utopia revealed several flaws and injustices in English society but that he would never recommend a complete replacement of his current system with this absurd, fantastical one.

This conclusion, however, doesn't fully represent the nature of *Utopia* as a philosophical work. More could have expressed his frustrations as a straightforward recommendation, or as a diatribe or manifesto. Yet he chose to tell a story instead, to incorporate dialogue and fictional characters. This literary style means that the author's politics aren't immediately apparent and the reader has to actively dig into the book to find its meaning. More employs several other distancing techniques throughout the work. For one, we have the double vision of More-as-author and More-as-character. We also have to contend with the fact that More's debate partner, who dominates the majority of the book with his seductive tales, is named Hythloday, which translates as "speaker of nonsense." In its rhetorical and literary stylistics, *Utopia* both is reminiscent of Plato's dialogues and looks forward to Kierkegaard's employment of multiple pen names. Like the works of Kierkegaard and Plato, *Utopia* cannot be reduced to a summation of More's apparent politics. The interpretive journey of the reader is part and parcel of the book's philosophical experience.

The unsettled form of *Utopia* reflects a larger trend in More's life and work. More was always concerned with the question of how one could be both a philosopher and a politician and with the problem of reconciling idealism with pragmatism. More could never exist purely in one realm or the other: he was always juggling, always questioning, and always debating. By following along with the characters of Hythloday and More, we can experience for ourselves the tension between idealism and pragmatism. We can experience the seduction of an idealistic narrative and the wistfulness of having to modify those principles in the face of practicality and the cold, hard facts of human nature. By the time we reach the end of *Utopia*, we can appreciate more fully the nature of More's lifelong dilemma.

René Descartes

(1596–1650)

THEMES, ARGUMENTS & IDEAS

- The Unreliability of Sense Perception
- Science Based on Reason
- Reason as the Essence of Humanity
- The Attainability of Knowledge

SUMMARY & ANALYSIS OF MAJOR WORKS

- *Discourse on the Method*
- *Meditations on First Philosophy*
- *Rules for the Direction of the Mind*

René Descartes is generally considered the father of modern philosophy. He was the first major figure in the philosophical movement known as rationalism, a method of understanding the world based on the use of reason as the means to attain knowledge. Along with empiricism, which stresses the use of sense perception rather than pure reason, rationalism was one of the main intellectual currents of the Enlightenment, a cultural movement spanning the seventeenth and eighteenth centuries that revolutionized the Western world. In tandem with men like John Locke, John Hobbes, and Voltaire, Descartes spurred society to re-examine its traditions and institutions, leading to massive social upheaval. Both the American and French Revolutions were based on Enlightenment theories, and the ways we approach science, math, philosophy, and the idea of the self were radically transformed during the period.

Descartes was born in 1596 in La Haye, a small village near Tours, France. The son of an aristocratic family, Descartes was enrolled at age six in the Jesuit College at La Flèche in Anjou. Because Descartes had always been somewhat sickly, his teachers allowed him to stay in bed until noon every day. Descartes attributed his most important ideas to this habit, and said he did his best thinking when he spent the morning in bed. Despite the religious underpinnings of the school, it was open to the free study of humanities and science. Descartes immersed himself in a wide range of subjects, excelling especially in mathematics.

At La Flèche, Descartes' professors favored the Aristotelian method of study, which held that nature was inherently stable and ordered and that one could rely on information derived from sense perceptions to deduce truths. Descartes would later question this fundamental tenet of his education. The college also taught mathematics separately from the study of physical world, which was founded on philosophy instead of what we now consider scientific method. Descartes had doubts about this divide, and one of the major results of his later work was the use of mathematics in the study of physics.

After leaving La Fleche, Descartes enrolled in the University of Poitiers, where he obtained a law degree in 1616. Despite his ill health, he then enlisted in the military. His military service, along with his family's modest wealth, gave Descartes the opportunity to travel. He happily settled in one foreign locale after another for most of his life. While in Holland in 1618, Descartes composed a brief treatise on music, titled *Compendium Musicae*, not published until after his death. The next year, Descartes traveled in Germany, where, in a stove-heated room on November 10, 1619, he had a vision of a new system of mathematics and science. He would later tell the story of this revelation in *Discourse on the Method*.

In 1628, Descartes began to compose *Rules for the Direction of the Mind*, a short treatise outlining a new method of thought. By using a set of rational principles, Descartes was able to eliminate many of his own doubts about fundamental ideas. Although the book was originally intended to be composed of three sections of twelve rules, Descartes only completed the first twelve. These first twelve deal with simple propositions. The incomplete second set covers a method for dealing with "perfectly understood problems"—that is, problems that can be expressed through simple mathematical equations. The third section was intended to deal with "imperfectly understood problems"—problems too complex to be reduced to an equation. Descartes hoped to show that even these problems could be expressed through mathematics.

In 1633, the Inquisition issued a formal condemnation of the work of the Italian scientist Galileo, who argued, contrary to the traditional notion that Earth was the center of the universe, that the Earth revolves around the sun. The church condemned Galileo to death for heresy but later reduced his sentence to house arrest. At the time, Descartes was working on *The World*, a study he thought would revolutionize the study of physics. After Galileo's house arrest, Descartes voluntarily suppressed *The World*, fearing the wrath of the Catholic Church.

It wasn't until 1636, when Descartes was forty, that he published his first full book, *Discourse on the Method*, a discussion of how he had made use of the rules he had begun to lay out in *Rules for the Direction of the Mind*. *Discourse on the Method* relates the series of revelations Descartes had in 1619 while in the stove-heated room in Germany. After confessing how he came to *doubt* all his knowledge, Descartes shows how he used his rules to solve profound problems. He resolves the problem of personal existence in one of the most famous philosophical statements of all time, *Cogito ergo sum*, or "I think, therefore I exist." He also offers rational proofs that the human mind is separate from the body, that the mind outlives the body, and that God exists. The *Discourse* was meant to serve as an introduction to three essays Descartes had been laboring over—*Optics, Meteorology,* and *Geometry*—which contain science now regarded obsolete. The *Discourse*, however, remains one of the world's most influential works of philosophy.

The work that cemented Descartes' fame was *Meditations on First Philosophy* (1641). Here Descartes addresses the concerns and attempted refutations that various readers sent to him after reading the *Discourse*. Although the theories in *Meditations* would change the way people thought about their minds and bodies and the relationship between the two, *Meditations* also contains arguments that later became known as the "Cartesian Circle" because of the apparent circularity of their logic. *Meditations* was followed by *Principles of Philosophy* (1644), which attempts to reduce the universe to its mathematical foundation. By the time *Principles* was widely read in Europe, Descartes was the toast of continental intellectual circles and was awarded a pension by the king of France.

Themes, Arguments & Ideas

THE UNRELIABILITY OF SENSE PERCEPTION

Descartes did not believe that the information we receive through our senses is necessarily accurate. After the revelation he experienced on November 10, 1619, Descartes undertook his own intellectual rebirth. His first step was to throw out everything he thought he knew, refusing to believe in even the most basic premises until proving them to himself satisfactorily. In this act of demolition and reconstruction, Descartes felt it would be a waste of time to tear down each idea individually. Instead, he attacked what he considered the very foundation: the idea that sense perception conveys accurate information. He developed several arguments to illustrate this point.

In the Dream argument, Descartes argues that he often dreams of things that seem real to him while he is asleep. In one dream, he sits by a fire in his room, and it seems he can feel the warmth of the fire, just as he feels it in his waking life, even though there is no fire. The fact that he feels the fire doesn't really allow him to tell when he is awake and when he is dreaming. Moreover, if his senses can convey to him the heat of the fire when he does not really feel it, he can't trust that the fire exists when he feels it in his waking life.

Likewise, in the Deceiving God and Evil Demon arguments, Descartes suggests that, for all he knows, he may be under the control of an all-powerful being bent on deceiving him. In that case, he does not have a body at all but is merely a brain fed information and illusions by the all-powerful being. (Fans of the *Matrix* films may recognize this concept.) Descartes does not intend these arguments to be taken literally. His point is to demonstrate that the senses can be deceived. If we cannot trust our senses to convey true information about the world around us, nor can we trust deductions we've made on the grounds of sense perception.

Descartes' casting of doubt on the reliability of sense perception was a radical position at the time. He was proposing that scientific observation had to be an interpretive act requiring careful monitoring. The proponents of the British empiricist movement especially opposed Descartes' ideas. They believed that all knowledge comes to us through the senses. Descartes and his followers argued the opposite—that true knowledge comes only through the application of pure reason.

SCIENCE BASED ON REASON

Although Descartes mistrusted the information received through the senses, he did believe that certain knowledge can be acquired by other means, arguing that the strict application of reason to all problems is the only way to achieve certainty in science. In *Rules for the Direction of the Mind*, Descartes argues that all problems should be broken up into their simplest parts and that problems can be expressed as abstract equations. Descartes hopes to minimize or remove the role of unreliable sense perception in the sciences. If all problems are reduced to their least sense-dependent and most abstract elements, then objective reason can be put to work to solve the problem.

Descartes' work combining algebra and geometry is an application of this principle. By creating a two-dimensional graph on which problems could be plotted, he developed a visual vocabulary for arithmetic and algebraic ideas. In other words, he made it possible to express mathematics and algebra in geometric forms. He also developed a method for understanding the properties of objects in the real world by reducing their shapes to formulae and approaching them through reason rather than sense perception.

REASON AS THE ESSENCE OF HUMANITY

Descartes' most famous statement is *Cogito ergo sum*, "I think, therefore I exist." With this argument, Descartes proposes that the very act of thinking offers a proof of individual human existence. Because thoughts must have a source, there must be an "I" that exists to do the thinking. In arguments that follow from this premise, Descartes points out that although he can be sure of nothing else about his existence—he can't prove beyond a doubt that he has hands or hair or a body—he is certain that he has thoughts and the ability to use reason. Descartes asserts that these facts come to him as "clear and distinct perceptions." He argues that anything that can be observed through clear and distinct perceptions is part of the essence of what is observed. Thought and reason, because they are clearly perceived, must be the essence of humanity. Consequently, Descartes asserts that a human would still be a human without hands or hair or a face. He also asserts that other things that are not human may have hair, hands, or faces, but a human would not be a human without reason, and only humans possess the ability to reason.

THE ATTAINABILITY OF KNOWLEDGE

Descartes firmly believed that reason is a native gift of humans and that true knowledge can be gleaned not from books but only through the methodical application of reason. The expressed aim of many of his books was to present complex scientific and philosophical matters in such a way that the least sophisticated readers could understand them. Because Descartes believed that every human possesses the "natural light" of reason, he believed that if he presented all his arguments as logical trains of thought, then anyone could understand them and nobody could help but be swayed. In the original edition of *Discourse on the Method*, in fact, Descartes declares his aim with the subtitle "*In which the Author... explains the most abstruse Topics he could choose, and does so in such a way that even persons who have never studied can understand them.*" In an attempt to reach a wider audience, Descartes occasionally wrote in French, the language of his countrymen, rather than Latin, the language of scholars, so that people without a formal education could understand him.

Summary & Analysis

Summary

Discourse on the Method is Descartes' attempt to explain his method of reasoning through even the most difficult of problems. He illustrates the development of this method through brief autobiographical sketches interspersed with philosophical arguments.

Part 1 contains "various considerations concerning the sciences." First, all people possess "good sense," the ability to distinguish truth from fiction. Therefore, it is not a lack of ability that obstructs people but rather their failure to follow the correct path of thought. The use of a method can elevate an average mind above the rest; in fact, Descartes considered himself a typical thinker improved by the use of this method. Descartes benefited from a superior education but believed that book learning also clouded his mind. After leaving school, he set off traveling to learn from "the great book of the world" with an unclouded mind. He comes to the conclusion that all people have a "natural light" that can be obscured by education and that it is as important to study oneself as it is to study the world.

In part 2, Descartes describes his revelation in the "stove-heated room." Contemplating various subjects, he hits on the idea that the works of individuals are superior to those conceived by committee because an individual's work follows one plan, with all elements working toward the same end. He considers that the science he learned as a boy is likely flawed because it consists of the ideas of many different men from various eras. Keeping in mind what he has learned of logic, geometry, and algebra, he sets down the following rules:

1. To never believe anything unless he can prove it himself
2. To reduce every problem to its simplest parts
3. To always be orderly in his thoughts and proceed from the simplest part to the most difficult
4. When solving a problem, to create a long chain of reasoning and leave nothing out

He immediately finds this method effective in solving problems that he had found too difficult before. Still fearing that his own misconceptions might be getting in the way of pure reason, he decides to systematically eliminate all his wrong opinions and use his new method exclusively.

In part 3, Descartes puts forth a provisional moral code to live by while rethinking his views:

1. To obey the rules and customs of his country and his religion and never take an extreme opinion
2. To be decisive and stick with his decisions, even if some doubts linger
3. To try to change himself, not the world
4. To examine all the professions in the world and try to figure out what the best one is

Not surprising, Descartes determines that reasoning and searching for the truth is, if not the highest calling, at least extremely useful. For many years after his revelation, Descartes traveled widely and gained a reputation for wisdom, then retired to examine his thoughts in solitude.

In part 4, Descartes offers proofs of the existence of the soul and of God. Contemplating the nature of dreams and the unreliability of the senses, he becomes aware of his own process of thinking and realizes it is proof of his existence: I think, therefore I exist (*Cogito ergo sum*). He also concludes that the soul is separate from the body based on the unreliability of the senses as compared with pure reason. His doubts lead him to believe that he is imperfect, yet his ability to conceive of perfection indicates that something perfect must exist outside of him—namely, God. He reasons that all good things in the world must stem from God, as must all clear and distinct thoughts.

Part 5 moves from discussion of a theory of light to theories about human anatomy. Descartes considers the fact that animals have many of the same organs as humans yet lack powers of speech or reason. He takes this difference to be evidence of humankind's "rational soul." He considers the mysterious connection of the soul to the body and concludes that the soul must have a life outside the body. Therefore it must not die when the body dies. Because he cannot conceive of a way that the soul could perish or be killed, he is forced to conclude that the soul is immortal.

In part 6, Descartes cautiously touches on possible conflicts with the church over his ideas about physical science. Finally, he implores his readers to read carefully, apologizes for writing in French rather than Latin, and vows to shun fame and fortune in the name of pursuing truth and knowledge.

Analysis

Discourse on the Method (1637) was Descartes' first published work. He wrote the book in French rather than Latin, the accepted language of scholarship at the time, because he intended to explain complex scientific matters to people who had never studied them before.

Descartes' education was based on the Aristotelian model of reasoning, which held that scientific knowledge is deduced from fixed premises. This model is based on the syllogism, in which one starts with a major premise ("Virtues are good") and a minor premise ("kindness is a virtue"), then draws a conclusion from the two ("therefore, kindness must be good"). Descartes wondered whether he could be certain of the premises he had been taught. He was reasonably convinced of the certainty of mathematics (at which he excelled), but the other sciences seemed shaky to him because they were based on philosophical models rather than rational tests, which seemed to Descartes the only sound method of discovery. His revolutionary step was to attempt to solve problems in the sciences and philosophy by applying the rules of mathematics. His work, however, is remembered for his development of a method rather than his work in the physical sciences, which is now considered flawed and obsolete.

Descartes initiated a major shift away from Aristotle with the notion that individuals should examine problems for themselves rather than rely on tradition. The four rules for individual inquiry he outlines in Part Two are a summary of the thirty-six rules he intended to publish as *Rules for the Direction of the Mind* (published posthumously). In essence, the first rule is about avoiding the prejudices that come with age and education. The second rule is a call for breaking every problem into its most basic parts—a practice that signals the shift from the traditional approach to science into an approach more in line with mathematics. The third rule is about working from simple elements to the more complicated elements—what math teachers call "order of operations." The fourth rule prescribes attention to detail.

Descartes' imposition of this method on scientific inquiry signals the break between Aristotelian thought and continental rationalism, a philosophical movement that spread across parts of Europe in the seventeenth and eighteenth centuries, of which Descartes is the first exemplar. Aristotelian science, like rationalism, proceeds from first principles that are assumed to be absolutely true. Aristotelians, like Descartes, proceed from those first principles to deduce other truths. However, the principle truths accepted by Aristotelians are less certain than the ones Descartes hopes to establish. By undertaking to doubt everything that cannot be deduced with pure reason, Descartes undermines the Aristotelian method. For centuries, scholars had based their philosophy on sense perception in combination with reason. Descartes' new philosophy instead proceeds from doubt and the denial of sensory experience.

Continental rationalism held that human reason was the basis of all knowledge. Rationalists claimed that if one began with intuitively understood basic principles, like Descartes' axioms of geometry, one could deduce the truth about anything. Descartes' method is now used most often in algebraic proofs, geometry, and physics. The gist of the method is that, when attempting to solve a problem, we have to formulate some sort of equation.

Descartes' moral rules demonstrate both his distrust of the material world and his confidence in his mind's ability to overcome it. He has near-absolute faith in his ability to control his own mind and believes that he only needs to change his mind to change reality. If he wants something he can't have, he won't struggle to get it or be miserable about not having it. Instead, he'll just decide not to want it. Descartes' resolution to become a spectator rather than an actor in the events of the world around him amounts almost to a renunciation of his physical existence. Long after

Descartes, scientific study was governed by the ideal of detached observation that Descartes advanced.

Part 4 of *Discourse* is a precursor to his later work, *Meditations on First Philosophy,* and the major ideas he provides here—that the self exists because it thinks and that God exists because the self is imperfect and there must be a source for the idea of perfection outside the self—are mere sketches of the detailed explanation he provides in *Meditations*.

MEDITATIONS ON FIRST PHILOSOPHY

Summary

Meditations on First Philosophy begins with two introductions. The first is addressed to the theology faculty at the Sorbonne (a university in Paris), the second to his lay readers. He outlines some of the objections to the *Discourse* and asserts that his critics generally ignored his chains of logic and only attacked his conclusions. He pledges to return to the two criticisms he finds worth considering. He asks his readers to approach the rest of the book with an unbiased mind.

The first meditation reiterates material from the *Discourse*. Responding to an objection to his critique of the senses, Descartes agrees that he would seem a madman if he argued he was not sure that he possessed a body. But he also points out that in his dreams he experiences a reality as convincing as his waking reality. He can find no sure way to distinguish between waking life and sleep. He then goes on to argue that if we dream of hands, feet, eyes, and bodies, then they must actually exist. When we dream, he continues, we use information we gathered from reality. Even if particular complex objects do not exist, at least the basic colors and shapes that compose them exist. In the same way, we can say the physical sciences are uncertain because they study composites. Arithmetic and geometry study simple objects (shapes, angles, numbers) and are therefore trustworthy. He trusts his perceptions of self-evident truths, such as simple shapes and numbers, because he believes in an all-powerful God who created these things.

Descartes admits that he cannot be sure that God is not playing some sort of trick on him. However, because he believes that God is good, he knows that God would not deliberately deceive him. Therefore, to rebuild his knowledge on the basis of doubt, he decides to pretend that a "malignant demon" is bent on tricking him. This powerful demon has created the illusions of the physical world to deceive him. With this in mind, Descartes sets out to prove, using only reason, that some things are beyond doubt.

Most of meditation II is devoted to discovering whether there is anything about which Descartes can be absolutely certain. First he decides he can be certain that he exists, because if he doubts, there must be a thinking mind to do the doubting. He does not yet accept that he is a thinking mind inside a body. After all, the demon could have convinced him that his body and the physical world exist. He moves to another question: what is the "I" that is doing the thinking?

The answer is that the mind is a purely thinking thing. Descartes concedes, however, that though what he perceives with his senses may be false, he cannot deny that he perceives. So the human mind is capable of both thought and perception. He explains this using the example of a piece of wax. We understand that solid wax and wax melted by a candle are both wax. Therefore perception is not strictly a function of the senses. It must be the reasoning mind that makes this judgment. Because the senses can be deceived, physical objects, including bodies, are properly perceived only by the intellect, and the mind is still the only thing he can be certain exists.

In meditation III, Descartes says he can be certain that perception and imagination exist, because they exist in his mind as "modes of consciousness," but he can never be sure whether what he perceives or imagines has any basis in truth. He then expands on his argument for the existence of God from the *Discourse*. He examines his own mind to see whether there is anything in him that would allow him to make God up. God is not only perfect but also infinite and all-powerful. Descartes knows that he himself is finite. He reasons that it is not possible for a finite being to dream of infinity. Therefore the idea of the infinite must come before the idea of the finite, before any person can begin to think of what he or she is.

Meditation IV deals almost entirely with the nature and origin of truth and error. Descartes asserts that knowledge of God will lead us to knowledge of other things. Because God is perfect, it is impossible that God would deceive Descartes, because deception is an imperfection. But Descartes knows himself to be capable of error, so he has to examine the nature of his own ability to err. He concludes that God must have created him so that he could be wrong. Imperfect things, like him, may occupy their place in the world perfectly. In other words, Descartes' imperfections may be what make him perfect for his role in God's plan. He further reasons that his own propensity to err must be his own failure to use his method to approach the knowledge sent to him by God.

Descartes decides in meditation V to begin to examine whether he can believe in the material world by examining the essence of material things in relation to God. He looks at his own ideas about the material world and separates them into two categories: distinct and confused. Mathematical ideas are distinct and there-fore exist. He further concludes that no truth, no science, and no certitude can exist without the knowledge of the existence of God. He realizes that the existence of everything depends on God and reasons on that basis that he doesn't have to doubt every-thing anymore. Descartes knows that God has given him the capac-ity to learn the truth about both intellectual and corporeal things.

Meditation VI is devoted to investigating whether material things exist. Finally, Descartes finds that it seems safe to believe that his God-given senses convey the truth to him. Above all, his senses convey to him that he has a body. He maintains that, though there is some mysterious link by which the mind is joined to the body, the mind and body are different things, and the mind will outlive the body. Having decided this, Descartes dismisses all his doubts of the past and determines, at last, that he can trust his senses.

Analysis

In the first introduction, to the theologians of the Sorbonne, Descartes takes pains to avoid charges of heresy. He had already seen, in the case of Galileo, what could happen if the church dis-approved of scholarly work. Although Descartes ultimately comes to conclusions that would be acceptable to the theologians—God exists; the human soul is eternal—it might have been considered heretical to feel that it was even necessary to prove God's existence through logic. The Catholic Church, after all, considers God's existence to be a matter of fundamental, unquestionable truth. The introduction to the reader reiterates his intention of publishing for an audience of logically thinking but uneducated readers.

One way in which Descartes tried to make his work acceptable to a conservative Catholic audience was to structure the meditations in a form similar to that of the *Spiritual Exercises* of St. Ignatius of Loyola, the founder of the Jesuit Order. The *Spiritual Exercises* recommends a six-step path in which the Christian begins by releasing all attachment to the material world, but after gaining confidence in God, the Christian returns to the material world with a renewed sense of purpose. Descartes' purpose was radically different, but the *Meditations* follow a sixfold structure that is, on the surface, similar. The first meditation proves that all things are subject to doubt. The second asserts that if we doubt, there must be a mind to do the doubting. The third meditation concerns Descartes' proof of the existence of God. The fourth explains how to distinguish what is true from what is false. The fifth explains corporeal nature and further proves the existence of God. The sixth explains the difference between understanding and imagination and proves that the human mind is distinct from the body. As with the *Spiritual Exercises*, the steps go from detachment from the material world to establishment of confidence in God to the achievement of confidence in the existence of the material world.

The three arguments that Descartes uses to make us doubt our own knowledge—the Dream argument, the Deceiving God argument, and the Evil Demon argument—are not meant to be taken literally. To prove anything beyond a shadow of a doubt, Descartes has to call everything into doubt. This strain of thinking in philosophy is called *skepticism*, the practice of critically examining one's own knowledge and perception to determine whether they are true. But skeptics also have to ask whether there is such a thing as true knowledge—in other words, whether it is possible to know anything for certain. Descartes was not the first person to employ skepticism; indeed, the tradition reaches back as far as the history of philosophy.

Descartes hopes to come to one irrefutable truth on which he can build his philosophy. The truth that he eventually reaches is often called the "cogito argument," after Descartes' triumphant declaration in *Discourse on the Method, Cogito ergo sum.* Through this argument, he decides that he is a "thing that thinks." In doing so, he reasons that we can only be certain of our minds and cannot be certain of our bodies' existence.

With the wax argument, Descartes advances a new conception of the mind and its properties. Aristotle had held that the mind is only intellect and that sensation and imagination are properties of the body. Descartes insists that sensation and imagination, though they involve the body, are actually properties of the mind. Although we receive information through our senses when looking at unmelted wax and melted wax, neither our senses nor our imagination can tell us that both of these things are wax or that the wax started out unmelted and ended up melted. Only intellect can make that judgment. Without intellect, our perceptions and imaginings are meaningless and tell us nothing about the world.

The arguments expressed in meditation III are often called, derogatorily, "the Cartesian Circle." Descartes argues that realizations such as *Cogito ergo sum* are "clear and distinct perceptions" and therefore certain. Essentially, Descartes claims that such perceptions are true because they are clear and distinct, and they are clear and distinct because it is obvious that they are true. This is called circular logic, and Descartes doesn't want to be caught in this circle. He therefore attempts to legitimize all clear and distinct truths by claiming they are provided by God.

If God exists, then truth is possible, since God is truth and perfection. But Descartes attempts to prove that God exists by relying on his own clear and distinct perception of God's existence. He is arguing that it is possible to have clear and distinct perception because we know that God exists and that we know that God exists because we have a clear and distinct perception of his existence. This logic is, again, circular. Descartes attempts to bolster this argument by saying that the idea of perfection, or God, must come from something outside of his own imperfect mind. He reasons that perfection must come from one source, and that source must be the perfect, all-powerful God. This argument has never held much philosophical weight, and it is tempting to see it as merely the result of caution on Descartes' part about going too far with his doubt and exposing himself to censure.

Descartes' idea that God can't deceive us because God is good comes from ancient Greek ideas of virtue and truth, specifically from Plato. In this scheme, truth, existence, and virtue are inextricably linked. Good things are true and real, and bad things are unreal and false. Since God exists infinitely (the ultimate reality), we know that God cannot participate in deception. If Descartes makes mistakes, then it must be somehow helpful to the universe for mistakes to exist. Otherwise, they would not be allowed. A page torn from a book of poetry might seem meaningless, but when the page is in the book, the book as a whole makes sense.

Descartes makes an important distinction between the intellect and the human will. The intellect, crafted by God, is the source of understanding, sensation, and imagination. The will is our ability to either affirm or deny what our intellect tells us. If the will affirms something that is not true with the information the intellect delivers, then the will—not the intellect—is always at fault. The difficulty lies in discerning when the will has made a mistake. Descartes, therefore, returns to the idea that we can only know what is true if we have had a clear and distinct perception. If we resolve to only believe what we have proved to ourselves, then we will be able to distinguish between what is clear and distinct and what is false and uncertain. Once we arrive at that point, the whole world of knowledge will open up to us.

Meditation V is an intermediary step in figuring out whether the material world exists. First, Descartes has to figure out whether he can believe even in things about which he has had clear and distinct perception. Naturally, he turns first to geometric and mathematical problems. Descartes, in the rationalist manner, argues that we learn the essence of things not through our interaction with them on a physical level but through our intellect. A triangle is a triangle *because* it has three sides, not because our senses tell us that a triangle has three sides. Because they are concepts and they exist in our intellect, we can be sure that triangles exist and have three sides. For Descartes, this is a "clear and distinct perception." Essences of things are always clearly and distinctly perceived.

Turning to the physical world, Descartes asserts we can clearly and distinctly perceive that bodies are "extended." *Extended* is a word that Descartes uses to describe something like "has physical mass" or "takes up space." Therefore, if we so clearly perceive that bodies are extended, then extension must be an essential part of bodies. Part of their essence is to exist in the physical realm. His acceptance of the existence of the body and the physical world in meditation VI is similarly predicated on clear and distinct perceptions of them, ultimately provided by God.

We may find it strange that one of the greatest works of a genius who founded a revolutionary school of philosophy would conclude by agreeing that, yes, we do have bodies after all, but for Descartes, what matters is not the conclusion we reach but the method by which we reach it. His conclusion is the hard-won result of years of study. Obviously, Descartes' years of study were not undertaken simply to prove that we have bodies and that the world exists. He never seriously doubted either of these things. His study was undertaken to prove that some form of truth existed and that it was possible to find it. He concludes with the truth that it is permissible to trust that our senses convey accurate information to our brains as long as we apply our intellect to all that information and rightly deduce information from it. And on this simple maxim, a whole new kind of thinking was born.

RULES FOR THE DIRECTION OF THE MIND

Summary

Rule 1 states that whatever we study should direct our minds to make "true and sound judgments" about experience. The various sciences are not independent of one another but are all facets of "human wisdom." Possession of any kind of knowledge—if it is true—will only lead to more knowledge. Rule 2 holds that we should only study objects about which we can obtain "certain and evident cognition." It is better not to study at all than to attempt a study when we can't tell what's right or wrong, true or false. All that is speculative or probable should be rejected, and knowledge should be defined as what can be proven by reason beyond doubt. Rule 3 states that we should study objects that we ourselves can clearly deduce and refrain from conjecture and reliance on the work of others.

Rule 4 proposes that the mind requires a fixed method to discover truth. A *method* is defined as a set of reliable and simple rules. The goal of study through the method is to attain knowledge of all things. The human mind begins life in a pure state, and from the moment learning starts, the mind grows clouded. The method's purpose is to return the mind to that pure state so that we can be certain of knowledge we attain.

Rule 5 holds that complicated problems should be reduced to their simplest parts. We then apply our "intuition" to the simplest parts and work our way back to the larger problem. According to Rule 6, we must not only find the simplest parts of the whole problem but also figure out how simple each nonsimple aspect of the problem is compared to the most simple. The simplest, or "absolute," things are universal and cannot be broken down into simpler parts. Nonsimple, or "relative," aspects of any problem share some qualities of the absolute parts and can be deduced from examination of the absolute parts.

Rule 7 demands that no steps be skipped in the examination of chains of relationships between simple and nonsimple aspects of a problem. After we have gone over the chain of relationships enough times, we will be able to see (without deducing) how each step relates to all of the others. Rule 8 calls for avoiding complexity to prevent confusion. Just as a blacksmith cannot forge a sword without first having tools, we cannot grasp truth without a method for attaining it. The method is a set of tools for learning, not a trick for leaping to complicated conclusions. Anyone who masters the method will either be able to come to the truth or be able to demonstrate that what he wants to know is beyond the grasp of human knowledge.

Rule 9 calls for focus on a problem's simplest elements. If we concentrate on these simple elements, we'll eventually be able to intuit their simple truths. Rule 10 states that the previous discoveries of others should be subjected to investigation. It is best for an individual to discover the truth by his own methods rather than accept the arguments of others. Not all minds are made for this, however. Therefore, the hardest problems should not be tackled first. Instead, students of the method should immerse themselves in simple, well-ordered tasks, such as embroidery, weaving, number games, and arithmetic. These activities train our minds to order, and human discernment is based almost entirely on the observance of order.

Rule 11 recommends that if a chain of simple intuitions leads us to deduce something else, we should subject this deduction to further scrutiny, reflecting on how each part is related to the others. If we think of the chain often enough as we run through our series of deductions, we will eventually be able to conceive of all aspects of a problem at once, thereby increasing our mental abilities.

Rule 12 holds that we must use our intellect, imagination, sense perception, and memory to their fullest extent. Using these tools well will help us to combine the matters we're investigating with knowledge we already have. Rule 12 contains a lengthy, inaccurate description of how the brain works and how memories are made, the point being that the brain learns to intuit simple things from experience. Descartes concludes Rule 12 (and the first set of rules) by saying that a problem can only be classed as perfectly understood if three things happen: we know what kind of problem it is when we come across it, we know what we need to deduce the answer, and we can see that the kind of problem it is and the means to deduce the answer depend on one another. The method for solving these simple problems was to be outlined in the second set of rules, which was never completed.

Analysis

The first three rules express the importance of certainty in Descartes' thinking. Descartes stresses the value of "true and sound judgments" and "certain and evident cognition" and goes so far as to argue that studying something that only serves to raise more questions is more harmful than not studying at all. If the information in your mind is jumbled, it is impossible to create any cohesive system of thought, and, as a result, everything you think you know is open to doubt. Rule 4 lays the groundwork for the intellectual rebirth that Descartes discusses in *Discourse on the Method*. Descartes' education was excellent but left him open to much doubt. He has read all the experts and enjoyed learning from them but finds that all too often the experts disagree. If two learned people hold opposing views on the same topic, how can it be determined who is right? According to Descartes, at least one party is wrong in such situations, and more often than not, both are wrong. For if one were right, he should be able to prove his point to the other through irrefutable logic.

In Rules 5 and 6, Descartes lays out several theories that fore-shadow other, grander thoughts he goes on to explain in *Discourse on the Method* and *Meditations on First Philosophy*. He asserts that every problem can be broken down into simple parts and that there exist parts so simple that they can't be broken down into simpler parts. These "absolute" ideas can be accurately perceived just by looking at them. These absolutes prefigure Descartes' later ideas of clear and direct perception. He ultimately concludes that whatever can be clearly and directly perceived is true. After breaking everything down into perfectly understandable parts, the next step is to figure out how the simple parts relate to one another. After that relation has been determined, the task is to find out how the compli-cated parts relate to the simple parts. In these rules, Descartes insists that repeated review of the chain of relationships among all the parts of a problem makes it easy to see at a glance how any single part relates to all the others.

Descartes' assurance, in Rule 8, that anyone can attain real knowledge by employing his method indicates that he was pro-moting the democratization of knowledge. Unlike most schol-ars of his time, Descartes occasionally switched from the scholarly language of Latin to publish in French, the language of his people. He always argued that he did so because a person who approached his writings with a mind unburdened by the prejudices that come with scholarship was the only person who would really be able to understand his points. Descartes held a firm belief in the native capacity for reason in every man. For Descartes, reason is what *makes* a man. So every man, from the lowliest plowherd to the most learned scholar, is endowed with the natural gift of reason. In fact, at this point in his career, Descartes felt that a plowherd, free of the burden of received ideas, might have an easier time using reason than a scholar.

Descartes often employs terms—such as "intuited," "natural light," and "clear and distinct perception"—that don't seem to fit in with his skeptical, rational view of the world. But these terms are used to describe a process that Descartes cannot fully explain. We intuit and have clear and distinct perceptions as a result of our reasoning. It happens when we have broken everything down so thoroughly that there appears in our mind something that we recognize to be true because it cannot be false. Reason, not divine inspiration, allows us to make these recognitions.

Something intuited is grasped in the same way one would grasp a simple math equation. Descartes' extensive work in geometry and algebra spurred his insistence that problems in the real world could be expressed in mathematical formulas—a radical view at the time that would revolutionize the way we study physics.

Descartes is famous for building his philosophy on the first premise that since he is thinking, he can be certain that he exists. Extrapolating form this original proposition, Descartes claimed that he could also prove the existence of God. How successful is this secondary conclusion?

Descartes' proof of God's existence follows closely on the heels of two earlier conclusions: that Descartes exists and that he is imperfect. Descartes buils his proof of God's existence on the back of these earlier conclusions, and in doing so he pulls a logical slight of hand. Rather than prove God's existence, Descartes leaves it further open to doubt by resting it on the strength of his earlier conclusions. He seems almost in a rush to prove God's existence, and his haste in doing so results in an argument that collapses on its own circular logic. Descartes' God is as reasonably defined as a mathematical equation, but that definition is not enough to prove God's existence.

By positing "I think, therefore I exist," Descartes identifies something undeniable—the activity of his own intellect—and deduces something further—his own existence. Similarly, he proves his own imperfection by pointing to his doubts and his lack of certainty. A perfect being, he believes, would never be uncertain. In fact, such a being would be all knowing. To arrive at his own perfection, Descartes claims, he must possess some idea of perfection, and that idea of perfection must have a perfect source outside his own imperfect intellect.

In other words, the idea of perfection necessarily proves the existence of a perfect being, God. This leap is the flaw in Descartes' argument. Whereas in proving his own existence and imperfection he deduced additional things about himself by extension from activities of his intellect, here he proves from one of his own ideas something outside his own being and apart from his intellect. Descartes may have been able to define what a perfect being, or God, would be in almost mathematical terms, but his ability to posit such a being does not necessitate its existence.

Student Essay

Similarly, we can define a triangle, or any other geometric shapes, solely by using the intellect, as Descartes demands of all things that are to be considered knowledge. However, just because we can define these ideas does not necessitate their actual existence in the world. For example, we can imagine and define the properties of a polygon with 1,000 sides, but that does not mean that such a shape actually exists anywhere. Therefore, God, as Descartes presents it, exists only as an idea. When Descartes argues that he can possess the idea of perfection only because it is somehow a perfect source outside him, he neglects to consider that the source of his idea might merely be his own imperfect mind. If his mind is imperfect, how can he be certain it is not the source of his idea of perfection? Or that his idea of perfection is correct?

Descartes employs the notion of essence to mean the property or set of properties that defined something. The essence of God, he argues, is existence. That argument fits with his definition of God as a perfect, all-knowing, and all-powerful being—the source of all good things—yet defining God as a being whose essence is existence goes no further in proving that God actually exists. What remains is only a definition, an idea of God that is clear and distinct but not provable. The leap that Descartes made in moving from his idea of perfection to proof of a perfect being's existence is closer to a leap of faith than to the rational chain of logic Descartes demanded in his intellectual inquiries. Descartes was anxious to use his methods to prove God's existence to ensure his acceptance by the church. It would fall to later thinkers, the British empiricists, to argue that the limits of our knowledge may make proving God's existence impossible.

Thomas Hobbes

1588–1679

THEMES, ARGUMENTS & IDEAS

- The Materialist View of Human Nature
- The Inadequacy of Observation as a Foundation of Knowledge
- Fear as the Determining Factor in Human Life
- Good and Evil as Appetite and Aversion
- Absolute Monarchy as the Best Form of Government

SUMMARY & ANALYSIS OF MAJOR WORKS

- *Leviathan*
  - Part I: "Of Man"
  - Part II: "Of Commonwealth"
  - Parts III & IV: "Of a Christian Commonwealth," "Of the Kingdom of Darkness"

Thomas Hobbes was born in Malmsbury, England, in 1588. As he noted in his autobiography, he was "born a twin of fear" because his mother went into premature labor out of fear that the Spanish Armada was about to attack England. Although the theme of fear and its overwhelming power would recur in his later work, Hobbes's early years were largely free of anxiety. He was educated in England's finest schools under the tutelage and patronage of some of its most prominent noblemen and intellectuals.

Hobbes lived through a tumultuous period in English history, and his most productive years as a philosopher coincided with a time of political turmoil and civil war. Early in the 1640s, when it became clear that Parliament was going to turn on King Charles I, Hobbes fled to France. As a devoted monarchist, Hobbes feared persecution if he stayed in an England run by Parliamentarians. He stayed in France for eleven years, during which he produced much of his most important writing. Hobbes's most famous work, *Leviathan*, was published in 1651, two years after Charles I had been executed by the administrators of the Long Parliament, the leaders of the first nonmonarchial government in English history. Although *Leviathan* won Hobbes a new notoriety, at the time of its publication Hobbes's political philosophy was already well known in Parliamentary circles, where he was generally vilified.

Throughout his professional life, Hobbes was more often derided than celebrated by his contemporaries. In England, his works were banned repeatedly, and "anti-Hobbism" reached such a peak that in 1666 his books were burned at his alma mater, Oxford. Because of his materialist philosophy and his opposition to the established church, Hobbes was often labeled an atheist, though he never professed to be one.

Hobbes was a supremely individual thinker. He attempted through his writing to influence the political conflicts of his day but managed to alienate himself even from those who might have been inclined to side with him. During the civil war, he chose not to tone down his rhetoric favoring absolutist monarchy as did many other royalists. At a moment when everyone on the king's side was at pains to proclaim their support for the Church of England, Hobbes trumpeted his distaste for the clergy. These indiscretions caused him to be banned from the court of King Charles when he was perhaps the most prominent royalist intellectual of the day. He also differentiated himself from his royalist cohorts by claiming that the king's right to rule came not from a divine right granted by God but from a social contract granted by the people. This iconoclastic position has led many to consider Hobbes to be among the first "liberal" political thinkers in Europe—despite the fact that many liberal philosophers held Hobbes's authoritarian view in disdain.

Hobbes's political philosophy was rooted in his fundamental conviction that all of philosophy needed to be overhauled. Hobbes believed that traditional philosophy had never been able to reach irrefutable conclusions or secure universal truth and that this failure was the cause not only of philosophical controversy but also of civil discord and even civil war. Hobbes set out to create a philosophical system that provided a secure and agreed-upon basis for all knowledge in the universe. This totalizing philosophy, which Hobbes developed over many years, was based on the materialist outlook that all phenomena in the universe are traceable to the physical properties of matter and motion. Hobbes, however, rejected the observation of nature and the experimental method as legitimate bases for philosophical knowledge. In this respect he diverged from his near-contemporary Francis Bacon, who also proposed a total reform of philosophy, but one based on the experimental method. Instead, Hobbes proposed a purely deductive philosophy that based its findings on previously stated, universally agreed-upon "first principles." Hobbes sought to create a philosophy capable of explaining absolutely everything that happens in the universe, and he produced original work that cut across virtually every academic discipline. He engaged in lengthy intellectual feuds (which he often lost) with figures as varied as the mathematician John Wallis, the philosopher René Descartes, and the scientist Robert Boyle.

Hobbes is primarily remembered today as a political theorist, and he has been enormously influential in political theory. The most durable components of his philosophy have been his appraisal of the role that power and fear play in human relations and his arresting portrait of humans in the state of nature. Political and ethical philosophers of all kinds have had to confront his theories.

Hobbes remained an incredibly prolific writer into old age, undeterred by widespread opposition to his work. He lived to the age of eighty-nine during an era when the average life expectancy was not much older than forty. Keeping busy to the end, in his eighties Hobbes produced new English translations of both the *Iliad* and the *Odyssey* and penned an autobiography in Latin verse. Despite the controversy he caused, he was something of an institution in England by the end of his life. As abhorrent or attractive as his views may be to readers, his brilliantly articulated theories are read by people across the political spectrum. Hobbes's ideas may be embraced or rejected, but they are never ignored.

Themes, Arguments & Ideas

THE MATERIALIST VIEW OF HUMAN NATURE

Hobbes believed that all phenomena in the universe, without exception, can be explained in terms of the motions and interactions of material bodies. He did not believe in the soul, or in the mind as separate from the body, or in any of the other incorporeal and metaphysical entities in which other writers have believed. Instead, he saw human beings as essentially machines, with even their thoughts and emotions operating according to physical laws and chains of cause and effect, action and reaction. As machines, human beings pursue their own self-interest relentlessly, mechanically avoiding pain and pursuing pleasure. Hobbes saw the commonwealth, or society, as a similar machine, larger than the human body and artificial but nevertheless operating according to the laws governing motion and collision.

In putting together this materialist view of the world, Hobbes was influenced by his contemporaries Galileo and Kepler, who had discovered laws governing planetary motion, thereby discrediting much of the Aristotelian worldview. Hobbes hoped to establish similar laws of motion to explain the behavior of human beings, but he was more impressed by Galileo's and Kepler's mathematical precision than by their use of empirical data and observation. Hobbes hoped to arrive at his laws of motion deductively, in the manner of geometrical proofs. It is important to note that Hobbes was not in any position to prove that all of human experience can be explained in terms of physical and mechanical processes. That task would have required scientific knowledge far beyond that possessed in the seventeenth century. Even today, science is nowhere near being able to fully explain human experience in physical terms, even though many people believe that science will one day be able to do just that. In the absence of such a detailed explanation, the image of the human being as a machine in Hobbes's writing remains more of a metaphor than a philosophical proof.

THE INADEQUACY OF OBSERVATION AS A FOUNDATION OF KNOWLEDGE

Hobbes rejected what we now know as the scientific method because he believed that the observation of nature itself is too subjective a basis upon which to ground philosophy and science. Hobbes contested the scientific systems of the natural philosophers Francis Bacon and Robert Boyle. These major figures in the Scientific Revolution in England base their natural philosophy on a process of inductive reasoning, making inferences and conclusions based on the observation of nature and the manipulation of nature through experimentation.

For Hobbes, the chief aim of philosophy is to create a totalizing system of truth that bases all its claims on a set of foundational principles and is universally demonstrable through the logic of language. He rejects the observation of nature as a means of ascertaining truth because individual humans are capable of seeing the world in vastly different ways. He rejects inductive reasoning, arguing that the results of contrived experiments carried out by a few scientists can never be universally demonstrable outside of the laboratory. Accordingly, Hobbes holds that geometry is the branch of knowledge that best approximates the reasoning that should form the basis of a true philosophy. He calls for a philosophy based on universally agreed-upon first principles that form the foundation for subsequent assertions.

FEAR AS THE DETERMINING FACTOR IN HUMAN LIFE

Hobbes maintained that the constant back-and-forth mediation between the emotion of fear and the emotion of hope is the defining principle of all human actions. Either fear or hope is present at all times in all people. In a famous passage of *Leviathan*, Hobbes states that the worst aspect of the state of nature is the "continual fear and danger of violent death." In the state of nature, as Hobbes depicts it, humans intuitively desire to obtain as much power and "good" as they can, and there are no laws preventing them from harming or killing others to attain what they desire. Thus, the state of nature is a state of constant war, wherein humans live in perpetual fear of one another. This fear, in combination with their faculties of reason, impels men to follow the fundamental law of nature and seek peace among each other. Peace is attained only by coming together to forge a social contract, whereby men consent to being ruled in a commonwealth governed by one supreme authority. Fear creates the chaos endemic to the state of nature, and fear upholds the peaceful order of the civil commonwealth. The contract that creates the commonwealth is forged because of people's fear, and it is enforced by fear. Because the sovereign at the commonwealth's head holds the power to inflict bodily punishment on anyone who breaks the contract, the natural fear of such harm compels subjects to uphold the contract and submit to the sovereign's will.

GOOD AND EVIL AS APPETITE AND AVERSION

Hobbes believed that in man's natural state, moral ideas do not exist. Thus, in speaking of human nature, he defines *good* simply as that which people desire and *evil* as that which they avoid, at least in the state of nature. Hobbes uses these definitions as bases for explaining a variety of emotions and behaviors. For example, *hope* is the prospect of attaining some apparent good, whereas *fear* is the recognition that some apparent good may not be attainable. Hobbes admits, however, that this definition is only tenable as long as we consider men outside of the constraints of law and society. In the state of nature, when the only sense of good and evil derives from individuals' appetites and desires, general rules about whether actions are good or evil do not exist. Hobbes believes that moral judgments about good and evil cannot exist until they are decreed by a society's central authority. This position leads directly to Hobbes's belief in an autocratic and absolutist form of government.

ABSOLUTE MONARCHY AS THE BEST FORM OF GOVERNMENT

Hobbes promoted that monarchy is the best form of government and the only one that can guarantee peace. In some of his early works, he only says that there must be a supreme sovereign power of some kind in society, without stating definitively which sort of sovereign power is best. In *Leviathan*, however, Hobbes unequivocally argues that absolutist monarchy is the only right form of government. In general, Hobbes seeks to define the rational bases upon which could be constructed a civil society that would not be subject to destruction from within. Accordingly, he delineates how best to minimize discord, disagreement, and factionalism within society—whether between state and church, between rival governments, or between different contending philosophies. Hobbes believes that any such conflict leads to civil war and holds that any form of ordered government is preferable to civil war. Thus he advocates that all members of society submit to one absolute, central authority for the sake of maintaining the common peace. In Hobbes's system, obedience to the sovereign is directly tied to peace in all realms. The sovereign is empowered to run the government, determine all laws, lead the church, determine first principles, and adjudicate in philosophical disputes. For Hobbes, this is the only sure means of maintaining a civil, peaceful polity and preventing the dissolution of society into civil war.

CHAPTER 7
HOBBES

Summary & Analysis

Summary

PART I: "OF MAN," CHAPTERS 1 TO 9 The opening of *Leviathan* is devoted to outlining the mechanics of the human mind and explaining the phenomena of sense perception, understanding, and processes of thought. Hobbes bases all his claims in his materialist conception of the universe as a plenum, filled with matter. All natural activity results from material bodies moving and colliding with one another, transferring motion from one body to another. All our sense perceptions result from material bodies colliding with our eyes, ears, nose, mouth, or body. The motions of the bodies with which we collide set off a series of motions between our sensory organs and our brain. Any body, once set in motion, will remain in motion until acted upon by another body.

Imagination results from continuing motion within the brain after the initial sensation of the foreign body causing that motion has passed. *Understanding* is a certain kind of imagination relating to the sense of signs and words. *Memory* is another kind of imagination, relating to the continuing motion set off by a sensation in the past. The motion of imagination continues until it is met by some hindrance, and in certain complex scenarios, it can build upon collisions with other motions to produce trains of thought. These trains of thought can be either *unguided*, as in dreams, or *regulated*, when the thinker intentionally directs his or her mental activity in a particular direction.

Hobbes moves on to discuss the various applications of regulated, or directed, thought. Language, reason, and science are chief among these applications. Language, or *speech*, was invented for the purpose of putting "mental discourse" into "verbal discourse." The transformation of the mental into the verbal allows us to name the conclusions reached by certain trains of thought without having to reconstruct the train of thoughts constantly and allows us to communicate mental discourse to other people. Speech has four principal uses:

1. To record knowledge of things

2. To communicate this knowledge to others

3. To communicate intentions and desires to others and ask for help

4. To entertain ourselves by playing with words

Speech can also be abused: the chief abuses of language include the use of lies, the use of metaphorical language, the shifting of meanings between words, and the use of language to injure other people.

Speech is composed primarily of names, or appellations, and the connections between them. Truth and falsity are categories that apply only to speech and do not exist outside of speech. The precise meanings we ascribe to different words must be consistent and commonly accepted for us to be able to recognize truth. Once common definitions are determined, true conclusions can be made by building logically on previous definitions. These accepted terms, and the truths they represent, are called first principles and are the necessary bases for meaningful philosophical discourse.

Our sensory experience of the world is not objective but is instead always influenced by our own subjective characteristics—physical, emotional, prejudicial. As long as differences remain in the approaches diverse individuals take toward reality, certain agreement regarding the meanings of words is impossible. It is impossible to simply look to nature itself as a basis of truth. Rather, there must exist in human society some central authority to decide the singular definitions of all words and to determine first principles. Although the faculty of reason allows us to apprehend the laws of nature, we do not all reason in exactly the same way. To maintain a peaceful and functional linguistic system of meaning—and a peaceful society—humans must agree to uphold the reasoned dictates of one central authority.

Hobbes elaborates on his description of the natural universe as a mechanical system in which motion is transferred from body to body. In living animals, two sorts of motion exist: *vital* and *voluntary*. Vital motions are those motions that take place unconsciously and that support life, including such basic bodily functions as breathing, circulating blood, and digesting food. Voluntary motions are invoked by active decisions, including moving limbs, speaking, and walking. The physical causes that precipitate these voluntary motions are the motions of thoughts and imagination. Hobbes calls these thoughts "endeavor." Endeavor can be broken down further into "appetite" (or "desire") and "aversion." Human nature essentially consists of the interplay between appetite and aversion. All humans are possessed of a great many appetites and aversions, including those we are born with that aid our survival and those we acquire from experience.

Varying configurations of appetites and aversions constitute the various human "passions." As Aristotle wrote, the metaphysical categories of good and evil are derived from our individual sensibilities of appetite and aversion: what we desire is "good" and what we avoid and direct our hate toward is "evil." When a person decides whether to act, he or she "deliberates" on the good or evil merits of the various options. At the end of deliberation, the decision is called the *will*.

Analysis

Hobbes's materialist view of the world is built upon the belief that the universe is a *plenum*, meaning that it is composed entirely of bodies (and no empty space, or vacuum) and that everything that happens is a result of the motion of those bodies. He takes this view to surprising lengths, suggesting that human nature, encompassing our physical, mental, and emotional faculties, is a product of physical motions. Even the various human passions are explained by Hobbes in quantitative physical terms. The quantity and type of passion possessed by an individual defines his or her condition in the world: to have weak passion is "dullness," to have indifferent passion is "giddiness," to have an overabundance or disproportionate amount of passion is "madness."

Another surprising and important assertion in the opening segment of *Leviathan* is that science and philosophy are equivalent endeavors. Hobbes is intent on illustrating the extent to which a proper philosophical method can explain and encompass all the varied areas of human knowledge. Unlike his contemporaries Francis Bacon and Robert Boyle, Hobbes does not believe in reaching true scientific knowledge through observation or experiment. Rather, he posits that all true science and philosophy must be based in language and in the solidity of definitions shared among many people, like the definitions of geometry. To Hobbes, "science is the knowledge of the consequence of words." He demands logically built definitions that take universally accepted first principles as their base, rather than subjective opinions or articles of faith. Following the form of geometry, Hobbes demonstrates how his own philosophical model can take under its umbrella the whole of human scientific inquiry.

Summary

PART I: "OF MAN," CHAPTERS 10 TO 16 Power, defined as "a man's . . . present means, to obtain some future apparent good," is divided into two kinds:

1. Natural, derived from inborn abilities of the body and mind, including intellect, strength, wit, and artistic ability
2. Instrumental, derived from the acquired faculties and advantages of friends, money, or reputation

The lifelong "perpetual and restless desire for power" is a fundamental quality shared by all humans. Along with power, fear of another's power acts as a counterbalance to the appetite for power and prevents people from constantly struggling to obtain power. Only fear of death and bodily harm causes humans to seek peace.

The mediation between power and fear, as manifested in human affairs, is called *manners*. The great variety of manners stem from confusions about the best way to mediate between power and fear, and ignorance of a "proper philosophy" that would grant such knowledge. Fear, Hobbes argues, stems from ignorance of causes, an ignorance for which people have tried to compensate by many artificial crutches, including custom, authority, and religion—all designed to dispel fear. Only proper philosophy can successfully dispel fear by granting scientific truth to the philosophy of causes and by enacting a peaceful society.

Reason dictates that a "prime mover" must have first set the universe in motion. Although our powers of reason are incapable of telling us the nature of this prime mover (or God), philosophy can help us to understand the prime mover's manifestation in the present motions of all bodies in the universe. However, human reason is by no means infallible. The only way for humanity to attain peace is through a universal religion based on the truths of philosophy.

Although men differ in the relative strength of their natural powers, they are all fundamentally equal in their ability to physically harm or kill another by various means. Fear may intervene, but if two people ever desire the same thing, the natural consequence of their mutual desire is war. Human nature is a purely mechanistic construct based in appetites and aversions, desires expressed in power struggles between men. Thus, life before civil society and law was characterized by continuous and total war, "every man against every man." This chaos is the state of nature, wholly lacking in culture and knowledge, a state in which human affairs are dominated by the continual fear and danger of violent death. "The life of man" in the state of nature, Hobbes famously writes, is "solitary, poor, nasty, brutish, and short."

In the state of nature, security is impossible for anyone, and the fear of death dominates every aspect of life. Being rational, humans naturally seek to be rid of fear. Reason teaches us that there are certain natural laws that dictate how a society may guarantee peace. One of these laws is the "Right of Nature," every man's inborn right to use whatever means available to preserve his own life. Natural law includes our right to self-preservation and forbids humans from taking actions destructive to their own lives. Although war may be necessary for self-preservation—and often is, in the state of nature—reason dictates that the first of all natural laws must be that humans seek peace to fulfill their right and obligation to preserve their own lives.

Building on the first law of nature, Hobbes elucidates other natural laws that he says can be discerned through reason. The second law states that in the state of nature "all men have a natural right to all things." However, to assure peace, men must give up their right to some things. The individual's transfer of some of his rights to another is offset by certain gains for himself. The mutual transfer of rights is called a *contract* and is the basis for all social organization and collective moral order. Although by contract we may give up all sorts of rights we possess in the state of nature—such as renouncing the right to kill another in exchange for not being killed—we may never give up our natural right to self-preservation, which is the basis for any contract.

The third law of nature proclaims that though the making of contracts is a necessary precondition to peace, we are obligated not only to make contracts but also to follow them. Out of these obligations and the consequences arising from their violation, we develop the concept of Justice. Only with the advent of the commonwealth, when such consequences can be systematized, are the concepts of justice and private property meaningful. Hobbes names sixteen additional natural laws for human conduct, totaling nineteen, that will uphold peace and together may be termed "moral philosophy." He says that the laws may be tested, or summed up, by the golden rule: "Do not that to another, which thou wouldst not have done to yourself."

The contract required by the most fundamental law of nature is forged and entered into by all persons. These persons can be divided into two categories: "natural persons" and "artificial persons." Natural persons are those whose words are their own, whereas artificial persons are those whose words are those of another. The contract, as the means by which the individual wills of all natural people are joined into one unified will, then becomes a kind of artificial person, whose words are those of many others not itself. Thus, the contract, and the commonwealth it forms, is an artificial person. This great iconographic person is the Leviathan.

Analysis

Hobbes leaves no doubt as to the absolute centrality of power relations in his scheme of human affairs. This emphasis is underscored by his defining many adjectives used to describe the worth of humans in terms of power. Indeed, Hobbes defines human "worth" as the measure of power possessed by an individual, in terms of how much would be exchanged to attain his power. All the relative qualities that may affect human esteem and conduct toward other people, for Hobbes, are based on the relative presence or absence of different sorts of power, and the recognition— or misrecognition—of the amount of power possessed by another person. Power's reciprocal companion, fear, dominates Hobbes's discussion of the state of nature. Fear both defines the state of nature and is the primary cause of its end: civil society. Most precisely, as Hobbes proclaims in *De Cive*, it is not mutual love between men that informs their decision to enter into society, it is their mutual fear.

In discussing the transition from state of nature to civil society, Hobbes speculates that natural laws perhaps shouldn't rightly be called "laws," because they don't come from commands but rather from innate faculties of reason. But then Hobbes states that since these laws are dictated by natural reason and that nature is ruled by God, "who commandeth all things," "law" is indeed a proper term after all. The important distinction between natural and civic laws is that natural laws are not commanded by a human power but are instead visible to all through right reason. Just the first three natural laws on their own provide all the necessary foundation for the forging of the contract that will create a civil society.

Summary

PART II: "OF COMMONWEALTH," CHAPTERS 17 TO 31 The first law of nature demands that humans seek peace—an end best met by the establishment of contracts. Yet the natural inclinations of men toward power always impel them to break contracts. Without the fear of punishment for breaking contracts, men will break them whenever it is immediately advantageous for them to do so. Thus the basic social contract of the commonwealth must vest power in one central, sovereign authority with power to punish those who break the contract. Under the rule of the sovereign, men are impelled, by fear, to keep the commonwealth functioning smoothly.

If the state is imagined as a person, the soul of that person is the concept of sovereignty, and sovereign himself is the person's head. Hobbes names this artificial person, representing the state in its totality, the Leviathan. Desiring to escape the state of the nature through contract, all persons erect a common power at the head of their commonwealth, whether one man or an assembly, and agree to submit to its will to escape fear of each other. The sovereign is charged with doing whatever necessary to defend the commonwealth. As all individual rights are transferred to him, all are compelled to follow the sovereign's commands regarding defense. Although Hobbes here states that the sovereign may be either an individual or an assembly, he does not yet state his preference for the sole sovereign ruler.

Commonwealths can be formed in two ways: through *institution*, or agreement, or through *acquisition*, or force. The group of people taken by force under a sovereign's rule may resist the acquisition and depose the sovereign before he takes control. However, if they do not do so initially, the sovereign in both acquisition and institution holds the same right of dominion over his subjects and the same responsibilities regarding the common defense. The sovereign is the foundation of all true knowledge and the embodied power underlying all civil peace. There are three possible forms of sovereign authority created by contract: monarchy, aristocracy, and democracy. Of these, Hobbes proclaims that monarchy is the best because it offers the greatest consistency and lowest potential for conflict, limiting the decision-making body to one.

Liberty may be defined as the ability to act according to one's own individual will without being physically hindered from acting as one wishes. From a strictly materialist perspective, only chains or imprisonment can prevent one from acting as such. Thus, under the rule of the sovereign, free subjects, unencumbered by chains, maintain their liberty. Although there may be certain laws and "artificial chains" arising from law under the sovereign, subjects have no right to complain about such chains because they have entered into a contract with the sovereign. Furthermore, since fear dominates the state of nature and hinders a person's ability to act as he wishes, true liberty does not exist in the state of nature. Only when the subject has forsworn his own fear and power to the sovereign to be used as tools is he absolutely free. If the sovereign ever loses his authority or ability to protect the commonwealth, then the soul will have gone out of the Leviathan, and subjects will be released from their contract and returned to the fear-filled state of nature—necessitating that they form a new contract if they don't wish to endure its horrors.

Hobbes identifies all the subunits of society as systems within that body: towns, trade organizations, and households that can be established by the sovereign or by groups of individual persons joined by some common interest. *Political systems* are always established by the sovereign, while systems created by independent subjects are termed *private systems*. Those ministers appointed by the sovereign to administer his systems are understood to be representatives of the sovereign's will. These "public ministers" act as joints in the Leviathanic body, manipulating the movements of all its limbs. Further expanding the bodily metaphor, Hobbes states that all goods produced within the commonwealth or obtained by trade are the "nutrition" on which the Leviathan's body subsists. Meanwhile, money, the liquidated form of commodities, is the blood of the body, circulating through all its various members to keep it functional. Last, the self-reproduction of the Leviathan is achieved by bearing versions of itself in miniature—offspring we know as plantations or colonies.

Through the last part of book 2, Hobbes elaborates on the specific functionalities of the Leviathan, particularly in relation to the creation and administration of laws. He also points out "birth defects" by which the Leviathan may be a dysfunctional body. The possible scenarios by which the Leviathan may be doomed and unhealthy include the sovereign lacking absolute power, subjects maintaining faith in the supernatural rather than submitting to the learned doctrine of the sovereign, matters of good and evil being decided by individuals rather than civil law, and civil and religious authority being divided and under different powers and imitating the governments of the Greeks and Romans. All of these problems have the potential to poison the commonwealth's body and dissolve it into civil war. A healthy and stable commonwealth depends on absolute respect and abeyance of the one sovereign's will.

Analysis

Hobbes's discussion of the complex functions of the Leviathan's body and its different possible forms of government all boils down to his strident belief that a body with two or more heads cannot function peacefully. He lists many other advantages inherent to absolutist monarchies. A monarch's interests are necessarily the same as the people's because he shares both a physical and a political body (the Leviathan) with the people, whereas in sovereign powers composed of groups, the members of a governing council do not share a body with their subjects.

Since a monarch can choose his own advisors and meet with them in private, he will receive better counsel than aristocratic or democratic governors. Conflicts over the succession of governmental power are impossible because the sovereign is solely empowered to determine his successor.

Crucially, no matter how the sovereign gains his sovereignty he holds the same rights and responsibilities. Whether by force or agreement, in both cases he gains his power through contract. The precise nature of the contract and dominion is all that differs, as the sovereign who gains his power through universal consent is backed by a contract resulting from the people's universal fear of one another, while the sovereign who gains his power through force is backed by a contract resulting from the people's fear of the sovereign himself. The form of dominion vested in contractual sovereignty is analogous to the dominion that a parent holds over a child.

Naturally, a child is "owned" by both its parents, yet since no subject can obey two masters, only one parent can have absolute dominion over the child. A mother will often enter into contract with a man, granting him absolute dominion and sacrificing personal rights to attain security. Just so, the contractual sovereign is granted his "paternal" authority. By contrast, the sovereign who acquires his power by force holds a dominion similar to that of a master over a servant. Although his power is called *despotical*, this sovereign, like the paternal sovereign and unlike the slave-holding master, holds his power by way of contract. Therefore, in the end, though the authority ascribed to different sovereigns may be termed paternal or despotical, the actual nature of their power is exactly the same. Above all, since both forms of sovereignty are consented to by a social contract grounded in fear, Hobbes considers them equally valid.

Summary

PARTS III AND IV: "OF A CHRISTIAN COMMONWEALTH" AND "OF THE KINGDOM OF DARKNESS" In part III, Hobbes addresses the problem of how the Christian faith relates to the Leviathan's ideal civic society. For Christians, who are compelled to follow the laws of God, a conflict arises from Hobbes's insistence that in the interest of peace, all knowledge, law, and belief must stem from the sovereign.

Hobbes asserts that the sovereign's laws may occasionally contradict God's *prophetical* laws, i.e., those Christian laws that cannot be known by reason alone—as God's natural laws are—but the sovereign's laws must still be obeyed by his subjects. Hobbes acknowledges that contradictory laws cannot both be followed, and in the face of this conflict, the sovereign's laws must be obeyed above all. Hobbes supports this position with a reading of biblical scripture, arguing that true Christian doctrine itself is not antithetical to his political philosophy but in fact supports it. There are some exceptions, such as the Christian belief in incorporeal spirits, and Hobbes counters that these are false beliefs. He concludes that religious and civic authority must be united under one source. The sovereign must be the head of the church in society as he is head of all else.

Part IV continues the project of discrediting false religious doctrine. Hobbes argues that the biblical Kingdom of Darkness in scripture must only be understood metaphorically as an allegorical term for the deceivers who lead men down wrong paths. He criticizes those Christians who propagate belief in spirits, labeling this belief a holdover from the "heathen religions" of pagan times. Once all false doctrine is banished from the church, larger society will be rid of falsity and will thus be capable of founding the utopian commonwealth of the Leviathan. Hobbes concludes by affirming the value of his book: "For such Truth, as opposeth no man's profit, nor pleasure, is to all men welcome."

Analysis

In Hobbes's attempt to reconcile Christian doctrine with civic philosophy, he expresses both his theories of power and human nature and his unique brand of Christian faith. Hobbes's view of human nature informs his belief that men will become hopelessly confused when confronted with "two masters"—the civil sovereign and God. The "double vision" Hobbes discusses here results from men dividing their loyalties between these two sources of power, simultaneously believed to be kings of the world. Although he bases his critique of this state of affairs in his political philosophy, he seeks to prove his argument by the citation of scripture. He selectively quotes Jesus to show that the Kingdom of God is not truly present until the end of the world. Accordingly, a person (like Hobbes) may believe in the ultimate sovereignty of God but recognize that his kingdom will not exist on the earth until the end of the world. As such, that person must obey the civil sovereign in the present. Although this maneuver conveniently adapts Christianity and his materialist worldview, it shocked and alienated once and for all the seventeenth-century Church establishment. The last book of Leviathan, which is not read or studied nearly so much today as the first two books, raises Hobbes's antichurch rhetoric to new heights. Despite his repeated denunciation of atheists, his radical assertion that God is not present in the current day guaranteed that he would always be a marginal figure among his contemporaries.

Enligtenment philosophers such as Lock and Rousseau are generally credited with being the inaugurators of modern democracy. Should Hobbes be grouped with these philosophers? Or does he belong to an older, more autocratic tradition?

Reading from the twenty-first century, the system of government outlined in *Leviathan* seems alarmingly totalitarian and fascistic. Hobbes's model seems to advocate a dictatorial system in which an absolute monarch holds and exercises sovereignty. The United States as the ultimate exemplar of modern democracy, seems to reject Hobbes's proposals outright by investing its populace with sovereignty, in the form of voting rights. However, despite the apparent structural differences, modern democracies actually come quite close to Hobbes's ideals of the preservation of peace and government through reason.

The truth of this assertion isn't immediately obvious. After all, Hobbes assumes that disagreement breeds strife and that any hint of discord is to be avoided scrupulously. However, disagreement is one of the fundamental characteristics of the American government. Our system values free speech, public demonstration, and open debate, and we hold as an unalienable right the ability to question our government's actions. The principle of disagreement also manifests itself in the practice of checks and balances. Various branches of the government—executive, legislative, and judicial in the case of the United States—restrain the others' excesses or spur the others on when they are lagging.

The system of checks and balances seems to completely negate Hobbes's notion of the absolute monarch, but in reality it simply modifies the principle. Hobbes' ultimate justification for absolute sovereignty lies in his assurance that only a total monarchy can adequately prevent civil strife. However, once he or she has been vested with supreme power, nothing prevents that monarch from turning predatory and becoming a source of danger rather than to security. Throughout history, countless totalitarian governments have borne out this dilemma. A sovereign, after all, is only human. He or she is susceptible to the same desire for power that Hobbes detected as endemic to the human condition.

Student Essay

Modern democracies answer the Hobbesian dilemma by investing its head executives with tremendous powers—as much as Hobbes's ideal monarch in some areas—but limiting that official's time in office. The welfare of the state remains a function of the quality of the executive's decision making, just as in Hobbes's *Leviathan*. The elected executive governs according to his reason and the advice he receives from his cabinet and appointed staff, just like Hobbes's sovereign. However, checks and balances prevent those executives from abusing their power. Government officials are answerable to the constituencies they represent through elections, which keeps their worst natures in check and encourages them to take reasonable actions. Their powers are further limited by laws and, typically, constitutions designed to perpetuate public order and stave off civil strife. In the case of modern democracies, fear can be translated into a positive situation: a leader, fearing that he or she will not be re-elected, will work harder to act according to the will of the population. This, too, reduces the threat of civil discord.

Hobbes's ultimate goal of domestic harmony is upheld further by democracy because the system of elections instills hope in the citizens and helps them stave off fear. When a leader makes an unpopular or harmful decision, the populace knows that, at the end of a set term, they will have the opportunity to replace those leaders if they so choose. With that assurance in mind, the threat of a violent revolt greatly diminishes. However, the institution of democracy does not inherently avoid Hobbes's dilemma. Only a strong democracy, with well-established institutions, has the power to diffuse fear and incapacitating conflict. After all, if a population cannot trust in its government's system of checks and balances, fear cannot be eradicated. We can witness this situation in several fledgling, developing democracies that are struggling to establish strong governmental infrastructures. The stability of both a Hobbesian Leviathan and a modern democracy eventually rests in the strength of its government and how adequately that government can instill either fear or hope.

John Locke

(1634–1704)

8

THEMES, ARGUMENTS & IDEAS
- The Moral Role of Government
- An Empirical Theory of Knowledge
- A Natural Foundation of Reason
- The Right to Private Property

SUMMARY & ANALYSIS OF MAJOR WORKS
- *An Essay Concerning Human Understanding*
- *Two Treatises of Government*

John Locke was born into a middle-class family on August 28, 1634, in Somerset, England. His father worked as an attorney and in local government, and owned properties that produced a modest income. Locke received an extraordinarily diverse education from early childhood on. His formal schooling began in 1647 at the prestigious Westminster School for Boys. Later, he studied a wide variety of literature, physical science, medicine, politics, and natural philosophy at Christ Church in Oxford, where he took up residence under a scholarship in 1652. Locke developed a particular interest in medicine and also studied the works of Descartes and Robert Boyle, the father of chemistry. Locke dabbled in chemistry using Boyle's rules and wrote short essays containing theological arguments against both the Roman Catholic Church and Protestant reformers.

In 1665, Locke met and befriended Lord Ashley, a prominent statesman who had come to Oxford for medical treatment. The two became fast friends, and Ashley invited Locke to join him in London at Exeter House as his personal physician. Locke agreed and left for London in 1667, where he lived for the next eight years. Locke's political interests had already begun to take precedence over his experiments in science and medicine, and they deepened while he lived with Ashley, one of England's most skilled politicians. Under Ashley's influence, Locke made financial investments that would secure his future and took a job working for the British government researching the relationship between trade opportunities and colonization. He worked closely with early colonists who left to found Carolina in the New World, assisting in the drafting and revision of the Fundamental Constitution (the original frame of government for the Carolinas, before they were split into North and South).

For the next several years, Locke worked in various government posts and received a hands-on education in public policy and politics while traveling extensively. When he returned to England in 1679, he found himself in the middle of political upheaval as Charles II struggled with Parliament for control. The threat of arrest spurred Locke to flee to Holland to join his friend Lord Ashley, now the Earl of Shaftesbury, and other political exiles. He returned to England when it became safe to do so in 1689. He lived with friends at Oates, held various government posts and civil service jobs, and published his philosophical works until his death on October 28, 1704.

Locke was born during the twenty-year English Civil War, which culminated in 1649 with the execution of Charles I and the dissolution of the House of Lords. England then reinvented itself as a commonwealth where both royalty and an elected parliament would work together to govern the country. In 1660, the Restoration period, which would last until the early 1700s, began. As a result of the Restoration, Charles II reclaimed the monarchy's former grip on both church and state institutions. Locke's early papers suggest that he welcomed these changes. These papers also reveal his sympathy with the concept of a state-appointed ("Anglican") religion, indicating that he still identified with the orthodoxy of his youth. He would almost completely reverse these views in later years.

The seeds of Locke's opinions on religion and government were planted during his childhood. His father's career had taught him a respect for the law, and his Puritan upbringing imparted him with strong religious convictions. A crucial turning point in his philosophical development was a 1665 trip abroad to Cleves, Germany, where he observed a community of different religious sects living together in harmony. This experience may have challenged his ideas about the necessity of state-appointed religion and led to the later writing of his *Letters Concerning Toleration* (1689). Locke held on to his deep-seated Christianity throughout his life and was disappointed in the public response to his essay, *The Reasonableness of Christianity* (1695). He did not view his critique of Christianity as a condemnation, but religious leaders disagreed and banned the book.

After a three-year visit to France, Locke returned in 1679 to an England in crisis. Rumors of a plot to assassinate Charles II and install his Catholic brother, James, on the throne had caused upheaval in the government. An insurrection, supposedly led by Lord Ashley (by now the Earl of Shaftesbury), mounted as it became clear that Charles II had no intention of reinstating Parliament. Correctly targeted by Charles II as an influential Whig, Shaftesbury survived a trial for treason and afterward fled to Holland. It is unclear how active Locke was in the affair, but his close friendship with Shaftesbury made him appear dangerous to Charles II. Locke followed Shaftesbury to Holland in 1683. In 1685, Charles II died, and the Catholic James II ascended the throne. In 1688, William of Orange invaded England in what is known as the Glorious Revolution, chasing James II to France and welcoming back the exiles, including John Locke, from Holland.

Locke's government work took him to France in 1675, where he learned the language well enough to read Descartes' works in the original French. His attention to Descartes in earlier years had been limited to scientific works. Now, Locke read more widely in Descartes' philosophy, which influenced his thoughts on the human experience in general. He stayed in France for just over three years, during which time he began several drafts of what would become his most famous work, *An Essay Concerning Human Understanding* (1689). During the unstable years before he too fled to Holland in 1683, Locke wrote his *Two Treatises of Civil Government* (1690). The *Treatises* are thought by some to be a direct reaction to the supposed Catholic plot and surrounding events. While in Holland, Locke wrote a series of letters to a close friend advising him how to govern his son's development. These were eventually published as *Some Thoughts Concerning Education* in 1693.

Themes, Arguments & Ideas

THE MORAL ROLE OF GOVERNMENT

According to Locke, political power is the natural power of each man collectively given up into the hands of a designated body. The setting up of government is much less important, Locke thinks, than this original social–political "compact." A community surrenders some degree of its natural rights in favor of government, which is better able to protect those rights than any man could alone. Because government exists solely for the well-being of the community, any government that breaks the compact can and should be replaced. The community has a moral obligation to revolt against or otherwise replace any government that forgets that it exists only for the people's benefit. Locke felt it was important to closely examine public institutions and be clear about which functions were legitimate and which areas of life were inappropriate for these institutions' participation or influence. He also believed that determining the proper role of government would allow humans to flourish as individuals and as societies, both materially and spiritually. Because God gave man the ability to reason, the freedom that a properly executed government provides for humans amounts to the fulfillment of the divine purpose for humanity. For Locke, the moral order of natural law is permanent and self-perpetuating. Governments are only factors contributing to that moral order.

AN EMPIRICAL THEORY OF KNOWLEDGE

For Locke, all knowledge comes exclusively through experience. He argues that at birth the mind is a tabula rasa, or blank slate, that humans fill with ideas as they experience the world through the five senses. Locke defines knowledge as the connection and agreement, or disagreement and repugnancy, of the ideas that humans form. From this definition it follows that our knowledge does not extend beyond the scope of human ideas. In fact, it would mean that our knowledge is even narrower than this description implies, because the connection between most simple human ideas is unknown. Because ideas are limited by experience, and we cannot possibly experience everything that exists in the world, our knowledge is further compromised. However, Locke asserts that though our knowledge is necessarily limited in these ways, we can still be certain of some things. For example, we have an intuitive and immediate knowledge of our own existence, even if we are ignorant of the metaphysical essence of our souls. We also have a demonstrative knowledge of God's existence, although our understanding cannot fully comprehend who or what he is. We know other things through sensation. We know that our ideas correspond to external realities because the mind cannot invent such things without experience. A blind man, for example, would not be able to form a concept of color. Therefore, those of us who have sight can reason that since we do perceive colors, they must exist.

A NATURAL FOUNDATION OF REASON

Locke argues that God gave us our capacity for reason to aid us in the search for truth. As God's creations, we know that we must preserve ourselves. To help us, God created in us a natural aversion to misery and a desire for happiness, so we avoid things that cause us pain and seek out pleasure instead. We can reason that since we are all equally God's children, God must want everyone to be happy. If one person makes another unhappy by causing him pain, that person has rejected God's will. Therefore, each person has a duty to preserve other people as well as himself. Recognizing the responsibility to preserve the rights of all humankind naturally leads to tolerance, the notion that forms the basis for Locke's belief in the separation of church and state. If we all must come to discover the truth through reason, then no one man is naturally better able to discover truth than any other man. For this reason, political leaders do not have the right to impose beliefs on the people. Because everything we understand comes through experience and is translated by reason, no outside force can make us understand something in conflict with our own ideas. Locke insists that if men were to follow the government blindly, they would be surrendering their own reason and thus violating God's law, or natural law.

THE RIGHT TO PRIVATE PROPERTY

The right to private property is the cornerstone of Locke's political theory, encapsulating how each man relates to God and to other men. Locke explains that man originally exists in a state of nature in which he need answer only to the laws of nature. In this state of nature, men are free to do as they please, so long as they preserve peace and preserve mankind in general. Because they have a right to self-preservation, it follows that they have the right to those things that will help them to survive and be happy. God has provided us with all the materials we need to pursue those ends, but these natural resources are useless until men apply their efforts to them. For example, a field is useless until it produces food, and no field will produce food until someone farms it.

Locke proposes that because all men own their bodies completely, any product of their physical labor also belongs to them. Thus, when a man works on some good or material, he becomes the owner of that good or material. The man who farms the land and has produced food owns the land and the food that his labor created. The only restriction to private property is that, because God wants *all* his children to be happy, no man can take possession of something if he harms another in doing so. He cannot take possession of more than he can use, for example, because he would then be wasting materials that might otherwise be used by another person. Unfortunately, the world is afflicted by immoral men who violate these natural laws. By coming together in the social–political compact of a community that can create and enforce laws, men are guaranteed better protection of their property and other freedoms.

Summary & Analysis

Summary

John Locke's *Essay* presents a detailed, systematic philosophy of mind and thought. The *Essay* wrestles with fundamental questions about how we think and perceive and even touches on how we express ourselves through language, logic, and religious practices. In the introduction, entitled "The Espistle to the Reader," Locke describes how he became involved in his current mode of philosophical thinking. He relates an anecdote about a conversation with friends that made him realize that men often suffer in their pursuit of knowledge because they fail to determine the limits of their understanding.

In Book I, Locke lays out the three goals of his philosophical project: to discover where our ideas come from, to ascertain what it means to have these ideas and what an idea essentially is, and to examine issues of faith and opinion to determine how we should proceed logically when our knowledge is limited. Locke attacks previous schools of philosophy, such as those of Plato and Descartes, that maintain a belief in a priori, or innate, knowledge. He begins by opposing the idea that we are all born knowing certain fundamental principles, such as "whatever is, is." The usual justification for this belief in innate principles is that certain principles exist to which all human beings universally assent. Locke contends that, on the contrary, no principle is actually accepted by every human being. Furthermore, if universal agreement did exist about something, this agreement might have come about in a way other than through innate knowledge.

Locke offers another argument against innate knowledge, asserting that human beings cannot have ideas in their minds of which they are not aware, so that people cannot be said to possess even the most basic principles until they are taught them or think them through for themselves. Still another argument is that because human beings differ greatly in their moral ideas, moral knowledge must not be innate. Finally, Locke confronts the theory of innate ideas (along the lines of the Platonic Theory of Forms) and argues that ideas often cited as innate are so complex and confusing that much schooling and thought are required to grasp their meaning. Against the claim that God is an innate idea, Locke counters that God is not a universally accepted idea and that his existence cannot therefore be innate human knowledge.

Having eliminated the possibility of innate knowledge, Locke in book II seeks to demonstrate where knowledge comes from. He proposes that knowledge is built up from ideas, either simple or complex. Simple ideas combine in various ways to form complex ideas. Therefore, the most basic units of knowledge are simple ideas, which come exclusively through experience. There are two types of experience that allow a simple idea to form in the human mind: sensation, when the mind experiences the world outside the body through the five senses, and reflection, when the mind turns inward, recognizing ideas about its own functions, such as thinking, willing, believing, and doubting.

Locke divides simple ideas into four categories:

1. Ideas we get from a single sense, such as sight or taste

2. Ideas created from more than one sense, such as shape and size

3. Ideas emerging from reflection

4. Ideas arising from a combination of sensation and reflection, such as unity, existence, pleasure, pain, and substance

Locke goes on to explain the difference between primary and secondary qualities. Ideas of primary qualities—such as texture, number, size, shape, and motion—resemble their causes. Ideas of secondary qualities do not resemble their causes, as is the case with color, sound, taste, and odor. In other words, primary qualities cannot be separated from the matter, whereas secondary qualities are only the power of an object to produce the idea of that quality in our minds.

Locke devotes much of book II to exploring various things that our minds are capable of, including making judgments about our own perceptions to refine our ideas, remembering ideas, discerning between ideas, comparing ideas to one another, composing a complex idea from two or more simple ideas, enlarging a simple idea into a complex idea by repetition, and abstracting certain simple ideas from an already complex ideas. Locke also discusses complex ideas, breaking them down into four basic types:

1. Modes, which are ideas that do not exist in and of themselves, such as qualities, numbers, and other abstract concepts

2. Substances, either self-subsisting things (such as a particular man or a sheep) or collections of such things (an army of men or a flock of sheep)

3. Relations, such as "father," "bigger," and "morally good"

4. Abstract generals, such as "man" or "sheep" in general

Complex ideas are created through three methods: combination, comparison, and abstraction.

In book III, Locke discusses abstract general ideas. Everything that exists in the world is a particular "thing." General ideas occur when we group similar particular ideas and take away, or abstract, the differences until we are left only with the similarities. We then use these similarities to create a general term, such as "tree," which is also a general idea. We form abstract general ideas for three reasons: because it would be too hard to remember a different word for every particular thing that exists, because having a different word for everything that exists would obstruct communication, and because the goal of science is to generalize and categorize everything.

Locke argues against the notion of *essences*, a concept that had been widely accepted since at least Plato's time. Plato argued that we can only recognize individuals as members of a species because we are aware of the essence of that species—for example, we recognize a particular tree as a tree because we understand what a tree is in its essence. Locke argues that essences don't actually exist as ideal entities but are instead nothing more than the abstract, general ideas that we form about the things we observe—things that actually exist in the world. Human beings decide which differences and similarities they will use to separate and classify particular things into categories—they choose how to define categories rather than discover the essence of a given species.

Despite having just criticized the traditional concept of essences, Locke decides to adopt the term into his own philosophy and proceeds to distinguish between real essences and nominal essences. Nominal essences are the specific collections of observable properties from which we create an abstract, general idea. For example, we observe similarities among many different individual dogs and from these observations form our idea of what a dog is. Real essences are the invisible structures and arrangements of corpuscles or atoms that allow for those observable properties to be observable in the first place. For example, to return to the case of dogs, if we could fully understand the biological structures and processes that make a dog a dog—whether those would include DNA or other things as well—then we would understand the real essence of dogs. Unlike the nominal essence, the real essence has a basis in reality.

Locke moves on to discuss language, pointing out natural weaknesses and common abuses of language. The most significant problem with words is that they do not immediately and obviously mean the same thing to all people. This problem has four main causes:

1. A word may imply a very complex idea

2. The ideas that words stand for may have no constant standard anywhere in nature to judge them against

3. The standard that ideas refer to may not be easily known

4. The meaning of a word and the real nature of the thing referred to by the word may not be exactly the same

Locke also identifies six common abuses:

1. People often use words without really knowing what these words mean

2. People use words inconsistently

3. People purposefully make terms obscure by using old words for new and unusual uses or by introducing new terms without defining them

4. People mistakenly believe that words refer to things rather than ideas

5. People try to use words incorrectly to change their meaning

6. People assume that others know what they are saying when they are not really being clear

Locke suggests four remedies to counteract the natural shortcomings and the abuses of language:

1. Never use a word without having a clear idea of what it means

2. Try to recognize the same meaning for words as others do so that we can communicate with a common vocabulary

3. If there is the slightest chance that the meaning of your words will be unclear, define your terms

4. Always use words consistently

In book IV, Locke addresses the nature of knowledge itself, asking what knowledge is and in which areas we can hope to attain it. For Locke, knowledge is what the mind is able to perceive through reasoning out the connection, or lack of connection, between any two or more of our ideas. Because knowledge only has to do with relations between ideas, which are in the mind, the knowledge we are capable of is not actually knowledge of the world itself. Locke identifies four sorts of agreement and disagreement that reason can perceive to produce knowledge:

1. Identity (blue is blue) and diversity (blue is not yellow)

2. Relation (two triangles with equal bases located between the same two parallel lines are equal triangles)

3. Coexistence (iron is always susceptible to magnets)

4. Realization that existence belongs to the ideas themselves and is not in the mind (the idea of God and of the self)

Locke distinguishes among three grades or degrees of knowledge: intuition, when we immediately perceive an agreement or disagreement the moment the ideas are understood; demonstration, which requires some sort of proof; and sensitive knowledge, which is about the existence of an external world, roughly resembling the world as we perceive it.

Locke argues that we can never really develop a system of knowledge in natural philosophy. The best that we can do is observe certain qualities in the world that tend to occur together on a regular basis. The kind of connection he demands is the sort that we find between properties occurring together regularly in geometrical figures. Although he doesn't seem to think we will ever be able to know more about the true nature of things, Locke is hopeful that we can understand existence, and the properties of things that exist in the world, much more thoroughly.

Locke outlines three strategies for dealing with the problem of skepticism, or doubt about whether the world exists outside of our minds. This problem arises naturally from Locke's theory of knowledge. If we only have access to the ideas in our minds, which only exist in our minds, how do we know there is a real world outside of our minds? Locke's first strategy is to refuse to take the skeptic seriously. Can anyone really doubt, he asks, that there is an external world out there? His second strategy is to say that it doesn't matter whether we doubt the existence of an outside world or not. All that matters is that we know enough to enable us to get around in the world.

Locke's third line of attack involves seven marks of our experience that can best be explained by the existence of an external world:

1. There is a certain realness and strength of clarity to perception of an immediate object that memories or products of the imagination do not have.

2. We cannot get these ideas without the sense organ appropriate to them.

3. We are able to receive ideas of this sort only in certain situations so it cannot be the organs themselves that are responsible for producing the ideas.

4. We receive ideas passively.

5. Some ideas are accompanied by pleasure or pain but the memories of those ideas are not.

6. Our senses often bear witness to the truth of each other's reports.

7. Two different people can share the same experience.

Locke argues that almost all science (with the exception of mathematics and morality), and most of our everyday experience is subject to opinion or judgment. We base our judgments on the similarity between propositions to our own experience and to the experiences we have heard described by others. Locke examines the relation between reason and faith. He defines reason as the faculty we use to obtain judgment and knowledge. Faith is the acceptance of revelation and has its own truths, which reason cannot discover. Reason, however, must always be used to determine which revelations truly are revelations from God and which are the constructions of man. Finally, Locke divides all human understanding into three sciences: natural philosophy, or the study of things to gain knowledge; ethics, or the study of how it is best to act; and logic, or the study of words and signs.

Analysis

Locke effectively shifted the focus of seventeenth-century philosophy from metaphysics to the more basic problems of epistemology, or how people are able to acquire knowledge and understanding. Locke rigorously addresses many different aspects of human understanding and of the mind's functions. His most striking innovation in this regard is his rejection of the theory that human beings are born possessing innate knowledge, which philosophers such as Plato and Descartes had sought to prove.

Locke replaces the theory of innate knowledge with his own signature concept: the tabula rasa, or blank slate. Locke tries to demonstrate that we are born with no knowledge whatsoever—we are all blank slates at birth—and that we can only know that things exist if we first experience them.

Locke builds a strong case against the existence of innate knowledge, but the model of knowledge he proposes in its place is not without flaws. By emphasizing the necessity of experience as a prerequisite for knowledge, Locke downplays the role of the mind and neglects to adequately address how knowledge exists and is retained in the mind—in other words, how we remember knowledge and what happens to our knowledge when we aren't thinking about it and it is temporarily out of our consciousness. Though Locke is thorough in his discussion of what objects of experience can be known, he leaves us with little idea of how the mind works to translate experiences into knowledge and to com-

bine certain experiences with other bits of knowledge to categorize and interpret future information.

Locke presents "simple" ideas as a basic unit of human understanding, claiming that we can break down all of our experiences
into these simple, fundamental parts that cannot be broken
down any further. For example, the idea of a plain wooden chair
can be broken down into simpler units that our minds receive
through one sense, through multiple senses, through reflection,
or through a combination of sensation and reflection. We thus
perceive and understand "chair" in several ways: as brown, as
hard, as according to its function (to be sat upon), and as a certain shape that is unique to the object "chair." These simple ideas
allow us to understand what "chair" is and to recognize it when
we come into contact with it.

Locke's theory of primary and secondary qualities is based on the
Corpuscular Hypothesis of Robert Boyle, Locke's friend and contemporary. According to the Corpuscular Hypothesis, which
Locke considered the best scientific picture of the world in his
day, all matter is composed of tiny particles, or corpuscles, that
are too small to see individually and that are colorless, tasteless,
soundless, and odorless. The arrangement of these invisible particles of matter gives an object of perception both its primary and
secondary qualities. An object's primary qualities include its size,
shape, and movement; they are primary in the sense that these
qualities exist regardless of whether anyone perceives them.

Secondary qualities include color, odor, and taste; they are secondary in the sense that they may be perceived by observers of the
object but are not inherent in the object. For example, a rose's
shape and the way it grows are primary because they exist regardless of whether they are observed, but the rose's redness only
exists for an observer under the right conditions of lighting and if
the observer's eyesight is functioning normally. Locke suggests
that because we can explain everything using the existence only
of corpuscles and primary qualities, we have no reason to think
that secondary qualities have any real basis in the world.

According to Locke, every idea is an object of some action of perception and thinking. An idea is an immediate object of our
thoughts, something we perceive and to which we are actively

paying attention. We also perceive some things without ever thinking about them, and these things do not continue to exist in our minds because we have no reason to think about them or remember them. The latter are nonimmediate objects. When we perceive an object's secondary qualities, we are actually perceiving something that does not exist outside of our minds. In each of these cases, Locke would maintain that the act of perception always has an internal object—the thing that is perceived exists in our mind. Moreover, the object of perception sometimes exists *only* in our minds. One of the more confusing aspects of Locke's discussion is the fact that perception and thinking are sometimes, but not always, the same action. To add to the confusion, Locke claims in book II that an action of perception *may* have a nonimmediate object, not that it *must* have one. This makes it difficult to pin down a rule for what perception is and isn't, and how perception works.

We may find Locke's discussion of essence, or substance, confusing because Locke himself doesn't seem convinced of its existence. Locke may have chosen to retain this concept for several possible reasons. First, he seems to think that the idea of essence is necessary to make sense of our language. Second, the concept of essence solves the problem of persistence through change: that is, if a tree is just a bundle of ideas such as "tall," "green," "leaves," and so on, what happens when a tree is short and leafless? Does this new collection of qualities change the essence from "tree" to something new? In Locke's view, the essence persists through any change, remaining the same despite changes in the object's properties. A third reason Locke seem to be compelled to accept the notion of essence is to explain what unifies ideas that occur at the same time, making them into a single thing, distinct from any other thing. Essence helps clarify this unity, though Locke is not very specific about how this works. For Locke, essence is what qualities are dependent on and exist in.

Locke's view that our knowledge is much more limited than was previously supposed was shared by other seventeenth- and eighteenth-century thinkers such as Descartes and Hume—even though Locke differs sharply from Descartes about why that knowledge is limited. For Locke, the fact that our knowledge is limited is a philosophical rather than practical matter. Locke points out that the very fact that we do not take such skeptical doubts about the existence of the external world seriously is a sign of how overwhelmingly probable we feel the existence of the world to be. The overwhelming clarity of the idea of an external world, and the fact that it is confirmed by everybody except madmen, is important to Locke in and of itself. Even so, Locke holds that we can never have real knowledge when it comes to natural science. Rather than encourage us to stop bothering with science, Locke seems to say instead that we should be aware of its limitations.

TWO TREATISES OF GOVERNMENT

Summary

Locke's *First Treatise* is a criticism of Robert Filmer's *Patriarcha*, which argues in support of the divine right of kings. According to Locke, Filmer cannot be correct because his theory holds that every man is born a slave to the natural born kings. Locke refuses to accept such a theory because of his belief in reason and in the ability of every man to virtuously govern himself according to God's law. The *Second Treatise* is Locke's proposed solution to the political upheaval in England and in other modern countries. This text laid the foundation for modern forms of democracy and for the Constitution of the United States.

The *Second Treatise* consists of a short preface and nineteen chapters. In chapter i, Locke defines political power as the right to make laws for the protection and regulation of property. In his view, these laws only work because the people accept them and because they are for the public good. In chapter ii, Locke claims that all men are originally in a state of nature. A man in this original state is bound by the laws of nature but is otherwise able to live, act, and dispose of his possessions as he sees fit. More important, human beings, free from the arbitrary laws of other men, have an obligation to protect one another's interests, since they are all equally children of God. They also have an obligation to punish anyone who goes against God's will and attempt's to harm another by compromising his life, liberty, or possessions.

In chapters iii and iv, Locke outlines the differences between the state of nature and the state of war. The state of nature involves people living together, governed by reason, without need of a common superior. The state of war occurs when people exert unwelcome force on other people, interfering with their natural rights and freedom, without common authority. The difference between war in society and war in nature depends on when they end. In society, war ends when the act of force, such as fighting, is over. When the last blow has been thrown, both parties can appeal to common authorities for the final resolution of past wrongs. But in nature, war does not end until the aggressive party offers peace and offers to repair the damage done. Locke claims that one of the major reasons people enter into society is to avoid the state of war.

Chapter v deals with the definition and function of property. Whether by natural reason or the word of the Bible, the Earth can be considered the property of all the people in the world to use for their collective survival and benefit. But Locke also believes in individual property. For individual property to exist, there must be a way for individuals to take possession of the things around them. Locke explains that the best theory of right to ownership is rooted in the fact that each person owns his or her own body and all the labor that he or she performs with that body. Therefore, when an individual adds his own physical labor, which is his own property, to a foreign object or material, that object and any resulting products become his property as well. Locke defines labor as the determining factor of value, the tool by which humans make their world a more efficient and rewarding place for all. Locke explains that money fulfills the need for a constant measure of worth in a trading system but is still rooted in the property of labor.

The rest of the *Treatise* is devoted to a more specific critique of government, stressing the rule of the majority as the most practical choice for government. He identifies three elements necessary for a civil society: a common established law, a known and impartial body to give judgment, and the power to support such judgments. He calls for a government with different branches, including a strong legislature, and an active executive who does not outstrip the lawmakers in power. Toward the end of the *Treatise*, Locke finally arrives at the question of forming a new government. When the state ceases to function for the people, it is dissolved or is overthrown and may be replaced. When the government is dissolved, the people are free to reform the legislative to create a new civil state that works in their best interest. Locke insists that this system protects against random unrest and rebellion because it allows the people to change their legislative and laws without resorting to force.

Analysis

The ideas expressed in the *Treatises* arose in the middle of England's political drama involving Charles II. Locke hoped to provide a convincing critique of England's current form of government and lay the groundwork for a better option. At the time, Locke's good friend and ally Lord Ashley, the Earl of Shaftesbury, was working from within the aristocracy to overthrow Charles II. Shaftesbury and many others wanted to prevent Charles II from allowing James II, his Catholic brother, to ascend to the throne. Locke worked on both treatises over several years, finally publishing them when William of Orange invaded and seized the throne in what was called the Glorious Revolution. Locke hoped that his new model of government would support William's revolution as the necessary solution to a monarchy that had abused its privileges.

Robert Filmer's *Patriarcha* had argued for the divine right of kings, and the refutation of this position, which had the weight of centuries of tradition behind it, was one of Locke's major tasks. Locke describes government as a human invention organized chiefly to further and protect the right of personal property. Human beings have an obligation in accordance with natural, divine, and moral law to care for one another and support the whole human race. Locke's explanation for the responsibility of community essentially boils down to the Golden Rule: "Do unto others as you would have done unto you." Despite various forms and complicated expansions, no philosopher or political thinker has provided a simpler, more obvious standard than Locke.

The first few chapters of the *Second Treatise* reveal some of Locke's most basic beliefs about human nature. Certain problems necessarily arise in a state of nature, such as the fact that some people will always make war or come into conflict with one another, steal from one another, act aggressively toward one another, and so on. But Locke firmly believes that all people have the ability to use reason to find the correct moral path. He insists that we are rational enough to know what is, and is not, in our best interest.

Belief in this universal ability is essential to Locke's remedy for war—civil government. Locke believes that people voluntarily create societies and governments all over the world because government provides certain things that the state of nature cannot, like protection and stability. For Locke, maintaining personal liberty is the key to a proper government, which should work toward the individual's and the commonwealth's best interests at all times.

The *Second Treatise* expresses even more emphatically that the key to all of Locke's political theories is property and the right to individual ownership of goods. Locke doesn't directly discuss the importance of property until chapter ix, but once he does, property quickly becomes the center of his model for government. After all, Locke says, the primary reason that people join together to form societies is that they have property to protect. Those same people become willing to give up some of their natural rights to the governing of a central authority, since those with property need a higher central authority to protect it. We may note, however, that this explanation leaves those without property out in the cold. Although Locke's ideas were revolutionary for his time, they have sometimes been criticized as lacking equal treatment for landowners and nonlandowners (i.e., the rich and the poor) alike.

Locke supports the right of the people to overthrow rulers who betray them. The executive and the legislature coexist independently to keep each other in check. Further, Locke asserts that if a leader violates the community's trust, the people can and should replace him immediately. Similarly, if the legislative body does not fulfill the needs of the people, it should be dissolved and replaced with whatever form of government the people think best.

John Locke tried to construct a theory of knowledge built solely upon individual experience and sensory input. How successful was he at eliminating the abstract entities that earlier philosophers, such as Plato, relied on?

Locke advocated an empiricist take on epistemology, in that he believed all human knowledge to be rooted in particular, specific sensory experiences. Therefore, he was suspicious of concepts like Forms or essences. These notions posit that somewhere in the universe exist entities that we can know and understand, though they remain completely invisible and intangible to us. Locke roundly rejected these theories, presenting the notion of abstract general ideas as their replacement. However, he never managed to dismantle the concept of essence completely and thus was not entirely successful at his epistemological project.

Locke begins his project by dismantling the classical notion of essences, a concept descended from Plato's Theory of Forms. Locke found the concept suspect because he did not believe in the possibility of innate knowledge. Both the Theory of Forms and the concept of essence require humans to have some mystical knowledge of an intangible, abstract entity. But according to Locke and other empiricists, we can only have knowledge of things that we experience through our senses. It would be impossible, then, to have true knowledge of a Form or an essence.

However, Locke realized that essence served an important function by allowing humans to categorize their world. Without this ability, science and communication would break down completely. To replace the discredited concept of essence, then, Locke proposed his theory of abstract general ideas. Locke argued that category defining terms like *cat*, *dog*, and *man* are actually concepts that humans create. We observe particular objects in the world around us and notice similarities among some of them. We then subtract the variant differences between those comparable objects and are left with certain qualities that, as we see it, define the category in question. So despite the fact that individual cats may differ in weight, size, and color, we distinguish their shared anatomical features, their tendency to purr, and their similar gait, and we classify them according to our abstract general idea of a cat. Human thought imposes categories on the world, and as such, those categories are unmoored from any objective, preexisting entity such as an essence, a Form, or an otherwise naturally occurring category.

Locke's theories get discouragingly complicated at this point. After summarily dismissing the concept of essence, he then reintroduces the term, but it is unclear precisely how the term has been transformed or why Locke feels the need to adopt it. An object's nominal essence is more or less equivalent to its abstract general idea. Nominal essences are constructed by humans and are relative according to those humans' needs. They are not based in any kind of objective reality, so it is unclear why Locke felt the need to confuse the issue by calling them a kind of essence at all.

Even more confusing, Locke then introduces something he calls a *real essence*. The real essence of an object is that object's internal arrangement of microscopic particles. In the scientific terminology of Locke's day, these particles were called corpuscles. This arrangement of corpuscles gives rise to the object's observable properties, which we then draw on to form our abstract general idea of the object. This seems to double back and contradict Locke's earlier assertion that abstract general ideas were imposed by humans on the world and had no basis in reality.

Locke justifies this arrangement by claiming that not all the microscopic properties of an object count as that object's real essence. Rather, only those elements that directly give rise to the object's nominal essence can be regarded as that object's real essence. So only the structural elements of the cat that create its anatomical features, its purr, and its gait are considered the cat's real essence. Those that lead to the cat's weight, size, or color can be discounted. The real essence is thus based in real, existent material, but it is still defined by the man-made categories of the abstract general ideas.

David Hume

(1711–1776)

THEMES, ARGUMENTS & IDEAS

- The Uncertainty of Causation
- The Problem of Induction
- Religious Morality Versus Moral Utility
- The Division of Reason and Morality
- Finding God in an Orderly Universe
- The Bundle Theory of the Self

SUMMARY & ANALYSIS OF MAJOR WORKS

- *A Treatise of Human Nature*
  - Book I: "Of the Understanding"
  - Book II: "Of the Passions"
  - Book III: "Of Morals"
- *An Enquiry Concerning Human Understanding*
- *An Enquiry Concerning the Principles of Morals*
- *Dialogues Concerning Natural Religion*

9

David Hume was born David Home on April 26, 1711, in Edinburgh, Scotland. Hume's father, lawyer Joseph Home, died in 1713, and Hume's mother, Katherine, raised their three children alone. With his Calvinist family, young Hume faithfully attended services in the Church of Scotland, where his uncle served as pastor. The boy's family had a comfortable life and a moderate income, enough to provide him with a good education. He left home at age twelve to study law at the University of Edinburgh.

Although Hume's earliest letters reveal that he took religion seriously, he developed a stronger interest in philosophy and literature while a student at Edinburgh. In 1729, Hume left Edinburgh to pursue a self-directed education. He worked briefly for a sugar merchant in England and left for France in 1734, where he wrote his first book,

A Treatise of Human Nature. When he returned to Britain, he anonymously published three of the five volumes of the *Treatise*: books I and II in 1739, and book III in 1740—a remarkable accomplishment for a twenty-nine-year-old. Although many scholars today believe that the *Treatise* is Hume's masterpiece, it was not well received by the English public, was not widely reviewed, and failed to arouse the public debate Hume hoped for.

In 1741 and 1742, Hume published his two-volume *Essays, Moral and Political*, which met with better success than the *Treatise*. Hume decided that the problem with his *Treatise* was its style, not its content, so he reworked it into several smaller publications. Two of these pulications became major works: *An Enquiry Concerning Human Understanding* and *An Enquiry Concerning the Principles of Morals*. This time, Hume caused a stir by advocating a system of morality based on utility, or usefulness, instead of God's authority. His newfound success encouraged him to seek a department chair position at the University of Edinburgh, but the town council rejected him because of his antireligious philosophy. Although the new books established Hume as the founder of the moral theory of utility and inspired the utilitarian movement, they also made him known as an atheist, and he was rejected from yet another chair position at the University of Glasgow.

In 1752, Hume became a librarian for the College of Advocates in Edinburgh, where he wrote and published his six-volume *History of England*. Although it was not a philosophical work in the strictest sense, Hume felt that *History* was the next step in his philosophical evolution. He described the series as the practical application of his ideas about politics. During this period he also published *Four Dissertations: The Natural History of Religion, Of the Passions, Of Tragedy, Of the Standard of Taste*. These works aroused controversy in the religious community before they became public. Early copies were passed around, and someone of influence threatened to prosecute Hume's publisher if the book was distributed as it was. Hume deleted two essays and removed some particularly offensive passages, then published the book to moderate success. But the larger success of *History of England* restored Hume's reputation and provided him with the income he needed to live comfortably.

In 1763, Hume left the library and returned to the world of politics, accompanying Lord Hertford, the British ambassador to

France, as his personal secretary. Hume was a controversial figure in England, but Enlightenment Paris received him warmly. In 1766, Hume returned to London as undersecretary of state, bringing along the persecuted writer Jean-Jacques Rousseau. Despite the generosity of his good-natured host, Rousseau eventually grew paranoid and bitter over his enemies' public attacks against him and broke with Hume in 1767. Rousseau wrote a public pamphlet accusing Hume of plotting against him while he was Hume's guest. Hume effectively cleared his name by publishing a response that explained the reasons for their dispute.

Another secretary appointment took Hume abroad for a year, but in 1768 he retired to Edinburgh, where he spent his remaining years revising his works and socializing. He died from a painful internal disorder on April 26, 1776, at age sixty-five. After his death, several of his unpublished works appeared in print. The first was the short autobiography *My Own Life*, in which he finally acknowledges that he had authored the *Treatise*. The autobiography aroused immediate religious controversy because of his professed happiness as an atheist. In 1779, Hume's *Dialogues Concerning Natural Religion* appeared his closest friends had suppressed it for years. Again, the response was mixed. Admirers of Hume considered it a masterful work, whereas critics railed against its hostility to religion. In 1782, Hume's last two suppressed essays, *Of Suicide* and *Of the Immortality of the Soul*, appeared to overwhelmingly negative criticism.

Hume is widely regarded as the third and most radical of the British empiricists, after John Locke and George Berkeley. Like Locke and Berkeley, Hume argued that all knowledge results from our experiences and is not received from God or innate to our minds. This kind of empiricism led to today's scientific method, which holds that knowledge should be based on observations rather than intuition or faith. Radical empiricism went further, arguing that our knowledge is nothing more than the sum of our experiences. Unlike Locke and Berkeley, Hume removed God from the equation completely and argued forcefully against the possibility of his existence as his contemporaries envisioned it.

Hume excelled as a moral philosopher, historian, and economist. He was the leader of the Scottish Enlightenment, a movement that took place between 1740 and 1790. This period was a very stable one in Scottish history, free of the civil strife and turmoil of earlier eras, and it gave rise to a remarkable number of notable intellectuals. The French Enlightenment had already spread throughout continental Europe and was beginning to influence Scottish academics, including Hume. Although they shared the French spirit, the Scottish philosophers practiced extreme skepticism and identified more strongly with utilitarianism, which posits that actions should be measured by their effect on the greater good of the world, not their consequences for the individual.

Despite Hume's nay-saying contemporaries, his theories of the "evolution" of ethics, institutions, and social conventions proved highly influential for later philosophers. Attention to his works grew after the great philosopher Immanuel Kant credited Hume with awakening him from "dogmatic slumber."

Themes, Arguments & Ideas

THE UNCERTAINTY OF CAUSATION

Hume observes that while we may perceive two events that seem to occur in conjunction, there is no way for us to know the nature of their connection. Based on this observation, Hume argues against the very concept of causation, or cause and effect. We often assume that one thing causes another, but it is just as possible that one thing does *not* cause the other. Hume claims that causation is a habit of association, a belief that is unfounded and meaningless. Still, he notes that when we repeatedly observe one event following another, our assumption that we are witnessing cause and effect seems logical to us. Hume holds that we have an instinctive belief in causality, rooted in our own biological habits, and that we can neither prove nor discount this belief. However, if we accept our limitations, we can still function without abandoning our assumptions about cause and effect. Religion suggests that the world operates on cause and effect and that there must therefore be a First Cause, namely God. In Hume's worldview, causation is assumed but ultimately unknowable. We do not *know* there is a First Cause, or a place for God.

THE PROBLEM OF INDUCTION

Induction is the practice of drawing general conclusions based on particular experiences. Although this method is essential to empiricism and the scientific method, there is always something inherently uncertain about it, because we may acquire new data that are different and that disprove our previous conclusions. Essentially, the principle of induction teaches us that we can predict the future based on what has happened in the past—which we cannot. Hume argues that in the absence of real knowledge of the nature of the connection between events, we cannot adequately justify inductive assumptions. Hume suggests two possible justifications and rejects them both. The first justification is functional: it is only logical that the future must resemble the past. Hume pointed out that we can just as easily imagine a world of chaos, so logic cannot guarantee our inductions. The second justification is that we can assume that something will continue to happen because it has always happened before. To Hume, this kind of reasoning is circular and lacks a foundation in reason.

Despite the efforts of John Stuart Mill and others, some might argue that the problem of induction has never been adequately resolved. Hume left the discussion with the opinion that we have an instinctual belief in induction, rooted in our own biological habits, that we cannot shake and yet cannot prove. Hume allows that we can still use induction, like causation, to function on a daily basis as long as we recognize the limitations of our knowledge.

RELIGIOUS MORALITY VERSUS MORAL UTILITY

Hume proposes the idea that moral principles are rooted in their utility, or usefulness, rather than in God's will. His version of this theory is unique. Unlike his Utilitarian successors, such as John Stuart Mill, Hume did not think that moral truths could be arrived at scientifically, as if we could add together units of utility and compare the relative utility of various actions. Instead, Hume was a moral sentimentalist who believed that moral principles cannot be intellectually justified as scientific solutions to social problems. Hume argues that some principles simply appeal to us and others do not. Moral principles appeal to us because they promote our interests and those of our fellow human beings, with whom we naturally sympathize. In other words, humans are biologically inclined to approve and support whatever helps society, since we all live in a community and stand to benefit. Hume used this simple but controversial insight to explain how we evaluate a wide array of phenomena, from social institutions and government policies to character traits and individual behavior.

THE DIVISION OF REASON AND MORALITY

Hume denies that reason plays a determining role in motivating or discouraging behavior. Instead, he believes that the determining factor in human behavior is passion. As proof, he asks us to evaluate human actions according to the criterion of "instrumentalism"—that is, whether an action serves the agent's purpose. Generally, we see that they do not and that human beings tend to act out of some motivation other than their best interest. Based on these arguments, Hume concludes that reason alone cannot motivate anyone to act. Rather, reason helps us arrive at judgments, but our own desires motivate us to act on or ignore those judgments. Therefore, reason does not form the basis of morality—it plays the role of an advisor rather than that of a decision-maker. Likewise, immorality is immoral not because it violates reason but because it is displeasing to us. This argument angered English clergy and other religious philosophers who believed that God gave humans reason to use as a tool to discover and understand moral principles. By removing reason from its throne, Hume denied God's role as the source of morality.

FINDING GOD IN AN ORDERLY UNIVERSE

Hume argues that an orderly universe does not necessarily prove the existence of God. Those who hold the opposing view claim that God is the creator of the universe and the source of the order and purpose we observe in it, which resemble the order and purpose we ourselves create. Therefore, God, as creator of the universe, must possess intelligence similar, though superior, to ours. Hume explains that for this argument to hold up, it must be true that order and purpose appear only as a direct result of design. He points out that we can observe order in many mindless processes, such as generation and vegetation. Hume further argues that even if we accept that the universe has a design, we cannot know anything about the designer. God could be morally ambiguous, unintelligent, or even mortal. The design argument does not prove the existence of God in the way we conceive him: all-knowing, all-powerful, and all-beneficent. The existence of evil, Hume holds, proves that if God exists, God cannot fit these criteria. The presence of evil suggests God is either all-powerful but not completely good or he is well-meaning but unable to destroy evil, and thus not all-powerful.

THE BUNDLE THEORY OF THE SELF

Hume asks us to consider what impression gives us our concept of self. We tend to think of ourselves as selves—stable entities that exist over time. But no matter how closely we examine our own experiences, we never observe anything beyond a series of transient feelings, sensations, and impressions. We cannot observe ourselves, or what we are, in a unified way. There is no impression of the "self" that ties our particular impressions together. In other words, we can never be directly aware of ourselves, only of what we are experiencing at any given moment.

Although the relations among our ideas, feelings, and so on, may be traced through time by memory, there is no real evidence of any core that connects them. This argument also applies to the concept of the soul. Hume suggests that the self is just a bundle of perceptions, like links in a chain. To look for a unifying self beyond those perceptions is like looking for a chain apart from the links that constitute it. Hume argues that our concept of the self is a result of our natural habit of attributing unified existence to any collection of associated parts. This belief is natural, but there is no logical support for it.

Summary & Analysis

A TREATISE OF HUMAN NATURE

Summary

BOOK I: "OF THE UNDERSTANDING" Hume begins by arguing for the validity of empiricism—the premise that all of our knowledge is based on our experiences—and using this method to examine several philosophical concepts. First, he demonstrates that all of our complex ideas are formed out of simpler ideas, which were themselves formed on the basis of impressions we received through our senses. Therefore, ideas are not fundamentally different from experiences. Second, Hume defines "matters of fact" as matters that must be experienced, not reasoned out or arrived at instinctually. Based on these two claims, Hume attacks metaphysical systems used to prove the existence of God, the soul, divine creation, and other such ideas. Since we have no experience of any of these things and cannot receive a direct impression of them, we have no real reason to believe that they are true.

Hume systematically applies the idea that ideas and facts come from experience in order to analyze the concepts of space, time, and mathematics. If we have no experience of a concept, such as the size of the universe, that concept cannot be meaningful. Hume insists that neither our ideas nor our impressions are infinitely divisible. If we continued to try to break them down ad infinitum, we would eventually arrive at a level too small for us to perceive or grasp conceptually. Since we have no experience of infinite divisibility, the idea that things or ideas are infinitely divisible is meaningless. Mathematics, however, is a system of pure relations of ideas, so it retains its value even though we cannot directly experience its phenomena. Many of its principles do not hold in matters of fact, but it is the only realm of knowledge in which perfect certainty is possible anyway.

Hume introduces two of his three tools of philosophical inquiry, the "microscope" and the "razor." The microscope is the principle that to understand an idea we must first break it down into the various simple ideas that make it up. If any of these simple ideas is still difficult to understand, we must isolate it and reenact the impression that gave rise to it. The razor is the principle that if any term cannot be proven to arise from an idea that can be broken into simpler ideas ready for analysis, then that term has no meaning. Hume uses his razor principle to devalue abstract concepts pertaining to religion and metaphysics.

Despite his apparent hostility to abstract ideas of a metaphysical nature, Hume does not deem all abstract ideas worthless. He argues that the mind naturally forms associations among ideas from impressions that are similar in space and time. In the mind, a general term becomes associated with further specific instances of those similar impressions and comes to stand for all of them. This process explains why we can visualize particular events that we may not have actually experienced, based on their association with those events that we have experienced.

Hume's third philosophical tool is the "fork," the principle that truths can be divided into two kinds. The first kind of truth deals with relations of ideas, such as true statements in mathematics—for example, that the sum of the angles in a triangle equals 180 degrees. These kinds of truth are necessary—once proven, they stay proven. The second kind of truth with matters of fact, which concerns things that exist in the world.

Analysis

The theories that Hume develops in the *Treatise* have their foundations in the writings of John Locke and George Berkeley—the other two great British empiricists. Like Hume, Locke denied the existence of innate ideas, dividing the sources of our ideas into two categories: those derived from sensation through the use of our sense organs and those derived from reflection through our own mental processes. Hume makes use of Locke's distinction in his own theory of ideas, though he alters the terminology. For Hume, sensations and reflections both fall under the term *impressions*, while he reserves the term *ideas* for the results of mental processes such as imagination and memory. Hume's discussion of abstract ideas rests on his acceptance of Berkeley's claim that the idea we have of a general term always springs from a specific experience, though used in a general way. Hume praised this explanation but further clarified how a general term could stand for several similar, but specific, experiences.

Prior to Hume, many philosophers made exceptions for metaphysics or held it to different standards than other areas of inquiry. Hume insisted that metaphysical issues, such as the existence of God, the possibility of miracles, and immortality of the soul, be held up to the same process of inquiry as investigations in the realm of ethics or physical science. For example, we can logically say that we can't conceive of what life might be like on a planet with no oxygen because our experience involves only forms of life that utilize oxygen. Why, then, should we allow for the existence of a being such as God, which is supposed to be the only example of his kind? We have no experience of anything even remotely like what we suppose God to be. We cannot assume that the existence of the universe automatically proves the existence of a creator because we have no experience that tells us that this has been proven. By this reasoning, the concept of God has no real meaning, and we cannot rationally accept it as certain.

Summary

BOOK II: "OF THE PASSIONS" Hume sets out to classify the passions in much the same way he classifies impressions and ideas in book I. First, he distinguishes between original impressions and secondary impressions. We receive original impressions through the senses. They are internal, in the form of physical pleasures or pain, and original because they come from outside of us, from physical sources, and are in that sense new to us. Secondary impressions are always preceded by either original impressions or ideas, which arise from original impressions. The passions, according to Hume, are properly found in the realm of secondary impressions. Hume describes both direct passions, such as desire, aversion, grief, joy, hope, and fear, and indirect passions, such as pride, humility, love, and hatred. Hume then distinguishes between the cause and the object of the passions.

Hume notes that since moral decisions affect actions (while decisions of reason do not), morality must not be based on reason. For Hume, beliefs about cause and effect are beliefs about connections among objects we experience. Our belief in such relations can affect our actions only if the objects being related are of some particular interest to us, and objects are of interest to us only if they cause us pleasure or pain. Hume concludes that reasoning regarding supposedly connected objects is not what makes us act. Rather, pleasure and pain, which give rise to passions, motivate us. Hume also says we cannot claim that actions are the result of passions that are reasonable or unreasonable, because passions themselves have nothing to do with reason. They are feelings that instigate actions. They may themselves be informed by reasoning, but reason is and should be the "slave" of passions.

Analysis

Hume's discussion of passions and reason sets the stage for book III and his discussion of morality. Passions, because they don't represent anything real and are not arguments in and of themselves, cannot be contrary to experience and cannot cause contradictions. Since these are two of Hume's most important measures, we can conclude that, following his argument, passions are completely different from reason and cannot be categorized as reasonable or unreasonable. This conclusion presents a dilemma for rationalists who view morality as the result of God-given reason. In fact, reason influences our actions in only two ways: by directing passions to focus on proper objects and by discovering connections between events that will create passions. The judgments a person makes about relations of ideas or about ideas themselves may be reasonable or unreasonable, but the judgments do not result in anything except opinions. For the moral process to complete itself, the judgments must incite passions, or feelings, which then lead us to act.

Summary

BOOK III: "OF MORALS" Hume stresses that his theory of morals follows naturally from the philosophy he elaborates in the first two books. Hume attempts to distinguish between vice and virtue, arguing that such moral distinctions are in fact impressions rather than ideas. He then describes how to distinguish these impressions from other common impressions, such as sounds and colors. First, the impression of vice is pain, while that of virtue is pleasure. Second, moral impressions are caused only by human actions, not the actions of animals or inanimate objects. Third, moral impressions are worth considering only from a social point of view because our actions are considered moral or immoral only with regard to how they affect others, not how they affect ourselves. This concept leads Hume to classify sympathy, feeling for fellow human beings, as the foundation of moral obligation.

For Hume, morality is not a matter of fact derived from experience. To prove his point, he suggests we examine ourselves with regard to any supposed moral misdeed, such as murder. If we examine the act of murder, we can discover no idea of that quality of immorality, or "vice." Rather, we discover only the strong feeling of dislike we have for murder. This supports the idea that morality resides in passions, or "sentiment," not in reason. Although reason does help us explain those feelings, it is not their origin.

Analysis

Hume makes the point that though we may not like it when one person kills another, there is nothing contradictory or illogical about the act of murder. This does not mean that Hume condones murder, merely that immoral actions are not immoral because they are irrational. Within Hume's system, murder would be banned on the grounds that it is not an action that can be universally justified as good for everyone. Hume also proposes the example of the man who would rather see the whole world destroyed rather than injure his own fingers. Hume claims this man is not in contradiction to himself or following illogical inferences, but this man also falls afoul of Hume's dictum that methods of justification and rationality must be universal. Other people in the same situation must be able to justify their actions in the same way. No one but the man will approve of his reasons for forsaking the world to save his own fingers. It is unlikely that this man would approve or desire that another person make the same decision.

Hume ascribes moral decisions to the passions for several reasons. First, passion appears to be the only viable alternative to reason, which he has already ruled out. Second, Hume's examination of his own feelings about conventionally transgressive acts such as murder reveals that while he can isolate his own feelings about such behavior, he cannot isolate clear and distinct ideas about it. Therefore, moral decisions must arise from or in some way be congruent with passions. Hume's connection of moral decisions to feelings, which leads him to the separation of morality from reason, put him at odds with religious leaders and philosophers of his time. Hume effectively dethroned reason, removed God from a place of necessity, and robbed religious theorists of an undisputed foundation for religious belief.

AN ENQUIRY CONCERNING HUMAN UNDERSTANDING

Summary

Hume begins by noting the difference between impressions and ideas. Impressions come through our senses, emotions, and other mental phenomena, whereas ideas are thoughts, beliefs, or memories that we connect to our impressions. We construct ideas from simple impressions in three ways: resemblance, contiguity, and cause and effect.

Next, Hume distinguishes between relations of ideas and matters of fact. Relations of ideas are usually mathematical truths, so we cannot negate them without creating a contradiction. Matters of fact are the more common truths we learn through our experiences. We understand matters of fact according to causation, or cause and effect, such that our experience of one event leads us to assume an unobserved cause. But Hume argues that assumptions of cause and effect between two events are not necessarily real or true. It is possible to deny causal connections without contradiction because causal connections are assumptions not subject to reason.

We cannot justify our assumptions about the future based on past experience unless there is a law that the future will always resemble the past. No such law exists. We can deny the relationship without contradiction and we cannot justify it with experience. Therefore, we have no rational support for believing in causation. Hume suggests that our assumptions are based on habit, not reason, and that ultimately our assumptions about matters of fact are based in probability. If experience teaches us that two events occur together repeatedly, we will assume a link between them. So, Hume explains, we must be able to reduce all meaningful concepts to the simple impressions on which they are built. Since no simple impression of causation or necessary connection exists, these concepts might appear meaningless.

Rather than dismiss these assumed connections entirely, however, Hume acknowledges their usefulness and limits them to being nothing more than simple observations of repeated conjunction between two events. Further, he concludes that if there is no cause and effect, then our actions are not predetermined, and we enjoy true free will.

At the end of the *Enquiry*, Hume pursues a number of tangential discussions. He argues that humans and animals possess similar capacities and methods for reason. He denies that any rational justification exists for belief in either miracles or most forms of religious and metaphysical philosophy. Although we can rationally justify our skepticism regarding the existence of an external world, that doubt destroys our ability to act or judge. The instinctual beliefs formed by custom help us get along in the world. As long as we restrict our thinking to relations of ideas and matters of fact, we are acting within the limits of reason, but we should abandon all metaphysical speculations as useless, impossible to resolve, and nonsensical.

Analysis

Hume seeks to explain our understanding of the world rather than try to justify our beliefs or prove anything. Here, he does not address the existence of necessary connections between events but states merely that we cannot know what those connections are. Ultimately, Hume argues for a mitigated skepticism. We have no good reason to believe much of what we believe about the world, but human nature helps us function in all the ways that reason cannot. However, we must limit ourselves by accepting that matters of fact are our sole source of true information. If past experience cannot teach us about the future, it becomes difficult to function on a practical level. The elimination of causation would make it impossible for us to function, if it meant that we began to act as if causation didn't exist. Whether or not we can *know* of a necessary connection between two events is not worth arguing about. Similarly, Hume does not think we should spend time and energy on questions such as whether God exists, what the soul is, or whether the soul is immortal. He claims that because the mind is not meant to help us discover and define truths, we will never be able to come to any definite and rational conclusions about abstract matters.

CHAPTER 9
HUME

Hume is skeptical about his own explanation of why we cannot rationally make necessary connections between two events. He stops short of saying that it is impossible to predict future events based on past experience and explains only that we lack any solid reason to believe this is the case. Hume admits that if we observe that one event repeatedly follows another, it is natural that we assume the two events will always occur together in this pattern. He also admits that we must necessarily make such assumptions to live our lives. Such assumptions are practical and useful but not completely reliable or passable as proof. We are wrong to justify these beliefs by claiming that reason supports them or that we can absolutely know that one event causes the other.

AN ENQUIRY CONCERNING THE PRINCIPLES OF MORALS

Summary

The subject of the *Enquiry* is the contributions that moral sense and reason make to our moral judgments. Hume claims that moral sense makes the ultimate distinction between vice and virtue, though both moral sense and reason play a role in our formation of moral judgments. Reason is important when we have to make a judgment about what is useful, for reason alone can determine how and why something is useful to us or to others. Hume briefly addresses what moral judges usually include in their lists of virtues, what they leave out, and how they make these lists. He then returns to the classification of virtues he proposed first in the *Treatise*.

Hume first distinguishes between artificial and natural virtues. Artificial virtues depend on social structures and include justice and fidelity to promises; allegiance; chastity and modesty; and duties of sovereign states to keep treaties, respect boundaries, protect ambassadors, and otherwise subject themselves to the law of nations. Hume defines each of these virtues and explains how each manifests itself in the world. He notes that artificial virtues vary from society to society.

Natural virtues, on the other hand, originate in nature and are more universal. They include compassion, generosity, gratitude, friendship, fidelity, charity, beneficence, clemency, equity, prudence, temperance, frugality, industry, courage, ambition, pride, modesty, self-assertiveness, good sense, wit and humor, perseverance, patience, parental devotion, good nature, cleanliness, articulateness, sensitivity to poetry, decorum, and an elusive quality that makes a person lovely or valuable. Some of these virtues are voluntary, such as pride, while others are involuntary, such as good sense.

As in the *Treatise*, Hume explains that reason does not cause our actions. Rather, moral sentiments, or passions, motivate us to act. In the *Enquiry*, however, Hume goes further to state that our actions are caused by a combination of utility and sentiment. In other words, we must care about the outcome if we are to care about the means by which it is achieved. Several sections of the *Enquiry* are devoted to utility, the first and most important of the four kinds of virtue, which Hume calls "virtuous because useful." He also addresses benevolence and its role in the moral process. Specifically, Hume says that benevolent acts are virtuous because they are useful to many others.

Analysis

Because he locates the basis of virtue in utility rather than in God-given reason, Hume's list of virtues implicitly forms a rejection of Christian morality. Items such as ambition are vices under the old model, so Hume's acceptance of them into his catalog is an insult to religious theorists. However, Hume is consistent in his theory that these traits are virtues because they fulfill his two requirements for moral sentiments: they must be useful to ourselves or others, or they must be pleasing to ourselves or others. Furthermore, Hume rejects the concept of morality as strictly voluntary. Rather, he divides his list into voluntary and involuntary virtues, claiming that separating them is necessary only when devising a system of reward and punishment. He is not interested in creating or endorsing such a system, so he makes no such distinctions in his moral philosophy.

DIALOGUES CONCERNING NATURAL RELIGION

Summary

The *Dialogues* are a series of discussions about the rationality of religious belief—among the fictional characters Cleanthes, Philo, and Demea—Demea represents religious dogmatism and insists that we cannot come to know the nature of God through reason. Philo, the philosophical skeptic, agrees with Demea that God is incomprehensible but insists that he might be morally corrupt. Cleanthes argues that we can know about God by reasoning from the evidence we find in nature.

Demea argues that although God clearly exists, we cannot know his nature, because God's nature is beyond the capacity of human understanding. Philo seems to agree. Demea goes on to explain that God is the First Cause, meaning that the world operates on a system of cause and effect, so there must be an original cause to have started the world in motion, and that First Cause is God. But this still tells us nothing about God's nature, which Cleanthes insists we can learn by examining nature. Cleanthes states that the only rational argument for God's existence is one based on experience. The design and order of nature reveal that there must be an intelligent designer, or creator, whose intelligence resembles our own. Cleanthes also states that things that are very familiar and present to us such as the knowledge that food nourishes the body need no reason to establish their truth.

Philo disagrees with Cleanthes and argues that just because the world is ordered, there is no reason to believe that this order is a result of intelligent design. He explains that the example of the design of the universe supposes an acceptance of cause and effect, which in turn supposes that the future will resemble the past. However, since there is nothing with which to compare our situation, we cannot assume the necessary connection based on past experience or other examples. Philo goes further, claiming that even if God is an intelligent designer, this fact does not explain why nature has order. Finally, even if the argument from design were valid, nature does not provide us with any knowledge about God other than that he designed it.

Philo next turns his attention to God's possible moral attributes and the question of whether we can discover these by examining nature. Together, Demea and Philo explain that the world is filled with evil. Philo says that if there is so much evil, there cannot be a God who is completely beneficent, or else he would have eliminated evil. If he cannot eliminate evil, he cannot be all-powerful. If he is unaware of the evil, he cannot be all-knowing. If nature itself provides evidence of God's nature, then we must conclude that he doesn't care about us at all and is therefore morally ambiguous. Demea leaves the room, upset by these claims.

Although Philo has successfully torn down Cleanthes' argument from design, Philo finishes the dialogue by declaring that the ordered world obviously has some intelligence behind it and that this intelligence does in fact resemble human intelligence. His real disagreement, he claims, concerns how strong this resemblance really is. He then attacks religious dogma as both morally and psychologically harmful. The most rational position, he says, is a philosophical belief in some unknowable higher power. Finally, Philo tells Cleanthes that philosophical skepticism is the only proper route to true Christianity because it forces us to rely on faith instead of the false connection between reason and theism.

Analysis

Hume clearly intends to point out that the question of God's existence and the supposed religious origin of morals are in fact two different issues and that a positive stance on the first issue does not necessarily confirm the second. The true question is whether enough evidence exists in the world to prove that there is an infinitely good, wise, and powerful God from whom morality naturally springs. Philo argues that there is not, and his explanation that the existence of evil poses a problem for this view of God is worth considering seriously. It seems impossible that an all-good, all-powerful, and all-knowing God could exist in a world as painful as ours. However, Cleanthes' position also seems cogent. We don't need to justify the existence of things that are universal truths. For example, we cannot prove that motion exists without referring to an example of motion itself. If both man and the universe exhibit form and order, we may logically consider that a similar intelligence lies behind both. However, from that claim we could argue that this intelligence, or God, possesses both good and evil, as man does.

CHAPTER 9
HUME

Imagine that you are taking part in an experiment in which you are asked to push a button repeatedly. At the other end of the room, behind a one-way mirror, is a person sitting in a chair. Each time you press the button, the person in the chair convulses violently. According to Hume, is it moral to continue with the experiment?

After reading Hume's theories of causation, we might be tempted to claim that Hume would find nothing objectionable about this experiment. However, though he might find himself arguing that the button pusher cannot truly be held responsible for the other person's pain, Hume would most likely reject the experiment on other grounds.

One of the most controversial elements of Hume's philosophy lies in his rejection of causation as a knowable phenomenon. Despite the fact that British empiricism provided the philosophical underpinnings for the modern scientific method, Hume did not believe that experimentation and the observation of patterns could genuinely produce real knowledge. When we throw a ball into the air a thousand times and subsequently watch it fall to the earth a thousand times, we may believe that we can induce a scientific rule from this regarding gravity and the behavior of moving objects. However, it is entirely possible that, on toss number 1,001, the ball would fail to follow its previous trajectory. It might baffle us to watch a ball float up and into outer space, but Hume argued that logical organization is an instinctual habit and not a guaranteed reality. Just because something has happened in the past does not mean that it will necessarily happen in the future.

Hume's rejection of causality gives rise to the bleakest elements of his philosophy, such as his dismissal of God and his refutation of the unified self. In the given situation, it is entirely possible to extend Hume's philosophy and argue that, since causation cannot be proven, I cannot know that I am actually responsible for the shocks my experiment partner receives. The question of morality is moot, since implicating my morality automatically assumes my responsibility. We can watch a pattern seem to emerge, but when all is said and done, we have no rational foundation for believing

Student Essay

that the pattern will continue to hold true. A nihilistic reading of Hume would suggest that the question of pushing or not pushing the button remains outside the realm of morality. The entire situation represents a cruel mockery of the scientific method and its inherent uncertainties.

Of course, having witnessed the pattern ourselves and having been warned of its potential consequences, pushing the button a final time would make all but the most callous of us uncomfortable. It would also be a huge gamble and would fundamentally garble one of Hume's most salient points. Hume, after all, didn't properly reject causation. Rather, he rejected a rational belief in causation. Hume argued that though we can never prove causation exists, we are equally unable to disprove it and biologically unable to discard it as a functional category. When Hume took his philosopher hat off, he too relied on a belief in causation to make it through his everyday life. Given this dilemma, it seems unlikely that Hume would advocate a pitiless adherence to philosophical rigor in this scenario.

Paying attention to our emotional responses is also crucial when determining the moral character of a given action. The fact that pushing the button would make most of us uncomfortable suggests that pushing the button would, in fact, be an immoral act. Hume denied the notion that morality should be based on reason, or on any kind of God-given, church-sponsored moral code. Passion and sentiment, he argued, are the true foundations of morality. Hume elicited two requirements for moral sentiments: that they be useful to us or to others or be otherwise pleasing to us or to others. The argument just outlined—that pushing the button is invalid as a moral choice, since we cannot know for certain that it would cause our partner's death—is a wrongheaded argument. It attempts to locate moral certainty in questions of reason, and as Hume argued, reason may influence our moral sentiment, but it is not synonymous with it. Sympathy, or feeling for our fellow humans, is the root of moral obligation. Pushing the button would demonstrate a profound lack of sympathy; if it also distressed and offended our emotions, the act would be immoral by definition.

Jean-Jacques Rousseau

(1712–1778)

10

THEMES, ARGUMENTS & IDEAS

- The Necessity of Freedom
- Defining the Natural and the State of Nature
- The Danger of Need
- The Possibility of Authenticity in Modern Life
- The Unnaturalness of Inequality
- The General Will and the Common Good
- The Idea of Collective Sovereignty

SUMMARY & ANALYSIS OF MAJOR WORKS

- *Discourse on Inequality*
- *The Social Contract*
- *Émile*
- *The Confessions*

Jean-Jacques Rousseau was born in Geneva, Switzerland, on June 12, 1712. His mother died soon after his birth, and his father, a watchmaker virtually abandoned him at the age of twelve. Orphaned at such an early age, Rousseau spent many years as an itinerant, living in the homes of various employers, patrons, and lovers, working variously as a clerk, an engraver, and a private tutor. By 1742, when he was thirty years old, he had made his way to Paris, where he eked out a living as a teacher and a copier of music. Here, he befriended Diderot, a major figure in the fledgling intellectual movement that would later be called the Enlightenment.

Rousseau had his first success as a writer when he was forty years old, relatively late in life for a man of his day. In 1752, he won a prize from the Academy at Dijon for his *First Discourse* on the Arts and

Sciences, which he composed in response to the Academy's question, "Has the advancement of civilization tended to corrupt or improve morals?" Rousseau answered in the negative, provocatively arguing that the advance of civilization mostly corrupted human morals and goodness. This thesis would run through all of his later philosophical works.

Immediately following his reception of the Dijon prize, Rousseau had an opera and a play performed to wide acclaim. In 1755, his first major political work, the *Discourse on Inequality*, was released. In 1761, Rousseau gained an unprecedented level of popular notoriety with the publication of his sentimental novel *Julie, ou la Nouvelle Héloïse*, but his fortunes were to change in the following year.

In 1762, Rousseau released both *The Social Contract* and *Émile*, a novelistic take on education. Both works were violently scorned by official forces and intellectuals alike, and both were publicly burned in Paris and Geneva. The French monarchy ordered that Rousseau be arrested, so he fled to the Swiss town of Neachatel. There, he formally renounced his Genevan citizenship and began work on his great autobiography, the *Confessions*. Rousseau spent much of the subsequent years seeking to escape continued attacks from French authorities and many of his contemporaries.

On July 2, 1778, a few years after returning to France from Scotland, where he had been seeking refuge with the British philosopher David Hume, Rousseau suddenly died. Although his passing was undoubtedly met with relief by many of his enemies in the French establishment, it also set off a great outpouring of regret by many of his readers. The esteem in which he was held by the people of Paris and all opponents of the monarchy was reaffirmed in 1794, when the French revolutionary government ordered that he be honored as a national hero and his ashes placed in the Pantheon.

Although never formally educated, Rousseau read widely throughout his years in obscurity, in philosophy, political science, and modern and ancient literature. His many influences as a thinker are evident in his own work. As a political philosopher, the area of his thought for which he is best known, Rousseau thoroughly engaged the work of immediate predecessors such as Hobbes, Grotius, Montesquieu, and Locke and sought to mediate between the thoughts of theorists on both ends of the political spectrum. In certain instances, he seems to embrace the view of conservatives such as Hobbes and Grotius, who claimed that consenting subservience to an absolute sovereign, or monarch, is the only means by which human beings can escape the brutality of the state of nature. At the same time, however, Rousseau shared the concerns of liberals such as Montesquieu and Locke, who argued for maintaining individual rights and protecting naturally free human beings from the abuses of an artificial state.

Although he respected these conflicting modern influences, Rousseau was in many ways a devoted classicist. His profound admiration for Aristotle's *Politics* and the civil societies of antiquity is clear throughout his political work. Although he betrays an affinity for the direct democracy modeled in a city-state such as Sparta, he acknowledges that such a form of government may not be possible in the modern age of nations. Above all, Rousseau's philosophical project was to describe the passage of human beings from their natural state into a civil society and to understand the differing virtues of each state and the ways they could be mediated between to provide for the common good.

The key philosophical context for Rousseau's work was the historical epoch in western Europe known as the Enlightenment. The Enlightenment was centered in France, and its key thinkers, often called the Lumieres, or "enlighteners," included Voltaire, Diderot, and d'Alembert. These writers held a diverse array of ideas and opinions, but the common current running through their thought was a great faith that human reason, rationality, and knowledge could be the key factors in human progress. Accordingly, they were hostile to religious dogma, received knowledge, superstition, and blind faith of any sort.

Although Rousseau is sometimes regarded as a key figure of the Enlightenment, he in fact had a complex relationship with many of its famous representatives and their mode of thought. At the start of his career, Rousseau maintained an intellectual friendship with Voltaire and even contributed some articles to Diderot's *Encyclopedie*, which purported to compile the entirety of recorded human knowledge to that point. In later years, however, he fell out with both men because of personal and intellectual differences. In much of his writing, Rousseau departs from their key intellectual tenets, such as in his very un-Enlightenment habits of occasionally defending religious faith and denigrating the potential benefits of human reason and "progress."

Rousseau's thought had a wide historical impact. As a writer on politics, his rhetoric laid much of the intellectual groundwork for the American and French Revolutions brought to completion in the years following his death. As a memoirist, his *Confessions* in many ways inaugurated the modern genre of autobiography and has greatly influenced literary theory and narrative technique for over two centuries. As a theorist, Rousseau rigorously attempted to describe the rational foundations underlying modern civil society, in all its imperfections, and his echo has been felt in the work of the most influential social philosophers since his time, from Hegel to Marx to Foucault.

Themes, Arguments & Ideas

THE NECESSITY OF FREEDOM

In his work, Rousseau addresses freedom more than any other problem of political philosophy and aims to explain how man in the state of nature is blessed with an enviable total freedom. This freedom is total for two reasons. First, natural man is physically free because he is not constrained by a repressive state apparatus or dominated by his fellow men. Second, he is psychologically and spiritually free because he is not enslaved to any of the artificial needs that characterize modern society. This second sense of freedom—the freedom from need—makes up a particularly insightful and revolutionary component of Rousseau's philosophy. Rousseau believed that modern man's enslavement to his own needs was responsible for all sorts of societal ills, from exploitation and domination of others to poor self-esteem and depression.

Rousseau believed that good government must have the freedom of all its citizens as its most fundamental objective. *The Social Contract* in particular is Rousseau's attempt to imagine the form of government that best affirms the individual freedom of all its citizens, with certain constraints inherent to a complex, modern, civil society. Rousseau acknowledged that as long as property and laws exist, people can never be as entirely free in modern society as they are in the state of nature—a point later echoed by Marx and many other Communist and anarchist social philosophers. Nonetheless, Rousseau strongly believed in the existence of certain principles of government that, if enacted, can afford the members of society a level of freedom that at least approximates the freedom enjoyed in the state of nature. In *The Social Contract* and his other works of political philosophy, Rousseau is devoted to outlining these principles and how they may be given expression in a functional modern state.

DEFINING THE NATURAL AND THE STATE OF NATURE

For Rousseau to succeed in determining which societal institutions and structures contradict man's natural goodness and freedom, he must first define the "natural." Rousseau strips away all the ideas that centuries of development have imposed on the true nature of man and concludes that many of the ideas we take for granted—such as property, law, and moral inequality—actually have no basis in nature. For Rousseau, modern society generally compares unfavorably to the "state of nature."

As Rousseau discusses in the *Discourse on Inequality* and *The Social Contract*, the state of nature is the hypothetical, prehistoric place and time in which human beings live uncorrupted by society. The most important characteristic of the state of nature is that people have complete physical freedom and are at liberty to do essentially as they wish. That said, the state of nature also carries the drawback that human beings have not yet discovered rationality or morality.

In different works, Rousseau alternately emphasizes the benefits and shortfalls of the state of nature, but by and large he reveres it for the physical freedom it grants people, allowing them to be unencumbered by the coercive influence of the state and society. In this regard, Rousseau's conception of the state of nature is entirely more positive than Hobbes's conception of the same idea, as Hobbes, who originated the term, viewed the state of nature as essentially a state of war and savagery. This difference in definition indicates the two philosophers' differing views of human nature, which Rousseau viewed as essentially good and Hobbes as essentially base and brutal. Finally, Rousseau acknowledged that although we can never return to the state of nature, understanding it is essential for society's members to more fully realize their natural goodness.

THE DANGER OF NEED

Rousseau includes an analysis of human need as one element in his comparison of modern society and the state of nature. According to Rousseau, "needs" result from the passions, which make people desire an object or activity. In the state of nature, human needs are strictly limited to those things that ensure survival and reproduction, including food, sleep, and sex. By contrast, as cooperation and division of labor develop in modern society, the needs of men multiply to include many nonessential things, such as friends, entertainment, and luxury goods. As time goes by and these sorts of needs increasingly become a part of everyday life, they become necessities. Although many of these needs are initially pleasurable and even good for human beings, men in modern society eventually become slaves to these super-fluous needs, and the whole of society is bound together and shaped by their pursuit. As such, unnecessary needs are the foundation of modern "moral inequality," in that the pursuit of needs inevitably means that some will be forced to work to fulfill the needs of others and some will dominate their fellows when in a position to do so.

Rousseau's conception of need, and especially the more artificial types that dominate modern society, are a particularly applicable element of his philosophy for the present time. Given the immense wealth that exists in a country such as the United States and the extent to which consumerism is the driving force behind its economy, Rousseau's insights should provoke reflection for anyone concerned about the ways the American culture nurtures a population of people increasingly enslaved by artificial needs.

THE POSSIBILITY OF AUTHENTICITY IN MODERN LIFE

Linked to Rousseau's general attempt to understand how modern life differs from life in the state of nature is his particular focus on the question of how authentic the life of man is in modern society. By *authentic*, Rousseau essentially means how closely the life of modern man reflects the positive attributes of his natural self. Not surprisingly, Rousseau feels that people in modern society generally live quite inauthentic lives.

In the state of nature, man is free to simply attend to his own natural needs and has few occasions to interact with other people. He can simply "be," while modern man must often "appear" as much as "be" so as to deviously realize his ridiculous needs.

The entire system of artificial needs that governs the life of civil society makes authenticity or truth in the dealings of people with one another almost impossible. Since individuals are always trying to deceive and/or dominate their fellow citizens to realize their own individual needs, they rarely act in an authentic way toward their fellow human beings. Even more damningly, the fact that modern people organize their lives around artificial needs means that they are inauthentic and untrue to themselves as well. To Rousseau's mind, the origin of civil society itself can be traced to an act of deception, when one man invented the notion of private property by enclosing a piece of land and convincing his simple neighbors "this is mine," while having no truthful basis whatsoever to do so. Given this fact, the modern society that has sprung forth from this act can be nothing but inauthentic to the core.

THE UNNATURALNESS OF INEQUALITY

For Rousseau, the questions of why and how human beings are naturally equal and unequal, if they are unequal at all, are fundamental to his larger philosophical enquiry. To form his critique of modern society's problems, he must show that many of the forms of inequality endemic to society are in fact unnatural and can therefore be remedied. His conclusions and larger line of reasoning in this argument are laid out in the *Discourse on Inequality*, but the basic thrust of his argument is that human inequality as we know it does not exist in the state of nature. In fact, the only kind of natural inequality, according to Rousseau, is the physical inequality that exists among men in the state of nature who may be more or less able to provide for themselves according to their physical attributes.

Accordingly, all the inequalities we recognize in modern society are characterized by the existence of different classes or the domination and exploitation of some people by others. Rousseau terms these kinds of inequalities *moral inequalities* and devotes much of his political philosophy to identifying the ways in which a just government can seek to overturn them. In general, Rousseau's meditations on inequality, as well as his radical assertion of the notion that all men are by and large equal in their natural state, were important inspirations for both the American and French Revolutions.

THE GENERAL WILL AND THE COMMON GOOD

Perhaps the most difficult and quasi-metaphysical concept in Rousseau's political philosophy is the principle of the general will. As Rousseau explains, the general will is the will of the sovereign, or all the people together, that aims at the common good—what is best for the state as a whole. Although each individual may have his or her own particular will that expresses what is good for him or her, in a healthy state, in which people correctly value the collective good over their own personal good, the amalgamation of all particular wills, the "will of all," is equivalent to the general will. In a state in which the vulgarities of private interest prevail over the common interests of the collective, the will of all can be something quite different from the general will. The most concrete manifestation of the general will in a healthy state comes in the form of law. To Rousseau, laws should always record what the people collectively desire—the general will—and should always be universally applicable to all members of the state. Further, they should exist to ensure that people's individual freedom is upheld, thereby guaranteeing that people remain loyal to the sovereign at all times.

Rousseau's abstract conception of the general will raises two difficult questions. The first, how can we know that the will of all is really equivalent with the common good? The second, assuming that the general will is existent and can be expressed in laws, what are the institutions that can accurately gauge and codify the general will at any given time? Tackling these complex dilemmas occupied a large portion of Rousseau's political thought, and he attempts to answer them in *The Social Contract*, among other places.

THE IDEA OF COLLECTIVE SOVEREIGNTY

Until Rousseau's time, the sovereign in any given state was regarded as the central authority in that society, responsible for enacting and enforcing all laws. Most often, the sovereign took the form of an authoritative monarch who possessed absolute dominion over his or her subjects. In Rousseau's work, however, sovereignty takes on a different meaning, as sovereignty is said to reside in all the people of the society as a collective. The people, as a sovereign entity, express their sovereignty through their general will and must never have their sovereignty abrogated by anyone or anything outside their collective self. In this regard, sovereignty is not identified with the government but is instead opposed against it. The government's function is thus only to enforce and respect the sovereign will of the people and in no way seek to repress or dominate the general will.

Summary & Analysis

DISCOURSE ON INEQUALITY

Summary

Rousseau's project in the *Discourse on Inequality* is to describe all the sorts of inequality that exist among human beings and to determine which sorts of inequality are "natural" and which "unnatural" (and therefore preventable). Rousseau begins by discussing man in his state of nature. For Rousseau, man in his state of nature is essentially an animal like any other, driven by two key motivating principles: pity and self-preservation. In the state of nature, which is more a hypothetical idea than an actual historical epoch, man exists without reason or the concept of good and evil, has few needs, and is essentially happy. The only thing that separates him from the beasts is some sense of unrealized perfectability.

This notion of perfectability is what allows human beings to change with time, and according to Rousseau it becomes important the moment an isolated human being is forced to adapt to his environment and allows himself to be shaped by it. When natural disasters force people to move from one place to another, make contact with other people, and form small groups or elementary societies, new needs are created, and men begin to move out of the state of nature toward something very different. As individuals have more contact with one another and small groupings begin to form, the human mind develops language, which in turn contributes to the development of reason. Life in the collective state also precipitates the development of a new, negative motivating principle for human actions. Rousseau calls this principle *amour propre*, and it drives men to compare themselves to others. This drive toward comparison to others is not rooted only in the desire to preserve the self and pity others. Rather, comparison drives men to seek domination over their fellow human beings as a way of augmenting their own happiness.

Rousseau states that with the development of *amour propre* and more complex human societies, private property is invented, and the labor necessary for human survival is divided among different individuals to provide for the whole. This division of labor and the beginning of private property allow the property owners and nonlaborers to dominate and exploit the poor. Rousseau observes that this state of affairs is resented by the poor, who will naturally seek war against the rich to end their unfair domination. In Rousseau's history, when the rich recognize this fact, they deceive the poor into joining a political society that purports to grant them the equality they seek. Rather than grant equality, however, it sanctifies their oppression and makes an unnatural moral inequality a permanent feature of civil society.

Rousseau's argument in the *Discourse* is that the only natural inequality among men is the inequality that results from differences in physical strength, for this is the only sort of inequality that exists in the state of nature. As Rousseau explains, however, in modern societies the creation of laws and property have corrupted natural men and created new forms of inequality that are not in accordance with natural law. Rousseau calls these unjustifiable, unacceptable forms of inequality *moral inequality* and concludes by making clear that this sort of inequality must be contested.

Analysis

Although Rousseau would later develop many of the main points of the *Discourse* more expansively, the *Discourse* is significant as the first work to contain all the central elements of his philosophy. In the moral and political realm, the fundamental concept here is moral inequality, or unnatural forms of inequality that are created by human beings. Rousseau is clear that all such forms of inequality are morally wrong and as such must be done away with. The means by which moral inequality is to be banished is not a topic Rousseau broaches here, though this is a question that was hotly debated during the French Revolution and subsequent revolutions in the centuries since.

In the *Discourse on Inequality*, Rousseau uses Hobbes's concept of the state of nature but describes it in a very different way. Whereas Hobbes described the state of nature as a state of constant war populated by violent, self-interested brutes, Rousseau holds that the state of nature is generally a peaceful, happy place made up of free, independent men. To Rousseau, the sort of war Hobbes describes is not reached until man *leaves* the state of nature and enters civil society, when property and law create a conflict between rich and poor. Aside from foreshadowing the work of Marx and later theorists of class relations and societal inequality, Rousseau's conception of natural man is a key principle in all his work: man is naturally good and is corrupted only by his own delusions of perfectability and the harmful elements of his capacity for reason. The means by which human beings are corrupted and the circumstances under which man agrees to leave the state of nature and enter human civil society are the focal points of Rousseau's masterpiece, *The Social Contract*.

THE SOCIAL CONTRACT

Summary

Rousseau begins *The Social Contract* with the most famous words he ever wrote: "Men are born free, yet everywhere are in chains." From this provocative opening, Rousseau goes on to describe the myriad ways in which the "chains" of civil society suppress the natural birthright of man to physical freedom. He states that the civil society does nothing to enforce the equality and individual liberty that were promised to man when he entered into that society. For Rousseau, the only legitimate political authority is the authority consented to by all the people, who have agreed to such government by entering into a social contract for the sake of their mutual preservation.

Rousseau describes the ideal form of this social contract and explains its philosophical underpinnings. To Rousseau, the collective grouping of all people who by their consent enter into a civil society is called the *sovereign*, and this sovereign may be thought of, metaphorically at least, as an individual person with a unified will. This principle is important, for while actual individuals may hold different opinions and wants according to their individual circumstances, the sovereign as a whole expresses the *general will* of all the people. Rousseau defines this general will as the collective need of all to provide for the *common good* of all.

For Rousseau, the most important function of the general will is to inform the creation of the laws of the state. These laws, though codified by an impartial, noncitizen "lawgiver," must in their essence express the general will. Accordingly, though all laws must uphold the rights of equality among citizens and individual freedom, Rousseau states that their particulars can be made according to local circumstances. Although laws owe their existence to the general will of the sovereign, or the collective of all people, some form of government is necessary to carry out the executive function of enforcing laws and overseeing the day-to-day functioning of the state.

Rousseau writes that this government may take different forms, including monarchy, aristocracy, and democracy, according to the size and characteristics of the state, and that all these forms carry different virtues and drawbacks. He claims that monarchy is always the strongest, is particularly suitable to hot climates, and may be necessary in all states in times of crisis. He claims that aristocracy, or rule by the few, is most stable, however, and in most states is the preferable form.

Rousseau acknowledges that the sovereign and the government will often have a frictional relationship, as the government is sometimes liable to go against the general will of the people. Rousseau states that to maintain awareness of the general will, the sovereign must convene in regular, periodic assemblies to determine the general will, at which point it is imperative that individual citizens vote not according to their own personal interests but according to their conception of the general will of all the people at that moment. As such, in a healthy state, virtually all assembly votes should approach unanimity, as the people will all recognize their common interests. Furthermore, Rousseau explains, it is crucial that all the people exercise their sovereignty by attending such assemblies, for whenever people stop doing so, or elect representatives to do so in their place, their sovereignty is lost. Foreseeing that the conflict between the sovereign and the government may at times be contentious, Rousseau also advocates for the existence of a *tribunate*, or court, to mediate in all conflicts between the sovereign and the government or in conflicts between individual people.

Analysis

Rousseau's central argument in *The Social Contract* is that government attains its right to exist and to govern by "the consent of the governed." Although this idea may not seem too extreme today, it was a radical position when *The Social Contract* was published. Rousseau discusses numerous forms of government that may not look very democratic to modern eyes, but his focus is always on figuring out how to ensure that the general will of all the people could be expressed as truly as possible in their government. He is always aiming to figure out how to make society as democratic as possible. At one point in *The Social Contract*, Rousseau admiringly cites the example of the Roman republic's *comitia* to prove that even large states composed of many people can hold assemblies of all their citizens.

Just as he did in his *Discourse on Inequality*, Rousseau borrows ideas from the most influential political philosophers of his day, though he often comes to very different conclusions. For example, though his conception of society as being akin to an individual person resonates with Hobbes's conception of the Leviathan (see Chapter 7, Hobbes), Rousseau's labeling of this metaphorical individual as the sovereign departs strongly from Hobbes, whose own idea of the sovereign was of the central power that held dominion *over* all the people. Rousseau, of course, believed the sovereign to *be* the people and to always express their will. In his discussion of the tribunate—the court that mediates in disputes between governmental branches or among people—Rousseau echoes ideas about government earlier expressed by Locke. Both Locke's and Rousseau's discussions of these institutions influenced the system of checks and balances enshrined in the founding documents of the United States.

The Social Contract is one of the single most important declarations of the natural rights of man in the history of Western political philosophy. It introduced in new and powerful ways the notion of the "consent of the governed" and the inalienable sovereignty of the people, as opposed to the sovereignty of the state or its ruler(s). It has been acknowledged repeatedly as a foundational text in the development of the modern principles of human rights that underlie contemporary conceptions of democracy.

ÉMILE

Summary

Rousseau's *Émile* is a kind of half treatise, half novel that tells the life story of a fictional man named Émile. In it, Rousseau traces the course of Émile's development and the education he receives, an education designed to create in him all the virtues of Rousseau's idealized "natural man," uncorrupted by modern society. According to Rousseau, the natural goodness of a man can be nurtured and maintained only according to this highly prescriptive model of education, and Rousseau states that his aim in *Émile* is to outline that model—a model that differed sharply from all accepted forms of the time.

The system of education that Rousseau proposes details a specific pedagogy for each stage of life, an educational method that corresponds with the particular characteristics of that stage of human development. Accordingly, *Émile* is divided into five books, each corresponding to a developmental stage. Books I and II describe the Age of Nature up to age twelve; books III and IV describe the transitional stages of adolescence; and book V describes the Age of Wisdom, corresponding roughly to the ages of twenty through twenty-five. Rousseau claims that this stage is followed by the Age of Happiness, the final stage of development, which he does not address in *Émile*.

In books I and II, Rousseau insists that young children in the Age of Nature must emphasize the physical side of their education. Like small animals, they must be freed of constrictive swaddling clothes, breast-fed by their mothers, and allowed to play outside, thereby developing the physical senses that will be the most important tools in their acquisition of knowledge. Later, as they approach puberty, they should be taught a manual trade, such as carpentry, and allowed to develop within it, further augmenting their physical capabilities and hand–brain coordination.

Rousseau goes on to say that as Émile enters his teenage years, he should begin formal education. However, the education Rousseau proposes involves working only with a private tutor and studying and reading only that which he is curious about, only that which is "useful" or "pleasing." Rousseau explains that in this manner Émile will essentially educate himself and be excited about learning. He will nurture a love of all things beautiful and learn not to suppress his natural affinity for them. Rousseau states that early adolescence is the best time to begin such study, because after puberty, the young man is fully developed physically yet still uncorrupted by the passions of later years. He is able to develop his own faculties of reason, under the guidance of a tutor who is careful to observe the personal characteristics of his student and suggest study materials in accordance with his individual nature.

At this stage, Émile is also ready for religious education, and in a subsection of book IV called "The Creed of the Savoyard Priest," Rousseau describes that education. He describes Émile receiving a lesson from the Savoyard Priest, who outlines the proper relationship a virtuous natural man such as Émile should hold with God, the scripture, and the church. The main thrust of the priest's instruction is that Émile should approach religion as a skeptic and freethinker and that he should discover the greatness and truth of God through his own discovery of it, not through the forced ingestion of the church's dogma.

Rousseau writes that only after a final period of studying history and learning how society corrupts natural man can Émile venture unprotected into that society, without danger of himself being corrupted. Émile does venture out in book V and immediately encounters woman, in the form of Sophie. Rousseau devotes a large part of the concluding section to their love story as well as to a discussion of female education.

Analysis

Émile is remembered best as Rousseau's statement of his philosophy of education and as a groundbreaking work in educational reform. Rousseau's belief that any formal education, whether scholastic or religious, should not be started until adolescence was a radical suggestion at a time when well-bred children were expected to begin religious training in particular by the age of six or seven. Although *Émile* is certainly a powerful statement on education, it created great controversy due to Rousseau's radical approach to religion. Rousseau always denied that *Émile* was "a work of education," insisting it was essentially a "philosophical work" devoted to defending his fundamental belief in man's natural goodness. In any case, *Émile* serves as a useful elaboration of Rousseau's philosophical system. Although Rousseau recognizes that the natural man, as described in his *Discourse on Inequality*, cannot possibly exist in modern society, he insists that many of the best characteristics of that natural man can coexist with the obligations of citizenship in civil society. His aim in *Émile* is to show how this can happen.

Émile initially received the most attention for the Creed of the Savoyard Priest. Rousseau's insistence that God and religion should be discovered freely—rather than preached to small children—was anathema to the eighteenth-century church and its clergy, who viewed any questioning or critique as a grave threat. Ironically, among his fellow Enlightenment *philosophes*, many of whom were ardent secularists and even atheists, Rousseau was the least hostile to the church. In fact, he identified as a Christian his entire life and always sought to reconcile his philosophy with his faith, which is the essential aim of this passage.

Émile brought vigorous attacks against Rousseau's character and ideas, but it was also widely read, and it is credited with bringing about some concrete changes in the way children of the educated classes across western Europe were raised. Through the latter part of the eighteenth century, many observers credited *Émile* with prompting aristocratic mothers to recognize the benefits of breast-feeding their own infants, not keeping them constrained in swaddling clothes at all times, and allowing older children to play outside and exercise their bodies. Although the extent to which such changes can be attributed to *Émile* is arguable, the work has definitely served as a foundational template for numerous works of educational philosophy that have appeared in the centuries that followed it. Indeed, many of the ideas concerning human development and the wonders of childhood that Rousseau forwarded in *Émile* presage the work of many of the most highly regarded psychologists and educators of the present day.

THE CONFESSIONS

Summary

Rousseau begins his *Confessions* by claiming that he is about to embark on an enterprise never before attempted: to present a self-portrait that is "in every way true to nature" and that hides nothing. He begins his tale by describing his family, including his mother's death at his birth. He ruminates on his earliest memories, which begin when he was five, a dawning of consciousness that he traces to his learning to read. He discusses his childhood in the years before his father left him and his own decision to run away to see the world at the age of sixteen. He often dwells for many pages on seemingly minor events that hold great importance for him.

Throughout the *Confessions*, Rousseau frequently discusses the more unsavory or embarrassing experiences of his life, and he devotes much of the early section to these types of episodes. In one section, he describes urinating in a neighbor's cooking pot as a mischievous child. He also discusses the revelatory experience he had at age eleven of being beaten by an adored female nanny twice his age—and desiring to be beaten again, which he analyzes as being his entry into the world of adult sexuality.

Rousseau continues to describe his life and eventually reaches adulthood. The narrative continues in a similar vein in the later sections, with Rousseau focusing less on places traveled and jobs held than on his personal trials, unrequited loves, and sexual frustrations. He speaks at length of his significant relations with women, including his rather unremarkable longtime companion Thérése le Vasseur and the older matron Madame de Warens, at whose home he often stayed as a young man.

In the last of the twelve books that make up the work, Rousseau speaks about his intellectual work, his writing, and his relations to contemporary philosophers. Rousseau concludes the *Confessions* in 1765, when he is fifty-three. At this point, all his major philosophical works have been published, and his fears of persecution are growing.

Analysis

A few notable autobiographies existed in Europe before Rousseau published the *Confessions*, but his work in many ways represented an entirely new literary form. Although works such as St. Augustine's own *Confessions* (A.D. 397) had previously been widely read and celebrated, religious works of that kind differed greatly from Rousseau's own, since they sought to convey an inspirational story of religious virtuosity. By contrast, Rousseau's *Confessions* sought to bare the entire life of its author subject, detailing all his imperfections, virtues, individual neuroses, and formative childhood experiences as a means of explaining and justifying the views and personality of his adult self.

Although Rousseau states that the *Confessions* should not be read as an unerring account of dates and events and admits that most likely he often gets such factual data wrong when his memory fails him, dates and exact events are not the point of the work. He says that though he may mix up the dates of certain happenings, he will never get wrong his feelings about them, and his feelings—and what his feelings have led him to do—are the subject of his story. He does not engage in the comprehensive unburdening of his whole self, with all its frailties, prurient desires, and natural failings, as an act of pure humility and self-deprecation. Rather, he does it as a way of saying that even with all his weaknesses, he is, as we all are, fundamentally a good and honest being. This principle is at the heart of Rousseau's entire philosophy, and it connects the *Confessions* to the rest of his work. The *Confessions* is key to understanding Rousseau's work as a whole.

The influence of the *Confessions* reaches well beyond philosophy. As a work of literature, it inaugurated the modern genre of autobiography and influenced narrative technique in the great novels that would appear in the following century. Rousseau's emphasis on the effects of childhood experiences on adulthood, especially in relation to the development of sexuality, foreshadows the revolutionary psychological work of Sigmund Freud. The *Confessions* is also the work considered most responsible for Rousseau's frequent accreditation as the father of the romantic movement, for the degree to which he emphasizes the importance of subjective, individual, and sensory experience of the world.

Your sister is pregnant with her first child. She has just read Rousseau's *Emile* and is considering educating her child according to the system outlined in the book. What would you say to this decision?

Like Rousseau, Americans tend to believe that education should foster independent thought, self-expression, and an excitement for learning. Yet despite its appeal, the system outlined in *Émile* remains both unworkable and undesirable. To rescue children from the harmful effects of society, Rousseau advocates raising them in more or less total isolation from other potentially corrupting people. However, Rousseau makes a fundamental mistake when he assumes that man's best, most natural state involves solitude. In trying to create a more natural child, his system would actually end up creating the most unnatural of children.

In *Émile*, Rousseau's fundamental distrust of society causes him to advocate an extreme form of negative education. Émile is kept isolated from other children and from potentially exciting stimuli in order to keep him in the natural state for as long as possible. Like Émile's parents, many modern American parents educate their children at home, so that they can tailor curriculum to their children's specific needs, or protect them from the corrupting influence of modern society. However, without the socialization that collective education affords, a child grows into an adult with no sense of how to engage with the world around him. Most homeschooling families recognize the need for their children to interact with other young people. Homeschooled children are often active in scouting troops, sports teams, and arts programs in order to develop their social skills, and as such they have little difficulty integrating into society at large.

Émile, however, emphasizes that children should always be kept away from other people in order to escape corruption and foster total independence. The company of other children—not to mention art, literature, or even too much learning—makes a child dependent on others and vulnerable to inauthentic, externally created needs. The aim of Émile's education is, essentially, a negative one. Rather than teach a child the way the proper way to navigate society and adulthood, Rousseau's system keeps him in guarded innocence for as long as possible. My sister should only implement the *Émile* system

Student Essay

if she wants her child to grow into a happy and self-sufficient but mediocre and unimaginative adult.

The problem with Rousseau's pedagogy can be traced to a deeper, more crucial problem in his philosophy: the unquestioning acceptance of the natural state's inherent superiority. Rousseau admits that the natural state only exists as a hypothetical construct, yet his rhetoric assumes a belief in the natural state's essential reality. Rousseau's word choice ends up doing much of the arguing for him, since the very term *natural* comes loaded with certain preconceptions. Even today, in our increasingly techno-logical world, the word natural implies goodness, wholesome-ness, and healthiness. When *civilized* is put in opposition to *natural*, the contrast implies that a civilized society is inherently unnatural, abnormal, and corrupted. Rousseau's system would seem very different if he termed the stages of human development *primitive* and *civilized*, for example.

This tension arises because, though an interesting and potentially clarifying concept, the natural state as defined by Rousseau denies the true history of humankind. Humans are social creatures, and they developed as such over several millennia. There was no spontaneous transition between individual man and collective society, as Rousseau suggests. His system may seek to create an authentic person, but his notion of authenticity rests on an inauthentic historical picture.

If the natural state is a hypothetical construct, then the values Rousseau tries to pass off as natural, inherent, and authentic are similarly hypothetical. If we question his evolutionary model of the human species, then we are free to question the hierarchy of morals he based on that model. We can sense this problem in *Émile*, as achieving a natural state for Émile seems extraordinarily difficult and complicated. The tu-tor has to be both unseen dictator and guardian angel and must carefully control the student's environment and activity at all times. It seems ironic that freedom from society could only be inculcated through such a carefully monitored system and that a natural state could only be regained through such conscientious engineering. While my sister should be free to make decisions about how she wants to raise her child, she should think carefully about what exactly she finds appealing about *Émile* before she submits my niece or nephew to Émile's life.

Immanuel Kant

(1724–1804)

11

THEMES, ARGUMENTS & IDEAS

- Philosophy as Critique
- The Philosophy of Transcendental Idealism
- The Category of the Synthetic A Priori
- Deontological Ethics
- The Ethics of Autonomy

SUMMARY & ANALYSIS OF MAJOR WORKS

- *Critique of Pure Reason* and *Prolegomena to Any Future Metaphysics*
- *Critique of Practical Reason* and *Groundwork for the Metaphysic of Morals*
- *Critique of Judgment*

Immanuel Kant is probably the most important philosopher of the past 2,000 years, yet he lived a remarkably boring life. He was born, lived, and died in the provincial Prussian university town of Königsberg (now Kaliningrad in Russia). He was so regular in his habits that locals set their clocks by his afternoon walk. Kant was the first great modern philosopher to be a university man and spent his entire student and professional life at the University of Königsberg.

Kant studied the rationalist metaphysicians, such as Leibniz and Christian Wolff, who were fashionable at the time, as well as mathematics and physics, in particular the physics of Isaac Newton. In his early career, he published mainly in the field of natural science, and for the most part he accepted the rationalist metaphysics he had been taught. He became a full professor in 1770 and for the next ten years published nothing, as he painstakingly worked out his mature philosophy.

During this time, he studied the works of David Hume carefully, crediting Hume with awakening him from the "dogmatic slumber" that had kept him from questioning rationalist metaphysics.

In 1781, Kant published his *Critique of Pure Reason*, a long and very difficult volume that was met with great interest and criticism. To this day, it remains one of the most discussed and influential works in philosophy. Kant continued to write prolifically throughout the 1780s, publishing almost all of his most important works in that decade: the *Prolegomena to Any Future Metaphysics* in 1783, the *Groundwork for the Metaphysic of Morals* in 1785, the *Critique of Practical Reason* in 1788, and the *Critique of Judgment* in 1790. Kant continued to think and write well into his old age and was at work on a fourth *Critique* at the time of his death in 1804.

Kant lived near the end of the Enlightenment, a European cultural movement that spanned the eighteenth century. Enlightenment figures such as Voltaire and David Hume sought to replace the traditions and superstitions of religion and monarchy with a worldview that relied primarily on the powers of reason. Kant's work belongs to this tradition. His three *Critiques* investigate the scope and powers of reason and emphasize that the proper study of metaphysics is our own rational faculties, not the sort of theological questions that occupied earlier generations.

Kant is generally credited with effecting a synthesis between the empiricist philosophy that had dominated Great Britain and the rationalist philosophy that had dominated the European continent for the previous 150 years. Although he was trained in the rationalist tradition, Kant was heavily influenced by the empiricist philosophy of David Hume. The mature philosophy we find in Kant's *Critiques* is his attempt to answer Hume's skepticism regarding the powers of human reason: both in morals and in metaphysics, Kant turns his philosophical eye inward, investigating or critiquing the powers of the human intellect itself. Instead of asking what we can know, Kant asks how we can know what we can know.

Kant's influence has been immense. No philosopher since has remained entirely untouched by his ideas. Even when the reaction to Kant is negative, he is the source of great inspiration. German idealism, which arose in the generation after Kant, draws heavily on Kant's work even as it rejects some of his central ideas. Similarly, the tradition of analytic philosophy, which has dominated the English-speaking world for the past century, takes its start from Gottlob Frege's criticisms of Kant.

Themes, Arguments & Ideas

PHILOSOPHY AS CRITIQUE

Kant's three major volumes are entitled *critiques*, and his entire philosophy focuses on applying his critical method to philosophical problems. The correct method in philosophy, according to Kant, is not to speculate on the nature of the world around us but to perform a critique of our mental faculties, investigating what we can know, defining the limits of knowledge, and determining how the mental processes by which we make sense of the world affect what we know. This change in method represents what Kant calls a Copernican revolution in philosophy. Just as Copernicus turned astronomy on its head in the sixteenth century by arguing that the sun, not the Earth, is the center of the solar system, Kant turns philosophy on its head by arguing that we will find the answers to our philosophical problems in an examination of our mental faculties rather than in metaphysical speculation about the universe around us. One part of this revolution is the suggestion that the mind is not a passive receptor but that it actively shapes our perception of reality. Another is a general shift, which remains to this day, from metaphysics toward epistemology. That is, the question of what reality actually consists of has become less central than the question of what we can know about reality and how we can know it.

THE PHILOSOPHY OF TRANSCENDENTAL IDEALISM

Kant's emphasis on the role our mental faculties play in shaping our experience implies a sharp distinction between *phenomena* and *noumena*. Noumena are "things-in-themselves," the reality that exists independent of our mind, whereas phenomena are appearances, reality as our mind makes sense of it. According to Kant, we can never know with certainty what is "out there." Since all our knowledge of the external world is filtered through our mental faculties, we can know only the world that our mind presents to us. That is, all our knowledge is only knowledge of phenomena, and we must accept that noumena are fundamentally unknowable. *Idealism* is the name given to the various strands of philosophy that claim that the world is made up primarily of mental ideas, not of physical things. Kant differs from many idealists in that he does not deny the existence of an external reality and does not even think that ideas are more fundamental than things. However, he argues that we can never transcend the limitations and the contextualization provided by our minds, so that the only reality we will ever know is the reality of phenomena.

THE CATEGORY OF THE SYNTHETIC A PRIORI

Kant inherits from Hume the problem of how we can infer necessary and universal truths from experience when all experience is by its nature contingent and particular. We actually experience individual sights and sounds and so on; we cannot "experience" a physical law or a relation of cause and effect. So if we cannot see, smell, or hear causation, how can we infer that some events cause others? Kant phrases this question more generally as the question of how synthetic a priori knowledge is possible. That is, how can we know things that are necessary and universal but not self-evident or definitional? Kant's ingenious solution is that synthetic a priori knowledge is possible because our mental faculties organize experience according to certain categories so that these categories become necessary and universal features of our experience. For instance, we do not find causation in nature so much as we cannot *not* find causation in nature. It is a feature of the way our minds make sense of reality that we perceive causes and effects everywhere at work. For Kant, then, the category of the synthetic a priori is the key to explaining how we gain substantive knowledge about the world.

DEONTOLOGICAL ETHICS

Ethical theorists can be roughly divided into two camps: those who consider an action moral or immoral depending on the motive behind it and those who consider an action moral or immoral depending on the consequences it produces. Kant is firmly in the former camp, making him a deontologist rather than a consequentialist when it comes to ethics. (The word *deontology* derives from the Greek roots *deon*, "duty," and *logos*, "science.") Kant argues that we are subject to moral judgment because we are able to deliberate and give reasons for our actions, so moral judgment should be directed at our reasons for acting. While we can and should take some care to ensure that our actions produce good consequences, the consequences of our actions are not themselves subject to our reason, so our reason is not fully responsible for the consequences of the actions it endorses. Reason can only be held responsible for endorsing certain actions, so it is only the actions, and the motives behind them, that are open to moral judgment.

THE ETHICS OF AUTONOMY

Every theory of ethics must give an answer to the question "Or else what?" That is, we must be able to explain why good is good and bad is bad. Christians answer the "Or else what?" question with the threat of eternal damnation, while Utilitarians answer that, since happiness is the greatest good, bad actions produce unhappiness, and unhappiness is bad in and of itself. Kant, by contrast, argues that since reason is the source of morality, goodness and badness should be dictated by reason. To act badly, according to Kant, is to violate the maxims laid out by one's reason, or to formulate maxims that one could not consistently will as universal laws. In other words, immorality is a form of irrationality: badness results from violating the laws of reason. According to Kant, our rationality is what makes us human, so by acting irrationally, and hence immorally, we also compromise our humanity. Kant's answer to the question "Or else what?" is that we diminish ourselves as rational human beings by acting immorally. Only by behaving rationally do we show ourselves to be autonomous beings, in control of the passions and appetites that might lead us to act against our better judgment.

Summary & Analysis

CRITIQUE OF PURE REASON
AND PROLEGOMENA TO ANY FUTURE METAPHYSICS

Summary

Kant published the *Critique of Pure Reason* in 1781. It is very long and almost unreadable due to its dry prose and complex terminology. Kant tried to ease his readers' confusion by publishing the *Prolegomena to Any Future Metaphysics* two years later. While it is hardly a page-turner, the *Prolegomena* is much briefer than the *Critique* and much more accessible in style, making it a valuable entry point to Kant's metaphysics and epistemology.

Kant's primary aim is to determine the limits and scope of pure reason. That is, he wants to know what reason alone can determine without the help of the senses or any other faculties. Metaphysicians make grand claims about the nature of reality based on pure reason alone, but these claims often conflict with one another. Furthermore, Kant is prompted by Hume's skepticism to doubt the very possibility of metaphysics.

Kant draws two important distinctions: between a priori and a posteriori knowledge and between analytic and synthetic judgments. A posteriori knowledge is the particular knowledge we gain from experience, and a priori knowledge is the necessary and universal knowledge we have independent of experience, such as our knowledge of mathematics. In an analytic judgment, the concept in the predicate is contained in the concept in the subject, as, for instance, in the judgment, "a bachelor is an unmarried man." (In this context, *predicate* refers to whatever is being said about the subject of the sentence—for instance, "is an unmarried man.")

In a synthetic judgment, the predicate concept contains information not contained in the subject concept, so a synthetic judgment is informative rather than just definitional. Typically, we associate a posteriori knowledge with synthetic judgments and a priori knowledge with analytic judgments. For instance, the judgment "all swans are white" is synthetic because whiteness is not a part of the concept of "swan" (a black swan would still be a swan even though it isn't white), but it is also a posteriori because we can only find out if all swans are white from experience.

Kant argues that mathematics and the principles of science contain synthetic a priori knowledge. For example, "7 + 5 = 12" is a priori because it is a necessary and universal truth we know independent of experience, and it is synthetic because the concept of "12" is not contained in the concept of "7 + 5." Kant argues that the same is true for scientific principles such as "for every action there is an equal an opposite reaction": because it is universally applicable, it must be a priori knowledge, since a posteriori knowledge only tells us about particular experiences.

The fact that we are capable of synthetic a priori knowledge suggests that pure reason is capable of knowing important truths. However, Kant does not follow rationalist metaphysics in asserting that pure reason has the power to grasp the mysteries of the universe. Instead, he suggests that much of what we consider to be reality is shaped by the perceiving mind. The mind, according to Kant, does not passively receive information provided by the senses. Rather, it actively shapes and makes sense of that information. If all the events in our experience take place in time, that is because our mind arranges sensory experience in a temporal progression, and if we perceive that some events cause other events, that is because our mind makes sense of events in terms of cause and effect. Kant's argument has a certain parallel to the fact that a person wearing blue-tinted glasses sees everything in a bluish light: according to Kant, the mind wears unremovable time-tinted and causation-tinted glasses, so that all our experience necessarily takes place in time and obeys the laws of causation.

Time and space, Kant argues, are pure intuitions of our faculty of sensibility, and concepts of physics such as causation and inertia are pure intuitions of our faculty of understanding. Sensory experience only makes sense because our faculty of sensibility processes it, organizing it according to our intuitions of time and space. These intuitions are the source of mathematics: our number sense comes from our intuition of successive moments in time, and geometry comes from our intuition of space. Events that take place in space and time would still be a meaningless jumble if it were not for our faculty of understanding, which organizes experience according to the concepts, like causation, that form the principles of natural science.

If time and space, among other things, are constructs of the mind, we might wonder what is actually "out there," independent of our minds. Kant answers that we cannot know for certain. Our senses react to stimuli that come from outside the mind, but we only have knowledge of how they appear to us once they have been processed by our faculties of sensibility and understanding. Kant calls the stimuli "things-in-themselves" and says we can have no certain knowledge about their nature. He distinguishes sharply between the world of noumena, which is the world of things-in-themselves, and the world of phenomena, which is the world as it appears to our minds.

After giving what he considers a satisfactory account of how synthetic a priori knowledge makes mathematics and science possible, Kant turns to metaphysics. Metaphysics relies on the faculty of reason, which does not shape our experience in the way that our faculties of sensibility and understanding do; rather, it helps us reason independent of experience. The mistake metaphysicians typically make is to apply reason to things in themselves and try to understand matters beyond reason's grasp. Such attempts tend to lead reason into contradiction and confusion. Kant redefines the role of metaphysics as a critique of pure reason. That is, the role of reason is to understand itself, to explore the powers and the limits of reason. We are incapable of knowing anything certain about things-in-themselves, but we can develop a clearer sense of what and how we can know by examining intensively the various faculties and activities of the mind.

Analysis

In the *Critique of Pure Reason*, Kant achieves a synthesis between the competing traditions of rationalism and empiricism. From rationalism, he draws the idea that pure reason is capable of significant knowledge but rejects the idea that pure reason can tell us anything about things-in-themselves. From empiricism, he draws the idea that knowledge is essentially knowledge from experience but rejects the idea that we can infer no necessary and universal truths from experience, which is Hume's conclusion. As a result, he avoids the metaphysical speculations of the rationalists, for which any definite proof seems unattainable but maintains the rationalists' ambitious agenda, which attempts to give some answer to the sorts of questions that inevitably occur when we think philosophically. By locating the answers to metaphysical questions not in the external world but in a critique of human reason, Kant provides clear boundaries for metaphysical speculation and maintains a sensible, empirical approach to our knowledge of the external world.

Kant achieves what he calls a Copernican revolution in philosophy by turning the focus of philosophy from metaphysical speculation about the nature of reality to a critical examination of the nature of the thinking and perceiving mind. In effect, Kant tells us that reality is a joint creation of external reality and the human mind and that it is only regarding the latter that we can acquire any certain knowledge. Kant challenges the assumption that the mind is a blank slate or a neutral receptor of stimuli from the surrounding world. The mind does not simply receive information, according to Kant; it also gives that information shape. Knowledge, then, is not something that exists in the outside world and is then poured into an open mind like milk into a cup. Rather, knowledge is something created by the mind by filtering sensations through our various mental faculties. Because these faculties determine the shape that all knowledge takes, we can only grasp what knowledge, and hence truth, is in its most general form if we grasp how these faculties inform our experience.

The lynchpin to Kant's critical philosophy is his category of the synthetic a priori. Although distinctions similar to Kant's a priori–a posteriori distinction and his synthetic–analytic distinction have been made by thinkers such as Hume and Leibniz, Kant is the first to apply two such distinctions to generate a third category for knowledge. Hume, for instance, does not distinguish between what Kant calls the analytic and the a priori and what he calls the synthetic and the a posteriori, so that, for Hume, all synthetic judgments are necessarily a posteriori. Since only a priori truths have the important qualities of being universal and necessary, all general truths about reality—as opposed to particular observations about unconnected events—must be a priori. If our a priori knowledge is limited to definitional analytic judgments, then Hume is right in concluding that rationally justified knowledge of universal and necessary truths is impossible. Kant's coup comes in determining that synthetic judgments can also be a priori. He shows that mathematics and scientific principles are neither analytic nor a posteriori, and he provides an explanation for the category of the synthetic a priori by arguing that our mental faculties shape our experience.

Kant differs from his rationalist predecessors by claiming that pure reason can discern the form, but not the content, of reality. Rationalists, such as Descartes, Spinoza, and Leibniz, speculated about the nature of time, space, causation, God, and the universe, and they believed at least on some level that they could come up with relatively confident answers through the exercise of pure reason. Kant, who was educated in this tradition, argues that his predecessors have not given any clear grounding for their metaphysical speculation, but that is because they assume that time, space, causation, and the like are the content of an external reality that the mind must reach out and grasp. Kant turns this assumption on its head, suggesting that time, space, and causation are not found in experience but are instead the form the mind gives to experience. We can grasp the nature of time, space, and causation not because pure reason has some insight into the nature of reality but because pure reason has some insight into the nature of our own mental faculties.

Kant has earned the great compliment of having detractors who criticize him with great insight and ingenuity. German idealism, which dominated nineteenth-century philosophy, finds its footing by attacking Kant's conception of things-in-themselves. Idealists such as Hegel argue that there is something deeply suspicious about these mysterious entities, which Kant claims are the source of our sensations while claiming we can have no direct knowledge of them. Idealism jettisons things-in-themselves and the whole noumenal realm, arguing instead that reality consists primarily of mental phenomena.

Analytic philosophy, which is one of the leading schools of twentieth-century philosophy, also gets its start through an attack on Kant. The logician Gottlob Frege criticizes Kant for basing the analytic–synthetic distinction on the subject-predicate form of grammar, which is not a necessary feature of the logical structure of language or reality. Frege argues that we should base the analytic–synthetic distinction on whether we justify a given judgment by appealing to its logical form or to empirical investigation and that, according to this distinction, the category of the synthetic a priori becomes unnecessary. Kant is only able to argue that geometry, for instance, relies on synthetic a priori knowledge because he fails to distinguish between pure geometry (the stuff of mathematical axioms and proofs) and empirical geometry (the application of geometrical principles to science). Pure geometry is a priori, but it is also analytic, since it is justified according to logical principles alone. Empirical geometry is synthetic but is also a posteriori, since we only learn from experience what sort of geometry applies to the real world.

CRITIQUE OF PRACTICAL REASON AND GROUNDWORK FOR THE METAPHYSIC OF MORALS

Summary

Groundwork for the Metaphysic of Morals, published in 1785, is Kant's first major work in ethics. Like the *Prolegomena to Any Future Metaphysics,* the *Groundwork* is the short and easier-to-read version of what Kant deals with at greater length and complexity in his *Critique.* The *Critique of Practical Reason*, published three years later, contains greater detail than the *Groundwork* and differs from it on some points—in the *Critique of Practical Reason,* for instance, Kant places greater emphasis on ends and not just on motives—but this summary and analysis will cover only the general points of Kant's ethics, which both his major works share in common.

Morality applies to all rational beings, and a moral action is defined as one that is determined by reason, not by our sensual impulses. Because an action is moral on account of its being reasoned, the moral worth of an action is determined by its motive, or the reason behind the action, not by its consequences. We can determine the worth of the motive behind any given moral action by asking whether we could turn that motive into a universally applicable maxim. Reason is the same at all times and for all people, so morality too should be universal. Therefore, an action is moral only if it embodies a maxim that we could will to be a universal law.

Kant calls it a "categorical imperative" that we must act in such a way that we could will the maxim according to which we act to be a universal law. He contrasts this with the "hypothetical imperative," which would demand that we act to achieve certain ends. The maxim of a hypothetical imperative would assert, "do such-and-such *if* you want to achieve such-and-such result." There are no ifs in moral action, according to Kant. Morality works according to a categorical imperative because we must act in a given way simply because the motive is admirable, not because we have calculated that we can achieve certain ends as a result.

Once we recognize the universality of moral law, we must also recognize that it applies equally to all people. Acting morally, then, requires that we recognize other people as moral agents and always treat them as ends in themselves, not as means by which we can achieve our own ends. We must also ensure that our actions do not prevent other people from acting in accordance with moral law. Kant envisions an ideal society as a "kingdom of ends," in which people are at once both the authors and the subjects of the laws they obey.

Morality is based in the concept of freedom, or autonomy. Someone with a free, or autonomous, will does not simply act but is able to reflect and decide whether to act in a given way. This act of deliberation distinguishes an autonomous will from a heteronomous will. In deliberating, we act according to a law we ourselves dictate, not according to the dictates of passion or impulse. We can claim to have an autonomous will even if we act always according to universal moral laws or maxims because we submit to these laws upon rational reflection.

Kant answers the tricky question of free will and determinism—how can we at once assert that we have a free will and that we live in a world that functions according to necessary physical laws?—by drawing on his distinction from the *Critique of Pure Reason* between the phenomenal world of appearances and the noumenal world of things-in-themselves. Physical laws apply only to appearances, whereas the will is a thing-in-itself about which we have no direct knowledge. Whether the will is actually free we can never know, but we still act in accordance with the idea of freedom.

Analysis

In Kantian ethics, reason is not only the source of morality, it is also the measure of the moral worth of an action. Like some of his predecessors, Kant recognizes that our status as moral beings follows from our status as rational beings. That is, our actions can be considered moral or immoral to the extent that they are reasoned. However, in saying that rational decisions are open to moral judgment, we have not determined the grounds on which we should judge them. Many of the ethical theorists who preceded Kant attempt to ground moral judgment in the law of God or of a sovereign monarch. Kant recognizes that grounding morality in an externally imposed law compromises the autonomy of the will: in such a case, we act under a feeling of compulsion to a will that is not our own, so we are not entirely accountable for our actions. We act autonomously only if we act in accordance with a law dictated by our own reason. Although earlier philosophers recognize that rationality is the source of morality, Kant is the first to argue that reason also provides the standard by which we make moral evaluations.

Kant's ethics is the most influential expression of an approach to ethics known as deontology, which is often contrasted with consequentialism. The distinctive feature of deontology is that it approves or disapproves of actions in and of themselves. For instance, according to Kant, lying is always wrong because we cannot will it as a universal maxim that lying is okay. The consequentialist view, by contrast, argues that moral value lies not in our actions but in their consequences. The utilitarianism of John Stuart Mill is one of the most influential forms of consequentialist ethics. Mill argues that we should always aim at ensuring the greatest happiness for the greatest number of people and that, for instance, telling a lie in particular consequences is good if telling that lie produces good consequences. The consequentialist view has the intuitive appeal that we presumably determine that actions are good or not depending on the effect they actually have. However, a Kantian would argue against this view, pointing out that we have full control only over our motives, not the consequences of our actions, so our autonomous will can only approve or disapprove of motives. An ethics that focuses on consequences, then, is not based in the autonomy of the will.

Kantian ethics rely on a universalist conception of reason and morality that is characteristic of the Enlightenment. Kant is quite clear that his ethics apply equally to all people. We can only consider an action moral if we could will that it apply as a universal law to everyone, and we should aspire to a "kingdom of ends" in which everyone is both author and subject to the moral laws dictated by reason. This conception of morality was first questioned by Hegel, who argued that morality varies depending on cultural and historical circumstances. Indeed moral relativism has become a cornerstone of the postmodern worldview. A postmodernist critique of Kant would suggest that Kant is insufficiently sensitive to the great variety of individual experience and that it is paternalistic, if not arrogant, to assume that one can apply one's own moral standards to peoples and cultures of which one has no understanding. A Kantian would reply that Kantian ethics are based in a shared humanity that applies to all people. Certainly, we adopt different practical identities, such that we might hold different values depending on whether we identify, say, as a Canadian, a postal worker, or a jazz aficionado. However, Kantian ethics are based not on these particular practical identities but on our shared identity as rational beings, which we cannot revoke without revoking our humanity.

CRITIQUE OF JUDGMENT

Summary

The *Critique of Judgment,* often called the Third Critique, does not have as clear a focus as the first two critiques. In broad outline, Kant sets about examining our faculty of judgment, which leads him down a number of divergent paths. While the *Critique of Judgment* deals with matters related to science and teleology, it is most remembered for what Kant has to say about aesthetics.

Kant calls aesthetic judgments "judgments of taste" and remarks that, though they are based in an individual's subjective feelings, they also claim universal validity. Our feelings about beauty differ from our feelings about pleasure and moral goodness in that they are disinterested. We seek to possess pleasurable objects, and we seek to promote moral goodness, but we simply appreciate beauty without feeling driven to find some use for it. Judgments of taste are universal because they are disinterested: our individual wants and needs do not come into play when appreciating beauty, so our aesthetic response applies universally. Aesthetic pleasure comes from the free play between the imagination and understanding when perceiving an object.

Kant distinguishes the beautiful from the sublime. While the appeal of beautiful objects is immediately apparent, the sublime holds an air of mystery and ineffability. While a Greek statue or a pretty flower is beautiful, the movement of storm clouds or a massive building is sublime: they are, in a sense, too great to get our heads around. Kant argues that our sense of the sublime is connected with our faculty of reason, which has ideas of absolute totality and absolute freedom. While storm clouds or a massive building might stretch our minds, they are nothing compared with reason's ideas of absolute totality and freedom. Apprehending sublime objects puts us in touch with these ideas of reason, so that sublimity resides not in sublime objects but in reason itself.

In a second part of the book, Kant wrestles with the concept of teleology, the idea that something has an end, or purpose. Teleology falls somewhere between science and theology, and Kant argues that the concept is useful in scientific work even though we would be wrong to assume that teleological principles are actually at work in nature.

Analysis

Although much of what Kant writes about aesthetics might strike us now as a bit dated, his work is historically very significant. Kant's Third Critique is one of the early works in the field of aesthetics and one of the most important treatises on the subject ever written. Aesthetics differs from literary criticism and art criticism, which have existed for millennia, in that it attempts to explain not only why things are or are not beautiful but also the concept of beauty and how the perception of beauty arises in us. Kant takes on the considerable task of making room for the concepts of the beautiful and the sublime in the complex account of the mind he gives in his first two Critiques.

Unfortunately for Kant, the success of this project can be understood only in the context of his complex and abstruse philosophical system, while its failures are immediately apparent. The close relationship between art and politics, which became clear in the twentieth century, casts doubt on Kant's assertion that our response to art is disinterested, and his claim that our sense of beauty is universal makes less sense in a world in which we are exposed to the diversity of artistic products of different cultures. Although his work continues to influence work in aesthetics, Kant falls victim to the same problem that touches everyone who tries to make general claims about art: the very concept of art has great historical fluidity so that we can never nail down for all time exactly what it is.

Kant's account of beauty as based in subjective feeling as well as his struggles with teleology stem from his desire to refute all metaphysical proofs of God. Kant is by no means an atheist, and he makes forceful arguments for why we ought to believe in God. However, God is the ultimate thing-in-itself, and so, according to Kant's epistemology, the nature and even the existence of God are fundamentally unknowable. In the *Critique of Pure Reason,* Kant provides refutations for all the main "proofs" of God's existence, one of which is the Argument from Design. According to this argument, the patterns and formal perfection in nature suggest the presence of an intelligent designer. Kant argues that our judgment of beauty is a subjective feeling, even though it possesses universal validity, in part because arguing that beauty is objective would play into the hands of those who make the Argument from Design. If beauty were an objective property of certain objects in nature, the question would naturally arise of how these objects were bestowed with beauty. This question would provide a toehold for the Argument from Design—an outcome that Kant is determined to avoid.

After seeing *The Matrix*, your sister becomes convinced that the world as she knows it is nothing more than a virtual projection, created by the giant supercomputer her "real body" is plugged into. What would Kant say about this?

In the 1999 film *The Matrix*, a mild-mannered computer programmer discovers that his world exists on two levels: a physical one and a virtual one. The virtual world, which he had always thought of as the real world, is in fact a program run by a supercomputer in the physical world. The film depicts the two-world scenario as a horrifying prospect. However, a student of Kant would understand that *The Matrix* should be read not as some terrifying science-fiction nightmare but simply as a colorful illustration of the world we already live in.

Two hundred years before *The Matrix*, Kant proposed that our own world simultaneously operates on two levels. As human beings, our perceptive power is limited. We can recognize only the world of phenomena, or things as they seem. Noumena, or things as they truly are, are beyond our comprehension. The noumenal world is the causal basis for the phenomenal, but understanding the nature of that world or the way in which that causal link operates is beyond our perceptive capabilities. The virtual world "inside" the Matrix represents the phenomenal world, which is the only world of which most of its inhabitants are aware. The noumenal world is completely inaccessible to the vast majority of the population. As in Kant, this noumenal world is the causal basis for the phenomenal world. It doesn't operate in the way most people imagine, but Kant would argue that it is a completely viable possibility. Indeed, anything remains a viable possibility, since there is no way to either confirm or deny the characteristics of the noumenal world.

Kant argued that given our restricted abilities it is pointless to concern ourselves with metaphysical issues such as the nature of God or of ultimate reality. The only thing philosophy can legitimately study is human mental capacity. So my first response

Student Essay

to my sister would be that—until the moment when she's actually confronted by a band of alternate-reality renegades—it's pointless to wring her hands over the situation. A million other mind-bending scenarios are equally possible. Maybe we're all characters in a novel. Perhaps, as Chinese philosopher Zhuang Zi mused, we're living inside the dream of a napping butterfly. But we can do no more than speculate detachedly about these possibilities. In the end, the only world we have is the world of appearances, and it is this world in which we must live with which we must and concern ourselves.

Even if the Matrix scenario turns out to be true, this is no cause for alarm or concern. In the world of the Matrix, humans are thoroughly at the whim of the programmers, and reality as they know it could be arbitrarily upended at any moment. Being afraid and angered by this possibility, however, means that we have failed to absorb Kant's ideas about causation, time, and space. Most of us believe that the laws of physics are somehow inherent in the design of the universe. Kant, however, argued that these frameworks are constructs of human consciousness. We organize our experiences according to these structures and thus make sense of those experiences. Time, space, and the law of cause and effect are not, by any means, necessary principles in our world any more than they are necessary principles in the Matrix world. In our world, we live our daily lives according to Hume's uniformity principle, assuming that the sun will rise, the days will pass, and objects dropped will fall to the floor because we believe that such relations are constant and unchanging. Inhabitants of the Matrix world live their lives according to the same assumptions, and for the most part, those assumptions are fulfilled. The Matrix world already operates like our own, so my sister has nothing to worry about.

Georg Wilhelm Friedrich Hegel

12

(1770–1831)

THEMES, ARGUMENTS & IDEAS

- Dialectic as the Fundamental Pattern of Thought
- Spirit as the Self-Awareness of Society
- Lordship and Bondage as the Basis of Social Relations
- Ethical Life as the Expression of an Age

SUMMARY & ANALYSIS OF MAJOR WORKS

- *Phenomenology of Spirit*
- *Science of Logic*
- *Elements of a Philosophy of Right*

Georg Wilhelm Friedrich Hegel was born in 1770 in Stuttgart, Wurttemberg, which was then one of numerous autonomous German principalities that would become the German state in 1871. His eventual preoccupation with the link between human experience and history can be traced to the uncertainties of the time and place in which he lived. The German urban middle class, which made up his early social environment, expressed Enlightenment optimism and faith in human progress but was numerically and politically weaker than the middle class elsewhere in northwestern Europe. Many young, cosmopolitan Germans viewed England and France with envy and resentment as their hopes for German progress and reform were consistently thwarted by an aristocracy that clung to old feudal privileges and institutions and suppressed criticism whenever it felt threatened. The old order was especially anxious after the

French Revolution began in 1789. Indeed the war would lead to the dissolution of aristocratic institutions and the execution of many aristocrats, including the French monarch. These events would have a profound impact on the worldviews of Hegel and other intellectuals of his generation.

In 1788, when he was eighteen, Hegel entered the protestant theological seminary in Tübingen, following in the footsteps of the several generations of Lutheran pastors from whom he had descended. However, he never really acclimated to seminary life. He learned more from his studies outside of official theology and, above all, from the friendships he made there with fellow students Friedrich Hoelderlin, who would become one of Germany's great Romantic poets, and Friedrich Shelling, the future idealist philosopher. The three friends exchanged ideas, excitedly watched the events in France unfold, and participated in societies in which students discussed and promoted revolutionary ideals.

Following his graduation, Hegel did not become a pastor. Instead, he worked as a private tutor for wealthy families in Berne and Frankfurt, devoting his free time to the study of philosophy and theology. Much of his writing represents an attempt to come to grips with Christianity, to wrestle with the significance of Christ and his teachings, and to outline the historical legacy of the Christian Church and its cultural and social implications as an institution. Hegel's lifelong claim that he was an orthodox Lutheran may be subject to question, as it could have easily been motivated by the religious intolerance of the Prussian state, but his philosophy is heavily influenced by theological language, and a theological outlook colors his vision of human experience.

When Hegel's father died, Hegel received a modest inheritance, which allowed him to pursue his academic career. In 1801, he went to the German city of Jena to work as a private professor. At the time, Jena was a center of intense intellectual and artistic creativity and one of the epicenters of German romanticism, a diverse movement that challenged the rationality and sobermindedness that characterized the Age of Enlightenment. Hegel consorted with philosophers and poets and began to envision his own unique philosophical approach. He sought to combine his diverse influences, including Kantian idealism, theology, romanticism, and contemporary political and social theory—all of which contribute to his philosophical voice. Early examples of this emerging voice include *The Difference Between the Philosophical Systems of Fichte and Shelling* (1801), in which he begins to critique some of the basic assumptions of Kantian idealism, and an 1802 essay on Natural Law, in which he formulates a philosophical approach to the analysis of culture, modernity, and modern institutions.

In 1807, the year after Napoleon marched into Prussia, Hegel published the *Phenomenology of Spirit*, an ambitious and difficult philosophical treatise. Here, Hegel fully elaborates some of his most striking and innovative concepts, such as the idea of Spirit, or collective consciousness, and his view that consciousness and knowledge develop dialectically, in a repeating pattern. After teaching in Bamberg and Nuremberg, where he met his wife, Hegel took up a professorship in Heidelberg and, later, took another at the new university in Berlin. Hegel's output from this period includes the three-volume *Encyclopedia of the Philosophical Science* (1817), in which he systematizes his approach to philosophy, and *Elements of a Philosophy of Right* (1821), which combines his philosophical insights with analysis and critique of modern society and modern political institutions. Hegel's students of this period include liberal civil servants in Prussian government, a fact that points to the widening and influential audience Hegel commanded in the years leading up to his death in 1831.

Although Hegel's status in the field of philosophy has fluctuated in the nearly two centuries since his death, his reflections have considerably influenced other disciplines as well, including literary and cultural theory, theology, sociology, and political science. His lifespan roughly coincides with the German composer Ludwig Von Beethoven (1770–1827), whose greatness rests partly in the way he took neoclassical musical conventions in new directions and incorporated diverse influences into his music in novel and idiosyncratic ways. Similarly, the originality of Hegel's insights stems partly from his adaptation of the available philosophical language to describe aspects of human experience that were beyond the immediate concerns of his philosophical predecessors. Like them, Hegel would devote a great deal of intellectual effort wrestling with the nature and possibilities of human knowledge. However, he also sought to understand his rapidly changing world and to describe the social, institutional, and historical dimensions of human experience.

Themes, Arguments & Ideas

DIALECTIC AS THE FUNDAMENTAL PATTERN OF THOUGHT

Before Hegel, the word *dialectic* referred to the process of argument and refutation through which philosophers sought to discover the truth. Plato's dialogues offer the prime example. One person advances a proposition or belief, and Socrates refutes it and shows why that proposition is wrong, which clears the way for a better, more convincing argument to take its place. The point of dialectical reasoning, before Hegel, was to clear away misconceptions and arrive at first principles—basic, fundamental truths on which we can all agree and that the philosopher can use as a starting point on which to base a philosophical system, such as Descartes' famous principle that if we're thinking, we can at least be sure that we exist.

Hegel used the dialectic for a different purpose than arriving at first principles. To understand what the dialectic means for Hegel, we have to first understand that Hegel was an idealist, in the tradition of his predecessor, Kant. Like Kant, Hegel believed that we do not perceive the world or anything in it directly and that all our minds have access to is ideas of the world—images, perceptions, concepts. For Kant and Hegel, the only reality we know is a virtual reality. Hegel's idealism differs from Kant's in two ways. First, Hegel believed that the ideas we have of the world are social, which is to say that the ideas that we possess individually are utterly shaped by the ideas that other people possess. Our minds have been shaped by the thoughts of other people through the language we speak, the traditions and mores of our society, and the cultural and religious institutions of which we are a part. *Spirit* is Hegel's name for the collective consciousness of a given society, which shapes the ideas and consciousness of each individual.

The second way that Hegel differs from Kant is that he sees Spirit as evolving according to the same kind of pattern in which ideas might evolve in an argument—namely, the dialectic. First, there is a thesis, an idea or proposition about the world and how we relate to it. Every thesis, or idea about the world, contains an inherent contradiction or flaw, which thus gives rise to its antithesis, a proposition that contradicts the thesis. Finally, the thesis and antithesis are reconciled into a synthesis, a new idea combining elements of both.

Essentially, Hegel sees human societies evolving in the same way that an argument might evolve. An entire society or culture begins with one idea about the world, which naturally and irresistibly evolves into a succession of different ideas through a dialectical pattern. Since Hegel believes that this succession is logical, meaning that it could only happen one way, he thinks that we can figure out the entire course of human history without recourse to archaeology or other empirical data, but purely through logic.

SPIRIT AS THE SELF-AWARENESS OF SOCIETY

The German word that is normally translated as "spirit" in English versions of Hegel is Geist, a word that can mean both "spirit" and "mind," depending on the context. Hegel uses it to refer to the collective consciousness of a society, in the sense that we might speak (following Hegel) of the spirit of the age. In both English and German, *spirit* can also mean a ghost, and it can be used to refer to religious phenomena as well. Both of these senses are relevant to Hegel's term because the collective dimension of consciousness—what we might call culture—is similarly intangible and mysterious. Spirit is located neither in objects nor in individual minds, but in a nonmaterial third realm that contains ideas that a whole society has in common.

Spirit does not exist from the earliest moments of human history but is instead a modern phenomenon toward which humanity had to evolve. According to the process outlined in the *Phenomenology of Spirit*, human consciousness starts from a position of trying to grasp objects through sensory inputs and moves on to more sophisticated ways of relating to the external world, until it finally reaches the level of Spirit. At this stage, consciousness understands that individuals are bound to other individuals in a single communal consciousness, or culture. Spirit is the self-consciousness of the community, the whole of which individuals are only a part. As the consciousness of spirit unfolds and changes, so do the values and actions of the individual parts of which it is made.

LORDSHIP AND BONDAGE AS THE BASIS
OF SOCIAL RELATIONS

Hegel agrees with other idealists, such as Kant, that consciousness of an object necessarily implies consciousness of a subject,
which is a self perceiving the object. In other words, human
beings are not only conscious of objects but also self-conscious.
Hegel takes this view a step further to suggest that self-consciousness involves not only a subject and an object but other subjects
as well. Individuals become aware of selves through the eyes of
another. Thus, true self-consciousness is a social process and
involves a moment of radical identification with another consciousness, a taking on of another's view of the world to obtain a
self-image. Consciousness of self is always consciousness of the
other. In relationships of inequality and dependence, the subordinate partner, the bondsman, is always conscious of his subordinate status in the eyes of the other, while the independent
partner, the lord, enjoys the freedom of negating consciousness
of the subordinate other who is unessential to him. However, in
doing so, the lord is uneasy because he has negated a consciousness with which he has radically identified in order to assure
himself of his independent and free status. In short, he feels
guilty for denying the moment of mutual identification and
sameness to preserve his sense of independence and superiority.
Social life is founded on this dynamic of competing moments of
mutual identification and objectification, of identifying with and
also distancing oneself from the other.

ETHICAL LIFE AS THE EXPRESSION OF AN AGE

Ethical life is a given cultural expression of Spirit, the collective
entity that transcends all individuals and determines their beliefs
and actions whether they are aware of it or not. Ethical life
reflects the fundamental interdependence among individuals in a
society and finds articulation in their shared customs and morals. Hegel argues that the tendency in modern life characterized
by economic individualism and the Enlightenment idea of the
individual as a subject possessing various rights represents a
movement away from the recognition of essential social bonds.
Before the Enlightenment, human beings were generally considered in terms of how they fit into social hierarchies and communal institutions, but following Enlightenment thinkers such as

Locke, Hobbes, Rousseau, and Kant, the individual on his own came to be considered sacred. In the *Philosophy of Right*, Hegel explains that the modern state is the institution that will correct this imbalance in modern culture. Although economic and legal individualism play a positive role in modern society, Hegel foresees the need for institutions that will affirm common bonds and ethical life while preserving individual freedom. He believes, for example, that the state must regulate the economy and provide for the poor in society and that there should be "corporative" institutions, somewhat similar to modern trade unions, in which different occupational groups affirm a sense of social belonging and a feeling of being connected to larger society.

Summary & Analysis

Summary

CHAPTERS 1 TO 3: "SHAPES OF CONSCIOUSNESS" In these first three chapters, Hegel attempts to outline the fundamental nature and conditions of human knowledge. He asserts that the mind does not immediately grasp the objects in the world, concurring with Kant, who said that knowledge is not knowledge of "things-in-themselves," or of pure inputs from the senses. A long-standing debate raged in philosophy between those who believed that "matter" was the most important part of knowledge and those who privileged "mind." Rationalists, such as Descartes (and before him, Plato), believed that we can only trust the truths that the mind arrives at on its own, while Empiricists, such as Locke, argued that all of our knowledge comes from our perceptions of actual objects, through our senses. Kant had sought to put this debate to rest by arguing that the meaning of objects derives from ideas, or "concepts," that stand between mind and matter. The information entering the mind via the senses is always "mediated" by concepts. In the first part of the *Phenomenology*, Hegel demonstrates that though concepts do in fact mediate matter, as Kant maintains, Hegel's own understanding of the way concepts come into being implies a certain instability or insecurity in knowledge, which Kant overlooks.

Whereas Kant seems to imply that an individual's mind controls thought, Hegel argues that a collective component to knowledge also exists. In fact, according to Hegel, tension always exists between an individual's unique knowledge of things and the need for universal concepts—two movements that represent the first and second of the three so-called modes of consciousness. The first mode of consciousness—*meaning*, or "sense certainty"—is the mind's initial attempt to grasp the nature of a thing. This primary impulse runs up against the requirement that concepts have a "universal" quality, which means that different people must also be able to comprehend these concepts. This requirement leads to the second mode of consciousness, *perception*. With perception, consciousness, in its search for certainty, appeals to categories of thought worked out among individuals through some kind of communicative process at the level of common language. Expressed more simply, the ideas we have of the world around us are shaped by the language we speak, so that the names and meanings that other people have worked out before us (throughout the history of language) shape our perceptions.

Consciousness is always pulled in two different directions. Our senses give us a certain kind of evidence about the world, and the categories through which we make sense of the world—categories that we learned when we learned language—tell us what the input of our senses means. The fact that a difference exists between perceptions and the meanings we give to them gives rise to a feeling of uncertainty or skepticism that is built into the very mechanism by which minds come to know objects. That is, to the extent that consciousness can grasp categories of thought, it is at the same time aware of the inadequacy of these categories and thus moved to find new ground for sense certainty, generating new concepts that smooth over the contradictions. This striving is constantly frustrated, the categories of thought reveal their inner contradictions, and consciousness is moved to posit more adequate categories. Although sense certainty is in some ways always elusive, this process of moving from less satisfactory to more satisfactory categories entails a kind learning process. Hegel calls this process *understanding*, the third and highest mode of consciousness.

Analysis

For the unprepared lay reader, *Phenomenology of Spirit*, the earliest of Hegel's major "mature" works, can be a frustrating introduction to his highly idiosyncratic and difficult philosophical style. The difficulty arises in part because Hegel, working within the tradition of German idealism, was attempting to grapple with dimensions of human experience that lie largely outside the scope of this tradition, which was established above all by Kant. While deeply indebted to Kant, Hegel did not find the language of idealism wholly adequate to explain what he felt needed explaining, and he had to invent his own philosophical terms, which at first seem unfamiliar and strange.

The difficulty of *Phenomenology* also lies in the work's extraordinary ambition. In one dizzying gesture, the twenty-seven-year-old Hegel attempts to outline and define all the diverse dimensions of human experience as he sees them: knowledge and perception, consciousness and subjectivity, social interaction, culture, history, morality, and religion. The result is chaotic, and his points are often difficult to grasp, but the work is ultimately highly rewarding for those with the right mix of patience and imagination required to "decode" Hegel.

"The spirit of man has broken with the old order of things" is the dramatic but fitting statement with which Hegel introduces *Phenomenology of Spirit*. Here he sets out his agenda for a systematic philosophy, the subject of which is not simply the knowing and perceiving individual mind (as it was for his immediate philosophical heirs, such as Kant) but social beings who are oriented to the world collectively through culture. The individual is not simply standing directly opposite objects but rather is forced to mediate between the subjective and the collective moments of understanding—that is, between his own immediate perceptions and the ideas about the world that he shares with the people around him. In these early sections of *Phenomenology of Spirit*, we get an early glimpse of this approach, the famous dialectic, the idea that knowledge is a process of striving to arrive at stable and truthful categories of thought. Knowledge-as-motion is a recurrent theme in Hegel's writings and forms the core of his highly original approach to epistemology.

Summary

CHAPTER 4: "SELF-CONSCIOUSNESS" Hegel moves from the discussion of consciousness in general to a discussion of self-consciousness. Like the idealist philosophers before him, Hegel believes that consciousness of objects necessarily implies some awareness of self, as a subject, which is separate from the perceived object. But Hegel takes this idea of self-consciousness a step further and asserts that subjects are also objects to other subjects. Self-consciousness is thus the awareness of another's awareness of oneself. To put it another way, one becomes aware of oneself by seeing oneself through the eyes of another. Hegel speaks of the "struggle for recognition" implied in self-consciousness. This struggle is between two opposing ten-dencies arising in self-consciousness—between, on one hand, the moment when the self and the other come together, which makes self-consciousness possible, and, on the other hand, the moment of difference arising when one is conscious of the "otherness" of other selves vis-à-vis oneself, and vice versa. Otherness and pure self-consciousness are mutually opposed moments in a "life and death struggle" for recognition. This tension between selves and others, between mutual identification and estrangement, plays out in the fields of social relations.

Hegel explains that the realization of self-consciousness is really a struggle for recognition between two individuals bound to each other as unequals in a relationship of dependence. One person is the bondsman, and one is the servant. The bondsman, or servant, is dependent on the lord. Because he is aware that the lord sees him as an object rather than as a subject (i.e., as a thing, rather than as a thinking, self-aware being), the lord frustrates his desire to assert his pure self-consciousness. He is stuck in a position of reflecting on his otherness. The independent lord, on the other end, is able to negate the otherness that he finds reflected through the subordinate bondsman, since the bondsman does not appear as a conscious subject to him. As the independent and superior partner in this relationship, his otherness does not bear down on him.

The lord occupies the position of enjoying his dominant status, whereas the bondsman must continuously reflect on his status as a subordinate "other" for the lord. At the same time, the lord does not find his position completely satisfying. In negating his own otherness in the consciousness of the bondsman, in turning the bondsman into an object unessential to his own self-consciousness, he has also to deny a fundamental impulse toward recognizing the bondsman as a consciousness equal to himself. At the same time, the bondsman is able to derive satisfaction in labor, a process of working on and transforming objects through which he rediscovers himself and can claim a "mind of his own."

Analysis

This section of the *Phenomenology*, and for that matter the rest of the book, is difficult because of its abstractness. Hegel writes about lords and bondsmen (or masters and slaves, as it is sometimes translated), and it is hard at first to see whom he is talking about and whether this is meant to describe social relations today or at some period in the past when slavery was more widespread.

Precisely because it is so abstract, the section has been interpreted in many different ways. It is possible to view the lord and bondsmen relationship as an early stage of history, since the *Phenomenology* describes the evolution of Spirit throughout the course of human civilization, culminating in modern society. However, the dialectical evolution of Spirit throughout history may also be seen as a metaphor for the process through which each individual develops psychologically. Thus, the images of the lord and bondsman may be interpreted not literally but as metaphors for positions in which we all find ourselves throughout life—sometimes as the objectified bondsman, sometimes as the objectifying lord.

The lordship and bondage section is among the most widely cited in all of Hegel's writings. The struggle for recognition between lord and bondsman inspired Marx's account of how class struggle naturally arises from the exploitation of one social class by another. A diverse array of twentieth-century thinkers, including psychoanalysts and existentialists, have drawn on Hegel's ideas here. Earlier idealists, such as Kant, pointed out the difference between subject and object, but Hegel believed that the subject, or the self, is aware of its self only as a distinct entity through the eyes of another self. The radical idea inherent in this view is that consciousnesses are inextricably interwoven and that one cannot have any concept of oneself without having actually experienced a moment of identification with the other. Many readers have found his notion of self-consciousness easier to grasp intuitively than many of Hegel's other concepts. His account seems to ring true with everyday experience. People come to know themselves through the image they suppose others hold of them. This image is positive or negative depending on who that person is, where he or she stands in society, and so forth, and gives rise to familiar stresses as individuals strive to assert their free individuality against the objectifying images that others have of them.

Summary

CHAPTERS 5 TO 8: "FREE CONCRETE MIND" AND "ABSOLUTE KNOWLEDGE" At the end of chapter 4, Hegel describes the "unhappy consciousness" that arises from individuals having to struggle for recognition from one another to realize themselves as self-conscious subjects. He asserts that various religious institutions and philosophical systems serve as a refuge from the fear and objectification that arise in this struggle. By turning toward a transcendent being (God), one can take comfort in a being that exists purely for itself, rather than in a struggle for recognition between beings, and thus isolate oneself from that struggle. This turn toward a transcendent being follows from the initial attempt of consciousness to grasp the nature of the object. The striving for sense certainty leads to perception and to the social nature of universal concepts.

Hegel's understanding of the dialectical movement of thought leads him to take issue with the idealist notion of reason. Reason is not, as the Kantian idealists claim, a matter of fitting isolated objects into universal categories. Reason involves a self-conscious ego struggling to assimilate objects while having to fend off their otherness, which it sees as a threat to its existence as a self-conscious being.

Like Kant, Hegel believes that reason leads consciousness to fit particular phenomena into universal categories. However, this process is not smooth and always involves an element of uncertainty and vagueness, since objects exist in a fluid spectrum of variations and do not readily conform to distinct universal categories. Thus, insofar as consciousness is oriented to those stable categories of thought, it is also aware of a set of standards governing how phenomena conform to such categories. These standards, or Laws of Thought, reside neither in the objects nor in the mind but in a third dimension, in the "organized social whole." When looking at the social dimension, we can see that every individual self-consciousness belongs to one collective self-consciousness, a locus of identity existing outside of every individual in the collective. Laws of thought, morality, and conventions belong to social life. Individual activities and interpretations conform to these laws as having a taken-for-granted existence, as "matters at hand," and individuals see these common laws not as alien but as emanating from their own selves, as a law of one's own heart. Hegel calls this dimension of collective consciousness Spirit.

Spirit is the location of the ethical order, the realm of the laws and customs, to which individual consciousnesses assent but that exist outside of individuals in the social being. Individuals interpret and act out laws and customs in an individual way, but they do so in tension with this communal spirit. The ethical communal spirit has two manifestations. First, it is the basis of the deep-seated ethical orientation of individuals, as an object of faith. Second, it has an outward existence as the culture and civilization of a given historical age. These two moments of ethical spirit, or ethical life, are in tension with each other. In modern Enlightenment culture, for example, the external cultural expression of ethical life, or Spirit, is a kind of individualism. An emphasis on education and the acquisition of wealth actually orients consciousness away from the social being and the deep ethical life of which it is a part. In its most extreme negative form, individualism in the modern world finds expression in despotism and political terrorism. When political life is no longer a true expression of common ethical life, factions merely pretending to represent the collective will enforce their rule through terror and the annihilation of opposing factions. In its more positive guise, individualism finds expression in individual rights.

The next stage in the development of consciousness is religion. Religion is essentially a collective Spirit conscious of itself, and as such it reflects a given culture's expression of ethical life and the balance between individual and collective. There are different phases in the development of religion represented in the various world religions and reflected in art, myth, and drama. But religion is not the highest stage of consciousness. This place is reserved for Absolute Knowledge. Whereas with religion, spirit is conscious of itself in pictorial or poetic form, in the state of Absolute Knowledge, consciousness combines attention to subjective knowledge with attention to objective truth. That is, in absolute knowledge, spirit becomes aware of its limitations and seeks to correct its contradictions and inadequacies by moving to a higher plane of understanding. Absolute Knowledge is self-conscious and critical engagement with reality. It is the standpoint of science and the starting point of philosophical investigation.

Analysis

The religious connotations of the Hegelian term *Spirit* have led many to believe that Hegel understands Spirit as a kind of supernatural or divine force guiding human civilization and history. As noted, *Spirit* is a translation of the German word Geist, which can also mean "mind," and while spirit is reflected in religion, in itself it is actually something more like culture, or the collective mind of a social being. "Ethical life" is an expression of sprit in everyday reality. The ethical encompasses the common understandings, customs, and moral codes of a culture, a supraindividual communal source of interpretation determining how people act, what they believe, and how they relate to the world and to the divine. Hegel says that even reason, which Kant treated as abstract and universal, is deeply embedded in collective culture.

One of Hegel's most original and influential ideas is that culture is a dynamic force and subject to change. While deeply influenced by Kant and German idealism, Hegel was also close to the Romantic movement that was strong in Germany when he came of age intellectually. German romantic philosophers such as Herder took issue with the image of the human experience that Kant and his students promoted. The Kantians and the rationalists of the Enlightenment sought to establish reason as a universal and unchanging bedrock of knowledge. The romantics thought the Kantians did not fully appreciate the profound differences in human experience from age to age and culture to culture. Hegel came along to fuse the insights of both camps, and the resulting view sees the human mind striving for stable categories of thought and referencing the common interpretations and customs of society to do so. In other words, one approaches the world through a common mind. This common mind operates as a consciousness in and of itself, seeking to understand the world, bumping up against contradictions in the process, sorting through these contradictions, and moving forward. One gets a glimpse here of Hegel's view of history as the dynamic unfolding of the collective mind or spirit.

SCIENCE OF LOGIC

Summary

Hegel begins by demonstrating that the categories of thought through which the mind grasps objects are not as stable or certain as his predecessor Kant seems to assume. This instability even applies to that apparently fundamental, universal category, "being." To be able to say that something "is," that it exists, implies another category: nothingness, or not being. Being always implies nothingness, and vice versa, such that one cannot call to mind one category without invoking the other. Being and nothingness are understood as both opposed and identical, a unity of being and nothing. Consciousness experiences this unity of opposites as contradiction, which it seeks to resolve by invoking a third category called "becoming," which captures both nothing and being at once. This dialectical process is how thought moves, according to Hegel's model. Consciousness posits a basic category that engenders a contradiction, is "negated," and falls apart, creating a need for a more complex category that smoothes over the contradiction. This new composite category in turn reveals its own contradiction and points to another category, and so on.

Essence, the subject of book II, is a higher, more complex mode by which consciousness grasps objects. Consciousness of being tries to get at objects through the simple binary of being/not being and through the outcome of the tension between these two categories—namely, becoming. Essence, on the other hand, points to qualities beyond mere existence or nonexistence, to particular qualities of the object. These qualities manifest themselves in the appearances of objects. Rather than being or not being, objects appear to have different natures. Being and essence are both features of objective logic—that is, they pertain to qualities of objects themselves. Subjective logic, on the other hand, gets at ideal properties of knowledge, those emanating from products of the mind—namely, concepts or notions—which make up the third and highest level of consciousness. It is at the level of concepts that subjective and objective are considered together. This is the domain of philosophy or metaphysics, where the concern is the interrelation of consciousness and inputs from the world of material objectivity.

Analysis

The *Phenomenology of Spirit* is regarded as Hegel's "first shot" at establishing his own unique philosophical approach. He covers a lot of ground and introduces many of the major themes that reappear in his later philosophical writings, but the work is very confusing. His *Science of Logic*, published in stages beginning in 1812, is no less difficult for the uninitiated, but it benefits from the five intervening years Hegel had to reflect carefully on his ideas. The latter book is widely understood to be a more systematic treatise on ontology, which is the study of being, and epistemology, which is the study of knowledge. Here Hegel explicitly lays out his famous dialectic—the concept that, along with the equally challenging concept of Geist, is most frequently associated with his name. The slogan "thesis–antithesis–synthesis" has long circulated as a useful shorthand for understanding the basic idea of Hegel's dialectical method. However, Hegel himself never uttered this construction, and most Hegel scholars agree that it is both helpful and potentially misleading.

In the *Science of Logic,* Hegel sets out to show that the process by which consciousness assimilates objects into mental concepts is more dynamic and, one might say, messier then Kant describes it. Just as he does in the *Phenomenology,* Hegel traces here the movement of consciousness, or the idea, from basic categories to more complex ones. Consciousness attempts to grasp objects at a most basic level, finds this first attempt somehow unsatisfying as exposing inadequacies or contradictions, and proceeds to a higher level, and so on. In the *Phenomenology* and elsewhere, Hegel seems to imply that this dialectical unfolding is an inherent feature of the world we inhabit, governing history and culture. In *Logic* we see that the dialectic is a phenomena of ideas. But the two dimensions of reality (i.e., history, culture, and the world in general) and our ideal, mental, or conceptual grasp of things are not really separable. The world we live in is a world created by ideas. But our ideas do not emanate from the mind of a single individual, as other idealists such as Kant seem to imply. Concepts have an objective status. They exist outside of any individual as taken-for-granted reality. They belong to common cultural understanding.

ELEMENTS OF A PHILOSOPHY OF RIGHT

Summary

I–II. ABSTRACT RIGHT AND MORALITY The basis of individual rights lies in property. Property is not merely material acquisition—it is central to an individual's assertion of identity and personality. Property is an expression of self and the locus of an individual's claim to rights, since it is through property that one can say "this is mine," a claim that others respect. Property is the "embodiment of personality," says Hegel. The system of private property establishes individuality and personality through contract and exchange. Contract establishes ownership through institutionalized norms of mutual respect of individual rights and obligations. Economic life governed by free exchange of commodities is based on an institutionalized notion of the individual as having some claim to recognition as a right-bearing person. If an exchange market is to function efficiently, economic actors must recognize universal standards by which a person can claim to own property. Established norms of reciprocal recognition in the modern economic sphere are internalized in economic actors and represent a "common will."

The concept of individual rights to which this common will gives its assent is an abstract concept. The individual it implies is a universal individual without particular traits and without reference to social or cultural environment. Thus, rights established by private property and exchange are "abstract rights" and engage individuals as abstract, universal subjects. The system of mutual recognition and abstract right is the basis of what Hegel calls *morality*. Morality is essentially the subjective side of the reciprocal social obligations institutionalized in contracts and the economic market. Individuals experience such reciprocal obligations as a moral obligation to respect universal rights. Morality gestures toward what ought to be and frequently is not. It is an abstract ideal, a vision of good based on mutual recognition of rights. People are morally motivated through a sense of duty to defend the universal rights of individuals.

Analysis

In *Elements of a Philosophy of Right*, Hegel attempts to fuse diverse elements of his philosophy and social thought into a grand statement about the nature of modernity. He traces a modern conception of individuality and of the individual as the bearer of rights to modern social, economic, and political institutions. He also describes how this modern notion of the individual, while positive in many ways, gives rise to certain stresses and to the alienation of the individual from the collective. In the first section, Abstract Right, Hegel returns to a theme of earlier writings in which he wrestles with the fairly common belief in "natural rights" that are present in the various "social contract" theories of, for example, John Locke, in which social or political order is said to derive its legitimacy from its ability to uphold and protect the rights of autonomous, sovereign individuals.

For Locke and others, the social contract is merely the outcome of a contract among autonomous individuals to respect one another's rights. In this view, the extent of one person's relationship to another can be summed up in the slogan, "Be a person and respect others as a person." Hegel believes this view of social life to be generally accurate, but he rejects the belief that contractual mutual recognition and the ideal of the universal-rights-bearing individual it supports is a basis of all societies throughout history. The worldview implied in contract theory and in the moral obligation to respect individual rights is not the foundation of social life but rather a reflection of the spirit of the modern age. This spirit resides in modern legal and economic institutions, which foster an idea of abstract rights and universal personhood. Hegel therefore applies his theory of history and culture to an analysis of the modern world. He also criticizes both contemporary political theory and idealist moral philosophy for not recognizing that the phenomena they recognize as universal laws are actually particular expressions of modern culture.

Summary

III. ETHICAL LIFE The morality that we see expressed in contracts and exchanges, which reflect a reciprocal respect between individuals for each other's rights, is only a particular expression of a wider and deeper dimension of moral life that Hegel calls ethical life. Ethical life is a system of norms and mores belonging to a social body, made up of spheres of social interaction and interdependence in which all individuals are embedded. Whereas morality turns people away from what is toward what ought to be, ethical life is merely what is—the set of meanings and practices that guide people in everyday activities whether they are aware of it or not. Ethical life is present in the three important levels of social life. In its most elementary form, it is present in the family and finds expression in basic emotions such as love and altruism. In civil society, a sphere of social interaction corresponds to economic life or the "system of needs." Civil society engages individuals as bearers of Abstract Rights, as owners of property and bearers of legal rights. In civil society, individuals relate to one another in universal terms.

Although private property as the basis of abstract right and morality is a positive force in promoting individual freedom, individualistic material interests, such as the pursuit of economic gain, could potentially destabilize society. When left unchecked, these destabilizing forces tend to polarize humanity into rich and poor. The individualism of private material acquisition also weakens the expression of the basic social bonds and common culture that hold society together. Certain institutions must be in place to prevent the system of private property and the individualist worldview it sustains from undermining society itself. Government authority, in addition to providing basic infrastructure and protection from crime, must both promote and protect society from economic individualism, ensuring that those without property or work are provided for. Corporate institutions, such as guilds or labor unions, must be in place not just to look after the economic needs of workers and tradesmen but to give them a sense of belonging and connection to the social whole of which they are a part.

After the family and civil society, the third and highest moment of ethical life is the institution of the state. The state is the medium through which individuals come to realize their location in the ethical life of society, as parts of a greater whole. The state is an expression of spirit unfolding in history through dialectical development. Whereas earlier forms of the state were imperfect expressions of collective spirit, the modern state has evolved as a rational adaptation to structures of modern life. Given the image of the universal person and the emergence of the autonomous rights-bearing individual, the modern state, as the highest form of collective association, serves to integrate this vision of individual freedom and autonomy into an appreciation of common social bonds, preventing these two opposed tendencies from pulling society apart and allowing freedom and rights to coexist with a full expression of communal spirit.

Analysis

Philosophy of Right is Hegel's most controversial work, as many readers have objected to the central role he attributes to the state in realizing a reconciliation of modern individuality and freedom with the need for collective belonging. However, Hegel's model of the rational state, though by no means purely democratic, does not invest power in authority simply to suppress individuality. Hegel understands the state in terms that are somewhat unfamiliar to modern readers, who, in the wake of the totalitarian states that arose during the twentieth century, tend to be skeptical of theories that give political institutions the task of solving society's problems. For Hegel, the state is not just a political and authoritarian entity but the broadest arena of social relations corresponding to common culture, or ethical life. It is in the institution of the state, therefore, that the contradictions of ethical life will reveal and fix themselves. In modern society, the role of the state is to reconcile the egoistic and individualizing tendencies of civil society with the need for common belonging.

Hegel largely adopts Kant's description of the moral, rational individual but believes that Kant's understanding of individuality is an expression of a particular historical epoch, namely of the modern world. Hegel is thus regarded as one of the first philosophers of modernity and of a particularly modern understanding of history. If there is a unifying ambition throughout his vast writings, this ambition lies in his attempt to describe the origins and implications of this image of the individual and how it relates to the religious, economic, and political aspects of modern life. Here he shows how this notion of individuality is rooted in practical life but also that it has a fundamental tension with the expression of ethical life.

Karl Marx, Hegel's most famous follower, used Hegel's philosophy to condemn the institutions of private property and the modern market economy. Was Hegel's view of these institutions similar to or different from Marx's?

In Hegel's view, the institution of private property is far from corrupting or unhealthy. Nevertheless, Hegel recognized that the modern market economy creates certain tensions within society, and in this regard his overall attitude toward economic life might be viewed as somewhat ambivalent. Modern civil society gives rise to such laudable concepts as freedom and individual rights, but these same benefits simultaneously threaten to destabilize a society's cohesion.

Following Enlightenment traditions, the modern economic sphere assumes and reinforces a belief in individual rights. Property, writes Hegel, is the "embodiment of personality." The ownership of property requires an individual to claim that something belongs to him and him alone. By respecting this claim, other individuals demonstrate that they respect the individual as a person and a possessor of certain rights. Thus, private property exists as an external, concrete expression of an individual's personhood and subjectivity. Taken as a whole system, the economic sphere engages actors as free individuals and reinforces the moral obligation to respect individual rights and freedom. Hegel regarded the evolution of this institutionalized concept of morality as a liberating development.

It is difficult to argue, therefore, that Hegel regarded the modern economic sphere as menacing or negative. In fact, much like Adam Smith and other classical liberal economic thinkers, Hegel saw modern economic life, and the notion of abstract right institutionalized therein, as forming an important dimension of the social interdependence he calls civil society. Although individuals in civil society are essentially self-interested, civil society can function properly only if actors respect this fundamental morality.

Student Essay

Yet despite his appreciation for the morality of civil society, as expressed through the legal–economic system, Hegel saw that its emphasis on individual subjectivity could potentially dismantle a modern society. As civil society engages persons only as abstract rights bearers, it turns them away from local customs and mores and undermines the sense of identity derived therein. The flip side of freedom and abstract right turns out to be alienation from collective, or ethical life. Thus, as Hegel famously asserted, man experiences the queasy sensation of not feeling at home in the modern world. The twin forces of freedom and alienation represent the defining contradiction of the modern age.

This contradiction defines the modern age but also provides the engine that will move the current era into the future. The dialectical nature of history necessitates an eventual reconciliation of these competing forces. According to Hegel, the agents of that reconciliation will be the institutions of the emerging modern state. Man must create institutions that reaffirm social and cultural bonds among individuals in a competitive market situation, which tends to undermine those bonds. Hegel advocated the establishment of corporations, which are somewhat like modern trade unions but actually operate more like medieval guilds. These corporations would create local communities of workers with their own shared culture and common identity. These collective organizations would also appoint leaders who will represent their interests in the political sphere. By organizing themselves around economic interests, corporations can support individualistic civil society while also enforcing life's collective, ethical dimension.

John Stuart Mill
(1806–1873)

13

THEMES, ARGUMENTS & IDEAS

- Logic as Induction
- The Subject of Experience
- Experience as the Ground
  of Knowledge
- Ethics vs. Behavior
- Government as a Force for Moral Education
- The Individual as a Product of Society

SUMMARY & ANALYSIS OF MAJOR WORKS

- *A System of Logic:
  Raciocinative and Inductive*
- *Principles of Political Economy*
- *On Liberty*

One of the most important thinkers and writers of the Victorian era, John Stuart Mill was also a political activist, involved in struggles for social reform throughout his life. Born in 1806 in London, Mill was the son of the prominent philosopher and historian James Mill. James Mill believed that the mind of a child is a blank slate that requires a strict regimen to be properly trained and educated. Accordingly, young John was isolated from boys his own age and kept under the austere eye of his father, who saw to it that his son was learning Greek by the age of three and had mastered Latin by the age of eight. Mill's day was filled with intellectual work, and he was allowed only one hour of recreation, which consisted of a walk with his father—who used the opportunity to conduct oral exams. By the age of fourteen, Mill had read extensively in history, logic, mathematics, and economic theory. When he was fifteen, he began studying the radical English philosopher Jeremy Bentham (1748–1832), the founder of utilitarianism.

Utilitarianism is the theory that laws and actions should be judged as good or bad based on their utility—that is, the results they produce. For a utilitarian, the best actions or laws are those that produce the greatest good for the most people and the greatest good over the least amount of pain. The influence of utilitarianism launched Mill on a lifelong pursuit of social reform.

Mill began publishing in 1822, and in 1823 he helped form the Utilitarian Society, which met at Jeremy Bentham's house. Mill took regular part in the London Debating Society, and by this time had adopted the views of Thomas Malthus, who had argued that the human population would eventually outgrow its food supply, leading to a dire catastrophe. Consequently, in 1824, Mill was arrested for distributing birth control literature to the London poor. In 1826, he suffered a severe bout of depression, which he attributed to the emotionally restricted life he had led as a child. He recovered and began an active intellectual life, but with a changed outlook. He now made room for a human dimension in his thought that offset the starkness of utilitarianism, stressing an intellectual approach to life at the expense of emotions.

In 1830, at the age of twenty-four, Mill met the woman he would love for the rest of his life. This woman, Harriet Taylor, was already married to a wealthy London merchant. The two waited patiently until the death of Taylor's husband in 1849, finally marrying two years later, in 1851. Harriet was Mill's constant companion from the time they met and took an active interest in his writing. The couple's years of happiness were brief, for Harriet died in 1858. Thereafter, Harriet's daughter from her first marriage, Helen, was Mill's companion. He remained a committed social reformer all his life and in 1865 was elected to Parliament, where he actively campaigned for women's rights and suffrage. He spent his last years in Avignon, France, with Helen, and died there in 1873. He was buried beside his wife.

Mill's philosophy is based on an empiricist approach to the world. Mill sees experience as the only true foundation of knowledge; thus, his philosophy allows no place for traditional or received ideas of right and wrong. As an empiricist, Mill continually privileges observation and experiment over theorizing, and his thought tends to be inductive (drawing general conclusions from particular instances) rather than deductive (drawing conclusions by extrapolating from general principles).

Although Mill was influenced by utilitarianism—a theory that directs people to work for the greatest happiness for the greatest number of people—Mill nevertheless worked to protect the rights of individuals, particularly women. Mill's interest in social reform stemmed from his belief that the majority often denies liberty to individuals, either through laws or through moral and social judgments.

Themes, Arguments & Ideas

LOGIC AS INDUCTION

Before Mill wrote his *System of Logic*, the system of logic outlined by Aristotle in his *Organon* (see chapter 2, Aristotle) had been accepted as authoritative. Aristotle's logic is a system of rules for creating syllogisms—arguments that start with a general premise and reach a conclusion about a particular instance, such as "All men are mortal. Socrates is a man. Therefore, Socrates is mortal." Mill, however, was an empiricist and believed that all knowledge comes to us through our senses and that we only come to believe in any general principles by experiencing many particular instances that bear them out. Although other empiricist philosophers, such as Locke, had argued that experience is the only basis of knowledge, no one before Mill had attempted to write a system of rules, comparable to Aristotle's, for how we arrive at general principles by starting with particulars. Mill established a distinction between *deductive* logic, in which we extrapolate from general principles, and *inductive* logic, in which we draw conclusions from specific cases. Mill maintained that inductive logic is the true basis of knowledge.

Although Mill defines many different types of induction, the basic principles of his system are fairly straightforward. The inductive method is based on the idea of causation; the goal of induction is to determine what causes something. Mill considers various kinds of evidence and proof, but the essential method for establishing a cause is elimination. If an event happens in one set of circumstances but does not happen in other circumstances that are the same except for one thing, that one thing must be the cause of the event. Complicated phenomena involving a number of causes may be explained using a more elaborate inductive method in which separate causes are identified through deduction, and then their combination is identified through deduction. For example, to explain what causes heart disease, we would use empirical evidence from experiments (i.e., induction) to establish many specific laws governing how diet, genetics, exercise, age, and other factors affect the heart, following which we would use deduction to arrive at a hypothesis for how these laws might work together. Finally, we would verify these hypotheses through induction (more experimentation and examination of empirical evidence).

Although Mill considered induction to be the basis of logic, today induction is not considered part of logic at all. The methods of evidence and proof that Mill wrote about are now considered part of the scientific method, whereas logic proper is limited to deduction.

THE SUBJECT OF EXPERIENCE

Mill sees experience as the exclusive and sole source of knowledge. He rejects the idea of what he calls intuitive knowledge, which could apply to any kind of knowledge that the mind grasps immediately and with certainty rather than verifying through observation over a period of time. Intuitive knowledge would include such things as Plato's Forms or Descartes' "I think, therefore I am." However, if the mind cannot intuitively perceive itself as a self, the question arises, what does the self consist of? Mill imagines the body as a permanent potentiality of sensations and the mind as a series of actual and possible states of being. In other words, neither the brain nor the body can be said to be a "person," in the sense we normally use that word, meaning a stable, consistent, identifiable self. Mill grapples with the problem of how a series of different states or impressions can be aware of itself. Mill observes that a bond seems to exist between the various parts of a series (such as the different states of mind through which a person goes), which allows us to say that these parts are the feelings of a person, who is the same person throughout. This bond constitutes the ego. However, Mill's argument here seems to depend on the existence of a faculty of perception very much like intuition—our minds apparently intuit the bond between elements in a series.

EXPERIENCE AS THE GROUND OF KNOWLEDGE

Experience for Mill is that which can be checked, tested, and proven by careful observation and analysis. Experience must be used to test the inferences we make from experience. Mill observes that the fundamental laws of mathematics and logic— to which the supporters of intuitive knowledge had long pointed as proof that there are some things we know that require no experience—are in fact no more than generalizations from experience. He argues that the law of contradiction—another supposedly innate idea which holds that nothing can be both true and not true—is purely a summary of the inherent incongruity of belief and nonbelief. He maintains that any accuracy of knowledge is only hypothetical, and thus fictitious. He views the law of causation (the fact that every event has a cause) as very important to his inductive system, as a generalization from the experience of an invariable and unconditional sequence. Further, Mill acknowledges only one kind of inference—that which occurs from particulars to particulars—and uses inference to interpret the record of particular experiences, since they alone provide evidence on which any kind of conclusion can rest.

ETHICS VS. BEHAVIOR

Mill considered the problem of what human beings do from two different perspectives. First, he observed that certain motives correspond to certain actions in consistent, even invariable sequences. This fact means that human actions are predictable and that a scientific study of human behavior is possible—from this insight, made by Mill and some of his contemporaries, the modern social and behavioral sciences arose. In particular, Mill observed that human beings always act to maximize their own pleasure. Since this observation is essentially a behavioral law, it would be useless to expect human beings to do otherwise, or to argue with them that they should do otherwise.

However, Mill also examined human actions from an ethical standpoint. On the surface, this second perspective would seem to conflict with the first. Ethics concerns what human beings *ought* to do and assumes freedom of choice, while the study of human behavior focuses on what human beings actually do and what makes them do it. Mill was able to combine these two perspectives because he believed that the pursuit of pleasure that actually motivates human beings does not necessarily conflict with acting for the general good of society—the greatest good for the greatest number of people. Different kinds of pleasures exist, and we can learn to eschew the baser in favor of the higher. Moreover, Mill saw the study of human behavior as being at the service of ethics. By scientifically studying the effects of human actions, we may discover those actions that most advance the happiness of all. Mill rejects the idea that we know right from wrong intuitively, arguing instead that we must judge our actions by their consequences.

GOVERNMENT AS A FORCE FOR MORAL EDUCATION

For Mill, government does not exist merely to promote and produce the maximum amount of pleasure, which its citizens like to have. Rather, government must continually seek to educate its citizens so that they pursue the higher, mental pleasures over the lower ones. In fact, it is the government's responsibility, as well as an individual responsibility, to undertake moral education so that the result may be a good society. This moral education must be implemented with the recognition that people are not merely hedonistic pleasure seekers but that they are progressive by their very nature and desire higher pleasures. Thus, a good government is one that encourages an active participation by all its citizens. A bad government is one that forces its citizens to be passively obedient to the wishes and whims of a ruling elite, no matter how sensible these wishes and whims may in fact be.

THE INDIVIDUAL AS A PRODUCT OF SOCIETY

Like many of the philosophers who preceded him in the eighteenth and nineteenth centuries, Mill saw the individual as sacred and as taking precedence over the state, in the sense that the state exists for the sake of individuals rather than the other way around. However, unlike Hobbes and Rousseau, Mill's interest in the individual was not as the individual might exist in a state of nature, before entering into society. Rather, Mill imagined the value of the individual as he or she would become with the proper education in a well-structured society. He sees the individual as filled with various potentials, and it is only in conjunction with society that an individual may develop these potentials so that he or she may benefit the community that he or she inhabits. Mill advocates the active life so that individuals may use their various gifts and talents to promote happiness for the greatest number. He sees the active life for the individual as morally superior to a passive one.

Summary & Analysis

A SYSTEM OF LOGIC: RACIOCINATIVE AND INDUCTIVE

Summary

A System of Logic was first published in 1843 and immediately enjoyed a wide circulation, going through numerous editions. Mill himself made substantial changes in the third edition, published in 1850, and the eighth edition, published in 1872, a year before his death. This book is Mill's most comprehensive and systematic philosophical work, elaborating his inductive method, which helped to free the empirical sciences from the rigidity of analysis by way of syllogisms. Syllogisms are arguments grounded in general principles, in which two premises are used to deduce a third premise, or conclusion. In *A System of Logic*, Mill breaks away from this age-old practice and instead proposes the use of a form of logic derived from the principles of the natural sciences. He uses his method to address questions of language and logic, induction, the relativity of knowledge, the structure of the scientific method, the structure of arithmetic and geometry, and the principles of the moral sciences. In effect, Mill provides a solid, scientific methodology for reasoning and for philosophy, derived from science and mathematics.

The introduction discusses the role and purpose of logic in human understanding. Logic is the art and science of reasoning, a means for the pursuit of truth. However, logic is only concerned with making inferences from observed phenomena, not with intuitive truths. Logic does not produce new evidence, but it can determine whether something offered as evidence is valid. Logic judges but does not observe, invent, or discover. Logic serves a purpose in some larger project of inquiry that gives it meaning. Fundamentally, logic is a method of evaluating evidence.

Book I defines logic as a method of proof. Proof always involves an assertion or proposition that must be proven. A proposition is a discourse that either affirms or denies something about some other thing. Thus, a proposition is a belief that depends on the ability to attach a name to something. When two names are joined together by a copula ("the sun is bright"), they form the proposition. Mill proceeds to examine the nature of predicates, which are properties that can be said to be possessed by substances. Predicates include such things as joy, fear, sound, smell, taste, pain, pleasure, thought, judgment, and conception. Mill suggests that feelings or states of consciousness are realities; that is, they are neither substances nor attributes. Mill proceeds to examine volition and action, substance and attribute, body, mind, quality, relation, resemblance, quantity, states of consciousness, and attributes of mind.

Book II discusses the place of logic within the field of knowledge, specifically denying that logic is related to metaphysics and stating that preconceived notions and speculative thought are foreign to the workings of logic, since they suggest that logic be reduced to consistency rather than truth. In book II, Mill opens up logic to include the various fields of science and knowledge and denies logic any kind of restrictive structure.

Book III introduces Mill's inductive method. An inductive inquiry begins with the analysis of things according to their elements. The first step in induction is the separation of a thing into its various elements through a process of experimentation and observation. Mill proceeds to examine the relationship between cause and effect and concludes that one effect may have several causes. Mill distinguishes between complex and compound effects, which brings him to examine the nature of generalizations and probable evidence, operations that, he says, are more useful in life than in science.

Book IV discusses the need for a philosophical language that would further the practice of induction by helping us to accurately observe, record, and communicate. Such a language must have a steady and determinate meaning for every general name, since names often have unclear connotations. Book V deals with various fallacies that must be resolved before logic can be firmly grounded. These include the fallacies of confusion; of ambiguous words; and the *petitio principii*, which states that the premise either appears to be the same as the conclusion or is proved from the conclusion. Mill concludes that this argument is a fallacy because it is nothing more than a circular argument, since the attempt to prove two propositions reciprocally from one another leads nowhere.

Book VI argues that the "moral sciences," meaning the study of ethics and human nature, require the same logical structure as the physical sciences. A discussion of the concepts of liberty, causation, and necessity as they apply to human affairs leads Mill to conclude that human nature is governed by scientific principles that logic can lay bare and that can be used to promote happiness. Mill argues that human psychology and behavior are governed by universal laws, as is the formation of each person's ethical character. However, these laws cannot be studied directly, through experiment and observation, but can only be known deductively.

Mill considers various scientific methods and the extent to which they may be applied to the social sciences. Although many of the methods of the natural sciences do not work for the social sciences, the methods of induction may still be applied to understand causes and effects, such as the effects of a given policy or legislative act. The social sciences can also be approached deductively, by starting with a priori laws of human nature and reasoning based on them. Mill divides the social sciences into two branches: those in which the causes and effects of human behavior are studied in a context that is assumed to be stable, and those sciences that examine progress and historical change.

Analysis

The most innovative aspect of *A System of Logic* is its rigorous, systematic explanation of induction. This explanation is a particularly impressive accomplishment given how unscientific and unsystematic induction seems to be at first glance, especially in comparison with the certainty of a deduction or syllogism. For example, in the famous syllogism, "All men are mortal. Socrates is a man. Socrates must be mortal," if you know for certain that all men are mortal and that Socrates is a man, you can be very certain of your conclusion—that Socrates will die at some point. However, if you work in the reverse direction, which induction requires you to do, you get a much less certain answer. Socrates died, and Socrates was a man, so perhaps all men are mortal—but maybe not. The fact that Socrates' friends Diabetes and Bursitis also died can be offered as further evidence that all men are mortal, but it still doesn't prove it. Nevertheless, for those who believe that all our ideas come from experience, induction is the source of every general principle that we think we know, so induction is the foundation on which deduction is based.

PRINCIPLES OF POLITICAL ECONOMY

Summary

Mill's *Principles of Political Economy* was first published in 1848 and went through various editions; the final edition was the seventh, which appeared in 1871. *Political Economy* is the term nineteenth-century writers use to refer to the study of what we today call macroeconomics, though its practitioners, such as Mill, Adam Smith, David Ricardo, and Karl Marx, were more philosophical and less empirical in their methods than modern economists. In this book, Mill examines the fundamental economic processes on which society is based: production, the distribution of goods, exchange, the effect of social progress on production and distribution, and the role of government in economic affairs.

Book I deals with production and begins by identifying the basic requisites that enable production to exist: labor and natural objects. Labor may be defined as an agent of production, though not all labor leads to the production of a material object. Labor produces three types of utilities. The first is the creation of objects for human use, wherein labor invests external material things with properties that make these things usable. Second, some labor renders human beings serviceable to society and to themselves, such as the labor of teachers and doctors. The third utility is the labor of giving pleasure or entertainment, which does not make other people more productive or result in a tangible product.

In addition to labor and natural objects, production requires capital, without which it would cease. In essence, capital is the accumulated stock of the products of labor. After discussing such aspects and manifestation of capital, such as fixed versus circulating capital, Mill examines the social forms of production, such as cooperation, combination of labor, production on a small and large scale, and the increase of labor, which results in the increase of capital as well as production. Last, Mill examines production from land and recognizes that such production is markedly different from the one achieved through labor and capital, since production from land is limited and not likely to greatly increase.

Book II examines distribution as it is manifested in the allocation of property and produce. Mill discusses the effect on distribution of such factors as competition; customs; slavery; ownership by peasants; and the various types of laborers, wages, profits, and rents. Mill acknowledges the difference between workers and capitalists (he includes landowners in this category), both of whom share the products of labor.

In book III, Mill addresses the topics of exchange and value, defining the latter in terms of supply and demand. Mill sees value as relative, since it depends on the quantity of another thing or things. There is no general rise and fall of value, for it rises only when a fall is supposed and falls only when a rise is supposed. Mill considers money and its relationship to supply and demand, cost of production, and credit (which is a substitute for money). Further, he looks at the influence of credit on prices, the function of currency, international trade and values, and rates of interest.

Book IV deals with the relationship between a society's progress and its economic affairs. Mill defines social progress in terms of the increase of knowledge, the improved protection of citizens and property, the transformation of taxes so they are less oppressive, the avoidance of war, and the increase in the prosperity of the people brought about by improvements in business capacities, including the more effective employment of the citizens through education. Mill notes that social progress is not infinite and that a given state of affairs may become stationary if production does not improve and if the overflow of capital from the affluent to the less affluent countries becomes suspended. This recognition of a state of stagnation leads Mill to speculate on the future of the laboring classes, which he foresees rising beyond the patriarchal values of society and becoming emancipated through education. The newly empowered working class will generate massive change in society.

Book V analyzes the influence of government on society, arguing that the functions of government can be divided into the necessary and the optional. The necessary is that which is inseparable from the very of idea of government, such as security, protection, and taxation. Everything else that government does is optional and subject to question. Mill concludes by considering the question of a government's interference with individual liberty. Mill asserts that government should always restrict itself to doing only what is necessary. First, a government should prohibit and punish individual behavior that harms other people, such as force, fraud, or negligence. Second, a government should work to limit or even eliminate the great amount of energy being spent on the harming of one nation by another. Third, a government should turn such destructive behavior into bettering human faculties, namely, transforming the powers of nature so they serve the greatest physical and moral good. Finally, Mill proposes that governments should adopt a laissez-faire policy, in which they abstain from interfering with individual choice and grant unconstrained freedom to people, who should be allowed to pursue their happiness without restrictions.

Analysis

In *Principles*, Mill turns economics into a viable philosophical area of inquiry by exploring what people really want and what economics can measure and assess. Mill's approach to economics is based on his belief in the superiority of socialism, in which economic production would be driven by cooperatives owned by the workers. To this end, Mill argues that the laws of production may be natural laws, but the laws of distribution are created and enacted by human beings. In other words, wealth is the natural end product of labor, but the distribution of wealth is determined by the decisions and the will of actual people (the elite) and is not simply part of the order of nature. Mill carries this view quite far, maintaining that human laws and institutions can and should determine how wealth is distributed. Thus, for Mill, economics is closely tied to social philosophy and politics.

Mill believes that society will continue to grow and change, but he recognizes that such change is limited by the capabilities of the land and of labor. Both land and labor have to be handled with care since neither can continue to produce an increasing amount in order to satisfy a growing demand. Mill agrees with Malthus that population must be controlled so that it does not outgrow its food supply.

Mill does discuss the benefits of free competition and the useful and favorable social energies that competition releases. He goes so far as to note that if a society becomes too entrenched in protecting its members from competition, the result will be stagnation and mental inertia in its citizens. Therefore, it is important to encourage self-initiative and individual responsibility, and government policy should never weaken or discourage this positive force. Although this does not free the state from its responsibilities of providing security and well-being for its citizens, Mill does modify his generally laissez-faire stance by stating that private monopolies must be prevented, the poor must be properly looked after, and the education of children must be suitably available. Mill firmly believes that it is only the well educated and therefore enlightened citizen who can help society grow, change, and progress. Moreover, education allows the lower classes to become more socially active and responsible.

One of the most remarkable facets of *Principles* is its call for equal rights for women. Just as the poor need to be emancipated from their dependence on the vicissitudes of a class-structured society, which reflect a patriarchal orientation, women need to be freed from the dependence on men. Thus, Mill advocates that women not be barred from seeking employment in areas traditionally the preserve of men.

The most important aspect of *Principles* is the use of a scientific method in the analysis of politics, thus giving a practical application to theoretical ideas. This gave a fresh impetus to liberal thought by placing its various concepts and ideals firmly within the realm of social and political action, grounded in the rigor of science.

ON LIBERTY

Summary

On Liberty is one of Mill's most famous works and remains the one most read today. In this book, Mill expounds his concept of individual freedom within the context of his ideas on history and the state. *On Liberty* depends on the idea that society progresses from lower to higher stages and that this progress culminates in the emergence of a system of representative democracy. It is within the context of this form of government that Mill envisions the growth and development of liberty.

Chapter I defines civil liberty as the limit that must be set on society's power over each individual. Mill undertakes a historical review of the concept of liberty, beginning with ancient Greece and Rome and proceeding to England. In the past, liberty meant primarily protection from tyranny. Over time, the meaning of liberty changed along with the role of rulers, who came to be seen as servants of the people rather than masters. This evolution brought about a new problem: the tyranny of the majority, in which a democratic majority forces its will on the minority. This state of affairs can exercise a tyrannical power even outside the political realm, when forces such as public opinion stifle individuality and rebellion. Here, society itself becomes the tyrant by seeking to inflict its will and values on others.

Next, Mill observes that liberty can be divided into three types, each of which must be recognized and respected by any free society. First, there is the liberty of thought and opinion. The second type is the liberty of tastes and pursuits, or the freedom to plan our own lives. Third, there is the liberty to join other like-minded individuals for a common purpose that does not hurt anyone. Each of these freedoms negates society's propensity to compel compliance.

Chapter II examines the question of whether one or more persons should be allowed to curtail another person's freedom to express a divergent point of view. Mill argues that any such activity is illegitimate, no matter how beyond the pale that individual's viewpoint may be. We must not silence any opinion, because such censorship is simply morally wrong. Mill points out that a viewpoint's popularity does not necessarily make it correct—this fact is why we must allow freedom of opinion. Dissent is vital because it helps to preserve truth, since truth can easily become hidden in sources of prejudice and dead dogma. Mill defines dissent as the freedom of the individual to hold and articulate unpopular views.

Chapter III discusses whether people who hold unpopular views should be allowed to act on them without being made social outcasts or facing a legal penalty. Actions cannot be as free as ideas or viewpoints, and the law must limit all actions whose implementation would harm others or be an outright nuisance. He states that human beings are fallible and therefore need to experiment with different ways of living. However, individual liberty must always be expressed in order to achieve social and personal progress.

Chapter IV examines whether there are instances when society can legitimately limit individual liberty. Mill rejects the concept of the social contract, in which people agree to be a part of society and recognize that society can offer certain forms of protection while asking for certain forms of obligations. However, he does suggest that because society offers protection, people are obliged to behave in a certain way, and each member of society must defend and protect society and all its members from harm. In brief, society must be given power to curtail behavior that harms others, but no more.

Chapter V summarizes and elucidates Mill's twofold argument. First, individuals are not accountable to society for behavior and actions that affect only them. Second, individuals *are* answerable for any type of behavior or action that harms others, and in such cases it is the responsibility of society to punish and curtail such behavior and action. However, Mill does note that there are some types of actions that certainly harm others but bring a larger benefit to society, as when one person succeeds in business more than his rival. In the rest of the chapter, Mill examines particular examples of his doctrine.

Analysis

The key concept in *On Liberty* is the idea that liberty is essential to ensure subsequent progress, both of the individual and society, particularly when society becomes more important than the state. This state of affairs would be attained in a representative democracy in which the opposition between the rulers and the ruled disappears, in that the rulers only represent the interests of the ruled. Such a democracy would make the liberty of the individual possible but would not guarantee it. When society becomes free of the constraints of government, it begins to entrench the interests of a select and powerful few, which threatens individual liberty in a new way. Mill grapples with the problem of envisioning society progressing in such a way as to prevent the repression of the individual by the ever more powerful and confident majority. Social progress can only take place if limits are placed on individual liberty, but progress also necessitates the freeing of the individual from such limits.

Mill sidesteps this dilemma by delving into moral theory, in which the only important thing is the happiness of the individual. Such happiness may only be attained in a civilized society, in which people are free to engage in their own interests, with all their skills and capabilities, which they have developed and honed in a good system of education. Thus, Mill stresses the fundamental value of individuality, of personal development, both for the individual and society for future progress. For Mill, a civilized person is one who acts on what he or she understands and who does everything in his or her power to understand. Mill holds this model out to all people, not just the specially gifted, and advocates individual initiative over social control. He asserts that things done by individuals are done better than those done by governments. Moreover, individual action advances the mental education of that individual—something that government action cannot ever do, for government action always poses a threat to liberty and must be carefully watched.

According to Mill, can human society improve itself?
If so, how?

To Mill, history is the story of human progress. Human beings
have transitioned from barbarity to civilization, and history
records the move toward intellectual and moral excellence,
increasingly democratic institutions, and greater equality between
individuals. Mill believed that it was possible to actually chart out
the various stages through which society would and should pass,
thereby arriving at a systematic pattern of historical change. This
pattern could be used to determine the forthcoming stages of
progress and development and guide humankind into successively
higher stages of civilization. Mill had a strong belief in the
possibility of progress, though he could not vouch for its certainty.

Mill recognized that there were some problems with his theory
of a definable, chartable map for social progress. It is one thing to
suggest that a primitive society should undertake particular steps
to achieve the status of a civilized society. After all, civilized
societies are not a hypothetical construct. They exist today, and
we generally have a sense of what distinguishing qualities make
them civilized. It would be theoretically possible, then, to
extrapolate a path that a primitive society could follow to reach a
higher level of advancement. This becomes profoundly more
difficult, however, when dealing with a society that is already
highly advanced. We have no extant models or examples of a
superadvanced society, so we don't know ahead of time what the
next stage will look like. For a highly civilized society, the pattern
of social progress will necessarily be conjectural.

Mill solved this problem by working deductively from his
concept of an ideal society. By articulating what an ideal society
would look like, Mill could work backward to determine the steps
contemporary society should follow. Thus, Mill believed that a
highly civilized society has to work toward ensuring that its rulers
are those individuals best suited to rule and, second, that those
individuals exercise the primary authority in society.

Student Essay

According to Mills, social progress and individual liberty are thoroughly inextricable. Mill believed that human beings are inherently progressive, with a natural inclination toward experimentation and self-development. If allowed to flourish freely, this innate tendency would cause these individual citizens to experiment in countless directions, elevating the character of human desires and fostering cultural and social development. He observed that, at each stage of civilization, certain states of affairs need to result in order to ensure the possibility of reaching the next stage of development. However, the existence of these conditions alone does not guarantee progress. Society also requires the active moral and intellectual leadership provided by superior men and women. These high-quality thinkers and activists can only be produced in conditions of liberty. Thus, Mill claimed that liberty alone is the chief guarantor of progress.

From this conclusion, Mill constructed a straightforward philosophy of social progress. Progress hinges on the emergence and creation of new ideas, which are the result of challenges to old ideas and conventionally accepted modes of behavior. These challenges can only occur when a society supports individual liberty. The free expression of action and behavior must be encouraged, so that viable alternatives to old constructs and systems may be both suggested and implemented.

Mill anticipated the criticism that existing beliefs and paradigms provide society with stability. Challenging those concepts could undermine social cohesion, creating a potentially dangerous and threatening environment. However, Mill stated that a representative form of government would be able to deal effectively with such instability. A truly healthy, progressive society requires a certain amount of flux and volatility to avoid stagnation.

Søren Kierkegaard

(1813–1855)

14

Søren Kierkegaard lived the majority of his life alone. He left his native Copenhagen only three times—each time to visit Berlin—and never married, though he was engaged for a short time. Despite his solitary existence, Kierkegaard's writings are some of the most impassioned and controversial in all of philosophy. He is sometimes called a "poet-philosopher" in honor of both his passion and his highly literary experiments in style and form. Kierkegaard is known for his critiques of Hegel, for his fervent analysis of the Christian faith, and for being an early precursor to the existentialists.

Kierkegaard was born in 1813, the year Denmark went bankrupt. Although Kierkegaard's father had personally managed to escape financial ruin, Denmark as a nation struggled for much of the early to mid-1800s. The people put increasing pressure on the monarchs to institute a democracy, and a free constitution was finally established in 1848. The changes leading up to the governmental restructuring resulted in an explosion of wealth and learning and afforded citizens like Kierkegaard the leisure and environment necessary to pursue a life of writing and thinking.

However, democratization also helped inspire one of Kierkegaard's most enduring philosophical themes: that freedom could actually lead to fear. While the new religious and social freedoms available in Denmark brought many positive changes, they also had psychological repercussions that toubled Kierkegaard. He felt that having the freedom to choose inevitably involved feeling anxiety over *which* path to choose, even as it simultaneously inspired joy. Kierkegaard also worried that too many people squandered that freedom by blindly following public opinion.

Kierkegaard was born into a wealthy and respected family, the youngest of seven siblings. His mother was an unassuming figure: quiet, plain, and not formally educated. Kierkegaard's father, on the other hand, was melancholic, anxious, deeply pious, and fiercely intelligent. Kierkegaard's father believed that a youthful denunciation of God had brought a curse upon his family and that all his children would die before the age of thirty-four (a fate that only Søren and his brother Peter escaped). Kierkegaard ended up inheriting a great deal of his intellectual and psychological character from his father.

In 1830, Kierkegaard enrolled at Copenhagen University and began to study theology, per his father's wishes. His mother died while he was at university, and despite keeping a remarkably detailed set of journals, Kierkegaard never mentioned her death. He didn't take his theological studies very seriously, though he was reading a great deal of literature and philosophy. Kierkegaard was highly social during this period, attending dinners, concerts, and the theater and becoming well known for his wit and good humor. When his father died in 1838, however, Kierkegaard settled down and devoted himself to the study of theology.

Kierkegaard received his doctoral degree in theology in 1840. He had inherited a large sum of money from his father, and as a rich, accomplished, young man, Kierkegaard was considered one of Copenhagen's most eligible bachelors. He became engaged to the beautiful Regine Olsen, the seventeen-year-old daughter of a politician, but later broke off their engagement. Despite their deep love for one another, Kierkegaard apparently believed that his life as a thinker made him unsuitable for marriage, particularly to a young, inexperienced girl. Kierkegaard had strong feelings for

Olsen throughout his life, despite her having married another man and leaving Copenhagen with him. His relationship with Olsen—like his relationship with his father—is a major biographical influence on his philosophical work.

After breaking off his engagement with Olsen, Kierkegaard retired to a solitary life of writing, publishing a prodigious amount of work over the next several years. At first he felt that his books weren't being noticed outside elite literary circles, which was rendering his work politically and socially ineffectual. To bring attention to his books, he tried to provoke the satirical paper *The Corsair* to attack him in its pages. Kierkegaard succeeded in 1845, although *The Corsair* focused its criticisms mainly on his personal rather than intellectual life. Kierkegaard was lampooned in *The Corsair* for years, which significantly damaged his social standing. It did, however, spur him into a highly productive phase of writing and publishing. Kierkegaard published his first major book, *Either/Or*, in 1843 and his last, *The Changelessness of God*, in 1855, the year of his death. Between these two books, Kierkegaard produced more than thirty volumes of philosophy, theology, and criticism.

Themes, Arguments & Ideas

THE PROBLEMS OF BOREDOM, ANXIETY, AND DESPAIR

Boredom, anxiety, and despair are the human psyche's major problems, and Kierkegaard spends most of his writing diagnosing these three ills. People are bored when they are not being stimulated, either physically or mentally. Relief from boredom can only be fleeting. Passion, a good play, Bach, or a stimulating conversation might provide momentary relief from boredom, but the relief doesn't last. Boredom is not merely a nuisance: a psychologically healthy human *must* find some way to avert boredom.

Anxiety stems from conflicts between one's ethical duty and one's religious duty. Social systems of ethics often lead one to make choices that are detrimental to one's spiritual health, and vice versa. The tension between these conflicting duties causes anxiety, and like boredom, anxiety must be escaped for a person to be happy.

Finally, despair is a result of the tension between the finite and the infinite. Humans are frightened of dying but are also frightened of existing forever. Kierkegaard believed that everyone would die but also that everyone had an immortal self, or soul, that would go on forever. Boredom and anxiety can be alleviated in various ways, but the only way to escape despair is to have total faith in God. Having total faith in God, however, is more than simply attending church regularly and behaving obediently. Faith requires intense personal commitment and a dedication to unending self-analysis. Kierkegaard thought that having total faith in God, and thus escaping despair, was extremely difficult but also extremely important.

THE AESTHETIC AS THE FIRST STAGE ON LIFE'S WAY

Kierkegaard proposed that the individual passed through three stages on the way to becoming a true self: the aesthetic, the ethical, and the religious. Each of these "stages on life's way" represents competing views on life and, as such, potentially conflicts with one another. Kierkegaard takes the unusual step of having each stage of life described and represented by a different pseudonymous character. Thus, it becomes too difficult to ascertain which propositions Kierkegaard himself upholds. This ambiguity fits with Kierkegaard's characteristic tendency to avoid dictating answers. He preferred that readers reach their own conclusions.

The aesthetic is the realm of sensory experience and pleasures. The aesthetic life is defined by pleasures, and to live the aesthetic life to the fullest, one must seek to maximize those pleasures. Increasing one's aesthetic pleasures is one way to combat boredom, and Kierkegaard describes many methods of doing so. He proposes that the anticipation of an event often exceeds the pleasure of the event itself, so he suggests ways of drawing out anticipation. One suggestion is to leave all of your mail for three days before opening it. Unplanned events can, at times, lead to pleasures as great as anticipation, but the pleasure of planned events is almost entirely in the anticipation.

Kierkegaard acknowledges the importance of the aesthetic but also presentes it as an immature stage. The aesthete is only concerned with his or her personal enjoyment, and because aesthetic pleasure is so fleeting, an aesthete has no solid framework from which to make coherent, consistent choices. Eventually, the pleasures of the aesthetic wear thin, and one must begin to seek the ethical pleasures instead. The ethical life offers certain pleasures that the aesthetic life cannot. An aesthete can never do something solely for the good of someone else, but we all know that doing things for others without personal motives can actually be incredibly enjoyable.

THE ETHICAL AS THE SECOND STAGE ON LIFE'S WAY

Ethics are the social rules that govern how a person ought to act. Although ethics are not always in opposition to aesthetics, they must take precedence when the two conflict. The aesthetic life must be subordinated to the ethical life, as the ethical life is based on a consistent, coherent set of rules established for the good of society. A person can still experience pleasure while living the ethical life. The ethical life serves the purpose of allowing diverse people to coexist in harmony and causes individuals to act for the good of society. The ethical person considers the effect his or her actions will have on others and gives more weight to promoting social welfare than to achieving personal gain. The ethical life also affords pleasures that the aesthetic does not. Aesthetics steers one away from consistency, since repetition can lead to boredom. An ethical person doesn't simply enjoy things because they're novel but makes ethical choices because those choices evoke a higher set of principles. Kierkegaard uses marriage as an example of an ethical life choice. In marriage, the excitement of passion can quickly fade, leading to boredom and a diminishing of aesthetic pleasure. However, by consistently acting for the good of one's spouse, one learns that there are enjoyments beyond excitement. Still, the ethical life does little to nurture one's spiritual self. The ethical life diverts one from self-exploration since it requires an individual to follow a set of socially accepted norms and regulations. According to Kierkegaard, self-exploration is necessary for faith, the key requirement for a properly religious life.

THE RELIGIOUS AS THIRD STAGE ON LIFE'S WAY

Kierkegaard considers the religious life to be the highest plane of existence. He also believes that almost no one lives a truly religious life. He is concerned with how to be a "Christian in Christendom"—in other words, how to lead an authentically religious life while surrounded by people who are falsely religious. For Kierkegaard, the relationship with God is exclusively personal, and the large-scale religion of the church (i.e., Christendom) distracts people from that personal relationship. Kierkegaard passionately criticized the Christian Church for what he saw as its interference in the personal spiritual quest each true Christian must undertake.

In the aesthetic life, one is ruled by passion. In the ethical life, one is ruled by societal regulations. In the religious life, one is ruled by total faith in God. One can never be truly free, and this causes boredom, anxiety, and despair. Although true faith doesn't lead to freedom, it relieves the psychological effects of human existence. Kierkegaard claims that the only way to make life worthwhile is to embrace faith in God, and that faith necessarily involves embracing the absurd. One has *faith* in God, but one cannot *believe* in God. We believe in things that we can prove, but we can only have faith in things that are beyond our understanding. For example, we believe in gravity: we feel its effects constantly, which we recognize as proof of gravity's existence. It makes no sense, though, to say we have *faith* in gravity, since that would require the possibility that, someday, gravity would fail to materialize. Faith requires uncertainty; thus, we can have faith in God because God is beyond logic, beyond proof, and beyond reason. There's no rational evidence for God, but this is exactly what allows people to have faith in him.

THE PLEASURES OF REPETITION AND RECOLLECTION

Repetition and recollection are two contrasting ways of trying to maximize enjoyment. Repetition serves multiple purposes for Kierkegaard. First, it has an important aesthetic function. People want to repeat particularly enjoyable experiences, but the original pleasure is often lost in the repeating. This is due to the expectation that things will be just the same the second time as the first time. The pleasure of expectation clouds the fact that the original experience wasn't undertaken with a specific idea of the joy it would cause. Repetition can produce powerful feelings but usually only when the experience occurs unplanned. In this case, the pleasure might even be magnified at the sudden resurgence of happy memories—in other words, the recollection. There is pleasure in planned repetition, but it is a comfortable pleasure, not an exciting one.

Whereas repetition offers the joy of anticipation—joy that seldom materializes in the actual event—recollection offers the joy of remembering a particularly happy event. Recollection can be cultivated along with the imagination to increase one's day-to-day aesthetic pleasure. Often, recalling a pleasant occurrence is more enjoyable than repeating the same event: remembering the Christmases of your childhood is often more pleasant than Christmas is in adulthood. Indeed, much of the pleasure of Christmas, for an older person, can come from nostalgia. The pleasures of recollection, which are best enjoyed alone, are well suited to the aesthetic life. Unplanned repetition is a truly aesthetic pleasure as well, while planned repletion, such as that represented by marriage, affords more ethical pleasures than aesthetic ones.

Summary & Analysis

EITHER/OR

Summary

Kierkegaard wrote *Either/Or* soon after receiving his doctorate and breaking his engagement with Regine Olsen. It is his first major work and remains one of his most widely read. Kierkegaard wrote the book under a series of pseudonyms. *Either/Or* has two parts: the first deals with the aesthetic, a word that Kierkegaard uses to denote personal, sensory experiences; the second part deals with ethics. In this second part, Kierkegaard discusses the merits of a social and morally proper life. Kierkegaard wrote the first section under the simple pseudonym "A," although he wrote the last section of part I, "The Diary of the Seducer," under the pseudonym "Johannes Climacus." Kierkegaard wrote part II under the interchangeable pseudonyms "B" and "the Judge." We know now that Kierkegaard himself wrote the entire book, but when *Either/Or* was first published, few people knew the author's actual identity. A claims that the aesthetic finds its highest expression in music, the theatre, and love. However, the source of love and the arts' aesthetic power lies in their ability to inspire the imagination. A considers the imagination to be the most useful tool in obtaining aesthetic pleasure. B argues that living an ethical life is preferable to the aesthetic life.

Music and drama create different kinds of aesthetic experiences. The aesthetic pleasure offered by music is the most direct. The very best music affects the imagination immediately. The pleasures to be found in drama—which is too concrete and intellectual to directly fire the imagination—lie in the viewer's opportunity to pretend to be someone else. The pairing of music and drama can be a particularly transcendent aesthetic experience. A praises Mozart's *Don Giovanni*, an opera based on the story of the great lover Don Juan. The music in *Don Giovanni* can be enjoyed on its own, and it is equally enjoyable to pretend to be Don Juan. However, the opera teaches a valuable aesthetic lesson as well, because Don Juan is the ultimate selfish aesthete. Repetition dulls the pleasure of an act, so Don Juan never repeats the act of love more than once with the same woman. Although he never sleeps with the same woman twice, by so doing he continually repeats the act of sleeping with a new woman. He can never enjoy the woman he is with because he is in such a hurry to get to the next one. A is devoted to pleasure as well and sees repetition as an enemy of pleasure. However, A believes that obtaining true aesthetic pleasure requires a more measured approach than blindly following one's passions, as Don Juan does.

The extreme difficulty of achieving true aesthetic pleasure leads A to claim that boredom is the most common, and unpleasant, human state. In fact, A goes so far as to claim that it is the root of all evil and makes a number of proposals for how it ought to be dealt with. One such plan is for Denmark to borrow a large sum of money and devote it explicitly to the entertainment of the masses. There are also more personal measures one can take to avoid boredom. A suggests that when receiving mail, one ought to leave it unopened for three days because the pleasure of imagining what is in the envelope far exceeds the pleasure to be gained from actually reading the letter.

Johannes Climacus, the pseudonymous author of the "The Seducer's Diary," which is the most famous section of *Either/Or*, further explores how to maximize aesthetic pleasure. "The Seducer's Diary" is Climacus's detailed, firsthand account of his wooing a young woman named Cordelia. For the majority of the diary, Climacus plots the seduction very slowly and deliberately. He takes great pleasure out of planning the seduction and doesn't even speak to Cordelia until the last quarter of the diary. Once Climacus makes his move, things happen very quickly, and he is soon engaged to Cordelia. He isn't satisfied with the success of his seduction, however, until he has deliberately driven Cordelia to break off the engagement and then, later, to come back to him. At this point he is finished with her and goes to find a new woman to seduce. Once Climacus has exhausted all the imaginative and exciting possibilities with Cordelia, continuing his relationship with her would lead him to boredom.

The second part of *Either/Or*, written under the pseudonyms B and the Judge—who eventually converge into a single character— takes the form of a letter written by the Judge to A. The letter is a response to part I of *Either/Or*; in it, the Judge attempts to persuade A that the ethical life is better than the purely aesthetic life. First, the Judge attempts to defend marriage. The Judge claims that the ethical life of being married is better than the aesthetic life of the seducer, and the Judge makes this claim on an aesthetic basis. The Judge says that there is actually more aesthetic pleasure to be found in a consistent marriage than in a bachelor life. The judge draws a distinction between the ethical, forward-looking repetition of the married life and the aesthetic, backward-looking recollection of the confirmed bachelor. He further points out that romantic literature always focuses on what happens before marriage but not what happens after, and he claims that the aesthetic fear of repetition is actually cowardly and selfish. The Judge argues that romantic love can exist in marriage and goes so far as to say that marriage is the highest form of romantic love. The ethical courage to submit to repetition is rewarded by the consistent, reliable aesthetic pleasure found in a loving marriage.

The Judge goes on to claim that A's devotion to the aesthetic prevents A from making any significant choices. Although A has a far wider range of options than the Judge, the Judge argues that since the Judge's choices are limited by ethics—by a consideration of other people—his choices are much weightier and mean much more to him than A's aesthetic choices mean to A. The aesthetic has its place, the Judge agrees, but the place of the aesthetic is beneath the ethical. The Judge's actual loving relationship with his wife is far better, the Judge argues, than the largely imaginary relationship between Johannes Climacus and Cordelia. The Judge experiences his pleasure with another person, while a seducer's pleasure is completely in his or her imagination. Part II ends with a sermon that the Judge has received from a friend. The sermon is entitled "The Edification Which Lies in the Fact that in Relation to God We Are Always in the Wrong." The sermon's key point is that humans, whether their choices are aesthetically or ethically motivated, are never in the right. Only by accepting that God is always right, and by trying to do God's will, can a person escape unhappiness.

Analysis

It is tempting, but incorrect, to read *Either/Or* as an explanation of how one can move from the aesthetic life into the ethical. True, the pleasures of the aesthetic are solipsistic, fleeting, and unreliable, whereas the pleasures of the ethical are empathetic, prolonged, and constant. However, both A and the Judge make good cases for their particular philosophies. A attempts to seduce the reader with his prose, just as Johannes Climacus attempts to seduce Cordelia, just as Don Juan seduces women, and just as music seduces the listener. A, through his attempted seduction of the reader, tries to lead the reader toward an appreciation of the aesthetic life. Alternatively, the Judge attempts to convince the reader that the ethical life is better than the aesthetic life, and he uses reason, not seduction, to accomplish this. Each writer's rhetorical strategy appropriately reflects his values.

However, a closer examination reveals inconsistencies in the positions of both A and the Judge. A speaks eloquently about the value of focusing solely on personal pleasure, but in doing so he is actually instructing the reader in how the reader might experience more aesthetic pleasure. A's apparent concern for the good of the reader is, though focused on the aesthetic, still an ethical concern, despite the fact that A makes it clear that the aesthete focuses on his or her own pleasure and not the pleasure of others. On the other hand, the Judge, in making the case for the ethical life, continually comes back to the point that the ethical life leads to even more aesthetic enjoyment than the purely aesthetic life.

In the end, A and the Judge are concerned with both aesthetic pleasures and ethical duties. Some think that *Either/Or* is about overcoming the aesthetic life for the ethical life. However, the Judge's arguments don't actually prove that the ethical life is wholly separate and better than the aesthetic life. There isn't actually an either/or choice between the aesthetic and the ethical: both are necessary. The either/or choice hinted at by the title *Either/Or* is actually a choice between the aesthetic/ethical life and the religious life. Either you choose the aesthetic and the ethical life or you choose the religious life. Aesthetics and ethics can coexist, but both detract from the religious. This is why *Either/Or* ends with the sermon on how people, in relation to God, are always wrong. Both A and the Judge make cases for how people should act in accordance with aesthetic and ethical systems, but any system designed by a human is necessarily flawed. Kierkegaard does not explore the religious very deeply in *Either/Or*, saving that for his later works, but *Either/Or* demonstrates that neither the aesthetic life nor the ethical life is complete without religion. A's groundless individuality and the Judge's principled marriage both interfere with the intense, faith-based introspection that exemplifies the religious life.

The final sermon in *Either/Or* is partially an attack on Hegel, who believes that the divine is played out through the actions of society. Kierkegaard emphatically does not believe this to be the case. If the divine is played out through society, then the social, ethical life would be, as a manifestation of the divine, the best life. Kierkegaard argues that only God is in the right and that to approach God requires introspective faith. There is no system, aesthetic or ethical, that can truly lead people in the right direction: people need religion, but they need it on a personal level, not a societal level. Kierkegaard feels that beliefs like Hegel's, and institutions like the church, claim to provide answers to people's troubles but in reality are simply providing excuses to avoid self-examination.

Kierkegaard's use of pseudonyms in *Either/Or* can be viewed as a concrete metaphor for Kierkegaard's internal confusion. In other words, although Kiekegaard wrote all of *Either/Or*, he made up authors for different parts to represent different aspects of his own personality. The conflict between the aesthetic and the ethical exists, to a certain extent, in every human. There are many systems in place to help mediate this conflict, but Kierkegaard demonstrates in *Either/Or* that the only escape from this conflict is to take a personal approach to religion.

FEAR AND TREMBLING

Summary

Fear and Trembling centers on the biblical story of Abraham. Abraham, childless after eighty years, prays for a son. God grants his wish, and Abraham has Isaac. Thirty years later, God orders Abraham to kill his son. Abraham prepares to kill Isaac, but at the last second God spares Isaac and allows Abraham to sacrifice a ram instead. *Fear and Trembling* includes four different retellings of the story, each with a slightly different viewpoint. In the first version, Abraham decides to kill Isaac in accordance with God's will. Abraham convinces Isaac that he's doing it by his own will, not by God's. This is a lie, but Abraham says to himself that he would rather have Isaac lose faith in his father than lose faith in God. In the second version, Abraham sacrifices a ram instead of Isaac. Even though God spares Isaac, Abraham's faith is shaken because God asked him to kill Isaac in the first place. In the third version, Abraham decides not to kill Isaac and then prays to God to forgive him for having thought of sacrificing his son in the first place. In the fourth version, Abraham can't go through with killing Isaac. Isaac begins to question his own faith due to Abraham's refusal to do what God commanded.

In the rest of *Fear and Trembling*, Kierkegaard examines his four retellings of the story of Abraham, focusing on the religious and the ethical. Kierkegaard claims that the killing of Isaac is ethically wrong but religiously right. Kierkegaard also uses his retelling of the Abraham story to distinguish between faith and resignation. Abraham could have been resigned to kill Isaac just because God told him to do so and because he knew that God was always right. However, Kierkegaard claims that Abraham did not act out of a resignation that God must always be obeyed but rather out of faith that God would not do something that was ethically wrong. Abraham knew that killing Isaac was ethically wrong, but he had faith that God would spare his son. Abraham decided to do something ethically wrong because having faith in God's good will was religiously right. Kierkegaard claims that the tension between ethics and religion causes Abraham anxiety.

Kierkegaard argues that his retellings of the story of Abraham demonstrate the importance of a "teleological suspension of the ethical." *Teleological* means "in regard to the end." If you are hungry and you eat something with the goal of no longer being hungry, then you made a teleological decision: you acted, by eating, in order to achieve the end of no longer being hungry. Abraham performs a teleological suspension of the ethical when he decides to kill Isaac. Abraham knows that killing Isaac is unethical. However, Abraham decides to suspend the ethical—in other words, to put ethical concerns on the back burner—because he has faith in the righteousness of the end (or *telos*) that God will bring about. Abraham's faith that God will not allow an unethical *telos* allows him to make what seems to be an unethical decision. Abraham puts religious concerns over ethical concerns, thus proving his faith in God.

Analysis

Fear and Trembling details the relationship between the ethical
and the religious in much the same way that *Either/Or* details the
relationship between the aesthetic and ethical. In *Either/Or*, the
aesthetic and the ethical are not entirely opposed. In *Fear and
Trembling*, the ethical and the religious are not directly opposed
either. However, the tension between ethics and religion produces anxiety. Abraham feels anxiety because it is his ethical duty
to spare Isaac, yet it is his religious duty to sacrifice Isaac. Ethics
are for the good of the many, and they transcend an individual's
personal aesthetic concerns, but Abraham recognizes that his
personal relationship to God transcends his social commitment
to ethics. If Abraham had desired to kill Isaac, this would have
been both immoral and irreligious. However, Abraham doesn't
decide to kill Isaac for personal aesthetic reasons or for social
ethical reasons. Abraham decides to kill Isaac because of Abraham's personal faith that God will not actually allow Isaac to die.

Kierkegaard believes that ethics are important to society but that
only an individual can approach God and that an individual can
only approach God through faith. Kierkegaard argues that Abraham's faith in God was a faith that God wouldn't really make
Abraham kill Isaac. If Abraham had not had enough faith, he
would have refused to kill his son. Abraham's faith allowed a teleological suspension of the ethical. Kierkegaard uses this story to
illustrate strong faith. Abraham's faith was tested by God, and
Abraham passed the test. In this way, Kierkegaard attempts to
draw a distinction between the blind obedience required by the
church and the true faith of the individual. Kierkegaard would
argue that if Abraham had only been willing to kill Isaac because
God ordered him to do so, this would have demonstrated obedience, not faith. Instead, the Abraham of Kierkegaard's retelling
is willing to kill Isaac because of his faith that God won't actually make him kill Isaac. This sounds like a paradox, or an
inherently contradictory situation. However, the seeming paradox highlights the distinction between faith and belief. Abraham has faith that God won't make him kill Isaac, but that
doesn't mean he believes it. To believe something is to be
assured of it; to have faith requires the possibility that you will
be proven wrong. If Abraham genuinely believed that God
wouldn't make him kill Isaac, the sacrifice would be no kind of

test. However, Abraham cannot be fully assured that his son will be spared. He must have *faith* that Isaac will not die, even though he *believes* that he must kill him.

Kierkegaard illustrates one of the essential paradoxes, or seeming impossibilities, of ethics. An ethical system consists of rules that are established to promote the welfare of large groups of people. However, sometimes the rules actually harm people, and following a rule may help one person but harm ten. Ethical systems are created to achieve certain ends, but humans lack the ability to see into the future. Therefore, no one can be completely certain of how to reach these desired ends. Faith in God answers this uncertainty because it removes the burden of prediction. Faith involves the teleological suspension of the ethical, in which faith allows one to believe that an unethical action will actually result in a better end. Humans alone have no access to this kind of information—only God does. Therefore, humans must put their trust in God whenever doing so conflicts with society's ethical systems. The decision to do this produces anxiety because a person can never know if he or she has passed the test until the test is complete. Kierkegaard thinks anxiety is a negative feeling, yet it can be taken as a positive sign that one is pursuing the correct relationship with God.

THE SICKNESS UNTO DEATH

Summary

Kierkegaard wrote *The Sickness Unto Death* under the pseudonym "Anti-Climacus"—the same pseudonym under which he wrote his other most important religious work, *Practices in Christianity*. The "sickness" in the title is despair —the sickness that everyone has until they die. Anti-Climacus defines despair primarily as a sickness of the self. He also says that everyone, whether they know it or not, is in despair. The most basic form of despair stems from not knowing you are in despair. A slightly more advanced form comes from a desire not to exist, and the most complex form of despair manifests in an attempt to escape the despair of not wanting to exist. All of these varieties of despair are caused by a tension between the infinite and the finite: Anti-Climacus claims that, although you will die and are thus finite, you also have an eternal self, which is infinite. After defining despair, Anti-Climacus questions whether it is a good or a bad thing. He comes to the conclusion that it is both. Despair is a type of suffering, so it must be bad. However, despair is a direct result of self-awareness, and increased self-awareness actually makes the self stronger. The stronger one's self, the closer one is to God. Anti-Climacus claims that only a "true Christian" can manage to live without despair. A true Christian is someone who places total faith in his or her relationship with God.

Anti-Climacus says that despair is sin and the only way to escape sin is to put complete faith in God. However, putting faith in God involves an increase of self-awareness and therefore an increase in despair. We are thus faced with the prospect that the closer to God one grows, the greater one's despair and the greater one's sin. Only by growing infinitely close to God can despair finally be defeated. The concrete sins, such as murder and stealing, arise from the sin of despair. However, to despair is the worst sin of all. This sounds like a tautology—a circular line of reasoning—but it is not. Anti-Climacus thinks of sin not as something you do but rather as something you are. All the bad things a sinner does (stealing, killing, cheating) are not sins themselves: they are the _results_ of being in sin. To despair over being in sin—in other words, to despair over being in despair—merely intensifies one's sin. The worst sin of all is to refuse forgiveness for one's sin: the only way to escape sin is to approach God with faith that forgiveness will be offered. Of course, approaching God in the first place intensifies sin. This is part of the paradox of faith.

Analysis

Much of _The Sickness Unto Death_ hangs on Kierkegaard's definition of "a self." Kierkegaard doesn't use the term the way we typically use it in everyday conversation. Kierkegaard's _self_ is not just synonymous with _person_. A self is, for Kierkegaard, a set of relations. On the simplest level, a self is a set of relations between a person and the world around him or her. A body and a brain constitute a person, but more is required for a self. The self is defined by external and internal relations. Although the idea of relating to oneself may sound contradictory, it isn't really. "A self relating to oneself" is just another way of describing self-awareness. Think of a person trying to decide whether to go running or watch TV. This is an internal conflict, and a conflict is, in essence, a relation. Different aspects of your personality are conflicting, but the conflict itself is part of what makes up the self. The will is synonymous with the self. The will binds together all of one's different aspects into a coherent whole. However, for Kierkegaard, the inability to make a choice is as much a part of one's self as the ability to make a choice. The self is the will—or possibly the lack of will. The highest and most important level of relation is not between the self and others, or the self and itself, but between the self and God.

Everyone has a self, whether they realize it or not, and having a self causes despair. Kierkegaard's notion of despair is not synonymous with unhappiness. One can be in despair and not even know it. Despair doesn't affect a *person*, it affects a self. Kierkegaard's self is similar to the common concept of the soul. Depression and unhappiness affect a person, but despair affects the self because despair is a spiritual sickness. Nonspiritual people—that is, people who don't know they have a self—suffer this sickness even though they aren't aware of it, because being unaware of one's self is the most basic form of despair. People who despair at *not* having a self are more aware of their spiritual aspect—as they at least recognize the *possibility* of having a self—but because they incorrectly believe they don't possess a self, they too suffer despair. Despairing at not having a self is like worrying that one doesn't have a coherent identity. The third kind of despair, despair at being a self, exists in someone who realizes that his or her identity is no greater than his or her relations, specifically his or her relationship to God. The closer one comes to realizing that one's self is actually just one's relation to God, the closer one comes to escaping despair.

Using his own philosophy, explain why Kierkegaard might have broken off his engagement to Regine Olsen.

Kierkegaard presents the aesthetic life and the ethical life as two competing value systems. While the two aren't always opposed, they often call for contradictory actions, and in such cases the ethical must always take precedence over the aesthetic. In *Either/Or*, marriage and bachelorhood are presented as examples of ethical and aesthetic lifestyles, respectively. Marrying Regine Olsen would have been an ethical act, so Kierkegaard must have had a reason to break it off that superseded the ethical concerns.

Kierkegaard may have believed that breaking the engagement would be more pleasurable than honoring it. Marriage is a form of repetition, and in the first part of *Either/Or* Kierkegaard claims that repetition ruins aesthetic enjoyment, which thrives on novelty, imagination, and recollection. A bachelor and confirmed aesthete, like Johannes Climacus in "The Seducer's Diary," can get far more enjoyment from thinking about past romances or imagining the possibility of future ones than from actually taking part in one.

But in the second part of *Either/Or*, the Judge stresses that aesthetic pleasure can be found in ethical choices as well. Aesthetic pleasures are solitary, whereas ethical ones are social. Climacus views romantic love as an essentially solitary endeavor. He feels pleasure by selfishly using women to feed his own imagination and recollection. This view of love, however, disregards the altruistic pleasures found in making others happy. The Judge makes it very clear that not only are there aesthetic pleasures to be had in the ethical life but that those aesthetic pleasures can even outweigh those found in the total aesthetic life.

Kierkegaard wrote both parts of *Either/Or* under pseudonyms, attributing neither part directly to himself. It stands to reason, then, that he was at least partly aware of the merits of both the bachelor life *and* the married life. Kierkegaard never actually got married, so perhaps he feared, as the wedding drew close, that his ideas about the joys of marriage were incorrect and that he would

Student Essay

lose the aesthetic pleasures he had cultivated as a bachelor. However, it is hard to believe that one who speaks so eloquently on the merits of the married life would be so uncertain of marriage's value. We are still left with the uncomfortable fact that, despite the fact that ethical considerations trump aesthetic ones, Kierkegaard committed a seemingly unethical act.

Kierkegaard, however, may not have been acting solely according to the ethical vs. aesthetic debate: he may have been applying the teleological suspension of the ethical, as described in *Fear and Trembling*. The teleological suspension of the ethical involves acting in a way that seems immediately unethical—such as breaking up with a fiancée for no obvious reason—to achieve a better end at some point in the future. Kierkegaard may have abandoned Olsen because he had faith that it would be better for both in the long run. Perhaps Kierkegaard felt that his melancholy nature would dampen Olsen's lively spirits. Maybe he worried that always having to care for her would hamper his work, thus depriving thousands of people the opportunity to benefit from his teachings.

Kierkegaard's biography seems to bear out the hypothesis that the engagement was broken off due to religious concerns. Kierkegaard's major religious works were written after breaking off his engagement with Regine Olsen, and in these he held that religion required intense degrees of introspection—the kind of introspection that could be very difficult to maintain when married. The religious life trumps both the ethical and the aesthetic life, and the religious life, Kierkegaard came to think, requires focusing as intently as possible on one's personal relationship with God. Other people could get in the way of this intense introspection. Marriage might have been a higher calling than a life devoted to aesthetic pleasure, but religion was a higher calling still.

Karl Marx

(1818–1883)

15

THEMES, ARGUMENTS & IDEAS

- Mode, Means, and Relations of Production
- Alienation
- Historical Materialism
- The Labor Theory of Value
- Commodity Fetishism

SUMMARY & ANALYSIS OF MAJOR WORKS

- Economic and Philosophic Manuscripts of 1844
- *The Manifesto of the Communist Party*
- *Capital*, Parts I–II: Commodities, the Labor Theory of Value, and Capital
- *Capital*, Parts II–V: Capital, Surplus Value, and Exploitation

Karl Marx was born in 1818 in the ancient city of Trier, in western Prussia. Marx's father was a prosperous lawyer, a Jew who converted to Lutheranism to advance his career at a time when unbaptized Jews did not have full rights of citizenship. Marx studied law at the University of Bonn and later at Berlin, where he switched to studying philosophy. He moved again to the University of Jena, where he wrote a doctoral dissertation on ancient Greek natural philosophy. Following the death of his father in 1838, Marx attempted to find a job as lecturer but ran into difficulties because of controversies surrounding his teacher and mentor Bruno Bauer (1809–1882), who had lost his professorship due to his unrepentant atheism. Marx decided instead to try journalism and became editor of the *Rhenish Gazette*, a liberal newspaper in Cologne, but the paper ran afoul of government censors and closed in 1843. Marx then married Jenny von Westphalen, the daughter of a wealthy industrialist, and moved to the more politically hospitable atmosphere of France. There he encountered another German émigré, Friedrich Engels, with whom he took up an interest in economics and class struggle.

One of Marx's most important intellectual influences was the philosophy of George Friedrich Hegel (1770–1831). Hegel's signature concept was that of the *dialectic*, a word that originally referred to the process of logical argumentation and refutation. Whereas earlier philosophers had treated dialectic as a process for arriving at true ideas, Hegel maintained that ideas themselves evolve according to a continual process of contradiction and resolution and that human history is driven by this dialectical evolution of ideas. Hegel's influence on Marx is evident in Marx's belief that history is evolving through a series of conflicts in a predictable, unavoidable direction. Hegel also influenced Marx in his characterization of the modern age. Hegel once famously declared that "man is not at home in the world," by which he meant that though human beings had achieved an unprecedented degree of personal autonomy and self-awareness in the modern age, this accomplishment had resulted in the individual's alienation from collective political and cultural institutions.

At the time of Marx's early career, socialism, an ideology advocating the abolition of private property, was gaining influence among the more politically radical European intellectuals. Although he was attracted to socialism, Marx was dissatisfied with the quality of socialist thought that he encountered in France, such as that of the utopian Socialist Saint-Simon (1760–1825). Feeling that most socialists were naïvely idealistic, Marx, following his meeting with Engels, set out to develop a theory of socialism grounded in a better understanding of both economics and philosophy. From that point on, Marx's project synthesizes these two distinct intellectual approaches, combining a Hegelian, philosophical view of historical evolution with an interest in capitalism that builds on the insights of classical economic theorists such as Adam Smith and David Ricardo.

Together with his coauthor Engels, Marx produced such important early works as *The German Ideology* (1846), which was a critique of Hegel and his German followers, and *The Communist Manifesto* (1848), in which Marx and Engels distinguish their idea of socialism from other currents of socialism and demonstrate how socialism arises naturally from the social conflicts inherent within capitalism. Shortly after the publication of *The*

Communist Manifesto, revolutionary unrest broke out in much of Europe. Although the Communist League of which Marx and Engels were leaders was in a state of disorganization, Marx took part in the the revolution in Germany as editor of a the *New Rhenish Gazette* in Cologne, which became a platform for radical political commentary. Following the unrest, Marx left Germany with his family and settled in London. The tumultuous events of 1848 and 1849 had impressed Marx deeply and formed the subject matter of later historical studies such as *The Eighteenth Brumaire of Louis Bonaparte* (1852).

While in London, Marx participated in the growing international workers' movement while working toward a new synthesis of his economic and social theories. In 1867, he published the first volume of *Capital* (*Das Kapital*), his mammoth treatise on economics. Having mastered all of the classical political–economic theorists, Marx intended in *Capital* to explain the modern class struggle in terms of economic principles. *Capital* remains Marx's greatest achievement, a powerfully insightful analysis of the nature of capitalism and its effects on human beings. Although most people no longer accept Marx's conclusion that the contradictions within capitalism will lead inevitably to a worker's revolution and the worldwide establishment of Socialism, *Capital* nonetheless remains a uniquely compelling book because of its ability to describe and explain the phenomenon of capitalism. Ironically, the proponents of capitalism are the people most likely to reject Marx as worthy of study, but it is to Marx that we owe the concept of capitalism and the perception that modern society is capitalist. (The word *capital* first acquired its importance with the publication of *Capital*.)

Themes, Arguments & Ideas

MODE, MEANS, AND RELATIONS OF PRODUCTION

Marx uses the term *mode of production* to refer to the specific organization of economic production in a given society. A mode of production includes the *means of production* used by a given society, such as factories and other facilities, machines, and raw materials. It also includes labor and the organization of the labor force. The term *relations of production* refers to the relationship between those who own the means of production (the capitalists or bourgeoisie) and those who do not (the workers or the proletariat). According to Marx, history evolves through the interaction between the mode of production and the relations of production. The mode of production constantly evolves toward a realization of its fullest productive capacity, but this evolution creates antagonisms between the classes of people defined by the relations of production—owners and workers.

Capitalism is a mode of production based on private ownership of the means of production. Capitalists produce commodities for the exchange market and to stay competitive must extract as much labor from the workers as possible at the lowest possible cost. The economic interest of the capitalist is to pay the worker as little as possible—in fact, just enough to keep him alive and productive. The worker, in turn, comes to understand that his economic interest lies in preventing the capitalist from exploiting him in this way. As this example shows, the social relations of production are inherently antagonistic, giving rise to a class struggle that Marx believes will lead to the overthrow of capitalism by the proletariat. The proletariat will replace the capitalist mode of production with a mode of production based on the collective ownership of the means of production, which is called Communism.

ALIENATION

In his early writings, which are more philosophical than economic, Marx describes how the worker under a capitalist mode of production becomes estranged from himself, from his work, and from other workers. Drawing on Hegel, Marx argues that labor is central to a human being's self-conception and sense of well-being. By working on and transforming objective matter into sustenance and objects of use-value, human beings meet the needs of existence and come to see themselves externalized in the world. Labor is as much an act of personal creation and a projection of one's identity as it is a means of survival. However, capitalism—the system of private ownership of the means of production—deprives human beings of this essential source of self-worth and identity. The worker approaches work only as a means of survival and derives none of the other personal satisfactions of work because the products of his labor do not belong to him. These products are instead expropriated by capitalists and sold for profit.

In capitalism, the worker, who is alienated or estranged from the products he creates, is also estranged from the process of production, which he regards only as a means of survival. Estranged from the production process, the worker is therefore also estranged from his or her own humanity, since the transformation of nature into useful objects is one of the fundamental facets of the human condition. The worker is thus alienated from his or her "species being"—from what it is to be human. Finally, the capitalist mode of production alienates human beings from other human beings. Deprived of the satisfaction that comes from owning the product of one's labor, the worker regards the capitalist as external and hostile. The alienation of the worker from his work and of the worker from capitalists forms the basis of the antagonistic social relationship that will eventually lead to the overthrow of capitalism.

HISTORICAL MATERIALISM

As noted previously, the writings of the German idealist philosopher Hegel had a profound impact on Marx and other philosophers of his generation. Hegel elaborated a dialectical view of human consciousness as a process of evolution from simple to more complex categories of thought. According to Hegel, human thought has evolved from very basic attempts to grasp the nature of objects to higher forms of abstract thought and self-awareness. History evolves through a similar dialectical process, whereby the contradictions of a given age give rise to a new age based on a smoothing over of these contradictions. Marx developed a view of history similar to Hegel's, but the main difference between Marx and Hegel is that Hegel is an idealist and Marx is a materialist. In other words, Hegel believed that ideas are the primary mode in which human beings relate to the world and that history

can be understood in terms of the ideas that define each successive historical age. Marx, on the other hand, believed that the
fundamental truth about a particular society or period in history
is how that society is organized to satisfy material needs. Whereas
Hegel saw history as a succession of ideas and a working out of
contradictions on a conceptual level, Marx saw history as a succession of economic systems or modes of production, each one
organized to satisfy human material needs but giving rise to
antagonisms between different classes of people, leading to the
creation of new societies in an evolving pattern.

THE LABOR THEORY OF VALUE

The labor theory of value states that the value of a commodity is
determined by the amount of labor that went into producing it
(and not, for instance, by the fluctuating relationship of supply
and demand). Marx defines a *commodity* as an external object
that satisfies wants or needs and distinguishes between two different kinds of value that can be attributed to it. Commodities
have a *use-value* that consists of their capacity to satisfy such
wants and needs. For the purposes of economic exchange, they
have an *exchange-value*—their value in relation to other commodities on the market, which is measured in terms of money. Marx
asserts that in order to determine the relative worth of extremely
different commodities with different use-values, exchange-value,
or monetary value, must be measurable in terms of a property
common to all such commodities. The only thing that all commodities have in common is that they are a product of labor.
Therefore, the value of a commodity in a market represents the
amount of labor that went into its production.

The labor theory is important in Marx's work not because it gives
special insight into the nature of prices (economists today do not
use this theory to explain why commodities are priced as they
are) but because it forms the foundation of Marx's notion of
exploitation. In the simplest form of exchange, people produce
commodities and sell them so that they can buy other commodities to satisfy their own needs and wants. In such exchanges,
money is only the common medium that allows transactions to
take place. Capitalists, in contrast, are motivated not by a need
for commodities but by a desire to accumulate money. Capitalists
take advantage of their power to set wages and working hours to

extract the greatest amount of labor from workers at the lowest possible cost, selling the products of the workers at a higher price than the capitalists paid for them. Rather than buy or sell products at their true exchange-value, as determined by the labor that went into making them, capitalists enrich themselves by extracting a "surplus-value" from their laborers—in other words, exploiting them. Marx pointed to the abject poverty of industrial workers in places like Manchester, England, for proof of the destructive effects of this exploitative relationship.

COMMODITY FETISHISM

The word *fetish* refers to any object that people fixate on or are fascinated by and that keeps them from seeing the truth. According to Marx, when people try to understand the world in which they live, they fixate on money—who has it, how is it acquired, how is it spent—or they fixate on commodities, trying to understand economics as a matter of what it costs to make or to buy a product, what the demand for a product is, and so on. Marx believed that commodities and money are fetishes that prevent people from seeing the truth about economics and society: that one class of people is exploiting another. In capitalism, the production of commodities is based on an exploitative economic relationship between owners of factories and the workers who produce the commodities. In everyday life, we think only of the market value of a commodity—in other words, its price. But this monetary value simultaneously depends upon and masks the fact that someone was exploited to make that commodity.

The concept of commodity fetishism applies both to the perceptions of normal people in everyday life and to the formal study of economics. Economists, both then and now, study the economy in terms of the movements of money, goods, and prices, which is essentially the point of view of the corporation. From this point of view, the social dimension of economic life is considered unscientific and unworthy of discussion. Marx argues that this commodity fetishism allows capitalists to carry on with day-to-day affairs of a capitalist mode of production without having to confront the real implications of the system of exploitation on which they depend.

Summary & Analysis

ECONOMIC AND PHILOSOPHIC MANUSCRIPTS OF 1844

Summary

FIRST MANUSCRIPT: "ESTRANGED LABOR" Under the economic system of private ownership, society divides itself into two classes: the property owners and the propertyless workers. In this arrangement, the workers not only suffer impoverishment but also experience an estrangement or alienation from the world. This estrangement occurs because the worker relates to the product of his work as an object alien and even hostile to himself. The worker puts his life into the object, and his labor is invested in the object, yet because the worker does not own the fruits of his labor—which in capitalism are appropriated from him—he becomes more estranged the more he produces. Everything he makes contributes to a world outside of him to which he does not belong. He shrinks in comparison to this world of objects that he helps create but does not possess. This first type of alienation is the estrangement of the worker from the product of his work.

The second type of alienation is the estrangement of the worker from the activity of production. The work that the worker performs does not belong to the worker but is a means of survival that the worker is forced to perform for someone else. As such, his working activity does not spring spontaneously from within as a natural act of creativity but rather exists outside of him and signifies a loss of his self.

The third form of alienation is the worker's alienation from "species-being," or human identity. For human beings, work amounts to a life purpose. The process of acting on and transforming inorganic matter to create things constitutes the core identity of the human being. A person is what he or she does in transforming nature into objects through practical activity. But in the modern system of private ownership and the division of labor, the worker is estranged from this essential source of identity and life purpose for the human species.

The fourth and final form of alienation is the "estrangement of man to man." Since the worker's product is owned by someone else, the worker regards this person, the capitalist, as alien and hostile. The worker feels alienated from and antagonistic toward the entire system of private property through which the capitalist appropriates both the objects of production for his own enrichment at the expense of the worker and the worker's sense of identity and wholeness as a human being.

Analysis

The 1844 Economic and Philosophical manuscripts remained unpublished during Marx's lifetime and did not surface until 1927, some forty-four years after his death. These manuscripts illustrate the young Marx's transition from philosophy to political economy (what is now called economics). Marx's emerging interest in the economy is apparent here—an interest that distinguishes him from other followers of Hegel—but his writing in these texts is much more philosophical, abstract, and speculative than his later writing. For example, the concept of species-being, of what it means to be human, is essentially a philosophical question. These manuscripts give us a glimpse into Marx's intellectual frame of reference and into the philosophical convictions that underlie his later, less explicitly philosophical work.

In the first manuscript, Marx adopts Hegel's concept of alienation, the idea that human beings can become out of sync with the world they live in, but he interprets this concept differently, arguing that alienation arises from the way human beings regard their own labor. In these early manuscripts, Marx reveals himself as the great philosopher of work, which he sees as a process of transforming physical matter (raw materials) into objects of sustenance. This process is fundamental to a person's identity and sense of place in the world, according to Marx. In capitalism, which is founded on the principle of private property, work as a source of identity and location is seriously undermined. Those without property (namely, workers in factories, etc.) must hand over their productive capacities, their essence as human beings, to another person, to the factory owners, the wealthy capitalists. This is not only inherently frustrating and unsatisfying but also turns workers against the capitalists and the system of private property that is the source of their frustration.

Summary

THIRD MANUSCRIPT: "THE MEANING OF HUMAN REQUIREMENTS" AND "CRITIQUE OF HEGELIAN DIALECTIC AND PHILOSOPHY AS A WHOLE" In a capitalist society, human needs are defined by the system of private ownership. Instead of mere food, clothing, and shelter, human beings need money. Moreover, capitalism mandates different needs for the different social classes that it creates. As capitalists accumulate wealth, their needs become increasingly more refined, even as the workers are forced to adjust their needs downward, making do with the bare minimum that the system pays them to stay alive. The modern system of ethics is shaped by the needs created by capitalism. In capitalism, self-denial becomes a cardinal virtue, with the moral ideal embodied by the miser and the thrifty worker scrimping and saving. Everything and everyone is treated in terms of utility and price. Capitalism demands that people be oriented to the world in this way simply to secure their own survival. In such a system, the worker quickly becomes conscious of his deprived and miserable status in relation to the capitalist. The solution to this situation of alienation is Communism, which does away with alienation by doing away with the system of private property that creates it.

Marx praises the philosopher Ludwig Feuerbach as the best of Hegel's followers, because of Feuerbach's demonstration that religion is a reflection of human alienation stemming from antagonistic social relationships. Marx approves of Feuerbach's criticism of Hegel for privileging religious belief, knowledge, abstract thought, and consciousness above the sensual, the real, and the material. Hegel correctly identifies labor as the essence of man but mistakenly defines labor as mental activity rather than actual physical labor. For Hegel, the dialectical process leads the mind in its search for certainty away from the world of the senses and objective reality, from nature to abstract self-awareness.

According to Hegel, the most highly evolved state of self-consciousness is a self-objectification that carries with it the experience of alienation. The function of religion, civil society, and the state is to enable the objectified, self-conscious subject to feel at home in the world. Marx sees this movement away from nature and toward a reliance on such institutions in order to ameliorate alienation as a mistake. For Marx, alienation results from estrangement from nature. In religious experience, the subject finds confirmation of his own alienation, he does not negate it. Human beings are motivated at a fundamental level by their relationship to natural objects through their senses. Their needs are sensual, and human passions stem from the excitements or frustrations of sensual desire for natural objects. This situation is the essence of human experience. Human beings seek self-realization by working on and transforming natural objects. Man is not at home in the world when this basic need does not find a proper outlet, which it lacks in capitalism. When one is estranged from nature, one is estranged from oneself.

Analysis

This manuscript is particularly dense and difficult because in it Marx is so deeply engaged in Hegelian philosophy, which is itself a difficult and abstract subject. Here we see Marx moving away from the idealism of Hegel, his main philosophical predecessor, toward the materialism that forms the bedrock of his own view of human nature and history. In these passages, Marx follows Hegel's dialectical method, beginning with the most basic concepts and abstracting toward more comprehensive ones. Marx differs from Hegel in rejecting ideas, or pure thought, as the mode through which human beings relate to the world. In Hegel's system, the mind's initial attempt to grasp at the nature of objects leads it away from the input of the senses toward more abstract concepts, to culture and religion and eventually to an objective understanding of self. Consciousness and self-consciousness represent abstractions from material reality.

In contrast, Marx argues that experience is built first and foremost around material needs and wants and that the organization of society grows out of this primary experience. In the manuscripts, this perspective leads him to focus on labor and the loss of control of one's labor as the defining moment of the modern age. In Marx's later works, this will be supplemented by an elaborated notion of exploitation.

THE MANIFESTO OF THE COMMUNIST PARTY

Summary

Marx and his coauthor, Friedrich Engels, begin *The Communist Manifesto* with the famous and provocative statement that the "history of all hitherto existing societies is the history of class struggle." They argue that all changes in the shape of society, in political institutions, in history itself, are driven by a process of collective struggle on the part of groups of people with similar economic situations in order to realize their material or economic interests. These struggles, occurring throughout history from ancient Rome through the Middle Ages to the present day, have been struggles of economically subordinate classes against economically dominant classes who opposed their economic interests—slaves against masters, serfs against landlords, and so on.

The modern industrialized world has been shaped by one such subordinate class—the bourgeoisie, or merchant class—in its struggle against the aristocratic elite of feudal society. Through world exploration, the discovery of raw materials and metals, and the opening of commercial markets across the globe, the bourgeoisie, whose livelihood is accumulation, grew wealthier and politically emboldened against the feudal order, which it eventually managed to sweep away through struggle and revolution. The bourgeoisie has risen to the status of dominant class in the modern industrial world, shaping political institutions and society according to its own interests. Far from doing away with class struggle, this once subordinate class, now dominant, has replaced one class struggle with another.

The bourgeoisie is the most spectacular force in history to date. The merchants' zeal for accumulation has led them to conquer the globe, forcing everyone everywhere to adopt the capitalist mode of production. The bourgeois view, which sees the world as one big market for exchange, has fundamentally altered all aspects of society, even the family, destroying traditional ways of life and rural civilizations and creating enormous cities in their place. Under industrialization, the means of production and exchange that drive this process of expansion and change have created a new subordinate urban class whose fate is vitally tied to that of the bourgeoisie. This class is the industrial proletariat, or modern working class. These workers have been uprooted by the expansion of capitalism and forced to sell their labor to the bourgeoisie—a fact that offends them to the core of their existence as they recall those workers of earlier ages who owned and sold what they created. Modern industrial workers are exploited by the bourgeoisie and forced to compete with one another for ever-shrinking wages as the means of production grow more sophisticated.

The factory is the arena for the formation of a class struggle that will spill over into society at large. Modern industrial workers will come to recognize their exploitation at the hands of the bourgeoisie. Although the economic system forces them to compete with one another for ever-shrinking wages, through common association on the factory floor they will overcome the divisions between themselves, realize their common fate, and begin to engage in a collective effort to protect their economic interests against the bourgeoisie. The workers will form collectivities and gradually take their demands to the political sphere as a force to be reckoned with.

Meanwhile, the workers will be joined by an ever-increasing number of the lower middle class whose entrepreneurial livelihoods are being destroyed by the growth of huge factories owned by a shrinking number of super-rich industrial elites. Gradually, all of society will be drawn to one or the other side of the struggle. Like the bourgeoisie before them, the proletariat and their allies will act together in the interests of realizing their economic aims. They will move to sweep aside the bourgeoisie and its institutions, which stand in the way of this realization. The bourgeoisie, through its established mode of production, produces the seeds of its own destruction: the working class.

Analysis

The Communist Manifesto was intended as a definitive programmatic statement of the Communist League, a German revolutionary group of which Marx and Engels were the leaders. The two men published their tract in February 1848, just months before much of Europe was to erupt in social and political turmoil, and the *Manifesto* reflects the political climate of the period. In the summer of that year, youthful revolutionary groups, along with the urban dispossessed, set up barricades in many of Europe's capitals, fighting for an end to political and economic oppression. Although dissenters had been waging war against absolutism and aristocratic privilege since the French Revolution, many of the new radicals of 1848 set their sights on a new enemy that they believed to be responsible for social instability and the growth of an impoverished urban underclass. That enemy was capitalism, the system of private ownership of the means of production. The *Manifesto* describes how capitalism divides society into two classes: the bourgeousie, or capitalists who own these means of production (factories, mills, mines, etc.), and the workers, who sell their labor power to the capitalists, who pay the workers as little as they can get away with.

Although the Communist League was itself apparently too disorganized to contribute much to the 1848 uprisings, *The Communist Manifesto* is a call to political action, containing the famous command, "Workers of the world unite!" But Marx and Engels also used the book to spell out some of the basic truths, as they saw it, about how the world works. In *The Communist Manifesto* we see early versions of essential Marxist concepts that Marx would elaborate with more scientific rigor in mature writings such as *Das Kapital*. Perhaps most important of these concepts is the theory of historical materialism, which states that historical change is driven by collective actors attempting to realize their economic aims, resulting in class struggles in which one economic and political order is replaced by another. One of the central tenets of this theory is that social relationships and political alliances form around relations of production.

Relations of production depend on a given society's mode of production, or the specific economic organization of ownership and division of labor. A person's actions, attitudes, and outlook on society and his politics, loyalties, and sense of collective belonging all derive from his location in the relations of production. History engages people as political actors whose identities are constituted as exploiter or exploited, who form alliances with others likewise identified, and who act based on these identities.

CAPITAL (DAS KAPITAL)

Summary

VOLUME I. PARTS I–II: COMMODITIES, THE LABOR THEORY OF VALUE, AND CAPITAL
Commodities are objects that satisfy human needs and wants.
Commodities are the fundamental units of capitalism, a form of
economy based on the intense accumulation of such objects. The
basic criterion for assessing a commodity's value is its essential
usefulness—what it does in the way of satisfying need and wants.
This usefulness is its use-value, a property intrinsic to the commodity. Commodities also possess an exchange-value—the relative value of a commodity in relation to other commodities in an
exchange situation. Unlike use-value, exchange-value is not
intrinsic to a commodity. Exchange-value allows one to determine what one commodity is worth in relation to another commodity, for example how many units of corn one might exchange
for a given unit of linen. In a complex market, all sorts of different commodities, though satisfying different needs and wants,
must be measurable in the same units, namely money.

Exchange-value as monetary value is what one means when one
says a commodity has "value" in a market. Marx poses the question of where this value comes from. How is it that commodities
with different use-values can be measurable in the same units?
His answer is that universal measure for value, expressed in terms
of money, corresponds to the amount of labor time that goes into
the making of each commodity. Labor time is the only thing that
all commodities with different use-values have in common and is
thus the only criterion by which they are comparable in a situation of exchange. This is Marx's labor theory of value. This theory
implies that commodities have a social dimension because their
exchange value is not intrinsic to them as objects but instead
depends on the society's entire division of labor and system of
economic interdependence, in which different people produce
different products for sale on a common market. Exchange-value
allows this market to function. As an expression the amount of
"congealed labor" in a given commodity, the value of that commodity, measured in monetary terms, always refers to the system
of social and economic interdependence in which it is produced.

Marx elaborates on the relationship between a commodity's value and its social dimension in a section on the "Fetishism of Commodities." Commodities are meaningful in two ways, first and most obvious as objects of exchange with a certain monetary value. The second, which is not so obvious and is in fact obscured by the first, is that commodities reflect not only the labor that went into making them but also the social relations of production in which the labor was performed.

This social aspect of commodities cannot express itself because in capitalist society the quality of a commodity is thought to emanate solely from its price—not from that which money expresses, namely social labor. The fact that people are moved to mistakenly reduce the quality of a commodity to money alone leads Marx to argue that modern capitalist society has invested the money-form with mystical or magical significance. Those who comment on the nature of economy—in particular bourgeois economists—reduce economics and the production and exchange of commodities to the behavior of money and, in so doing, always avoid looking at what commodities represent in social terms. As a result, the bourgeoisie is conveniently able to ignore the fact that commodities emerge through an inherently exploitative system of wage labor.

Analysis

The Labor Theory of Value is not Marx's invention; it originated with classical economist David Ricardo, who developed a labor theory of price, which states that the prices of commodities represent the labor that went into making them. However, Marx's labor theory of value differs from Ricardo's and is given a drastically different significance within the larger context of his work. Marx's focus on the nature of value is intended to show that the modern capitalist system of production and exchange is not what it seems. Although economic activity is apparently reducible to the behavior of money, to focus only on money is barely to scratch the surface. Production and exchange are social institutions, and their organization has social consequences. Capitalism, founded on a principle of private ownership, has the owners of the means of production (factories, raw materials) dependent on wage labor to create profits.

Modern economists do not accept the Labor Theory of Value as an explanation of prices, but that is not really the sense in which Marx intended the theory to be used. Marx's point is that the production of commodities is a social process, dependent on exploitation and giving rise to antagonistic relationships among classes, an idea that modern economics does not address at all.

Summary

VOLUME 1. PARTS II –V: CAPITAL, SURPLUS VALUE, AND EXPLOITATION Marx differentiates ordinary money from capital. In the simplest form of circulation of commodities, a commodity is transformed into money, which is then transformed back into a commodity as someone sells a commodity for money and then uses that money to buy a commodity they need. In this basic market arrangement, people produce commodities so that they can obtain money to buy the commodities that they need. This dynamic naturally emerges in societies with a simple division of labor, in which different people specialize in the production of different commodities. Capitalism operates in accordance with different principles. Capitalists see money not as a means of exchanging the commodities they produce for the commodities they need but as something to be sought after for its own sake. The capitalist starts with money, transforms it into commodities, then transforms those commodities into more money. Capital is money used to obtain more money. These two different arrangements are summed up respectively in the diagrams C-M-C and M-C-M (C = commodity; M = money). Capitalists are primarily interested in the accumulation of capital and not in the commodities themselves.

To increase their capital, capitalists rely on workers who put their labor power at the disposal of capitalists. Workers treat their labor power as a commodity and sell it to factory owners. The capitalist buys the workers' labor power and puts the worker to use making products. The capitalist appropriates the product, since it does not belong to the worker, and sells it on the market. Capital accumulates through the creation of surplus-value. Since a commodity's value equals the labor time congealed in it, this extra value can only come from the workers. In fact, says Marx, the capitalist forces the worker to work longer hours to generate this surplus value. The capitalist, to generate profits, must keep the working day at a certain length. Part of the day is spent generating value that keeps the workers fed and clothed, while the remainder is spent generating surplus value, which goes to the capitalist himself. This is the essence of exploitation.

The capitalist, who must submit his commodities to the exchange market at a competitive price, buys as much labor power from the worker at the lowest price possible, which is no more than the cost of keeping the worker alive. Where neither laws exist to regulate this system nor any mechanism for collective bargaining, the capitalist is in a position to decide the terms of this relationship to the detriment of the worker. For example, in industrial England prior to legislation limiting the length of the working day, workers had no power and were forced to work long days in horrible conditions for wages that barely kept them fed. This struggle over the length of the working day is illustrative of the struggles in capitalist society generally. The exploitative relationship has capitalists trying to get as much from the worker as possible and the worker trying to limit the capitalist's power to do so.

Analysis

Marx's account of the exploitative relationship of capitalist to labor remains powerfully compelling, and many believe that history has vindicated it. Essentially, Marx argues that the mechanism of exploitation built into the capitalist economic system is the source of social antagonisms that will eventually lead to the dismantling of capitalism itself. In Hegel's early writings, Marx looks to a notion of alienation, the estrangement of the worker from his humanity, to support the same prognosis. With the theory of exploitation and surplus value, Marx shifts away from philosophical language toward an economic frame of reference, while retaining a common element—the idea that the capitalist social relations of production will lead to a destruction of the capitalist mode of production. The later formulation is more effective than the earlier, as it accompanies an analysis of actual historical events rather than purely speculative thought.

Writing in exile in England, Marx was able to view firsthand the workings of the world's most advanced industrial economy. Scenes of textile laborers in industrial Manchester living in abject squalor and barely clinging to life along with the poet William

Blake's evocative and disturbing images of "dark satanic mills," impressed on many the downside of growing production and prosperity that had become evident in England and throughout much of Europe. Marx tried to show that such poverty was a permanent feature of capitalism and in fact would grow worse as capitalism advanced. With no means of defense, the working class's economic well-being is at the mercy of capitalists. But the capitalist, if he wishes to survive in a competitive market, cannot exercise mercy without endangering his enterprise. Classes grow out of this antagonistic relationship that exposes their bare economic interests. The bourgeoisie unites to defend its monopoly over workers using all the means at its disposal, including the state and even its religion. Meanwhile workers, through common association, gradually manage to unite to push back the capitalist. In England, the Parliament, through growing pressure of workers and their sympathetic advocates among the upper classes, finally decided to intervene in this exploitative relationship.

Marx predicted that modern capitalist society would eventually be replaced by international Communism. Given that such a state failed to emerge in the twentieth century—and seems unlikely to ever do so—is there any reason to keep reading Marx?

We can salvage certain aspects of Marxist theory by distinguishing between two linked, but ultimately distinct, dimensions in his work. To the extent that he was influenced by Hegel, Marx believed that history was dialectical and that the development of societies followed a pattern that was necessary and, therefore, predictable. According to this outlook, Socialism or Communism will be the final reconciliation of the dialectical contradictions in modern society. The other dimension consists of Marx's more concrete observations about the behavior of capitalist economies and the nature of exploitation and class conflict. Marx saw both dimensions as intimately related to one another, but even if we discount Marx's grand predictions about the inevitability of a proletariat revolution, we can still find much that is resonant and relevant in his analysis of capitalist societies.

Even if we accept that Marx was essentially correct about class antagonism under capitalism, we can still imagine scenarios in which these conditions would not necessarily lead to the dramatic revolution he predicted. Historical materialism's conjectures depend on the accumulation of intense social energy among the working class. However, many things can happen along the way to deflect and dissipate that energy. Take, for example, the kind of unionizing and legal reform that occurred in industrial England and that has continued to occur in many developed countries. Marx and Engels cited these amendments as the outcome of a successful working-class effort. Although labor organizations respond to and address Marxist ideologies, they may also have the effect of improving the life of the working class to such a degree as to disarm the threat of revolution. Bourgeois interests may also employ all manner of sophisticated tactics to divide the working class against itself, thereby undermining working-class solidarity. Capitalist institutions may also resort to various forms of

Student Essay

intimidation, all of which would decrease the possibility of a true revolution. Marx may have been naïve in his Hegelian view of history, as applied to modern class relations; however, though history has not borne out his predictions, it does seem to be consistently validating his essential analysis.

Societies in the twenty-first century participate in a global culture to an extent that Marx could not have foreseen, yet the situation seems to be corroborating Marx's basic analysis of the operations of capitalism. The rapid growth of communication and transportation technology makes it increasingly easy for corporations to spread labor across international borders. The relationship Marx described as existing between bourgeois owners and proletariat workers can be newly mapped onto the production system currently evolving between developed Western countries and developing non-Western countries. As corporations in the first world rely on production labor located in the third world, the gap between the two grows wider and more concrete.

The concept of alienation takes on a new intensity in the global situation, as the physical distance between workers and owners grows almost unfathomably wide. In this scenario, laborers and consumers almost never interact personally. This not only makes the worker even more alienated from his or her product, it also makes it that much easier for the capitalist consumer to ignore or erase the means of production. Dissatisfaction about the exploitative nature of these conditions grows, which has led many to speculate on the potential volatility of the current political and economic situation. If an international proletariat revolution truly emerges, it is possible that the actors in the conflict will be whole nations, not simply socioeconomic classes within individual countries.

Friedrich Nietzsche

(1844–1900)

THEMES, ARGUMENTS & IDEAS

- The Nihilism of Contemporary Europe
- The Doctrine of the Will to Power
- The Perspectivist Conception of Truth
- Christianity as a Life-Denying Force
- The Revaluation of All Values
- Man as Bridge Between Animal and Overman
- The Doctrine of the Eternal Recurrence

SUMMARY & ANALYSIS OF MAJOR WORKS

- *The Birth of Tragedy*
- *Thus Spoke Zarathustra*
- *Beyond Good and Evil*
- *On the Genealogy of Morals*

Friedrich Nietzsche was born in the small town of Röcken, Germany, in 1844. His father, a Lutheran pastor, died when Nietzsche was only four years old, and Nietzsche grew up in a family consisting of his mother, grandmother, two aunts, and a younger sister. He attended a top boarding school and studied philology at the universities of Bonn and Leipzig. He was such an exceptional student that he was offered an academic position at the University of Basel at the age of twenty-four, before he had even completed his doctorate. Around this time, he also met the great composer Richard Wagner, whom he idolized and with whom he became close friends.

Nietzsche volunteered to serve as a medical orderly in the Franco-Prussian War in 1870 and returned to Basel after having contracted dysentery, diphtheria, and perhaps syphilis. Health problems would plague him for the rest of his life. In 1872, he published his first book, The Birth of Tragedy, which met with controversy due to its unconventional style. He continued teaching at Basel until 1879, but his interest in philology waned in favor of philosophical interests. In the late 1870s, Nietzsche broke with Wagner, disgusted by the cult of personality surrounding Wagner as well as with Wagner's German nationalism and anti-Semitism.

Between 1879 and 1889, Nietzsche lived mostly in Switzerland and Italy, subsisting on a small university pension and writing furiously despite his declining health. He suffered constant migraines, insomnia, and indigestion, such that he could only read and write for a few hours each day, and his eyesight became so poor that he was partially blind. Despite these setbacks, Nietzsche wrote eleven books and thousands of pages of notebook jottings in the next ten years. Throughout this time, Nietzsche's books sold poorly, and he had only a handful of admirers.

In January 1889, Nietzsche saw a man beating his horse on the street in Turin and rushed to intervene. He collapsed in the street and never regained his sanity. He spent the last eleven years of his life as a vegetable, oblivious to his surroundings, and died in August 1900.

During his insanity, Nietzsche was cared for by his half sister, Elisabeth Förster-Nietzsche. She was married to Bernhard Förster, a prominent German nationalist and anti-Semite, whose political views she shared. Elisabeth published Nietzsche's writings selectively and used her close relationship with her brother to promote him as a kind of proto-Nazi saint. Though Nietzsche was unaware of it, he became suddenly famous during the 1890s, and by the time of his death he was a national celebrity. Due to his sister's influence, however, he was frequently and wrongly associated with the politics of the Nazi party, and it was only after the Second World War that his reputation was cleared.

Nietzsche lived during a time of rising German nationalism. After the Franco-Prussian War of 1870–1871, Germany was united for the first time as a single empire. The brutish nationalism and anti-Semitism that Nietzsche derides in his writings are precisely the sentiments that led Germany into two world wars.

Nietzsche also lived at a time when the scientific spirit was triumphant in the West. Physicists of the late nineteenth century were confident that they had essentially settled all the major questions their discipline had to offer, the social sciences were coming into their own, and Darwin's theory of evolution was making great waves in all variety of fields.

Despite the optimism his countrymen felt at Germany's rise as a world power and the triumph of the sciences, Nietzsche characterized his age as nihilistic. The scientific worldview does not require God, and while most Europeans were still practicing Christians, Nietzsche recognized that "God is dead": Christianity had given way to science as the primary means of making sense of the world. However, science is avowedly value-neutral: it had replaced Christianity without introducing any new values. As a result, Nietzsche saw a great void opening up in the realm of human values, which was in danger of being filled by narrow-minded nationalism. Much of his writing is concerned with this crisis in values that most of his contemporaries did not even recognize.

As a trained philologist, Nietzsche knew the Greek and Roman classics backward and forward. However, his philosophical tastes were atypical. He rarely mentions Aristotle, and he is mostly contemptuous of Plato. His attitude toward Socrates is more complex but mostly negative. Instead, he prefers Heraclitus, a pre-Socratic philosopher famous for the doctrine that one cannot step into the same river twice. Heraclitus contends that everything is in flux, such that we cannot make any fixed claims about any aspect of reality.

Nietzsche first became fascinated by philosophy when he read Arthur Schopenhauer's *The World As Will and Representation.* Schopenhauer argues that reality has two different aspects. The first is the "world as representation," which is the world as it appears to the senses. The second is the "world as will," which lies behind the senses. According to Schopenhauer, the world as will is the real world, and we must look behind appearances to see the wills at work in nature. Schopenhauer was also the first major Western philosopher to take seriously the philosophies of India, and it is thanks to Schopenhauer that we find Nietzsche conversant in the main ideas of Hinduism and Buddhism.

While Nietzsche drew some influence from thinkers, such as Heraclitus and Schopenhauer, and drew much negative influence from many other thinkers, most notably Plato, Kant, and the Christian tradition, he does not belong to any tradition.

CHAPTER 16
NIETZSCHE

Nietzsche is as much of an oddball as can be found among the great philosophers.

His peculiarities have not kept him from being tremendously influential in the twentieth century, however. Those philosophers who stand in his debt read as a "who's who" of twentieth-century continental philosophy: Jaspers, Heidegger, Sartre, Derrida, and Foucault, just to name a few. More than perhaps any other philosopher, Nietzsche has had a profound impact on literature and other fields. Joyce, Yeats, Freud, Shaw, and Mann are only some of the major thinkers deeply indebted to Nietzsche. In his preface to *The Antichrist*, Nietzsche writes, "Only the day after tomorrow belongs to me. Some are born posthumously." Given that Nietzsche was largely ignored while he wrote, and given his tremendous influence on twentieth-century thought, we can only conclude that Nietzsche was right on that count, and that he was, in a sense, born posthumously.

Themes, Arguments & Ideas

THE NIHILISM OF CONTEMPORARY EUROPE

While most of his contemporaries looked on the late nineteenth century with unbridled optimism, confident in the progress of science and the rise of the German state, Nietzsche saw his age facing a fundamental crisis in values. With the rise of science, the Christian worldview no longer held a prominent explanatory role in people's lives—a view Nietzsche captures in the phrase "God is dead." However, science does not introduce a new set of values to replace the Christian values it displaces. Nietzsche rightly foresaw that people need to identify some source of meaning and value in their lives, and if they could not find it in science, they would turn to aggressive nationalism and other such salves. The last thing Nietzsche would have wanted was a return to traditional Christianity, however. Instead, he sought to find a way out of nihilism through the creative and willful affirmation of life.

THE DOCTRINE OF THE WILL TO POWER

On one level, the will to power is a psychological insight: our fundamental drive is for power as realized in independence and dominance. This will is stronger than the will to survive, as martyrs willingly die for a cause if they feel that associating themselves with that cause gives them greater power. Likewise, it is stronger than the will to sex, as monks willingly renounce sex for the sake of a greater cause. While the will to power can manifest itself through violence and physical dominance, Nietzsche is more interested in the sublimated will to power, in which people turn their will to power inward and pursue self-mastery rather than mastery over others. An Indian mystic, for instance, who submits himself to all sorts of physical deprivation gains profound self-control and spiritual depth, representing a more refined form of power than the power gained by the conquering barbarian.

On a deeper level, the will to power explains the fundamental, changing aspect of reality. According to Nietzsche, everything is in flux, and there is no such thing as fixed being. Matter is always moving and changing, as are ideas, knowledge, truth, and everything else. The will to power is the fundamental engine of this change. For Nietzsche, the universe is primarily made up not of facts or things but rather of wills. The idea of the human soul or ego is just a grammatical fiction, according to Nietzsche. What we call "I" is really a chaotic jumble of competing wills, constantly struggling to overcome one another. Because change is a fundamental aspect of life, Nietzsche considers any point of view that takes reality to be fixed and objective—be it religious, scientific, or philosophical—to be life denying. A truly life-affirming philosophy embraces change and recognizes in the will to power that change is the only constant in the world.

THE PERSPECTIVIST CONCEPTION OF TRUTH

Nietzsche is critical of the very idea of objective truth. That we should think there is only one right way of considering a matter is only evidence that we have become inflexible in our thinking. Such intellectual inflexibility is a symptom of saying "no" to life, a condition that Nietzsche abhors. A healthy mind is flexible and recognizes that there are many different ways of considering a matter. There is no single truth but rather many.

At this point, interpreters of Nietzsche differ. Some argue that Nietzsche believes there is such a thing as truth but that there is no single correct perspective on it. Just as we cannot get the full picture of what an elephant is like simply by looking at its leg or looking at its tail or looking at its trunk, we cannot get a reasonable picture of any truth unless we look at it from multiple perspectives. Others, particularly those who value Nietzsche's early essay "On Truth and Lies in a Nonmoral Sense," argue that Nietzsche believes the very idea of "truth" to be a lie. Truth is not an elephant that we must look at from multiple perspectives under this view. Rather, truth is simply the name given to the point of view of the people who have the power to enforce their point of view. The only reality is the will to power, and truth, like morality, is just another fig leaf placed on top of this reality.

CHRISTIANITY AS A LIFE-DENYING FORCE

Throughout his work, particularly in *The Antichrist*, Nietzsche writes scathingly about Christianity, arguing that it is fundamentally opposed to life. In Christian morality, Nietzsche sees an attempt to deny all those characteristics that he associates with healthy life. The concept of sin makes us ashamed of our instincts and our sexuality, the concept of faith discourages our curiosity and natural skepticism, and the concept of pity encourages us to value and cherish weakness. Furthermore, Christian morality is based on the promise of an afterlife, leading Christians to devalue this life in favor of the beyond. Nietzsche argues that Christianity springs from resentment for life and those who enjoy it, and it seeks to overthrow health and strength with its life-denying ethic. As such, Nietzsche considers Christianity to be the hated enemy of life.

THE REVALUATION OF ALL VALUES

As the title of one of his books suggests, Nietzsche seeks to find a place "beyond good and evil." One of Nietzsche's fundamental achievements is to expose the psychological underpinnings of morality. He shows that our values are not themselves fixed and objective but rather express a certain attitude toward life. For example, he argues that Christian morality is fundamentally resentful and life-denying, devaluing natural human instincts and promoting weakness and the idea of an afterlife, the importance of which supersedes that of our present life. Nietzsche's aim is not so much to replace Christian morality with another morality but rather to expose the very concept of morality as being a fig leaf placed on top of our fundamental psychological drives to make them seem more staid and respectable. By exposing morality as a fiction, Nietzsche wants to encourage us to be more honest about our drives and our motives and more realistic in the attitude we take toward life. Such honesty and realism, he contends, would cause a fundamental "revaluation of all values." Without morality, we would become an entirely different species of being, and a healthier species of being at that.

MAN AS BRIDGE BETWEEN ANIMAL AND OVERMAN

Nietzsche contends that humanity is a transition, not a destination. We ceased to be animals when we taught ourselves to control our instincts for the sake of greater gains. By learning to resist some of our natural impulses, we have been able to forge civilizations, develop knowledge, and deepen ourselves spiritually. Rather than directing our will to power outward to dominate those around us, we have directed it inward and gained self-mastery. However, this struggle for self-mastery is arduous, and humanity is constantly tempted to give up. Christian morality and contemporary nihilism are just two examples of worldviews that express the desire to give up on life. We come to see life as blameworthy or meaningless as a way of easing ourselves out of the struggle for self-mastery. Nietzsche's concept of the overman is the destination toward which we started heading when we first reined in our animal instincts. The overman has the self-mastery that animals lack but also the untrammeled instincts and good conscience that humans lack. The overman is profoundly in love with life, finding nothing in it to complain about, not even the constant suffering and struggle to which he willingly submits himself.

THE DOCTRINE OF THE ETERNAL RECURRENCE

While it is hard to give a definitive account of the eternal recurrence, we can undoubtedly claim that it involves a supreme affirmation of life. On one level, it expresses the view that time is cyclical and that we will live every moment of our lives over and over an infinite number of times, each time exactly the same. In other words, each passing moment is not fleeting but rather echoes for all eternity. Nietzsche's ideal is to be able to embrace the eternal recurrence and live in affirmation of this idea. In other words, we should aim to live conscious of the fact that each moment will be repeated infinitely, and we should feel only supreme joy at the prospect.

On another level, the doctrine of the eternal recurrence involves Nietzsche's distinctive metaphysical notions. Nietzsche contends that there is no such thing as being: everything is always changing, always in a state of becoming. Because nothing is fixed, there are no "things" that we can distinguish and set apart from other "things." All of reality is intertwined, such that we cannot pass judgment on one aspect of reality without passing judgment on all of reality. In other words, we cannot feel regret for one aspect of our lives and joy for another because these two aspects of our lives cannot properly be distinguished from one another. In recognizing that all of life is one indistinguishable swirl of becoming, we are faced with the simple choice of saying *yes* to all life or *no* to all life. Naturally, Nietzsche contends that the *yes*-saying attitude is preferable.

Summary & Analysis

Summary

Artistic creation depends on a tension between two opposing forces, which Nietzsche terms the "Apollonian" and the "Dionysian." Apollo is the Greek god of light and reason, and Nietzsche identifies the Apollonian as a life- and form-giving force, characterized by measured restraint and detachment, which reinforces a strong sense of self. Dionysus is the Greek god of wine and music, and Nietzsche identifies the Dionysian as a frenzy of self-forgetting in which the self gives way to a primal unity in which individuals are at one with others and with nature. Both the Apollonian and the Dionysian are necessary in the creation of art. Without the Apollonian, the Dionysian lacks the form and structure to make a coherent piece of art, and without the Dionysian, the Apollonian lacks the necessary vitality and passion. Although they are diametrically opposed, they are also intimately intertwined.

Nietzsche suggests that the people of ancient Greece were unusually sensitive and susceptible to suffering and that they refined the Apollonian aspect of their nature to ward off suffering. The primal unity of the Dionysian brings us into direct apprehension of the suffering that lies at the heart of all life. By contrast, the Apollonian is associated with images and dreams, and hence with appearances. Greek art is so beautiful precisely because the Greeks relied on the appearances generated by images and dreams to shield themselves from the reality of suffering. The early, Doric period of Greek art is dull and prim because the Apollonian influence too heavily outweighs the Dionysian.

The Greek tragedies of Aeschylus and Sophocles, which Nietzsche considers to be among humankind's greatest accomplishments, achieve their sublime effects by taming Dionysian passions by means of the Apollonian. Greek tragedy evolved out of religious rituals featuring a chorus of singers and dancers, and it achieved its distinctive shape when two or more actors stood apart from the chorus as tragic actors. The chorus of a Greek tragedy is not the "ideal spectator," as some scholars believe, but rather the representation of the primal unity achieved through the Dionysian. By witnessing the fall of a tragic hero, we witness the death of the individual, who is absorbed back into the Dionysian primal unity. Because the Apollonian impulses of the Greek tragedians give form to the Dionysian rituals of music and dance, the death of the hero is not a negative, destructive act but rather a positive, creative affirmation of life through art.

Unfortunately, the golden age of Greek tragedy lasted less than a century and was brought to an end by the combined influence of Euripides and Socrates. Euripides shuns both the primal unity induced by the Dionysian and the dreamlike state induced by the Apollonian, and instead he turns the Greek stage into a platform for morality and rationality. Rather than present tragic heroes, Euripides gives his characters all the foibles of ordinary human beings. In all these respects, Nietzsche sees Socrates' influence on Euripides. Socrates effectively invented Western rationality, insisting that there must be reasons to justify everything. He interpreted instinct as a lack of insight and wrongdoing as a lack of knowledge. By making the world seem knowable and all truths justifiable, Socrates gave birth to the scientific worldview. Under Socrates' influence, Greek tragedy was converted into rational conversation, which finds its fullest expression in Plato's dialogues.

The modern world has inherited Socrates' rationalistic stance at the expense of losing the artistic impulses related to the Apollonian and the Dionysian. We now see knowledge as worth pursuing for its own sake and believe that all truths can be discovered and explained with enough insight. In essence, the modern, Socratic, rational, scientific worldview treats the world as something under the command of reason rather than something greater than what our rational powers can comprehend. We inhabit a world dominated by words and logic, which can only see the surfaces of things, while shunning the tragic world of music and drama, which cuts to the heart of things. Nietzsche distinguishes three kinds of culture: the Alexandrian, or Socratic; the Hellenic, or artistic; and the Buddhist, or tragic. We belong to an Alexandrian culture bound for self-destruction.

The only way to rescue modern culture from self-destruction is to resuscitate the spirit of tragedy. Nietzsche sees hope in the figure of Richard Wagner, who is the first modern composer to create music that expresses the deepest urges of the human will, unlike most contemporary opera, which reflects the smallness of the modern mind. Wagner's music was anticipated by Arthur Schopenhauer, who saw music as a universal language that makes sense of experience at a more primary level than concepts, and Immanuel Kant, whose philosophy exposes the limitations of Socratic reasoning. Not coincidentally, Wagner, Schopenhauer, and Kant all are German, and Nietzsche looks to German culture to create a new golden age.

We have no direct understanding of myth anymore but always mediate the power of myth through various rationalistic concepts, such as morality, justice, and history. So far, the tremendous influence of Greek culture has done very little to shift our own culture's opposition to art because we tend to interpret the Greeks according to our own standards and read tragedies as expressions of moral, rational forces rather than expressions of the mythic forces of the Apollonian and the Dionysian. Myth gives us a sense of wonder and a fullness of life that our present culture lacks. Nietzsche urges a return to our deeper selves, which are entwined in myth, music, and tragedy.

Analysis

Nietzsche's concept of the Dionysian, which he refines and alters over the course of his career, stands as a pointed counterbalance to the thoroughgoing rationality that is so prominent in most philosophy. In most scholarly investigations, the importance of truth and knowledge are taken as givens, and thinkers trouble themselves only over questions of how best to achieve truth and knowledge. By contrast, Nietzsche questions where this drive for truth and knowledge come from and answers that they are products of a particular, Socratic view of the world. Deeper than this impulse for truth is the Dionysian impulse to give free rein to the passions and to lose oneself in ecstatic frenzy. We cannot properly appreciate or criticize the Dionysian from within a tradition of rationality because the Dionysian stands outside rationality. As much as the civilized world may wish to deny it, the Dionysian is the source of our myths, our passions, and our instincts, none of which are bounded by reason. Though the civilizing force of the Apollonian is an essential counterbalance—contrary to some stereotypes of Nietzsche, he is firmly against the complete aban-

CHAPTER 16
NIETZSCHE

donment of reason and civilization—Nietzsche warns that we lose the deepest and richest aspects of our nature if we reject the Dionysian forces within us.

For Nietzsche, art is not just a form of human activity but is rather the highest expression of the human spirit. The thrust of the book is well expressed in what is perhaps its most famous line, near the end of section 5: "it is only as an *aesthetic phenomenon* that existence and the world are eternally *justified*." One of Nietzsche's concerns in *The Birth of Tragedy* is to address the question of the best stance to take toward existence and the world. He criticizes his own age (though his words apply equally to the present day) for being overly rationalistic, for assuming that it is best to treat existence and the world primarily as objects of knowledge. For Nietzsche, this stance makes life meaningless because knowledge and rationality in themselves do nothing to justify existence and the world. Life finds meaning, according to Nietzsche, only through art. Art, music, and tragedy in particular bring us to a deeper level of experience than philosophy and rationality. Existence and the world become meaningful not as objects of knowledge but as artistic experiences. According to Nietzsche, art does not find a role in the larger context of life, but rather life takes on meaning and significance only as it is expressed in art.

By attacking Socrates, Nietzsche effectively attacks the entire tradition of Western philosophy. Although a significant group of Greek philosophers predate Socrates, philosophy generally identifies its start as a distinctive discipline in Socrates' method of doubt, dialogue, and rational inquiry. While Nietzsche acknowledges that Socrates gave birth to a new and distinctive tradition, he is more interested in the tradition that Socrates managed to replace. Greek tragedy as Nietzsche understands it cannot coexist with a world of Socratic rationality. Tragedy gains its strength from exposing the depths that lie beneath our rational surface, whereas Socrates insists that we become fully human only by becoming fully rational. From Socrates onward, philosophy has been the pursuit of wisdom by rational methods. In suggesting that rational methods cannot reach to the depths of human experience, Nietzsche suggests that philosophy is a shallow pursuit. True wisdom is not the kind that can be processed by the thinking mind, according to

Nietzsche. We find true wisdom in the Dionysian dissolution of the self that we find in tragedy, myth, and music.

Nietzsche wrote *The Birth of Tragedy* at a time when he was most heavily under Wagner's influence. Nietzsche had met Wagner as a young man and was deeply honored when Wagner chose to befriend him. Wagner impressed his own views on life and art on Nietzsche, and *The Birth of Tragedy* is in many ways a philosophical justification for the work Wagner was carrying out in his operas. Over the course of the 1870s, however, Nietzsche became increasingly disillusioned with Wagner, and his mature works, starting with *Human, All-Too-Human*, show Nietzsche finding his own distinctive voice, free from Wagner's influence. In particular, Nietzsche became disgusted with Wagner's shallow pro-German nationalism and his anti-Semitism. In contrast to Nietzsche's later biting attacks on nationalism, *The Birth of Tragedy* bears Wagner's influence in its pride in German culture and its hope that a purified German culture can rescue European civilization from the deadening influence of Socratic rationalism.

THUS SPOKE ZARATHUSTRA

Summary

Zarathustra goes into the wilderness at the age of thirty and enjoys his freedom and solitude so much that he remains there ten years. Finally, he decides to return to society and share his wisdom. On his way down from his mountain, he encounters a saint, who has devoted his life to God. Zarathustra is startled that this man has not heard that God is dead. Zarathustra then descends into the town and preaches about the overman. Man, Zarathustra claims, is only a bridge between animals and the overman, and we must hasten the arrival of the overman by being faithful to this world and this life and abandoning the values that lead us to distrust them. Zarathustra also warns about the "last man," who is afraid of everything extreme and dangerous and lives a life of contented mediocrity. The people in the town are not very receptive to Zarathustra's teaching, so he resolves to seek out like-minded individuals who might break away from the herd rather than preach to the herd itself.

Zarathustra gives a number of sermons in a town called the Motley Cow. He emphasizes the struggle and suffering necessary to become a stronger person and encourages people to embrace this struggle and suffering cheerfully. He characterizes the progress toward the overman as proceeding through three stages. First is the stage of the camel, in which we renounce comfort and discipline ourselves harshly. Second is the stage of the lion, in which we defiantly assert our independence. Third is the stage of the child, in which we find a new innocence and creativity. Achieving this stage is like reaching the summit of a mountain: we can look down on everything around us and find lightness and laughter rather than seriousness and struggle. To become overmen, we must isolate ourselves from the mob. Our only companions should be friends who provide us not with comfort but with a constant goad to improve ourselves. The goal of the overman is to create his own values. To date, there have been a thousand peoples with a thousand different conceptions of good and evil. Each race's conception of good expresses the will to power of that race, or the goals it hopes to achieve. Everyone must obey something, and if one cannot command oneself, one will be commanded by others. The overman has sufficient will to power to create his own good and evil.

Zarathustra also preaches against those who promote ideas that are contrary to life. His primary target is religion, which focuses on the spirit and the afterlife. We are creatures of flesh and blood, and those who wish to turn attention elsewhere are fundamentally opposed to life. Meekness and pity are the virtues of the weak, promoted by those who resent the power of the strong. There is no virtue in being meek if one is too weak to be capable of being otherwise. Zarathustra praises the three things religion condemns the most: sex, the lust to rule, and selfishness. All three, when pursued with a good conscience, are celebrations of one's life and power. Religion, however, is not the only threat to leading a free and healthy life: the state, too, tries to mold people into a mediocre mob, and the egalitarian spirit of democracy is bred from the same resentment and hatred of life as religion.

Zarathustra asserts that life and wisdom are like dancing women: constantly changing, always seductive. Those with healthy attitude toward life and truth enjoy their constantly changing nature. People who see truth as fixed have grown tired of life. The only constant that Zarathustra can identify in his own life is his will: its constant drive to improve him and re-create him has changed every other aspect of him.

Zarathustra struggles to confront the idea of the eternal recurrence. If time is infinite, he reasons, then the present moment must have occurred in just this way an infinite number of times in the past and will recur an infinite number of times in the future. Therefore, each passing moment is not fleeting but is bound to be repeated eternally. It takes tremendous courage to accept the full implications of this idea. Zarathustra is troubled, for instance, by the thought that humanity in all its mediocrity will be repeated through eternity. Ultimately, he learns to accept the eternal recurrence joyfully, proclaiming, "I love you, O eternity!"

In book 4, Zarathustra encounters nine characters, each of whom has some obvious flaws but also shows potential for greatness. Zarathustra directs these characters one by one to his cave in the highest mountain. He then meets them in his cave where they have a "last supper," at which Zarathustra preaches to them about the overman. Now that God is dead, man is something that must be overcome, and this self-overcoming requires courage, evil, self-motivation, suffering, and solitude. Despite the difficulty of the task, the overman himself is characterized by lightness, enjoying laughter and dancing. Stepping into the evening air, Zarathustra sings a song out of a feeling of complete satisfaction with his life. Because all things are interconnected, our suffering and our joy are inseparable. We cannot wish for joy without also wishing for suffering. In this, Zarathustra finds a positive affirmation of all life.

The next morning, Zarathustra steps out of his cave and sees a lion. He takes this as a sign that the overman is coming. He leaves his cave with the triumphant feeling that he has overcome his last weakness: pity for the higher man.

Analysis

Thus Spoke Zarathustra is one of the strangest books ever to achieve the status of a classic and represents Nietzsche's boldest attempt to find a literary form appropriate to his revolutionary ideas. Zarathustra, known more commonly by his Greek name, Zoroaster, was an ancient Persian prophet who was the first to preach that the universe is engaged in a fundamental struggle between good and evil. Nietzsche appropriates Zarathustra because, as he explains in *Ecce Homo,* "Zarathustra created this most calamitous error, morality; consequently, he must also be the first to recognize it." Through Zarathustra, Nietzsche tries to preach a nobler alternative to the Judeo-Christian worldview. Throughout the text, we find Nietzsche playfully subverting elements from the Old and New Testaments, particularly in reference to the life and ministry of Jesus. For example, at the age of thirty, Jesus spends forty days in the wilderness being tempted by the devil. By contrast, Zarathustra happily spends ten years in the wilderness, suggesting that he is more cheerful in spirit and less needful of others. We also see Zarathustra preaching against "the herd," whereas Jesus portrays himself as a shepherd leading a flock, and toward the end we find a parody of the last supper.

We should be careful not to mistake Nietzsche's criticism of Christianity, and particularly his proclamation that "God is dead," for smug atheism. Certainly, Nietzsche has a great deal of venom to expend on Christianity, but he is perhaps even more troubled by the spiritless atheism that he fears will follow it. The claim that God is dead is more of a sociological observation than a metaphysical declaration. Christian morality and its attendant concepts of good and evil no longer have such a powerful hold on our culture as they once did. Nietzsche worries that the world is being increasingly consumed by nihilism, the abandonment of all beliefs. He expresses this worry in the figure of the last man, who represents the triumph of science and materialism. Nietzsche would likely recognize in early twenty-first century consumer culture a perfect expression of the last man, as we direct our tremendous wealth and power to insulating ourselves from all risks and passions. Zarathustra preaches about the overman not so much to replace Christianity as to fill the void that opens in a culture in which fundamental values are eroding.

The overman, sometimes translated as "superman" or rendered in the original German as *Übermensch,* is Nietzsche's ideal of a creative, independent, spiritual genius. The overman is often misconceived as any person who has an independent and revolutionary attitude toward ethics or politics, such as a Thomas Jefferson or Martin Luther King, Jr. Most likely, Nietzsche would have criticized these two figures, the first for advocating democracy and the second for advocating Christianity. Nietzsche dislikes both democracy and Christianity for the way they promote equality and defend the weakest in a society. Nietzsche instead has Zarathustra invoke a system of values in which the strongest and most original in a society can rise above the masses and shine. A great artist, then, is a closer approximation to the overman than a political leader. As expressed in the figures of the camel, the lion, and the child, an overman sets aside the values and assumptions he was raised with and develops his own creative vision of the world, much like an artist. However, the overman is more than just an artist in that his creativity is not limited to the page or the canvas. The overman's work of art is his own life, which he forges and lives according to his own creative will.

The will to power, which lies at the heart of Nietzsche's concept of the superman and of his mature philosophy generally, is the supreme drive behind all life. Contrary to alternative views—for instance, that we are fundamentally driven by sex or the need for survival—Nietzsche believes that all life is driven by a lust for power. Barbarians might express this will to power by raping and pillaging, whereas Christians might express it by turning the other cheek and showing that they have enough self-mastery to swallow their vengeful instincts, but the principle is the same. In all cases, living things do what they can to assert their power over themselves and over the world around them. Everyone has a will to power, but some have a healthier will to power than others. Nietzsche would criticize a barbarian's will to power for not exhibiting enough self-mastery and a Christian's will to power for being mistrustful of our natural instincts. The overman exhibits a supremely healthy will to power. He celebrates his strength of spirit, is free from guilt and resentment, and is profoundly in love with life.

The doctrine of the eternal recurrence is the profoundly life-affirming lynchpin of Nietzsche's philosophy. The idea is based on the supposition that if there is only a finite amount of matter in the universe, there are only a finite number of arrangements of that matter, so if time is infinite, each arrangement of matter will be repeated an infinite number of times. The idea as Zarathustra expresses it is logically unsound. Even assuming that there is a finite amount of matter and an infinite amount of time, there are still infinitely many possible configurations of matter, so it is by no means necessary that any given moment, let alone all moments, must repeat itself. However, Nietzsche's main interest in the eternal recurrence is the theoretical one of how a person would come to terms with this doctrine. In a sense, the eternal recurrence is a kind of litmus test for a potential overman. Faced with the prospect that every moment in one's life will echo for eternity, only an overman would rejoice. Only an overman is so in love with life that he would not take back a single moment.

BEYOND GOOD AND EVIL

Summary

Nietzsche opens with the provocative question, "Supposing truth is a woman—what then?" Then truth would need to be cajoled and flattered, not pursued with the tactless dogmatism of most philosophers. However, although philosophy must overcome its dogmatic thinking, it has at least provided our culture with the tension to spring forward into something new and better. Nietzsche catalogs a number of the dogmatisms inherent in philosophy, such as the separation of ideas into binary opposites like truth and falsehood; "immediate certainties," like Descartes' certainty that he is thinking; and the idea of free will. Philosophy is interested in giving us insight not into truth but into the minds of the different philosophers. Everything is governed by a will to power, and in philosophy, we see great minds trying to impose their will on the world by persuading others to see the world as they see it.

The will to power is the fundamental drive in the universe. Behind truth, thought, and morality lie drives and passions that we try to mask behind a veneer of calm objectivity. What we call truth, for instance, is just the expression of our will to power, in which we declare our particular perspective on reality to be objectively and universally true. Ultimately, all reality is best understood in terms of competing wills. Nietzsche praises "free spirits" who struggle to free themselves from the prejudices of others and to question their own assumptions. In particular, they will look beneath the "moral" worldview that examines people's motives and perceive instead the "extra-moral" worldview that examines the unconscious drives that determine our expressed motives.

Nietzsche characterizes his age as atheistic but religious. He identifies the religious spirit with a willingness to sacrifice, to assert one's power by submitting oneself to torture. In primitive societies, people sacrificed others, whereas the people of more advanced cultures sacrificed themselves through self-denial. The Christians went one step further in sacrificing God himself. While Europe is still nominally Christian, Nietzsche suggests that its faith in God has been replaced by a faith in science. He warns that this faith in science leads to nihilism and that we must find something more spiritually affirming.

Nietzsche traces our spiritual decline to the rise of Christianity, which he calls the "slave revolt in morality." Because most people are unable to handle the darker aspects of their natures, and we would be less safe if all people gave free rein to the violence and sensuality within them, Christianity declares that only meekness and timidity are holy and condemns these other things as evil. By majority rule, Christian morality condemns us to prefer tame, peaceful lives. Even in an atheistic age, this egalitarian spirit lives on in democracy. Nietzsche longs for a generation of "new philosophers" who can rescue us from our mediocrity. These philosophers will differ markedly from the "philosophical laborers" and scholars of the universities, who work to find new knowledge but lack the creative spirit to do anything with it. Nietzsche's new philosophers will rebel against the values and assumptions of their day and will have the strength of will and creativity to affirm something new.

Rather than think on egalitarian lines that the same rules apply to all people, Nietzsche argues that there is an "order of rank," among both people and philosophies. Some people simply have stronger and more refined spirits than others, and to hold those people to the same rules is to hold them back. Pity is just a refined form of self-contempt, whereby we show preference for weakness.

As a race, we have never lost our instinct for cruelty but have only refined it. We are unique among animals in being both creatures and creators, and the strongest among us turn our instinct for cruelty against ourselves. The creator within us reshapes the creature that we are by violently attacking its weaknesses. Suffering, then, is essential to growing stronger, and we must struggle constantly to remake ourselves by assailing our weaknesses and prejudices. However, at heart, we have certain stupid convictions and assumptions that we simply cannot change. As if to prove his point, Nietzsche launches a diatribe about how he hates women.

Nietzsche criticizes the narrow nationalism of many Europeans and praises the idea of the "good European," who foreshadows the future uniting of Europe. He discusses a number of different races, reserving particular venom for the English. He has high praise for the Jews, saying that though their religion is responsible for the slave morality that afflicts Europe, they also carry tremendous creative energy.

Modern culture is defined by a tension between two kinds of morality. Master morality comes from the aristocratic view that whatever one is and likes is good and whatever one dislikes and is unlike one is bad. Slave morality, by contrast, comes from a resentment of the power of the masters: slaves see masters as evil and see themselves, in their weakness and poverty, as good. Thus, the master's "good" is the slave's "evil," and the master's "bad" is the slave's "good."

Nietzsche believes that aristocratic nature is to some degree bred into us, so that some of us are simply born better off than others, and that society as a whole thrives with a strong aristocratic class. He suggests, however, that genius is perhaps not as rare as we suppose. What is rare is the self-mastery to remove oneself from others and discipline oneself to the point that one can refine one's genius. Nietzsche closes the prose section of his book by lamenting that all his thoughts seem so dead and plain on paper. Language can only capture ideas that are fixed in place: the liveliest thoughts are free and constantly changing, and so they cannot be put into words. The book closes with a poem in which the speaker has climbed a high mountain and awaits like-minded friends to join him.

Analysis

For Nietzsche, change is the predominant feature of reality. Everything is always changing: not just matter and energy but also ideas, wills, and hence truth. Philosophy and science tend to see the world as primarily made up of facts and things that we can observe and regulate, providing the illusion of stable, objective truths. Nietzsche rejects this metaphysics of facts and things, suggesting instead that the world is primarily made up of wills—some conscious and some unconscious—that constantly compete for dominance. Whatever we see as "true" at a given moment is not objectively so but rather represents the victory of a particular will over the others working within us. Nietzsche's main targets, from Christianity to science to democracy to traditional philosophy, are all guilty in one way or another of denying or avoiding the fact that reality is composed of a constantly shifting competition among wills. They wish to see the universe as fixed—whether by divine law or the laws of nature—and wish to slacken the struggle and competition that characterize existence. Nietzsche sees any effort to resist struggle and change as contrary to life.

While Nietzsche's account of the will to power applies to everything in existence, the concept is easiest to grasp if we think of it in terms of an inner struggle. We all live according to certain assumptions or fundamental beliefs, some more obvious than others. One person may hold fundamentalist religious views, while another may cling unquestioningly to the assumption that democracy is the best political system. For Nietzsche, the question of whether these assumptions and beliefs are true or false, just or unjust, is not an issue. What matters is that all beliefs and assumptions represent our identity—they are the bedrock from which we build ourselves.

The greatest power that we can have is power over ourselves, and we gain power over ourselves in the same way we gain power over external enemies: by attacking them and submitting them to our will. Strong-willed people, whom Nietzsche often refers to as free spirits, are always ready to attack their fundamental beliefs and assumptions, to question their very identity. There is great safety in resting assured that certain truths or beliefs are beyond question, and it takes great courage to question our fundamental "truths." Nietzsche writes that what is important is not the courage of our convictions but the courage for an attack on our convictions. Such courage exhibits a strong will to power, the will to choose self-mastery over safety.

Despite Nietzsche's denigration of Christianity and democracy, and his ardent praise of strife and violence, it is important to note that he is not the warmongering brute that the Nazi party, among others, proclaimed him to be. Nietzsche does not so much promote physical violence as admire the vigor of those who are capable of it. He thinks it hypocritical that people who lack the vigor to be violent condemn violence. However, physical violence is usually destructive and hardly ever useful. What Nietzsche admires most is the person who is capable of physical violence but sublimates this will to destroy others, directing it instead at himself or herself. Better than being ruthless with others is being ruthless with oneself and attacking all the petty beliefs and assumptions to which one clings for a feeling of safety and stability. A free spirit is free by having won an inner struggle, not an outer one. When Nietzsche writes approvingly of violence, it is not so much that he thinks of war as inherently good but rather that he thinks anything is preferable to the mediocrity of our cloistered modern lives. Better to suffer hardship, he believes, than lead a safe and unadventurous life.

The title of the book expresses Nietzsche's interest in an extramoral worldview. Concepts like good and evil come from a moral worldview, in which we question people's motives and judge them accordingly. However, as Nietzsche shows, our motives are themselves subject to analysis. For example, he criticizes the seemingly altruistic motives of Christian charity as a form of resentful vengeance by the powerless. Throughout the book, Nietzsche highlights the various drives and wills that lead us to adopt one or another moral worldview. In doing so, Nietzsche hopes to lead us to a point "beyond good and evil," where we see moral concepts as manifestations of deeper drives. At this point, we will no longer judge an action based on its motives but will judge motives based on the spirit in which they were formulated. For example, we should not condemn a violent act for being violent; rather, we should inquire about the will behind it. If the violent act were motivated by a spiteful, resentful will, then the violent act is contemptible, but if it were motivated by a healthy will, guiltlessly claiming what it wants, then the violent act is acceptable. Nietzsche advocates for a strong and healthy will, which acts cheerfully, independently, and free from resentment.

ON THE GENEALOGY OF MORALS

Summary

On the Genealogy of Morals, sometimes translated as *On the Genealogy of Morality*, consists of three essays, each of which questions the value of our moral concepts and examines their evolution.

The first essay, "'Good and Evil,' 'Good and Bad,'" examines the evolution of two distinctive moral codes. The first, "knightly-aristocratic" or "master" morality, comes from the early rulers and conquerors, who judged their own power, wealth, and success to be "good" and the poverty and wretchedness of those they ruled over to be "bad." Nietzsche associates the second, "priestly" or "slave" morality, primarily with the Jews. This morality originates with priests, who despise the warrior caste and condemn their lustful power as evil, while calling their own state of poverty and self-denial good. This slave morality turns master morality on its head. Driven by a feeling of *ressentiment,* or resentment, slave morality is much deeper and more refined than master morality. Its crowning achievement is Christianity: Christian love is born from hatred. While slave morality is deeper and more interesting than the casual self-confidence of the masters, Nietzsche worries that it has rendered us all mediocre. Modern humans, who have inherited the mantle of slave morality, prefer safety and comfort to conquest and risk. The slave morality of the priestly caste focuses the attention on the evil of others and on the afterlife, distracting people from enjoying the present and improving themselves.

Nietzsche illustrates the contrast between the two kinds of morality by reference to a bird of prey and a lamb. Nietzsche imagines that the lambs may judge the birds of prey to be evil for killing and consider themselves good for not killing. These judgments are meaningless, since lambs do not refrain from killing out of some kind of moral loftiness but simply because they are unable to kill. Similarly, we can only condemn birds of prey for killing if we assume that the "doer," the bird of prey, is somehow detachable from the "deed," the killing. Nietzsche argues that there is no doer behind the deed, taking as an example the sentence, "lightning flashes." There is no such thing as lightning separate from the flash. Our assumption that there are doers who are somehow distinct from deeds is simply a prejudice inspired by the subject–predicate form of grammar. Slave morality detaches subject from predicate, doer from deed, and identifies the subject with a "soul," which is then liable to judgment. Although slave morality is definitely dominant in the modern world, Nietzsche hopes that master morality will have a resurgence.

In the second essay, "'Guilt,' 'Bad Conscience,' and the Like," Nietzsche suggests that our concept of guilt originally had no moral overtones, identifying a similarity in the German words for *guilt* and *debt*. A person in debt was "guilty" and the creditor could make good on the debt by punishing the debtor. Punishment was not intended to make the debtor feel bad but simply to bring pleasure to the creditor. Punishment was cruel but cheerful: there were no hard feelings afterward. A society with laws is like a creditor: when someone breaks the law, they have harmed society, and society can exact punishment.

The concept of justice in effect takes punishment out of the hands of individuals by claiming that, in a society, it is not individuals but laws that are transgressed, and so it is the laws, not individuals, that must exact punishment. Reflecting on the many different purposes that punishment has served over the ages, Nietzsche observes that all concepts have a long and fluid history in which they have had many different meanings. The meanings of concepts are dictated by a will to power, in which concepts are given meanings or uses by the different wills that appropriate them.

Nietzsche identifies the origin of bad conscience in the transition from hunter–gatherer to agrarian societies. Our violent animal instincts ceased to be useful in a cooperative society, and we suppressed them by turning them inward. By struggling within ourselves, we carved out an inner life, bad conscience, a sense of beauty, and a sense of indebtedness to our ancestors, which is the origin of religion. At present, we direct our bad conscience primarily toward our animal instincts, but Nietzsche urges us instead to direct our bad conscience against the life-denying forces that suppress our instincts.

The title of the third essay poses the question, "What Is the Meaning of Ascetic Ideals?" Why have people from various cultures pursued an ascetic life of self-denial? Nietzsche suggests that asceticism enhances the feeling of power by giving a person complete control over him- or herself. In many cases, then, asceticism is ultimately life-affirming rather than life-denying. Ascetic ideals manifest themselves differently in different kinds of people. A sort of philosophical asceticism leads philosophers to claim that the world around them is illusory. This is one way of looking at things, and Nietzsche applauds looking at matters from as many perspectives as possible. There is no single right way to look at the truth, so it's best to be flexible in our viewpoints.

Nietzsche sees asceticism as being born of spiritual sickness. Those who find the struggle of life too hard turn against life and find it blameworthy. Nietzsche sees the majority of humanity as sick and sees priests as doctors who are themselves sick. Religion addresses this spiritual sickness partly by extinguishing the will through meditation and work but also through "orgies of feeling," manifest in the consciousness of sin and guilt. We condemn ourselves as sinners and masochistically punish ourselves. Science and scholarship are not alternatives to the ascetic ideals of religion; they simply replace the worship of God with the worship of truth. A healthy spirit must question the value of truth. Nietzsche concludes by observing that while ascetic ideals direct the will against life, they still constitute a powerful exercise of the will: "Man would rather will *nothingness* than *not* will."

Analysis

In his essay, "Nietzsche, Genealogy, History," Michel Foucault notes an important distinction in Nietzsche's work between the concepts of genealogy and origin. An origin suggests a fixed starting point and, hence, an original essence with which something is associated. For example, the Adam and Eve story of creation locates human origins in the Garden of Eden. Naturally, we have changed since the time of Adam and Eve, but certain essential features, such as original sin, remain with us. Genealogy fits more comfortably with the paradigm of Darwinian evolution. With genealogy, there is no fixed starting point and no essential features, just a gradual and often haphazard progression from one state to another. We might understand Nietzsche's main purpose in this book as being to shift our understanding of morality from an origins model to a genealogy model. That is, we tend to think of moral concepts like good and evil as stable, grounded in some distant origin. Nietzsche attempts to show that our moral concepts have always been fluid, to the point that the word *good*, for example, has had contrary meanings to different people. Our moral concepts have a long genealogy and are by no means fixed. By dislodging the idea that good and evil exist somehow independently of our wills, Nietzsche encourages a greater sense of agency with regard to our moral lives.

Nietzsche explains the fluidity of moral concepts by reference to the will to power. According to Nietzsche, the will to power is the fundamental drive in the universe. Every will has a desire for independence and to dominate other wills, though this will to power expresses itself in many different ways. For instance, the schoolyard bully achieves physical power over others, while the nerd studies hard to achieve an intellectual kind of power. Since all concepts are human inventions, Nietzsche argues, all concepts are ultimately the expression of some will or other. For example, the concept of good can mean wealth and vigor or it can mean meekness and charity, depending on who interprets it. If we seem to have relatively fixed moral concepts in this day and age, that is only a result of the triumph of slave morality over all other points of view. By assuming that these concepts have fixed meanings, we are surrendering our will to the wills of those who framed these concepts. Strong-willed people, according to Nietzsche, resist the categories of thought that are foisted upon them and have the independence and creativity to see the world from their own distinctive perspectives.

While it often seems as if Nietzsche praises the morality of ancient aristocratic cultures and condemns Judeo-Christian "slave" morality, he does not simply advocate a return to the older "master" morality. Although its net effect has been detrimental, slave morality has brought a number of benefits. While ancient conquerors had clearer consciences, they were also shallow. We have become deep and cunning and have acquired the characteristics that distinguish us from animals, as a result of the slave's turning inward. Those who cannot successfully project their will to power outward and dominate those around them project it inward instead and gain fearsome power over themselves. The dominance of Judeo-Christian morality in the modern age is evidence of how the slave's inner strength is much more powerful than the conqueror's outer strength. Nietzsche's concern with slave morality is not that it has turned us inward but that we are in danger of losing our inner struggle. Inner struggle is painful and difficult, and Nietzsche sees in the asceticism of religion, science, and philosophy a desire to give up the struggle or to minimize the hardship. Nietzsche insists that we must see humanity not as an end to be settled for but rather as a bridge to be crossed between animals and what he terms the overman. Properly directed against the life-denying forces within us, the inner strength brought about by slave morality can be our greatest blessing.

Nietzsche often laments that language is incapable of expressing what he wishes to express, and he lays principal blame on the subject–predicate form of grammar. Because all sentences divide into subject and predicate, we are lulled into thinking that reality, too, bears this form and that there are doers and deeds. In Nietzsche's view there are only deeds and no doers, and it is just as absurd to say that an eagle exists distinct from its act of killing as it is to say that lightning exists distinct from its act of flashing. An eagle *is* the act of killing just as much as lightning *is* the act of flashing: we are what we do. We might say Nietzsche's is a metaphysics of verbs rather than a metaphysics of nouns. While most metaphysics conceives of a universe made up of things, Nietzsche conceives of a universe made up of wills. We are inclined to believe that there are subjects who exercise their will only because our grammar demands that we give subjects to verbs. In fact, Nietzsche suggests, there is no "I" that makes decisions and acts on them. Rather, that "I" is the forum in which different wills assert themselves in the form of decisions and actions. Frustratingly, both for Nietzsche and his readers, it is difficult to wrap our minds around this idea that there is no doer behind the deed because every written expression of this idea relies on grammatical structures that reinforce the contrary idea.

In *Thus Spoke Zarathustra*, Zarathustra becomes wise by going up a mountain and isolating himself from his fellow human beings. To what extent is it possible for him to share his wisdom with others?

Nietzsche writes that for Zarathustra to share his wisdom with other people, Zarathustra must first "go down." At first, it seems that physically going down the mountain will be enough. However, Zarathustra finds that his task is somewhat more complicated. Zarathustra discovers that he will, in fact, have to "go down" to become an overman but that the phrase means much more than he had originally expected. Nietzsche had a tendency to freely mix his philosophy with metaphor, allusion, and wordplay. Thus, Zarathustra's journey becomes a kind of literary word game: to truly understand what it takes to become an overman, Zarathustra must puzzle out all the potential meanings of the term "to go down."

The proliferation of meanings begins almost immediately. In the decision to leave the mountaintop to preach to the people, Zarathustra makes two descents. Literally, he comes down from the physical mountain to preach in the village below. Metaphorically, he descends from the lofty realm of thought into the mundane world of everyday concerns. Zarathustra describes his decision with a simile. He decides that he must be like the setting sun, descending into the dark depths of the sea to illuminate what lies below. However, when Zarathustra goes and speaks to the people, he is met with derision.

Zarathustra's failure causes him to confront the necessarily paradoxical nature of his mission: that it will simultaneously involve both an ascent and a descent. Zarathustra's concern lies with the process of ascending to become an overman, or a human beyond all other humans. At first, he believes that his duty lies in paving the way for other humans to become overmen, or *übermenschen*, as well. In his descent to the level of the common people, Zarathustra imagines himself as a shepherd, coming to tend his flock. With the shepherd metaphor, Nietzsche consciously echoes the rhetoric of the Bible, which similarly describes Jesus's preaching as shepherding. Unsurprisingly, given Nietzsche's

Student Essay

rather hostile views on Christianity, Zarathustra's imitation of Jesus fails at its basic task of elevating other humans to the status of overmen. Zarathustra then realizes that it is not his burden to teach other humans. This seemingly charitable concept is, in fact, foolish, as the process cannot be taught as a doctrine.

Zarathustra's true going down involves a descent from this apparently moral behavior into something that seems immoral and depraved. Rather than a shepherd, Zarathustra decides to be a thief. He will steal from the flock of the shepherds, but not for the sake of leading his own flock; he will steal to have companions. Zarathustra's change of heart is expressed by his vision of an eagle flying with a snake wrapped around it. Zarathustra identifies the eagle as pride and the snake as wisdom, and he vows that the two will always go along together. In other words, Zarathustra rejects modesty, meekness, and humility—another move that distances his philosophy from that of Christianity. In Proverbs, it says that "pride goeth before the fall." This fall in Proverbs can be understood either as a general failing or specifically as a fall from the good graces of God. After all, it was Lucifer's pride that caused God to cast him out of heaven and into hell. In a sense, Zarathustra is painting himself as a sort of anti-Christ, whose going down involves a fall from grace and religion, just as it also involves an ascendance into the status of overman.

Throughout his philosophy, Nietzsche stressed how difficult and taxing self-actualization can be. This complicated process is visualized through the linked images of the camel, the lion, and the child. Moving among these three metamorphoses involves a series of goings-down, each of which differs significantly from another. As a camel, a person goes down on his or knees in submission and patience. As the lion, a person descends into pride and destructiveness. Finally, as a child, a person reverts to a state of innocence and purity. To realize one's full potential and become an overman, it is crucial that a person pass through each of these stages of going down.

Bertrand Russell

(1872–1970)

Although he was best known for his contributions to logic and philosophy, Bertrand Russell's range of interests was impressively wide. He was engaged in what seemed to be the entire extent of human endeavor: he was involved not only with mathematics, philosophy, science, and logic but also in political activism, social justice, education, and sexual morality. His influence has been so pervasive that in some ways it has become difficult for us to appreciate its full impact. Russell's work has fundamentally changed the way philosophy is practiced and the way we understand logic, mathematics, and science.

Bertrand Arthur William Russell was born into a privileged English family on May 18, 1872. He was the grandson of Lord John Russell, who was the first Earl of Russell as well as a former prime minister. Bertrand's early life was traumatic: orphaned by the age of four, he and his elder brother Frank were sent to live with their strict grandparents. Lord Russell died when Bertrand was six, and thereafter the boys were raised by their austerely religious, authoritarian grandmother. Russell's youth was filled with rules and prohibitions, and his earliest desire was to free himself from such constraints. His lifelong distrust of religion no doubt stems from this early experience. As was customary for children of his social class, Russell was initially tutored at home. Later, he attended Trinity College, Cambridge, where he achieved first-class honors in mathematics and philosophy.

At Cambridge, under the tutelage of the Hegelian philosopher J. M. E. McTaggart, Russell became a proponent of idealism, the belief that all reality is ultimately a product of the mind. Some years after graduating, however, Russell and his colleague G. E. Moore came to reject idealism in favor of realism, the belief that the external world exists independently of experience and consciousness. Russell became part of a general revitalization of empiricism, the belief that all human knowledge is derived from our sensory experience of the external world. By the time Russell published the philosophical works discussed here (*The Problems of Philosophy* and *Our Knowledge of the External World*), he was working firmly in the empiricist tradition.

Russell graduated from Cambridge in 1894 and was briefly an attaché at the British Embassy in Paris. In 1895, he returned to England, where he became a fellow of Trinity College and married his first wife, Alys Pearsall Smith. A year later, after a visit to Berlin, he published *German Social Democracy*, the first of his seventy-odd books.

Russell's important early work was concerned with mathematics. Russell's great contribution to logic and mathematics was his defense of logicism—that is, the theory that all mathematics can, in some fundamental way, be reduced to logical principles. The logicist project was important because, if it could be achieved, then mathematics would be established as a field of certain knowledge and not one of conjecture. Mathematics could legitimately be considered a priori knowledge, meaning knowledge that is necessary and self-evident, completely objective, and independent of human experience. The search for legitimately a priori knowledge has been a major occupation of philosophy throughout history.

Over the course of his career, Russell remained preoccupied with the questions of what we can know with absolute certainty and how we can know it. The *Principia Mathematica*, Russell's three-volume treatise on logicism, coauthored with A. N. Whitehead, is full of painstaking proofs that attempt to establish that numbers, arithmetic, and all mathematical principles can be derived from formal logic. This dedication to rigor and interest in justification is a recurring characteristic in Russell's work.

Along with G. E. Moore and with Russell's student Ludwig Wittgenstein, Russell is considered one of the founding proponents of analytic philosophy. Analytic philosophy describes both a historical tradition (the tradition following Moore and Russell) and a general approach to the practice of philosophy. Analytic philosophy—which has come to be virtually synonymous with "logical positivism"—refers to a belief that philosophy should be executed with the same rigor and precision as scientific inquiry. Analytic philosophy is characterized by a skeptical distrust of assumptions and a methodical system of analysis based on logic. Just as he used logic to describe the foundations of mathematics in *Principia Mathematica*, Russell would use logic to clarify philosophy, through his concept of logical atomism, and linguistics, through his theory of descriptions. Although the subject matter differed across his career, Russell's analytic methodology remained more or less constant. Many of the particulars of Russell's analysis have been challenged or refuted, but his legacy as an analyst remains undeniably influential.

Although Russell's intellectual reputation is based on his work as a mathematician, philosopher, and logician, Russell was also noted for his work as a social reformer. In fact, he first became known to the general public because of his political and social work rather than his publications. When the First World War broke out, Russell publicly voiced increasingly controversial political views. He became an activist for pacifism, which resulted in his dismissal from Trinity College in 1916. Two years later, his opposition to British involvement in the war landed him in prison. Stripped of his teaching job, he began to make his living by writing and lecturing independently. In 1919, Russell visited the newly formed Soviet Union, where he met many of the famous personalities of the revolution he had initially supported. The visit soured his view of the Socialist movement in Russia, and later that year he wrote a scathing attack titled *Theory and Practice of Bolshevism*. In 1921, he married his second wife, Dora Black, with whom he explored his interest in education. Russell and Black opened the progressive Beacon Hill School, and Russell wrote such works as *On Education* (1926) and *Education and the Social Order* (1932).

In 1931, Russell became the third Earl of Russell. Five years later, he divorced Dora Black and married his third wife, Patricia Spence. By this time, he was very interested in morality and had written on the subject in his controversial book *Marriage and Morals* (1932). He had moved to New York to teach at City College but was dismissed from the position because of his unconventional, liberal attitudes on sexuality. When Adolf Hitler came to power in Germany, Russell began to question his own dogmatic pacifism and by 1939 had rejected it in favor of a more relativist position. Believing Nazism to be an evil that needed to be stopped at all costs, he campaigned tirelessly against it throughout the Second World War. He returned to England from the United States in 1944. His teaching position at Trinity College was restored to him, and he was granted the Order of Merit by King George VI.

In the period that followed, Russell wrote several important books, including *An Enquiry into Meaning and Truth* (1940), *Human Knowledge: Its Scopes and Limits* (1948), and his best-known work from the period, *History of Western Philosophy* (1945). He also continued writing controversial pieces on social, moral, and religious issues. Most of these were collected and published in 1957 as *Why I Am Not a Christian*. From 1949 and for the rest of his life, he was an active advocate of nuclear disarmament. In 1950, Russell won the Nobel Prize in Literature. He spent his final years in North Wales, actively writing until the end. He died on February 2, 1970.

Themes, Arguments & Ideas

LOGICAL ATOMISM

The theory of logical atomism is a crucial tool in Russell's philosophical method. Logical atomism contends that, through rigorous and exacting analysis, language—like physical matter—can be broken down into smaller constituent parts. When a sentence can be broken down no further, we are left with its "logical atoms." By examining the atoms of a given statement, we expose its underlying assumptions and can then better judge its truth or validity.

Take, for example, the following sentence: "The King of America is bald." Even this deceptively simple sentence can be broken down into three logical components:

There exists a King of America.

There is only one King of America.

The King of America has no hair.

We know, of course, that there is no King of America. Thus the first assumption, or atom, is false. The complete statement "The King of America is bald" is untrue, but it isn't properly *false* because the opposite isn't true either. "The King of America has hair" is just as untrue as the original statement, because it continues to assume that there is, in fact, a King of America. If the sentence is neither true nor false, what kind of claim on the truth can it make? Philosophers have debated whether the sentence, in fact, has any meaning at all. What is clear is that applying the concepts of logical atomism to language reveals the complexity of the concepts truth and validity.

THE THEORY OF DESCRIPTIONS

The theory of descriptions represents Russell's most significant contribution to linguistic theory. Russell believed that everyday language is too misleading and ambiguous to properly represent the truth. If philosophy was to rid itself of mistakes and assumptions, a purer, more rigorous language would be required. This formal, idealized language would be based on mathematical logic

and would look more like a string of math equations than anything ordinary people might recognize as a language.

Russell's theory offers a method for understanding statements
that include definite descriptions. A definite description is a
word, name, or phrase that denotes a particular, individual
object. *That chair*, *Bill Clinton*, and *Malaysia* are all examples of
definite descriptions. The theory of descriptions was created to
deal with sentences such as "The King of America is bald," in
which the object to which the definite description refers is ambiguous or nonexistent. Russell calls these expressions *incomplete
symbols*. Russell showed how these statements can be broken
down into their logical atoms, as demonstrated in the previous
section. A sentence involving definite descriptions is, in fact,
just a shorthand notation for a *series* of claims. The true, logical form of the statement is obscured by the grammatical
form. Thus, application of the theory allows philosophers and
linguists to expose the logical structures hidden in ordinary language—and, it is hoped, to avoid ambiguity and paradox when
making claims of their own.

SET THEORY

The ability to define the world in terms of sets is crucial to Russell's project of logicism—or the attempt to reduce all mathematics to formal logic. A set is defined as a collection of objects,
called *members* or *elements*. We can speak of the set of all teaspoons in the world, the set of all letters in the alphabet, or the
set of all Americans. We can also define a set negatively, as in
"the set of all things that are *not* teaspoons." This set would
include pencils, cell phones, kangaroos, China, and anything else
that's not a teaspoon. Sets can have subsets (e.g., the set of all
Californians is a subset of the set of all Americans) and can be
added to and subtracted from one another. In early set theory,
any collection of objects could properly be called a set.

Set theory was invented by Gottlob Frege at the end of the nineteenth century and has become a major foundation of modern
mathematical thought. The paradox discovered by Bertrand Russell in the early twentieth century, however, led to a major recon-
sideration of its founding principles. Russell's Paradox showed
that allowing any collection of objects to be termed a set some-

times creates logically impossible situations—a fact that threatens to undermine Russell's greater, logicist project.

RUSSELL'S PARADOX

Russell's Paradox, which Russell discovered in 1901, reveals a problem in set theory as it had existed up to that point. The paradox in its true form is very abstract and somewhat difficult to grasp—it concerns the set of all sets that are not members of themselves. To understand what that refers to, consider the example of the set containing all the teaspoons that have ever existed. This set is not a member of itself, because the set of all teaspoons is not itself a teaspoon. Other sets may, in fact, be members of themselves. The set of everything that is not a teaspoon does contain itself because the set is not a teaspoon. The paradox arises if you try to consider the set of all the sets that are not members of themselves. This metaset would include the set of all teaspoons, the set of all forks, the set of all lobsters, and many other sets. Russell poses the question of whether *that* set includes itself. Because it is defined as the set of all sets that are not members of themselves, it must include itself because by definition it does not include itself. But if it includes itself, by definition it must not include itself. The definition of this set contradicts itself.

Many people have found this paradox difficult to fathom, so in philosophy textbooks it is often taught by analogy with other paradoxes that are similar but less abstract. One of the most famous of these is the barber paradox. In a certain town, there is a barber who shaves the men who do not shave themselves. The paradox arises when we consider whether the barber shaves himself. On one hand, he can't shave himself because he's the barber, and the barber only shaves men who don't shave themselves. But if he doesn't shave himself, he must shave himself, because he shaves all the men who don't shave themselves. This paradox resembles Russell's in that the way the set is defined makes it impossible to say whether a certain thing belongs to it or not.

Russell's Paradox is significant because it exposes a flaw in set theory. If any collection of objects can be called a set, then certain situations arise that are logically impossible. Paradoxical situations such as that referred to in the paradox threaten the entire logicist project. Russell argued for a stricter version of set theory, in which only certain collections can officially be called sets. These sets would have to satisfy certain axioms to avoid impossible or contradictory scenarios. Set theory before Russell is generally called *naïve set theory*, while post-Russell set theory is termed *axiomatic set theory*.

Summary & Analysis

PRINCIPIA MATHEMATICA

Summary

Principia Mathematica is one of the seminal works of mathematical logic. Russell coauthored it with the mathematician Alfred North Whitehead over a ten-year period beginning in 1903. Originally conceived as an elaboration of Russell's earlier *Principles of Mathematics*, the *Principia*'s three volumes eventually grew to eclipse *Principles* in scope and depth.

The goal of the *Principia* is to defend the logicist thesis that mathematics can be reduced to logic. Russell believed that logical knowledge enjoys a privileged status in comparison with other types of knowledge about the world. If we could know that mathematics is derived purely from logic, we could be more certain that mathematics was true. Russell and other philosophers believed that logical truths are special for several reasons. First, they have the distinguishing characteristic that they are true in virtue of their form rather than their content. Second, we have knowledge of them a priori, meaning without experience. Take, for example, the statement "Penguins either do or do not live in Antarctica." This is a logical truth, an example of what logicians call the Law of Excluded Middle. Regardless of whether we know anything about penguins or frogs or X, we can say with certainty that this statement is true. On the other hand, we cannot know whether penguins are good swimmers without having observed some penguins (or at least looking in a book). Logicians, beginning with Aristotle, have studied statements and arguments that have the quality of certainty and tried to distill what in their form makes them certain. The *Principia* is in some sense an extension of this project from general logical arguments to mathematical ones. It aims to show that mathematical truths like "two plus two equals four" are true for the same reasons as our first statement about penguins.

The *Principia*'s three massive volumes are divided into six sections. Like most modern logic texts, the *Principia* begins by laying out a formal system of propositional logic and then proceeds to develop the theorems (or consequences) of the system. The basic idea is to use symbols to stand for propositions. A proposition is a statement that can be deemed either true or false. For example, *P* could stand for the proposition that penguins live in Antarctica and ¬*P* (read "not P") for the proposition that penguins do not live in Antarctica. Russell and Whitehead introduce symbols like these and then add rules for combining them into complex statements using logical connectors, the English language equivalents of which are *and*, *or*, *not*, and *if . . . then*. Our original penguin statement would then read "*P* or ¬*P*." In addition to this vocabulary for formalizing propositions, there is also a set of rules for making deductions. A deduction is simply a way to express a valid argument using symbols. (Recall that an argument is valid if the truth of its premises or assumptions guarantees the truth of its conclusion.) A simple deduction rule used in *Principia* is called *modus ponens*:

If P, then Q.

P.

Therefore Q.

As in the penguin example, *P* and *Q* can stand for any propositions, so the following is a valid use of *modus ponens*:

If it rains, then the ground will be wet.

It has rained.

Therefore the ground is wet.

Typically, a formal system also contains a set of axioms or assumptions that form the starting point for applying deduction rules. In the case of *Principia*, the axioms are a select group of self-evident logical truths of the penguin type, except that they are about classes and sets instead of concrete physical objects.

After specifying these axioms and rules, Russell and Whitehead spend the bulk of *Principia* methodically developing their consequences. First, they develop their theory of types within the formal language. Next, they define the concept of number. Defining the concept of number is quite difficult to do without being circular. For example, it is hard to imagine how one would explain what the number 2 is without having to refer to the concept of 2. The key insight into this problem, which was originally conceived by the German philosopher Gottlob Frege and adopted by Russell and Whitehead, is to think of numbers in terms of concrete counting, not in terms of abstract numbers. When we first learn to count, we use our fingers to mark off the items as we count them. Each finger corresponds to one item. One can do the same thing to see whether two sets are the same size by marking off items two at a time, one from each set. If there are no items left over in either set after pairing everything, the sets are the same size. The technical expression of this operation is somewhat complicated, but the basic idea is that the "number" of a set is the set of all sets that are the same size, as measured by our counting procedure. Russell and Whitehead were able to prove that this procedure produces objects that behave just like numbers. In fact, Russell and Whitehead go even further and make the claim that numbers simply are these sets. The number 2 is a shorthand way of referring to "the set of all sets of couples," the number 3 is a shorthand for "the set of all sets of trios," and so on.

With the definition of number settled, Russell and Whitehead spend the rest of *Principia* deriving more complicated math, including arithmetic and number theory. However, to do this, Russell and Whitehead were forced to add two additional axioms to their system. The first is the axiom of infinity, which postulates that there is an infinity of numbers. This axion is necessary to derive real numbers. The second is the axiom of reducibility, which is necessary to avoid Russell's paradox. Using these two new axioms in combination with the original logical axioms and *modus ponens*, Russell and Whitehead spend the second and third volumes of *Principia* deriving much of pure mathematics in their system of formal logic.

Analysis

Russell and Whitehead's *Principia*, like Newton's similarly titled book two centuries earlier, was truly groundbreaking. Just as Newton's *Principia* revolutionized physics, Russell and Whitehead's treatise forever changed mathematics and philosophy. The *Principia* has produced at least three lasting, important effects. First, the *Principia* brought mathematical logic to the forefront as a philosophical discipline. It inspired much follow-up work in logic and led directly to the development of *metalogic*, or the study of what properties different logical systems have. Obscure as this may sound, many, if not most, of the interesting results in logic in the twentieth century are actually in metalogic, and these results have had profound implications for epistemology and metaphysics. Second, the methods of mathematical logic have had a great effect on the practice of *analytic philosophy*. Analytic philosophy refers to a method of doing philosophy by making arguments, the assumptions and structure of which are as explicit and clear as possible. This idea is directly parallel to the use of axioms and inference rules in formal systems. From metaphysics to the philosophy of science to ethics, modern philosophers in the Anglo-American tradition try to justify each step of their arguments by some clear assumption or principle. Third, both the technical apparatus of mathematical logic and its principles of rigorous, step-by-step reasoning have found application in fields ranging from computer science to psychology to linguistics. Computer scientists, for example, have used logic to prove the limits of what computers can do, and linguists have used it to model the structure of natural language. None of these advances would have been possible without Russell and Whitehead's pioneering work.

However, the modern *Principia* also resembles Newton's work in a less flattering respect. Just as Einstein's theory of relativity overthrew Newton's ideas about force, mass, and energy, the work of later logicians and philosophers such as Kurt Gödel and W. V. O. Quine has cast the results of *Principia* and the logicist project into doubt. Recall that the aim of *Principia* was to show that all mathematical knowledge could be derived from purely logical principles. It was with this goal in mind that Russell and Whitehead carefully selected logical axioms and rules of inference that appeared to be a priori logical truths. However, two of these axioms—the axiom of infinity and the axiom of reducibility—arguably do not fit the bill. Consider our statement about penguins: there either are or are not penguins in Antarctica. This statement seems impossible to deny. Now consider the assertion that there is an infinity of numbers. What makes this logically necessary? Is there an infinite number of atoms? How can we have any knowledge of infinites?

Some critics have argued that the axiom of infinity is not a priori in nature but is an empirical question whose answer depends on experience. If this is so, any mathematical results derived from it must also depend on experience, and the logicist program is in peril. Critics have also focused on the axiom of reducibility. This axiom is necessary to avoid Russell's Paradox, but apart from that it does not seem to have a purely logical justification. Critics have assailed it as ad hoc, or assumed just to get a desired result. If this is the case and it does not have a more fundamental nature, all of the results derived from it are in doubt or at least not logically self-evident, as Russell and Whitehead hoped to show.

The work of the logician Kurt Gödel has raised special doubts about the *Principia*'s supposed proof of the logicist program. Recall that one goal of the *Principia* was to show that all of mathematics could be captured in a formal system. This should be distinguished from the central logicist thesis that mathematics was reducible to logic, but it was still crucial to Russell and Whitehead's method of proving this thesis. Gödel, in a famous 1931 response to the *Principia*, showed that this goal was unachievable, that no formal system could capture all mathematical truths. This famous result is known as Gödel's Incompleteness Theorem. Its significance was in establishing that there are some mathematical truths that cannot be deduced in any formal system. This proved a major obstacle to logicists like Russell who hoped to show formally that mathematics was just logic. However, the logicist program is not yet completely dead, and the substantial contributions of the *Principia* are still being felt throughout math, philosophy, and beyond.

THE PROBLEMS OF PHILOSOPHY

Summary

The Problems of Philosophy is an introduction to the discipline of philosophy, written during a Cambridge lectureship that Russell held in 1912. In it, Russell asks the fundamental question, "Is there any knowledge in the world which is so certain that no reasonable man could doubt it?" Russell sketches out the metaphysical and epistemological views he held at the time, views that would develop and change over the rest of his career.

Russell begins by exploring the twin concepts of appearance and reality. Empiricists like Russell believe that all knowledge is ultimately derived from our sensory perceptions of the world around us. Individual perception, however, is easily affected and prone to error. If three people—one who's had three martinis, one with a high fever, and one who's color-blind—look at the same table, chances are they'll each see the same object somewhat differently. Submerge the same table underwater, or set it behind a wavy pane of glass, and once again the table will look different. There is, then, a distinction to be made between appearance and reality. If perception is so variable, what can it actually tell us about the stable, real object we assume lies behind it?

Russell coined the term *sense-data* in his attempt to discern the relationship between appearance and reality. Sense-data are the particular things we perceive during the act of sensation. When you walk into a café, the smell of the coffee, the redness of the awning, and the heat from the radiator are all examples of sense-data. Sense-data are the *mental images* (visual as well as auditory, olfactory, tactile, and gustatory) that we receive from a given object in the physical world. As we can see from the table example, the same object can produce variable sense-data. Sense-data are related to the physical objects they represent, but the exact nature of this relationship is unclear. The skeptical argument contends that sense-data tell us nothing about the reality of the object. Russell had a commonsense take on the matter: while he understood the skeptical arguments, he found no reason to believe them. A hundred different viewers may have a thousand different kinds of sense-data for a given table, yet each agrees that they are looking at the same table. This consistency suggests, to Russell, that we must at least believe in the existence of a single, particular, real table. To this "instinctive" belief, Russell also adds the hypothesis that physical objects *cause* the sense-data we receive and therefore correspond to them in some significant way.

During the act of sensation (i.e., the exercising of our five senses), we receive and process the sense-data produced by physical objects in our vicinity. The knowledge we gain during this process Russell calls "perceptual knowledge"—knowledge gained through experience. In contrast, Russell believes we are also in possession of certain kinds of a priori knowledge. These include the self-evident rules of logic, most important, and those of mathematics. Perceptual knowledge (the knowledge of things) and a priori knowledge (the knowledge of truths) work in concert: the first gives us empirical data, and the second tells us how to process that data.

Russell further divides human knowledge into knowledge by acquaintance and knowledge by description. To be acquainted with something is to be directly and immediately aware of it, without the action of an intermediary. When you sit on a red plastic chair, you become acquainted with lots of sense-data associated with that chair. You know its redness, its smoothness, its coolness, and its hardness. But to know that this thing is called a "chair" and that it's often found in the company of other "chairs" and something called a "table" requires more than just direct, immediate acquaintance with the physical object. To know all that requires us to make inferences, based on our general knowledge of facts and on our acquaintance with other similar objects. This kind of knowledge is derivative, and Russell terms it "knowledge by description." For instance, most of us know only by description that Everest is the tallest mountain in the world. Few of us have actually been there, so we have to rely on the testimony of others to "know" that fact. Indeed, to truly be acquainted with the fact of Everest's superior height, one would have to visit and measure *all* the mountains in the world. It's probably safe to say, then, that no one is truly acquainted with that particular piece of knowledge.

Just as we can know objects either immediately or derivatively, we can also know truths immediately or derivatively. Russell defines immediate knowledge of truths as *intuitive* truths. These are concepts that, to Russell, are so clearly self-evident that we just know they *must* be true. "1 + 1 = 2" is an example of such a self-evident truth. Derivative knowledge of truths involves deduction and inference from immediate, self-evident truths.

All knowledge is, in Russell's view, built on acquaintance. Without knowledge by description, however, we would never pass beyond the limits of our own individual experience. Thus, just like perceptual and a priori knowledge, knowledge by acquaintance and knowledge by description work together to create a totality of human knowledge.

Analysis

The Problems of Philosophy represents Russell's first major attempt at mapping out a theory of epistemology, or a theory of the nature of human knowledge. Russell's attempt to discern what kinds of knowledge, if any, could be considered reasonably certain is similar to the goal of *Principia Mathematica*, which is to find an undeniable reason for believing in the supposed truths of mathematics. Both branches of Russell's work—the mathematical and the more traditionally philosophical—have at their heart Russell's steadfast devotion to rigorous analysis and his reluctance to accept any proposition (no matter how obvious or commonsense seeming) without a concrete, logical reason for doing so.

Beginning with this work and continuing through *Our Knowledge of the External World* and beyond, Russell sought to describe the relationship between knowledge, perception, and physics (the study of the material, physical world). Fundamental to Russell's theories was a belief that the physical world does, in fact, exist. Almost two decades earlier, Russell had rejected idealism—the theory that reality is not physical but exists only in the mind—in favor of realism, the belief that objects exist independently of our perception or experience. The theories of epistemology described in *Problems of Philosophy* fit squarely within the British empiricist tradition in that they claim that the data gained from personal, immediate experience is the starting point of all human knowledge. In Russell's system, data gained from personal, immediate experience are termed "knowledge by acquaintance."

According to Russell, any proposition we know "by description" must be wholly made up of things we know by acquaintance. If we assume this, then there are some consequences for what, exactly, it is possible to know by description. Suppose you make a proposition about Julius Caesar: you say, for example, "Julius Caesar launched the first Roman invasion of Britain." You are not actually *acquainted* with Julius Caesar himself, since you have no direct, immediate experience of the man. What you hold in your mind is a *description* of him. You may know of him as "the founder of the Roman Empire," for example, or "the man assassinated on the Ides of March," or "the subject of the marble bust in my local library." Thus, when you say, "Julius Caesar launched the first Roman invasion of Britain," you're not really asserting something about the real Julius Caesar—you can't be, as you have no direct knowledge of him. Instead, you're asserting something about the collection of facts and ideas about Caesar with which you *are* acquainted. No matter how many facts we may learn about Caesar, we can still only know him by description. We can never reach a point where we directly know him by acquaintance.

The general thrust of this argument foreshadows Russell's work in logical atomism, which argues that statements can be broken down into a series of constituent assumptions. The argument also ties into Russell's Theory of Descriptions, which explains how definite descriptions—phrases like *that cat, Bill Cosby*, or *my mother*, that refer to specific, particular objects—are just shorthand for a series of logical claims. Similarly, when we use the phrase *Julius Caesar*, we're using the name to refer not to the man himself but to a series of facts and descriptions we have learned about him.

The Problems of Philosophy was meant to be an introduction to the field, and as such, Russell's arguments aren't as thorough as we might expect from the founder of analytic philosophy. He often errs on the side of "illustrating" his points rather than meticulously mapping them out. Though the book makes strong appeals to common sense, there are still elements that have greatly troubled critics. One such problem lies with Russell's notion of intuitive knowledge. Russell never satisfactorily explains what, exactly, makes a truth self-evident, and he does not provide sufficient examples of these intuitive, immediate truths. Russell also provides no plan for distinguishing between two apparently self-evident truths that nevertheless contradict each other.

The concept of sense-data, as set out by Russell, has also proved problematic. Russell takes it as a given that sense-data are the building blocks of perception. We look at a table and we sense its brownness, its hardness, and its rectangularity. From these sense-data, we construct our idea of the table. Other philosophers argue that, upon seeing a table, we are immediately aware of the object *as a table*, and it is only later, when we stop to concentrate on what we see, that we consciously notice the object's color, texture, or shape. According to these thinkers, sense-data as defined by Russell cannot be the most primitive, direct element of experience because it requires too much conscious effort to be aware of them.

Finally, a major issue in *Problems of Philosophy* lies in the fact that, to Russell, all knowledge is built on knowledge by acquaintance, or the things we know through direct, personal experience. Russell accepts a fundamentally Cartesian point of view, which means he accepts that the proper foundation for philosophical inquiry is individual consciousness and perspective. But how can a theory of knowledge be built on private experiences if this theory is supposed to apply to all beings? This problem (among others) bothered Russell, and in his next major epistemological work, *Our Knowledge of the External World*, he begins to push his inquiry into the public sphere.

OUR KNOWLEDGE OF THE EXTERNAL WORLD

Summary

Russell wasn't completely satisfied with his theories as laid out in *The Problems of Philosophy* and continued his work on knowledge and perception over the next several decades. One of his important contributions to the field is *Our Knowledge of the External World*, a collection of lectures published in 1914. In this book, Russell continues to struggle with the implications of his Cartesian assumption—that private experience is the proper place to begin philosophical inquiry. Russell doesn't reject that notion wholeheartedly but is very aware of the difficulties it raises. He is aware that crossing over from the "private space" of personal experience and sensation into the "public space" of science and the physical world is a difficult leap to logically justify.

Following from *Problems*, one thrust of *Our Knowledge of the External World* concerns itself with the relation of perception and physics. Russell continues to ask, can we come to know things about the physical world through the actions of our senses? And if so, *how* do we know these things? In both this book and in an article titled "The Relation of Sense-Data to Physics" (also from 1914), Russell returns to the concept of sense-data, which he described earlier in *Problems*. Sense-data are the characteristics and qualities we primitively, immediately sense about physical objects: color, shape, texture, temperature, and so forth. Previously, Russell had argued that sense-data were the functions of physical objects. That is to say, physical objects *cause* sense-data, which we then perceive when we exercise our five senses. A cat exists in the real, physical world, and from that cat we sense warmth, softness, grayness. The problem with this theory, however, is that we are only *acquainted* with the sense-data of warmth, softness, and grayness—we *infer* that a cat is causing these things, but we cannot know for sure that such a thing exists.

Russell argued that the most fundamental principle of scientific reasoning is that, "whenever possible, logical constructions are to be substituted for inferred entities." With this in mind, Russell executes a kind of flip. Rather than say that physical objects create sense-data, he turns the matter around and argues that *sense-data* construct the physical object. Sense-data don't just testify to the existence of physical objects, they essentially *create* the physical world. They do so in tandem with what Russell calls *sensibilia*. Sensibilia are "unsensed sense-data"—that is, how an object appears when no one is perceiving it at a given moment. This accounts for an object's continued existence in the absence of perceivers. An important consequence of this theory is the notion that sense-data are not simply images held in the mind but are instead the actual building blocks of physics. Thus, sense-data inhabit the public space of science as well as the private space of experience.

A second major component of *Our Knowledge of the External World* is Russell's presentation of logical atomism. This is his most important discussion of the theory, although logical atomism is also covered in several of Russell's other publications.

In terms of physics, atomism is the theory that all matter in the universe is made up of tiny, finite particles that cannot be broken down into anything smaller. The cup sitting in front of me *looks* like a solid, whole object but is in reality a swarm of individual whizzing atoms. The idea of a "cup" is a convenient fiction that obscures the reality of the atomic situation. Even if we know that the cup is made up of millions of tiny particles and a lot of empty space, it's easier to simply accept that it is a solid cup and move on with our day. The physicist doesn't have that luxury, of course, and neither does the dedicated philosopher. Logical atomism proposes that the theory of atomism extends to other areas beyond matter—most important for Russell, to the fields of language and of knowledge. In terms of linguistics, Russell showed how seemingly ordinary statements could be analyzed to reveal a string of simpler, more elemental assumptions, which could then individually be judged either true or false (see the section Logical Atomism, page 399).

In *Our Knowledge of the External World*, Russell shows how logical atomism applies to the question of knowledge and the physical world. Russell combines logical atomism with empiricism. He proposes that the "atoms" of our knowledge are the sense-data with which we are directly acquainted. Our immediate sensory experience is the only knowledge we can genuinely claim; all other knowledge is inferred or deduced from it. Consider the cat described earlier. The cat's sense-data—warmth, softness, grayness—are the "atoms" of our knowledge about that object. The cat that we infer *from* that sense-data is only a "logical fiction." Objects are nothing more than systems of sense-data. Here, we can see a seemingly logical basis for Russell's assertion that sense-data *create* rather than simply testify to the existence of physical objects.

Analysis

After advancing his theory of how sense-data create the physical world, Russell abandoned it in future works and reverted to the notion that physical objects could legitimately be inferred from sensory experience. This was partially due to scientific advances in physics and human physiology, which were asserting that perception is, in fact, caused by the effects of the physical world on our sense organs. Russell also sensed other difficulties in his theories on physics and perception. For one, his notion of sensibilia is difficult to establish: what, exactly, does it mean for there to be "unsensed sense-data"? How can there be an element of perception when no one is present to do the perceiving? Russell was unable to adequately describe his system of private and public spaces or to explain how sense-data and sensibilia interact with that system. In later work like *The Analysis of the Mind* (1921), Russell stops treating sense-data and the act of sensation as separate entities. He does, however, maintain the classic empiricist position that physical objects are not directly knowable; only their sensory effects (what he took to calling *percepts*, as opposed to sense-data) are available to us. Eventually, Russell abandoned his inquiries into the relationship of matter and perception, though he continued to work in other areas of epistemology.

Critics also found flaws with Russell's presentation of logical atomism, which was often sketchy in areas. His former student Ludwig Wittgenstein, for example, disagreed with the idea that logical atomism should be tied to empiricism, and in his *Tractacus Logico-Philosophicus* Wittgenstein treated logical atomism as a purely formal theory. Critics have also taken issue with how Russell defines the "simple" elements of the world's structure. Russell says that the basic atomic facts of the world with which we can become acquainted are of two kinds: particulars and universals. Particulars are individual instances of sense-data, whereas universals are concepts that apply to many objects. These include qualities (like redness, softness, heaviness) and temporal and spatial relations (before, on top of, next to). Russell contends that particulars and universals are atomic "simples"— that is, they are finite and individual and cannot be analyzed or broken down further. However, it is difficult to see how this definition could apply to a universal like "redness." The very concept of redness requires us to compare different objects and classify them as similar; this being so, it is impossible for "redness" to be an independent entity.

Other critics have refuted Russell's logical atomism in myriad ways, many of which are too complex to cover here. Although Russell's presentation of logical atomism may have proved untenable, it remains an important moment in the history of philosophy. Like the *Principia Mathematica*— another of Russell's projects that eventually proved largely unjustifiable—Russell's defense of logical atomism is spurred by an intense interest in justification. Russell's work throughout his career can be characterized by an extreme reluctance to believe any proposition without a firm, sound reason to do so.

Logical atomism was one of the earliest manifestations of analytic philosophy, which (in its most general sense) holds that philosophy should aspire to the precision and exactitude of the sciences. As Russell was one of the founders of analytic philosophy, his work inspired philosophers to rigorously examine their own assumptions and to avoid taking seemingly self-evident truths for granted. It is this dedication to constant, consistent analysis that is Russell's greatest legacy to philosophy.

CHAPTER 17
RUSSELL

If you were to inform Bertrand Russell that Santa Claus wears a blue suit, how would Russell evaluate this statement?

Most of us would immediately say that this statement is false. Everyone knows that Santa Claus wears a red suit, not a blue one. Bertrand Russell would agree with that verdict, but he would disagree with our reasoning. To Russell, the statement is false because it rests on the kind of faulty, hidden assertions that consistently plague everyday language.

Russell would argue that both the statement "Santa Claus wears a blue suit" and the proposed alternative, "Santa Claus wears a red suit," are equally false because they assume the existence of a nonexistent thing. Russell's work in linguistics focused on analyzing statements such as "Santa Claus wears a blue suit" in order to determine their truth or validity. By analysis, he means the systematic separation of an object into its constituent parts in order to study the structure of the whole. The notion that language, like physical material, can be broken down in this manner lies at the heart of logical atomism, a key tool in Russell's philosophical method. The first step to understanding "Santa Claus wears a blue suit," then, is to break it down.

Applying Russell's theory of descriptions to the statement reveals the exact location of the logical glitch. Russell's theory describes statements that involve definite descriptions, or phrases that refer to a particular, specific individual or object. Russell proposed that statements involving definite descriptions are, in fact, *compound* statements. The statement "Santa Claus wears a blue suit," for example, makes several separate assertions:

1. There exists an individual called Santa Claus.

2. There exists only one individual called Santa Claus.

3. Santa Claus wears clothing.

4. Santa Claus's clothing is a suit.

5. Santa Claus's suit is blue.

Student Essay

Immediately, we can see that the first assertion is false, because no such person as Santa Claus exists. Russell would argue that this, in turn, renders the entire statement "Santa Claus wears a blue suit" false.

Santa Claus may be a fictional character, but it still seems that he must have some element of existence to him, because we can talk about him and be understood by other people when we do so. Santa Claus isn't a real person, in the sense that he doesn't have a physical body and isn't alive. Yet it still seems possible to make assertions about Santa Claus as well as other fictional characters. Most of us would agree that we can say "Hamlet is a prince of Denmark" or "The Cat in the Hat is a troublemaker" without being taken for liars. We gain knowledge about fictional characters in much the same way that we learn about famous people who died long ago. Although we cannot know Julius Caesar directly, we can know him by description, through stories and biographies and plays. We cannot become acquainted with Julius Caesar, but we can become acquainted with a body of knowledge *about* him. We are acquainted with a similar body of knowledge about Santa Claus.

Russell would probably agree with these arguments, but his steadfast commitment to logic would maintain that the arguements don't make "Santa Claus wears a blue suit" any less false. We are still talking about a nonexistent object as if he were real. We could say, however, "The character Santa Claus is often depicted wearing a red suit" and have it be a true statement. This assertion doesn't require us to admit, however tacitly, that Santa Claus has any kind of reality or existence about him, and it frees us to either assert or deny the fact presented.

The change may seem trivial, and Russell didn't claim that, in everyday conversation, we need to be this rigorous about challenging our own language. For philosophers, however, he sets the bar much higher. To Russell, the lurking ambiguities of daily language are philosophical obstructions, and it is only by consistently routing them out that we can close the representative gap between language and truth.

Ludwig Wittgenstein

(1889–1951)

18

THEMES, ARGUMENTS & IDEAS

- Early vs. Later Wittgenstein
- Language as a Source of Philosophical Confusion
- The Dissolution of Philosophical Problems
- Philosophy as an Activity of Clarification
- The End of Philosophy?

SUMMARY & ANALYSIS OF MAJOR WORKS

- *Tractatus Logico-Philosophicus*
- *The Blue and Brown Books*
- *Philosophical Investigations*
- *On Certainty*

Ludwig Wittgenstein was born in 1889 into one of the richest families in Austria. His father was a self-made man and a steel magnate. Ludwig was the youngest of eight children and grew up in a very musical family: his brother Paul had a successful career as a concert pianist even after losing his right arm in the First World War. As a child, Ludwig was not an exceptional student, and he was sent to a technical school in the hope that he would learn engineering and follow his father in the family business. For one year, he was a pupil at the same school as a younger boy named Adolf Hitler.

Wittgenstein developed an interest in the nascent field of aeronautics and went to the University of Manchester to study aeronautical engineering. While he was there, he became increasingly preoccupied by mathematical and philosophical questions. Understanding that the highest authority on these questions at the time was Bertrand Russell, Wittgenstein impulsively traveled to Cambridge in

1911 and requested that Russell take him on as a student. Russell was hesitant at first but was soon impressed by Wittgenstein's intelligence. Within a year, the roles were reversed, and Russell was looking up to the young Wittgenstein as the greatest hope for the field of logic.

Wittgenstein's work on logic was interrupted by the First World War, during which Wittgenstein enlisted in the Austro-Hungarian army and served on the eastern front. Driven by a desire to face his own mortality, he constantly requested the most dangerous assignments and was twice decorated for bravery. While in the trenches, Wittgenstein completed his *Tractatus Logico-Philosophicus,* which he believed solved all the problems of logic and philosophy. After the war, Wittgenstein gave his large fortune away to his siblings and, satisfied that he had nothing more to offer philosophy, took a position as a schoolteacher in the mountains of rural Austria. Gradually, he became convinced that the *Tractatus* was flawed and that he had more to contribute to philosophy, and by 1929 he found himself back at Cambridge.

For nearly twenty years, Wittgenstein taught on and off at Cambridge, never entirely happy with his role as philosopher but unable to abandon his calling. He was known for his severity and his unusual teaching style, and he persuaded many of his brightest students to abandon philosophy for more practical pursuits. During these years, he kept extensive notebooks outlining his thoughts. The only notes he deemed fit for publication are the 120-odd pages that make up the first part of the *Philosophical Investigations,* but many of his other notebooks have survived and have been published. Wittgenstein requested that none of his work be published during his lifetime. He died of cancer in 1951, and the *Investigations* were published in 1953.

Wittgenstein was brought into philosophy by Bertrand Russell, who was one of the founders of analytic philosophy. Russell and Gottlob Frege were the two foremost figures in the movement, which brought advances in the field of mathematical logic to bear on philosophical questions. They found that logical analysis could reveal the deep structure of language, which could in turn expose the source of much philosophical confusion. Russell and Frege shared what is known as a universalist conception of logic. They believed logic to be the most fundamental set of laws: while the laws of physics govern physical phenomena and the laws of grammar govern grammatical phenomena, the laws of logic are supremely universal and govern all phenomena. Exploring and codifying the laws of logic, then, is a supremely important activity.

Wittgenstein's *Tractatus* is largely a response to the work of Frege and Russell, and it is impossible to appreciate it fully without a strong grasp of the work of those two philosophers. By contrast, the *Philosophical Investigations* are interesting precisely in the way that they do not seem to fit into any particular context. In the *Investigations*, Wittgenstein is concerned primarily with the very impulse to think philosophically more than he is with any particular philosophical views. Nevertheless, we find in the *Investigations* a preoccupation with language, and we can see the enduring influence of Frege and Russell in Wittgenstein's conviction that a proper understanding of language will expose the hidden flaws in philosophical reasoning.

Themes, Arguments & Ideas

EARLY VS. LATER WITTGENSTEIN

Wittgenstein is famous for revolutionizing philosophy not once but twice. He claimed to have solved all the problems of philosophy in his *Tractatus Logico-Philosophicus*, only to return to philosophy ten years later, repudiate many of the central claims of the *Tractatus*, and reinvent philosophy a second time with the *Philosophical Investigations*. Among the central differences between the early Wittgenstein of the *Tractatus* and the later Wittgenstein of the *Philosophical Investigations* and his various notebook writings is a shift in emphasis regarding the importance of logic. In the *Tractatus,* logic is given central importance as determining the structure of language and reality, but in the *Investigations* it receives scarcely a mention. Wittgenstein's later philosophy abandons the rigidly structured world of the *Tractatus* in favor of a less pristine and more modest conception of a complex world that resists any simple articulation. Though the differences between the early and later philosophies of Wittgenstein go deep, significant similarities remain. The four themes that follow trace some of the most important points on which Wittgenstein's position does not change radically throughout his career.

LANGUAGE AS A SOURCE OF PHILOSOPHICAL CONFUSION

Though Wittgenstein repeats that ordinary language is fine as it is, he also identifies the misuse of that language as the source of much philosophical confusion. Language is suited to its everyday business of facilitating communication among people. Philosophers make the mistake of abstracting language from its ordinary contexts to understand the essences of things. For example, when people talk about knowing things, in most contexts it is perfectly obvious what they mean. But despite the fact that we can talk about what we know without complication, we are puzzled when confronted by a question such as "What is knowledge?" All of a sudden, we are faced with an abstract concept, "knowledge," divorced from the contexts in which this concept is used. When philosophers get confused over the question of what knowledge is, they are confused not because the essence of knowledge is difficult to identify; rather, they are confused because they have abstracted a word from the contexts in which it has a function and find that, outside these contexts, the word loses its meaning. If philosophers were careful about how they use language, Wittgenstein believes, philosophical confusion would cease to exist.

THE DISSOLUTION OF PHILOSOPHICAL PROBLEMS

The correct approach to philosophical problems, according to Wittgenstein, is not to attempt to solve them but rather to reach a point at which the problems dissolve of their own accord. The problems of philosophy, in this view, are in fact pseudoproblems. Where we think we perceive a problem, we are in fact caught in philosophical confusion. For example, in *On Certainty*, Wittgenstein attempts to unravel the problem of external-world skepticism, showing that the very question of how we can know that there is a world external to our senses only arises if we misunderstand the nature of propositions, such as "here is a hand"—in actual life, such propositions are not offered as knowledge that might be proven true or false. Wittgenstein's approach is not to say that external-world skepticism is false but rather to show that the very question of whether external-world skepticism is true or false arises out of a misunderstanding of the language we use. If we absorb Wittgenstein's teachings, we do not come to settled solutions to the philosophical problems that haunt us, but rather we reach a state where these problems cease to haunt us. What Wittgenstein seeks is not solutions so much as an end to theorizing.

PHILOSOPHY AS AN ACTIVITY OF CLARIFICATION

Wittgenstein emphasizes the difference between his philosophy and traditional philosophy by saying that his philosophy is an activity rather than a body of doctrine. We can identify definite positions and theories in the writings of most traditional philosophers, but not with Wittgenstein. In fact, Wittgenstein's writings are distinctly antitheoretical: he believes that the very idea of a philosophical theory is a sign of confusion. He conceives of the role of philosophy as an activity by which we unravel the sorts of confusion that manifest themselves in traditional philosophy. This activity carries with it no theories or doctrines but rather aims at reaching a point at which theories and doctrines cease to confuse us. In the *Philosophical Investigations,* Wittgenstein writes, "the work of the philosopher consists in assembling reminders for a particular purpose." That is, his ideal philosopher works to remind those confused by abstract theorizing of the ordinary uses of words and to set their thinking in order. The clarity achieved through this kind of activity is not the clarity of a coherent, all-encompassing system of thought but rather the clarity of being free from being too influenced by any systems or theories.

THE END OF PHILOSOPHY?

Wittgenstein scholars disagree as to whether his work ought to represent an end to philosophy. Certainly, his work has a conclusive feeling about it. In the preface to the *Tractatus*, he writes, "I am . . . of the opinion that the problems [of philosophy] have in essentials been finally solved." If we wholeheartedly embrace Wittgenstein's work—either the *Tractatus* or his later writings—we will no longer be able to speculate about the problems of philosophy as thinkers have done for the previous two and a half millennia. However, it is far from clear that Wittgenstein intends for all philosophical activity simply to cease. Rather, he seems to intend a new role for philosophy, as an activity of clarification. While the main target of this activity seems to be traditional philosophy, it would presumably continue to have a role even if everyone were to give up traditional philosophy. So long as we continue to think, we are liable to fall into intellectual confusion. Though philosophy is a particularly rich source of intellectual confusion, no field of thought is free from confusion. In his later writings, Wittgenstein devotes a great deal of energy to picking apart the confusion inherent in the nascent field of experimental psychology. We might conclude that Wittgenstein does not want to do away with philosophy so much as he wants to reinvent it.

Summary & Analysis

TRACTATUS LOGICO-PHILOSOPHICUS

Summary

The *Tractatus* consists of a series of terse propositions numbered in a decimal form from 1 to 7. It divides roughly into three parts: propositions 1 to 2.063 deal with the nature of the world; 2.1 to 4.128 deal with the nature of language; and 4.2 to 7 deal with the nature of logic and its implications for mathematics, science, philosophy, and the meaning of life.

Proposition 1.1 announces, "The world is the totality of facts and not things." A complete description of the world is not a list of all the objects in the world but a list of all the facts that are true of the world. In other words, facts are metaphysically prior to objects: an object only has being insofar as it is a constituent of a fact. Facts can be logically analyzed into constituent parts. Fundamental, atomic facts that cannot be further analyzed are called *states of affairs*, and they are all logically independent of one another. Any given state of affairs can be true or false regardless of the truth or falsity of any other state of affairs. Objects link together to form facts by virtue of their logical form, much as pieces of a jigsaw puzzle link together by virtue of their shape.

Language depicts reality by virtue of sharing a logical form in common with reality. We know that a picture of a sunset represents a sunset because both the picture and the sunset share a similar "pictorial form." Similarly, a proposition and what it represents share a similar "logical form": a proposition depicts a fact, and just as a fact can be analyzed into independent states of affairs, a proposition can be analyzed into independent elementary propositions.

Wittgenstein draws an important distinction between saying and showing: while a proposition *says* that such-and-such fact is the case, it *shows* the logical form by virtue of which this fact is the case. The upshot of this distinction is that we can only say things about facts in the world; logical form cannot be spoken about, only shown. Because logical form shows itself and cannot be spoken about, there is no need for the so-called logical objects, the connecting glue between different propositions that plays a central role in the logic of Frege and Russell. Wittgenstein asserts that most philosophical confusion arises from trying to speak about things that can only be shown.

At proposition 4.31, Wittgenstein introduces his method of truth tables, which show how logical form makes itself apparent without the need for logical relations or objects. One consequence of this view is that all the propositions of logic are tautologies—they are the set of propositions that are true no matter what. As such, they tell us nothing about the world, and they are all equivalent.

The foregoing reflections on the nature of the world, language, and logic lead Wittgenstein to address a series of long-standing philosophical problems. He suggests that solipsism, the belief that we have no knowledge of a world outside of our own minds, is technically valid but that there is no distinction between solipsism and realism that can properly be expressed in language. He claims that mathematics can be derived from the successive application of logical operations and that the laws of science are neither logical laws nor empirical observations but rather an interpretive method. Because language can speak about only facts in the world, we can say nothing about the world as a whole (metaphysics) or about the value of things in the world (ethics and aesthetics).

Philosophy has no propositions. Properly speaking, philosophy is the activity of clarifying language, and the correct method in philosophy is to remain silent and only to speak up to correct people who misuse language. Since Wittgenstein has already asserted that only propositions that depict facts in the world have meaning, he concludes that all the propositions in the *Tractatus* are meaningless. They are like a ladder that one can cast away once one has climbed up it. He concludes with the mystical reflection, "What we cannot speak about we must pass over in silence."

Analysis

The *Tractatus* opposes Frege and Russell's universalist conception of logic. In the universalist view, logic is the supremely general set of laws, the foundation on which the edifice of knowledge is built. Wittgenstein, by contrast, argues that logic is not a set of laws at all. Logic is not distinct from the sciences simply by virtue of being more general but by virtue of being something entirely different altogether from the sciences. According to Wittgenstein, logic has no laws, and there are no logical objects or relations. The assumption that there must be laws, objects, and relations is a holdover from the assumption that logic is like the sciences, only more general. Laws, objects, and relations are the content of a body of knowledge, and according to Wittgenstein, logic is all form and no content. If the universalist conception sees logic as the foundation on which the edifice of knowledge is built, Wittgenstein sees logic as the metallic framework around which the edifice is structured. Logic itself says nothing, but it determines the form and structure of everything that can be spoken about.

Relying on the say–show distinction, the *Tractatus* draws strict limits to what can be said intelligibly. Wittgenstein limits the sayable to empirical propositions: language is suited to describing facts in the world. By contrast, we cannot say anything that speaks about the world as a whole, that speaks about value, or that purports to speak from a perspective outside the world. Consequently, metaphysics, ethics, aesthetics, and most of philosophy go out the window. Wittgenstein does not claim that these things are useless, simply that language is unsuited to dealing with them. For instance, the attitude we hold toward the world and the way we go about living expresses our ethical worldview. Wittgenstein criticizes the notion that this worldview can be put into words in the form of ethical maxims or laws and still remain meaningful. For him, our ethical worldview can only be shown and cannot be said. In asserting that most of what we consider philosophy lies beyond the limits of what can be said, Wittgenstein reconceives the role of philosophy. Philosophy should stand as a watchdog at the limits of what can be said and correct those who try to say the unsayable.

The final few self-refuting propositions of the *Tractatus* are the subject of great scholarly controversy. What should we make of Wittgenstein's claim that all the propositions in the *Tractatus* are nonsense? One school of thought takes the *Tractatus* to be the last word in nonsense, so to speak. According to this interpretation, the propositions of the *Tractatus* are nonsense, strictly speaking, but it is only by understanding them that we can recognize that they are nonsense. Although they are nonsense, the propositions of the *Tractatus* point to deeper truths, and once we have recognized these deeper truths we can reject the *Tractatus* along with all the other nonsense that makes up philosophy. An alternative school of thought rejects this previous interpretation as being too soft. If the propositions of the *Tractatus* are nonsense, then they are nonsense, and that is all there is to it. The important thing, according to this second interpretation, is to grasp the frame of mind that would think that these propositions make sense and, by grasping it, to recognize the inconsistency of this frame of mind. According to this view, the propositions of the *Tractatus* do not point to deeper truths. There are no deeper truths, and we can only appreciate this once we have grasped that the propositions of the *Tractatus* are nonsense.

THE BLUE AND BROWN BOOKS

Summary

The *Blue and Brown Books* are transcripts of lecture notes Wittgenstein gave to his students in the early 1930s, shortly after returning to philosophy. They are so named because of the color of the paper in which they were originally bound.

The *Blue Book* criticizes the idea that the meaning of a word resides in some sort of mental act or act of interpretation. Calling meaning a "mental" act is just a means of obscuring the matter. If the meaning of language is a matter of how we use words, we could just as easily say that meaning resides in the voice box as in the head. Rather than identify meaning with a mental act, Wittgenstein identifies meaning with use: the meaning of a word is determined by the way we use it and nothing more.

Wittgenstein attacks the philosophical "craving for generality" that leads philosophers to try to make the most general claims without properly considering particulars. This craving leads philosophers to make such general claims as the Heraclitean doctrine that "all is in flux." Such claims amount to redefinitions: if all is in flux, for instance, the word *stable* ceases to have meaning. In their attempts to make grand metaphysical pronouncements, philosophers really just twist language out of shape.

Philosophers also often fail to distinguish between physical impossibility and grammatical impossibility, drawing on false analogies. If A has his mouth closed, it is physically impossible to know whether A has a gold tooth. Analogously, we might say that it is impossible to feel A's toothache and conclude that the feeling of A's toothache is a piece of knowledge to which we do not have access. In fact, feeling A's toothache is a grammatical impossibility: the grammar of the word *toothache* is such that only the person who has the toothache can feel it. If we think that our knowledge is somehow incomplete because we are unable to feel the pains of others, we are simply showing that we have allowed ourselves to become confused about the grammar of certain words. Toothaches are things that people feel when they have them. Toothaches are not objects of knowledge that we can know or not know.

The *Brown Book* develops Wittgenstein's concept of a "language game," in which he devises simpler forms of language to examine more closely the contrasts between different kinds of words. The upshot of these experiments is to show that most attempts to draw general theories of language are misguided and to draw our attention to the diversity of the uses and functions of words. Wittgenstein also examines the many different uses of such words as *compare*, *recognize*, and *understand*, showing that they have a variety of uses, all of which are related, but not in any definite way. He calls the relations among the various uses of a word *family resemblances* because, like the members of a family, the uses of a word share a certain resemblance, but that resemblance, is not based in any single feature.

The *Brown Book* contains a number of other significant ideas that are developed further in the *Philosophical Investigations*. Wittgenstein discusses rule following, arguing that there is no rock-bottom justification for the rules we follow and that we need not consciously follow or interpret a rule every time we obey a rule. He discusses the word *can* and the way that misunderstandings regarding this word give us mistaken notions about the past and future. He also discusses the distinction between *seeing* and *seeing as*, arguing that we can see a bunch of squiggles on a page *as* a face, but we cannot see a fork *as* a fork, since no alternative presents itself. In other words, when philosophers speak of seeing things "as themselves," in the sense of seeing things in their

CHAPTER 18
WITTGENSTEIN

essence, such statements have no meaning. For example, it would not make sense to speak of seeing someone "as a human being" or "as a person"—there's no difference between that and how we normally see people.

Analysis

The *Blue and Brown Books* represent a strong repudiation of some of the central ideas of the *Tractatus Logico-Philosophicus*. Wittgenstein's philosophy from the *Blue Book* onward is often referred to as his "later philosophy," in contrast to the "early philosophy" of the *Tractatus*. While the *Tractatus* argues that language corresponds to reality by virtue of sharing a common logical form, Wittgenstein's later philosophy abandons the idea of any abstract link between language and reality. Instead, Wittgenstein asserts that language has meaning simply by virtue of how it is used. Unlike the *Tractatus,* Wittgenstein's later philosophy does not present a grand, tidy theory that explains how everything falls into place. Instead, the later philosophy is profoundly antitheoretical and unapologetically asserts that there is no way to tidy up the various aspects of language and experience into a single, unified whole. However, the similarities between Wittgenstein's early work and his later work are possibly more revealing than the differences. Throughout his work, Wittgenstein asserts his conviction that the problems of philosophy only arise through confusion and that a proper understanding of the matter at hand will not answer philosophical problems so much as it will make the problems vanish.

The *Brown Book* marks the peak of Wittgenstein's interest in language games and their usefulness as a tool for attacking the idea of fixed meaning. Wittgenstein is wary of theories of language, fearing that they are too simplistic. Any attempt at discussing how words have meaning is liable to assert that there is a single, fundamental link between language and reality and that through this link the meanings of words are fixed in place. One of Wittgenstein's fundamental ideas is that words do not have fixed meanings but rather carry a family of related meanings. Wittgenstein develops the concept of language games as a tool for counteracting the tendency toward theorizing about language. Whereas theories of language seek to find unity in diversity, language games are diverse by their very nature. Wittgenstein invents series upon series of simpler forms of language, not to highlight the commonalities among all of them but to reveal the irresolvable differences among them. Language games are his tool for showing that no single theory of language can possibly account for the diversity of linguistic phenomena.

PHILOSOPHICAL INVESTIGATIONS

Summary

We are often tempted to think that language is fundamentally a relationship between names and objects. The danger is that we may conclude that the name–object relationship is the fundamental link that connects language to the world. In fact, names of objects can only be identified as such when we contrast them with other kinds of words, such as words for colors, prepositions, numbers, and the like. The supposedly fundamental relation between names and objects only makes sense within the broader context of language and cannot be abstracted from it. The meaning of words is determined not by an abstract link between language and reality but by how words are used.

By talking about meaning in the abstract, we are tempted to think of the meanings of words as fixed, with definite limits. However, the meanings of words are often vague and fluid without being any less useful as a result. Wittgenstein takes the example of *game*, showing that there is no rigid definition that includes everything we consider a game and excludes everything we do not consider a game, but we nevertheless have no difficulty in using the word *game* correctly. As far as Wittgenstein is concerned, ordinary language is perfectly adequate as it is. His aim is not to show the underlying structure of language but rather to show that all attempts at digging beneath the surface of language lead to unwarranted theorizing and generalization.

One of Wittgenstein's primary targets in the *Philosophical Investigations* is the language of psychology. We are tempted to think that words like *understanding, meaning, thinking, intending,* and the like denote mental states or processes. Wittgenstein conducts what he calls a "grammatical investigation," looking closely at the way these words are used to show that the criteria we use for judging whether someone has, for example, understood how to play chess have nothing to do with that person's mental state and everything to do with that person's behavior. That is not to label Wittgenstein as a behaviorist: he is trying to show the inevitable flaws in any theory of the mind, not to set up an alternative theory of his own.

Our language and customs are fixed not by laws so much as by what Wittgenstein calls "forms of life," referring to the social contexts in which language is used. In other words, the most fundamental aspect of language is that we learn how to use it in social contexts, which is the reason why we all understand each other. We do not understand each other because of a relationship between language and reality. Wittgenstein gives the example of a student who obeys the rule "add 2" by writing 1004 after 1000 and insisting that this is a correct application of the rule. In such an instance, there is nothing we can say or do to persuade the student otherwise because the misunderstanding lies at a deeper level than explanation can reach. Such examples do not occur in ordinary life not because there is some perfectly unambiguous explanation for "add 2" but because we share forms of life: people, on the whole, simply understand one another, and if this basic understanding were missing, communication would be impossible.

Elaborating on his view that language functions according to shared norms and forms of life, Wittgenstein denies the possibility of a private language. That is, it is inconceivable that someone could invent a language for his or her own private use that describes his or her inner sensations. In such a language, there would be no criteria to determine whether a word had been used correctly, so the language would have no meaning. Wittgenstein illustrates this point by arguing that the sentence, "I know I am in pain" makes no sense. The claim to know something carries with it further baggage that is inapplicable when talking about our own sensations. To claim to know something, we must also be able to doubt it, we must have criteria for establishing our knowledge, there must be ways other people can find out, and so on—all of which is absent when dealing with our inner sensations.

The last 300 sections of part I, as well as part II, of the *Investigations* deal with a number of related issues but lack a general thrust. Wittgenstein attacks the idea that we have privileged knowledge of our own mental states, suggesting that our relation to our mental states is not one of knowledge at all. This suggestion diminishes the thrust of "other minds skepticism," the philosophical claim that we have only imperfect knowledge of other minds, which is based on the premise that the subject is the only one with privileged knowledge of his or her own mind. Part II deals primarily with the grammar of the word *see*, discussing, among other things, the distinction between *see* and *see as*. We do not see a fork *as* a fork: we simply see the fork. The word *as* implies an act of interpretation, and we do not interpret what we see except in those cases where we really do entertain more than one possible interpretation.

Analysis

The philosophy that Wittgenstein preaches and practices in the *Investigations* is concerned primarily with dissolving problems rather than solving them. A philosophical problem, in Wittgenstein's view, is not a difficult question for which we must search long and hard for an answer. Rather, a philosophical problem is a mental knot we create by thinking theoretically, and untying it requires considerable mental clarity. For example, in the early sections of the *Investigations*, Wittgenstein criticizes the idea that there is a fundamental, abstract link between names and objects, but he does not criticize this theory in order to replace it with some other theory of language. Rather, he wants us to recognize that, when we consider language in the right light, there is no need to develop a theory to explain the connection between language and reality at all. Some commentators have observed that the *Investigations* is therapeutic in its aim. A therapist does not attempt to solve a patient's problems but rather attempts to help to shift the thinking of a patient so that the problems no longer seem like problems. Similarly Wittgenstein aims to shift our philosophical thinking so that the problems of philosophy no longer seem like problems.

Wittgenstein repeatedly draws our attention to the subtle line between everyday speech and philosophical theorizing—a line that he believes most philosophers cross unconsciously. Scientific disciplines, among others, have a very specific specialized vocabulary: a physicist uses words like *electron* and *gluon* to refer to phenomena that are distinct to the field of physics and are

CHAPTER 18
WITTGENSTEIN

unfamiliar to everyday experience. Philosophy, by contrast, carries the conceit of drawing only on familiar, everyday experience. (Philosophers may use specialized or unfamiliar words, but the things they talk about, such as knowledge and certainty, are things with which we are all familiar.) A skeptical argument, such as that in Descartes' first *Meditation*, draws its strength from beginning with ordinary observations that no one could deny and then reaching startling conclusions. If philosophy, unlike physics, has no specialized data and draws only on the world of everyday experience, then philosophers are in no position to draw up a specialized vocabulary and complex theories. The field of philosophy has something suspicious about it, in that it makes no claims to have specialized data and yet claims to be a form of specialized knowledge. Wittgenstein's response to this fact is to identify the purported specialized knowledge of philosophy as consisting of confusion and to reconceive the role of philosophy as clarifying precisely that sort of confusion.

One of Wittgenstein's main targets is the mental realm and the very idea of a sharp distinction between "inner" and "outer." When we think of inner and outer as two distinctive, parallel realms, we are tempted to think that the kinds of understanding we have about the outer world should apply similarly to our inner lives. There must be inner states and processes about which we can have knowledge or fail to have knowledge, and this knowledge must be based on some sort of data, and so on. Wittgenstein devotes a great deal of the *Investigations* to showing how these parallels between inner and outer break down. The relation a person has with his or her own inner life is far more intimate than the kind of knowledge-based relation we have with the world around us, but this more intimate relation does not simply translate as knowledge with greater certainty. Rather, it is the kind of relation with regard to which talk of knowledge and certainty, and language more generally, loses its hold. Much of our confusion as regarding psychology comes from attempts to theorize or speak about the mind using false analogies.

ON CERTAINTY

Summary

On Certainty is a series of notes Wittgenstein took toward the end of his life on matters related to knowledge, doubt, skepticism, and certainty. Although the notes are not organized into any coherent whole, certain themes and preoccupations recur throughout.

On Certainty takes as its starting point Wittgenstein's response to a paper given by G. E. Moore called "A Proof of the External World." In this paper, Moore tries to prove that there is a world external to our senses by holding up his hand and saying "here is a hand." Wittgenstein admires the boldness of Moore's approach, which implicitly questions the reasonableness of doubting such a claim, but he suggests that Moore fails because his claim that he *knows* he has a hand automatically invites the question of how he knows, a question that would embroil Moore in the sort of skeptical debate he wishes to avoid.

The idea of doubting the existence of a world external to our senses gains a foothold from the fact that any knowledge claim can be doubted, and every attempt at justification of a knowledge claim can also be doubted. Traditional epistemology has sought a bedrock of certain knowledge—knowledge that is immune to all possible doubt. But from Descartes to Moore, this search has always come across problems.

Wittgenstein asserts that claims like "here is a hand" or "the world has existed for more than five minutes" have the form of empirical propositions but in fact have more in common with logical propositions. That is, these sorts of propositions may seem to say something factual about the world, and hence be open to doubt, but really the function they serve in language is to serve as a kind of framework within which empirical propositions can make sense. In other words, we take such propositions for granted so that we can speak about the hand or about things in the world—these propositions aren't meant to be subjected to skeptical scrutiny. At one point, Wittgenstein compares these sorts of propositions to a riverbed, which must remain in place for the river of language to flow smoothly, and at another, he compares them to the hinges of a door, which must remain fixed for the door of language to serve any purpose. The key, then, is not to claim certain knowledge of propositions like "here is a hand" but rather to recognize that these sorts of propositions lie beyond questions of knowledge or doubt.

Analysis

Wittgenstein does not try to refute skeptical doubts about the existence of an external world so much as try to sidestep them, showing that the doubts themselves do not do the work they are meant to do. By suggesting that certain fundamental propositions are logical in nature, Wittgenstein gives them a structural role in language: they define how language, and hence thought, works. "Here is a hand" is an ostensive definition, meaning that it defines the word by showing an example. That statement explains how the word *hand* is to be used rather than making an empirical claim about the presence of a hand. If we begin to doubt these sorts of propositions, then the whole structure of language, and hence thought, comes apart. If two people disagree over whether one of them has a hand, it is unclear whether they can agree on anything that might act as a common ground on which they can debate the matter. Communication and rational thought are only possible between people when there is some sort of common ground, and when one doubts such fundamental propositions as "here is a hand," that common ground shrinks to nothing. Skeptical doubts purport to take place within a framework of rational debate, but by doubting too much, they undermine rationality itself and so undermine the very basis for doubt.

Behind Wittgenstein's belief that "here is a hand" is an odd proposition, either to assert or to doubt, lies his insistence on the importance of context. The very idea of doubting the existence of the external world is a very philosophical activity. A philosopher can doubt away, but it is impossible to live out this sort of skepticism. In essence, skepticism only has a foothold when we abstract it from the activity of everyday life. Similarly, skepticism gains its foothold by doubting propositions like "here is a hand" when these propositions are abstracted from the activity of everyday life. According to Wittgenstein, a proposition has no meaning unless it is placed within a particular context. "Here is a hand," by itself, means nothing, though those words might come to have meaning in the context of an anatomy class or of a parent teaching a child to speak. However, once we give propositions a particular context, the doubts cast by a skeptic lack the kind of generality that would throw the very existence of the external world into doubt. Only by removing language from all possible contexts, and hence rendering language useless, can skepticism function.

Your friend Monica, a robotics genius, is attempting to build the world's first talking robot. She invites you over to her laboratory to witness its progress. LUDWIG3000 can point to and name forty different objects around the laboratory. "And he can learn new words too!" Monica points to a desk and says, "Desk." LUDWIG3000 repeats, "Desk." "I've succeeded!" she exclaims happily. What do you think of that claim? Has Monica succeeded in building a true, talking robot?

When we teach small children to speak, we often do so through pointing, reciting, and repeating. We gesture toward a cat and say "Cat," then prompt the child to repeat the word. Often, however, that child gets so excited about her new word that she tries to use it all the time. She points to a dog and says "Cat!" or she runs up to the refrigerator and yells "Cat!" Each time, an adult has to say, "No, that's a dog," or "That's a refrigerator." Eventually she begins to learn, though she will still call a tiger or a lion a cat every now and again.

Parents and teachers base this model of language acquisition on the Augustinian picture of language. St. Augustine believed that words were, in essence, names and that each individual word pointed like an arrow to a specific thing in the real world. Thus, it becomes possible to teach language ostensively, or through pointing. Eventually students would learn to associate the proper word with the proper object, and language proficiency would be achieved. Monica has been relying on this routine to teach LUDWIG3000 how to speak English. However, as Wittgenstein showed, the Augustinian picture doesn't sufficiently explain human language capabilities.

For one thing, LUDWIG could learn to name every specific object in the laboratory and still not have learned language. Wittgenstein noted that there are things and concepts that exist but simply cannot be pointed to. How would you ostensively define *tomorrow* for LUDWIG? You could point at tomorrow's date on a calendar, but that would be pointing at a graphical representation of tomorrow, not tomorrow itself. Similarly, language has words that do not

Student Essay

express a single, unified referent. When we say the word *love*, for example, we know that single word has myriad meanings. We could mean romantic love, sexual love, love for the family, or love for our favorite television show. It would be impossible to draw a single arrow from the word *love*. Consequently, Wittgenstein insisted on the importance of context in understanding spoken utterances. The ability to grasp these complicated webs of meaning requires the ability to think abstractly, and it remains unclear whether LUDWIG has that capability.

Augustine believed that language was a map of reality and that it followed fixed and unchanging rules. Wittgenstein believed instead that language was a game, which we learn to play as we grow up within a given culture. Like all games, language has rules—it's just that the rules are forever changing without explicit warning. Think of the little girl who has learned the word *cat*. When she becomes an adult, she may indeed want to call a lion or a tiger a "cat" to emphasize the similarities between the different species. Or she might say, "Time is a cat," because time is stealthy and quick. The same woman might refer to a seemingly tough guy at her office as "a real pussycat." A mature language user would understand each of these expressions as proper uses of the word *cat*, even though none of them refers to an actual house cat. The potential for confusion always exists in language games, though we play with greater ease as we grow more experienced.

I would congratulate my friend for having planted the seeds of language in LUDWIG3000, but I would not say that he has mastered or even truly learned language any more than I would claim a toddler can speak English. For that to be the case, LUDWIG would have to move far beyond the infantile, ostensive stage of language.

Jean-Paul Sartre

(1905–1980)

19

Jean-Paul Sartre was born in Paris on June 21, 1905, the only child of Anne-Marie and Jean-Baptiste Sartre. Both of his parents came from prominent families. Sartre's paternal grandfather was a celebrated physician, and his maternal grandfather, Karl "Charles" Schweitzer, was a respected writer on topics of religion, philosophy, and languages. In 1906, Sartre's father died of entercolitis, a disease he'd contracted on a voyage to China while in the navy. After the death, Sartre and his mother moved into the highly disciplined home of Sartre's grandfather, Karl Schweitzer. Sartre maintained a complicated relationship with his grandfather throughout his childhood. Like his mother, the young Sartre resented Schweitzer's domineering presence and fallacious religiosity. However, Sartre was at least mildly receptive to the tutoring of his grandfather, who had recognized early on Sartre's lively, unique mind.

In 1924, Sartre enrolled at the École Normale Supérieure (ENS), an elite French university. In 1928, he made the acquaintance of a classmate named Simone de Beauvoir, who would become his lifelong companion and go on to become a tremendously important thinker herself. Her most famous work, *The Second Sex*, is regarded as one of the seminal texts of feminist thought. Although Sartre and de Beauvoir never married and never maintained an exclusive romantic relationship, they remained close both intellectually and emotionally until Sartre's death in 1980.

After finishing his studies at ENS, Sartre served briefly in the army, then accepted a teaching position at a high school in northwest France. In 1933, Sartre left for Berlin to study under the eminent German philosopher Edmund Husserl, a thinker who contributed greatly to the synthesis of Sartre's own philosophy. While in Berlin, Sartre also became acquainted with the work and, briefly, the person of Martin Heidegger, another leader of twentieth-century philosophy who also greatly influenced Sartre. In 1938, Sartre published *Nausea*, a philosophical novel heavily imbued with the ideas and themes of Husserl's philosophy.

At the start of World War II, Sartre was once again conscripted into the military. He was captured by the Nazis in June 1940 and held as a prisoner of war until March 1941, when he escaped and returned to Paris. There, he joined the French Resistance to Nazi occupation. During the months he spent in captivity, Sartre began work on what would become his magnum opus, the sprawling classic of existentialism entitled *Being and Nothingness*. Published in 1943, the work made Sartre famous and brought his existentialist philosophy to the forefront of the intellectual conversation that followed the war.

As an editor of the journal *Les Temps Moderne*, which was first published in 1945, Sartre had a constant and immediate outlet for his ideas, which evolved considerably over time as they adapted to the social and political context of the world in the decades that followed the war. While many of his peers, notably Albert Camus, supported America and its Western European allies in the Cold War, Sartre was a devoted socialist and stood with the Soviet Union. Although Sartre condemned the more totalitarian elements of Sovietism, in particular its imperialist authoritarian side, he believed that the proletariat, or working class, was better off there than anywhere in the capitalist West.

In seeking to unite his philosophical and political beliefs, Sartre maintained a firm belief in the idea that both literature and philosophy are inherently political, in function if not in content. He believed that the author or the artist must always create with the hope of changing the social order. Sartre himself enthusiastically lent his name and his writing to many causes, including, most famously, the struggle to end French colonialism in Africa.

In the last decades of his life, Sartre was perhaps better known for his leftist political beliefs than for the existentialist philosophy that had elevated him to iconic status in France and throughout Europe. In the 1960s, student radicals in both Europe and America embraced Sartre as a hero and appropriated him as a symbol in their resistance to war, imperialism, and other reactionary cultural–political forces. However, Sartre was never much more than an icon of the counterculture. Until his death in 1980, he remained a tremendously prolific and outspoken writer and embodied the conviction that philosophy, if it is to be serious, must be lived.

Sartre's basic philosophy, existentialism, is neither a narrowly definable school of thought nor limited to Sartre and his French contemporaries such as Camus. Although in a certain sense Sartre and Camus were the first to name and define existentialism, it is best understood as a long-running current in Europe's philosophical history—a current that emerged in the late nineteenth century. Existentialist philosophers believe that philosophy should emphasize the individual human experience of the world, and they consider ideas of individual freedom; individual responsibility; and how it is possible, if it is possible at all, for individual human beings to act meaningfully in the world.

CHAPTER 19
SARTRE

Themes, Arguments & Ideas

THE GIFT AND CURSE OF FREEDOM

In the early phase of his career, Sartre focused mainly on his belief in the sanctity of every individual consciousness, a consciousness that results from each person's subjective and individual experience of the world. He was particularly attuned to the ways that people are objectified by the gaze of others. As Sartre became more intimately involved in the concrete political questions of his day, he came to focus more on the various larger social structures that systematically objectify people and fail to recognize or affirm their individual consciousness and innate freedom. These structures include capitalist exploitation, colonialism, racism, and sexism.

Sartre's focus on individual freedom shaped his view of Marxism. Politically, Sartre was for many years closely allied to the French Communist Party. However, he never actually joined the party, largely because of his ever-present suspicion of authoritarian states and institutions of all kinds, especially after the Soviet invasion of Hungary in 1956. Sartre always harbored a libertarian or anarchist streak. He wanted the working class collectively to overthrow the capitalist system and believed that any political struggle should affirm and allow for the individual freedom of all human beings. In accordance with this view, Sartre never accepted Marx's view that economic and social realities define consciousness. Rather, Sartre affirmed that people are *always* essentially free. No matter how objectified they may be, the gifts of freedom and consciousness mean that they always have the possibility of making something out of their circumstance of objectification. In Sartre's view, individual freedom of consciousness is humanity's gift—as well as its curse, since with it comes the responsibility to shape our own lives.

THE BURDEN OF RESPONSIBILITY

Sartre believed in the essential freedom of individuals and also believed that as free beings, people are responsible for all elements of themselves, their consciousness, and their actions. That is, with total freedom comes total responsibility. He believed that even those people who wish not to be responsible, who declare themselves not responsible for themselves or their actions, are still making a conscious choice and are thus responsible for anything that happens as a consequence of their inaction. Sartre's moral philosophy maintains that ethics are essentially a matter of individual conscience. Sartre reveals much about his own ethics in his writings about oppressive societal structures and the ways in which individuals might ideally interact with each other to affirm their respective humanities, but he is dismissive of any version of universal ethics. He is clear in his belief that morals are always first and foremost a matter of subjective, individual conscience.

THE DIFFICULTY OF KNOWING THE SELF

For Sartre, for any individual to claim "that's just the way I am" would be a statement of self-deception. Likewise, whenever people internalize the objectified identity granted to them by other people or by society, such as servile woman or dutiful worker, they are guilty of self-deception. Every individual person is a "being-for-itself" possessed of self-consciousness, but he or she does not possess an essential nature and has only a consciousness and a self-consciousness, which are eternally changeable. Whenever people tell themselves that their nature or views are unchangeable, or that their social position entirely determines their sense of self, they are deceiving themselves. Sartre believed it is *always* possible to make something out of what one has been made into. This task of self-actualization, however, involves a complex process of recognizing the factual realities outside of one's self that are acting on the self (what Sartre calls *facticity*) and exactly how those realities are working, as well as knowing fully that one possesses a consciousness independent of those factors.

For Sartre, the only truly authentic outlook recognizes one's true state as a being possessed of self-consciousness whose future conscious state of being is *always* a matter of choice, even as that conscious state will itself always be in flux. That is, even though we are ultimately responsible for our own consciousness, consciousness of self is never quite identical to consciousness itself. This difficult paradox—that one is responsible for one's own consciousness, even though that consciousness is never quite graspable, since it is based on nothingness—goes to the heart of Sartre's existentialism and is crucial to his conceptions of human freedom and moral responsibility.

EN-SOI (BEING-IN-ITSELF) VS. POUR-SOI (BEING-FOR-ITSELF)

Sartre defines two types, or ways, of being: *en-soi*, or being-in-itself, and *pour-soi*, or being-for-itself. He uses the first of these, *en-soi*, to describe things that have a definable and complete essence yet are not conscious of themselves or their essential completeness. Trees, rocks, and birds, for example, fall into this category. Sartre uses *pour-soi* to describe human beings, who are defined by their possession of consciousness and, more specifically, by their consciousness of their own existence—and, as Sartre writes, by their consciousness of lacking the complete, definable essence of the *en-soi*. This state of being-for-itself is not just defined by self-consciousness—it would not exist without that consciousness. In Sartre's philosophical system, the interplay and difference between these two manners of being is a constant and indispensable point of discussion.

THE IMPORTANCE AND DANGER OF THE OTHER

Following Hegel, Sartre writes that an individual person, or being-for-itself, can become cognizant of his own existence only when he sees himself being perceived by another being-for-itself. That is, we can formulate a conscious state of being and an identity only when we are confronted by others who are also possessed of that consciousness and we apprehend ourselves in relation to them. As Sartre explains, however, the encounter with the Other is tricky, at least initially, because we may first believe that in being perceived by another conscious being we are being objectified or essentialized by that being, who may appear to be regarding us only as type, appearance, or imagined essence. In turn, we may seek to regard others as definable, simple objects not possessed of individual consciousness.

The notion of the Other plays a central role in Sartre's thinking and writing about large-scale systems of social objectification, such as colonialism, racism, and sexism. Such systems enable the Other to be falsely seen as an object, a definable being-in-itself, and not as a free individual, a being-for-itself, possessed of his or her own undefinable, conscious state of being.

Summary & Analysis

Summary

The main character in the novel *Nausea* is Antoine Roquentin, a historian who has retired to a small, depressing village called Bouville. The novel is made up of Roquentin's journal entries from 1932, in which he records his ever-intensifying struggle to understand the sickening anguish that overwhelms him as he observes the world and questions its meaning.

Nausea begins with a fictional editors' note, claiming that the diary was found in Roquentin's papers, and the actual diary then begins with a brief introduction by Roquentin that explains his thoughts about diary keeping. In the entries that follow, Roquentin describes an uncomfortable feeling that plagues him from time to time—a feeling he calls "the Nausea." He describes his daily life, in which he talks to few people, has casual sexual encounters with women, and thinks occasionally of a former lover named Anny. He interacts with the town and its people, often describing them and his interactions with them. He visits the library frequently and often sees and talks to someone he calls the Self-Taught Man. He wishes to escape the feelings of despair and hopelessness that overwhelm him, but he cannot repair the disconnect he feels with reason and the comforts of humanity. Failing to find salvation in his outward pursuits, he is forced to look inward, and he describes his confusion with what the world means and the Nausea that comes and goes.

In one entry, he reports receiving a letter from Anny, requesting that he meet her at a hotel. He remembers pieces of their past together and decides he'll go to see her when she arrives in one week. In subsequent entries, he describes occasionally thinking about her as he goes about his daily life.

In conversation one day with the Self-Taught Man, Roquentin is suddenly struck by the reality of a dessert knife he is holding in his hand—the feel of the handle and blade, its appearance. Believing he suddenly understands the Nausea, he says, "Now I know: I exist—the world exists—and I know that the world exists." He is overcome by the bare reality of existence. When he examines a stone on the seashore, the root of a chestnut tree, and other objects, he is taken aback by a revelation that exposes the things as pure existence rather than the "essence" of what they are. The discovery forces Roquentin to confront what he sees as the complete meaninglessness and nauseating purity of existence.

A few entries later, Roquentin describes his meeting with Anny, who looks older now. Their encounter is awkward, and Roquentin describes feeling uncomfortable in her hotel room. Although he is initially happy to see her, eventually the conversation becomes accusatory, with both of them bringing up hurts from the past. He dreads leaving her and knows he'll probably never see her again. The next day, he finds her at the train station, but they do not speak, and her train leaves.

In an entry near the end of *Nausea*, Roquentin describes sitting in a café and spotting the Self-Taught Man at a table with two young boys. A Corsican sees the Self-Taught Man make a sexual advance to one of the boys, and he and another café patron say this isn't the first time they've seen the Self-Taught Man do this kind of thing. The Corsican punches the Self-Taught Man in the face, and though Roquentin tries to help him, the Self-Taught Man orders him away.

Roquentin ultimately discovers at least the possibility of a way out of the emptiness that consumes him. He has decided to leave Bouville and return to Paris, and, sitting in a café, he is moved by the sublime melody of a jazz recording. Roquentin the historian, a recorder of deadness, pledges to write a novel. Art, perhaps, is the way to transcend the nauseating predicament of human nothingness in the face of pure existence. As Sartre emphasizes time and again, the human condition is that of complete freedom: we are our own maker. Through creatively exercising the freedom that man is condemned to, Roquentin can perhaps find a cure for his nausea.

Analysis

Along with the short story "The Wall" (1939), which details the psychological battles of a prisoner of war facing imminent execution, *Nausea* is considered an essential example of early Sartrean existentialism. *Nausea*, Sartre's earliest substantial work, serves as an introduction to many of the philosophical themes he contemplates in later works, particularly in *Being and Nothingness*. *Nausea* also contains many allusions to phenomenology, the study of objects as we consciously experience them—a philosophy that influenced Sartre greatly, particularly in the earlier stages of his career. Today, *Nausea* endures as one of the most significant works of "philosophical fiction" produced in the twentieth century.

Although it was only his first novel and not meant as a philosophical tract, *Nausea* is remarkable for the degree to which it contains many key tenets of Sartre's mature existentialist philosophy. Most important are the concepts of *pour-soi*, or being-for-itself, and *en-soi*, or being-in-itself. Being-for-itself, represented by Roquentin, is conscious and aware of its own selfhood and existence. Being-in-itself, represented by the stone on the shore and the entire nonhuman world, is that form of being that has a definable and complete essence yet does not possess consciousness and cannot be cognizant of its own existence. In *Nausea*, when being-for-itself is confronted by being-in-itself, the former is nauseated by the latter. Being-in-itself suffocates being-for-itself. Pure being is an undifferentiated, amorphous whole that knows no lack and no emptiness. Pure being sucks everything into itself—a fact that causes the being-for-itself to experience the feeling of nausea. For Roquentin, the world external to his body is meaningless, and world within him is nothingness. The way out of this sickening feeling of despair is a mystery, but Sartre alludes to the potential of art, both in its consumption and creation, to provide a place of respite at least.

BEING AND NOTHINGNESS

Summary

Sartre introduces *Being and Nothingness*, his single greatest articulation of his existentialist philosophy, as "an essay in phenomenological ontology." Essentially, it is a study of the consciousness of being. *Ontology* means the study of being; *phenomological* means of or relating to perceptual consciousness.

In the introduction to *Being and Nothingness*, Sartre details his rejection of Kant's concept of *noumenon*. Kant was an idealist, believing that we have no direct way of perceiving the external world and that all we have access to is our ideas of the world, including what our senses tell us. Kant distinguished between phenomena, which are our perceptions of things or how things appear to us, and noumena, which are the things in themselves, of which we have no knowledge. Against Kant, Sartre argues that the appearance of a phenomenon is pure and absolute. The noumenon is not inaccessible—it simply isn't there. Appearance is the only reality. From this starting point, Sartre contends that the world can be seen as an infinite series of finite appearances. Such a perspective eliminates a number of dualisms, notably the duality that contrasts the inside and outside of an object. What we see is what we get (or, what appears is what we know).

After dispensing with the concept of the noumenon, Sartre outlines the binary distinction that dominates the rest of _Being and Nothingness_: the distinction between unconscious being (_en-soi_, being-in-itself) and conscious being (_pour-soi_, being-for-itself). Being-in-itself is concrete, lacks the ability to change, and is unaware of itself. Being-for-itself is conscious of its own consciousness but is also incomplete. For Sartre, this undefined, undetermined nature is what defines man. Since the for-itself (like man) lacks a predetermined essence, it is forced to create itself from nothingness. For Sartre, nothingness is the defining characteristic of the for-itself. A tree is a tree and lacks the ability to change or create its being. Man, on the other hand, makes himself by acting in the world. Rather than simply be, as the object-in-itself does, man, as an object-for-itself, must _actuate_ his own being.

Sartre next introduces the related truth that the being-for-itself possesses meaning only through its perpetual foray into the unknown future. In other words, a man is not essentially what one might describe him as now. For example, if he is a teacher, he is not a teacher in the way that a rock, as a being-in-itself, is a rock. In truth, the man is never an essence, no matter how much he strives at self-essentialism. The way he interprets his past and foresees his future is itself a series of choices. As Sartre explains, even if an individual can be said to have a certain physical nature, as a chair does (e.g., "he is six feet tall, and the chair two"), the individual nonetheless projects himself by ascribing meaning to, or taking meaning from, his concrete characteristics and thus negating them. The paradox here is great. The for-itself, desiring to become one within the in-itself, imposes its subjectivity on the other's objectivity. The for-itself is consciousness, yet the instant this consciousness makes its own being a question, the irreconcilable fissure between the in-itself and the for-itself is affirmed.

Sartre explains that as a conscious being, the for-itself recognizes what it is not: it is not a being-in-itself. Through the awareness of what it is not, the for-itself becomes what it is: a nothingness, wholly free in the world, with a blank canvas on which to create its being. He concludes that the for-itself is the being through which nothingness and lack enter the world, and consequently, the for-itself is itself a lack. The absence it signifies is the absence of the unattainable synthesis of the for-itself and the in-itself. The being-for-itself is defined by its knowledge of being not in-itself.

Knowing is its own form of being, even if this knowledge is only of what one is not and cannot be, rather than what one is. The human can never know being as it truly is, for to do that, one would have to be the thing itself. To know a rock, we have to be the rock (and of course, the rock, as a being-in-itself, lacks consciousness). Yet the being-for-itself sees and intuits the world through what is not present. In this way, the being-for-itself, already wholly free, also possesses the power of imagination. Even if absolute beauty (to Sartre, the absolute union of being and consciousness) cannot be apprehended, knowing it through its absence, as in the way one feels the emptiness left by a departed loved one, is its own truth.

Delving into the ways individual beings-for-itself relate to one another, Sartre argues that we, as human beings, can become aware of ourselves only when confronted with the gaze of another. Not until we are aware of being watched do we become aware of our own presence. The gaze of the other is objectifying in the sense that when one views another person building a house, he or she sees that person as simply a house builder. Sartre writes that we perceive ourselves being perceived and come to objectify ourselves in the same way we are being objectified. Thus, the gaze of the other robs us of our inherent freedom and causes us to deprive ourselves of our existence as a being-for-itself and instead learn to falsely self-identify as a being-in-itself.

In the last segment of his argument, Sartre expands on the for-itself as a being of agency, action, and creation and a being devoid of concrete foundation. To escape its own nothingness, the for-itself strives to absorb the in-itself, or even, in more profane terms, to consume it. Ultimately, however, the in-itself can never be possessed. Just as the for-itself will never realize the union of for-itself and in-itself, neither will it succeed in apprehending or devouring the alien object. Thus, at the summation of Sartre's polemic, an incredible sense of hopelessness dominates the discussion: I am a nothingness, a lack, dehumanized by the other and deceived even by myself. Yet, as Sartre continually emphasizes, I am free, I am transcendent, I am consciousness, and I make the world. How to reconcile these two ostensibly unreconcilable descriptions of human ontology is a question Sartre does not attempt to definitively answer. This avoidance of reaching a definitive point of philosophic conclusion is in many ways intentional, however, in keeping with both Sartre's personal style and the existentialist maxim that there are no theories that can make a claim to universality.

As Sartre outlines in the conclusion to his work, perhaps the most essential characteristic of being is its intrinsic absence of differentiation and diversity. Being is complete fullness of existence, a meaningless mass of matter devoid of meaning, consciousness, and knowledge. Consciousness enters the world through the for-itself and with it brings nothingness, negation, and difference to what was once a complete whole of being. Consciousness is what allows the world to exist. Without it, there would be no objects, no trees, no rivers, no rocks: only being. Consciousness always has intentionality—that is, consciousness is always conscious of something. It thus imposes itself on being-in-itself, making consciousness the burden of the for-itself and of all being. On a similar note, the for-itself at all times depends on the in-itself for its existence. In Sartre's ontology, consciousness knows what it is only through the knowledge of what it is not. Consciousness knows it is not a being-in-itself and thus knows what it is—a nothingness, a nihilation of being. Yet, to Sartre, despite the fact that the for-itself is nothing, it exists only in its relation to being and thus is its own type of *is*.

Analysis

From the beginning of *Being and Nothingness*, Sartre displays his debt to Nietzsche through his rejection of the notion of any transcendent reality knowable to humans and lying behind or beneath the appearances that make up reality. That is, the experience of appearances *is* reality. Although this does imply an emptiness, Sartre does not see it as a negative truth. Freed of the search for some essential form being, we, as conscious beings (all beings-for-itself), are empowered in knowing that our personal, subjective experience of the world is all the truth there is. We are the ultimate judge of being and nonbeing, truth and falsity.

The key concepts of Sartre's vision of the world are the being-in-itself and the being-for-itself. One way of understanding how they relate to each other is to think of being-in-itself as another word for *object* and the being-for-itself as another word for *subject*. The being-in-itself is something that is defined by its physical characteristics, whereas the subject is defined by consciousness, or nonphysical and nonessentializable attributes. These concepts overlap to a certain degree, since the being-for-itself, or subject, is also possessed of some of the physical self, or some of the attributes of an object or being-in-itself. It thus follows that sometimes a being-for-itself can be harmfully and mistakenly regarded as a being-in-itself.

The interaction of beings possessed of consciousness is a major focus for Sartre, and as he describes a being-for-itself to interact with another being-for-itself, the key concepts are "the gaze" and "the other." Without question, in Sartre's view the gaze of the other is alienating. Our awareness of being perceived not only causes us to deny the consciousness and freedom inherent to us but also causes us to recognize those very qualities in our counterpart. Consequently, we are compelled to see the other who looks at us as superior, even if we recognize his gaze as ultimately dehumanizing and objectifying. In response to the gaze of the other, we assert ourselves as free and conscious and attempt to objectify the individual who objectifies us, thus reversing the relationship. The pattern of relations Sartre describes appears frequently in society. The assertion of freedom and transcendence by one party often results in the repression of those conditions in another. Race-based slavery and the treatment of women by men in patriarchal societies are two obvious examples.

Sartre brings up the ethical implications of the ontological vision set forth in *Being and Nothingness* only at the end of the work. In later works, notably the famous lecture "The Humanism of Existentialism," Sartre attempts to outline a philosophy of ethics based on an existentialist study of the nature of being. In short, he argues that values are never objective, as they are created by the choices and actions of free individuals. Herein lies the room for hope that Sartre inserts into a work so full of nothingness and lack: freedom is humanity's curse as well as its blessing, and what we make of that freedom is our own. In it lies great and indeterminate possibility.

NO EXIT

Summary

Sartre published the play *No Exit* in 1944, just as World War II was reaching its end. The play details the interactions of three people, Garcin, Inez, and Estelle, who are confined within a room in hell. The drama essentially serves as a backdrop for an exploration of Sartre's philosophical themes, notably the objectifying gaze of the other, self-deception, bad faith, and issues surrounding human freedom and responsibility.

The play begins with Garcin's arrival in hell, which appears to be a drawing room. A valet shows Garcin around, pointing out a bell that Garcin can use to summon the valet if needed. The valet warns, however, that the bell does not always work. A woman named Inez soon arrives, and she thinks Garcin is a torturer. She says his mouth is grotesque. The valet eventually brings in another woman, Estelle, and says no one else will arrive. Estelle insults the appearance of the room.

Garcin, Inez, and Estelle discuss how and when they died, but they initially refuse to confess their crimes. They hint at what they did by describing the moral principles behind their actions but not revealing the actions themselves.

The three eventually realize that although there are no physical torments and no actual torturer in hell, they have been put together to torment each other. There are no mirrors in the room, so each of them is seen only by the other two, not by him- or herself. They can neither avoid one another's gaze nor escape one another's judgment. They begin to tell the truths about themselves and what they did to be sent to hell: Garcin was executed by the army because he tried to leave the country without fighting, Inez was killed by a widow whom she taunted about the widow's husband's death, and Estelle threw her baby off a balcony.

The dynamics of the group become complex as each begins asking things of the others. Inez makes a sexual advance toward Estelle, who refuses her. Estelle expresses her desire to be with Garcin, and Garcin reciprocates. However, he stops short of kissing her and says he wants her trust. He asks Estelle if he was a coward for running from the army and expresses doubt about the rightness of his actions. He asks Estelle to have faith in him. Estelle says he loves him, and Garcin says they will climb out of hell. Inez warns Garcin that Estelle is lying. Garcin dismisses both women in disgust.

Garcin then approaches the door, searching for an escape. He rings the bell to summon the valet, but it doesn't work. As he continues pounding on the door, Estelle begs him not to leave and says she'll go with him.

The door swings open, and Inez taunts Garcin that he can now leave. However, he finds he doesn't want to, and the women hesitate as well. Estelle tries to convince Inez to leave so she and Garcin can be alone, but Garcin says he will stay because of Inez. He wishes to convince her he is not a coward. Garcin pledges that he will not leave unless Inez pronounces her faith in him. She does not, and Garcin, unable to exercise his freedom, instead chooses imprisonment. He concludes, "Hell is—other people!"

Inez reminds the other two that she is dead and stabs herself repeatedly with a knife. The three laugh, realizing they'll be in hell together forever.

Analysis

Both *No Exit* and *The Flies*, Sartre's other dramatic work of the period, which was published and performed during the German occupation of Paris, endure today as essential examples of the artistic response to World War II. Many people argue that the room in hell, occupied by Garcin, Inez, and Estelle, is a metaphor for the Nazi occupation of Paris. Although this is an overly simplistic interpretation in many respects, without question the play was influenced by the political realities of the time. In Paris during the war, a strong and profound resistance, of which Sartre was a part, served as an ever-present antidote to German militarism. At least in that instance, the people demonstrated their collective will for freedom. The characters in *No Exit*, save Inez, have resigned themselves to an (after)life characterized by a lack of freedom and the ubiquitous presence of alienation and despair. As in many Sartrean narratives, beyond all the deep cynicism of human existence and human relations, there exists a small but potentially liberating seed of hope.

Aside from these common characteristics, the other essential philosophical theme exhibited in the play relates to the politics and psychology of the gaze of the other, or the ways people recognize one another and formulate identities. As Sartre details in *Being and Nothingness*, the other perceives the subject of its gaze as a being-in-itself, robbing it of the freedom to create its own essence. As such, the characters in the drama search for mirrors so that they might avoid the dehumanizing stare of the other. However, as they have come to view themselves as objects being perceived above all else, a mirror will only confirm the way the other sees them. The process of degradation is complete: no longer a being-for-itself, free to create himself or herself, each character instead can see only the essentialisms that have been imposed on them. Worse, as actors in a play, Garcin, Inez, and Estelle are subject not only to the objectifying gaze of one another but also to the unflinching stare of the audience. The famous conclusion to the play, "hell is—other people," is certainly a misleading phrase if one takes it as the sum of Sartre's view of the human condition. However, the play does highlight the cynical veneer of Sartre's philosophy, as the characters wallow in an atmosphere of despair from which there is indeed no easy exit.

ANTI-SEMITE AND JEW

Summary

Sartre constructs his landmark postwar analysis of anti-Semitism around four feature characters: the anti-Semite, the democrat, the authentic Jew, and the inauthentic Jew. He presents their interactions as a kind of hypothetical drama. Sartre examines how the four actors in the "drama" create the others—or more precisely, how each character both defines the others and is defined by them.

Sartre first explains that the anti-Semite character represents the most reactionary tendencies of a French cultural nationalist. He hates modernity and sees the Jew as the representative of all that is new and mysterious within society. In this way, the anti-Semite creates for himself a Jew that is representative of all that he loathes. In turn, the presence of the Jew, the object of his hatred, forms the anti-Semite and gives him his very reason for being. In perhaps the most famous passage of the work, Sartre declares that even if the Jew did not exist, the anti-Semite would create him.

Sartre then explains that the democrat is the proud upholder of the Enlightenment, a believer in reason and the natural equality of man. However, the democrat is blind to the true effects of anti-Semitism: he expounds on the virtues of the universal rights of humanity while denying the Jew his identity as a Jew. While the anti-Semite creates the Jew to destroy him, the democrat negates the Jew to pretend the problem of anti-Semitism does not exist. In Sartre's analysis of the democrat, his contempt for all things bourgeois is plainly evident, as is his rejection of the Enlightenment as the ultimate savior.

Finally, Sartre discusses the Jews themselves, who are divided into two representatives—the authentic and inauthentic Jew—who represent slightly different ways of confronting and dealing with anti-Semitism and contemporary society. Sartre describes all the Jewish people as without a civilization of their own, without a history save for martyrdom and suffering. Thus, they are the perfect candidates for assimilation, wherever they may find themselves in the Diaspora. Both the authentic Jew and the inauthentic Jew, in Sartre's view, live wholly in the present. The reason they exist in the present, as opposed to the anti-Semite, who dwells in the past, and the democrat, who inhabits the future, is that the anti-Semite has placed them firmly in the here and now. The Jew, Sartre argues, affirms his role in the drama by believing the Jewish identity that is imposed on him by the other, the anti-Semite, who acts as the oppressor.

Analysis

Toward the end of World War II, Sartre observed that no one seemed to be talking about the potential return of the French Jews deported by the Nazis. With *Anti-Semite and Jew*, Sartre sought to deconstruct the causes and effects of anti-Semitism in France. *Anti-Semite and Jew* is an extraordinarily important and ambitious work in Sartre's oeuvre. It represents an attempt to incorporate existentialist psychoanalysis into the discussion of what had traditionally been viewed as a social, cultural problem. *Anti-Semite and Jew* is also notable as one of the first works in which the Sartre's Marxism is evident, foreshadowing his later embracing of the Marxian class analysis.

Anti-Semite and Jew is also significant to Sartre's body of existentialist work for its determination to explore the idea of individual freedom in a social context that is undeniably deterministic. Sartre believed that man is inherently and totally free and that we are nothing less than the sum of the choices we make. However, social circumstance at least partially facilitates the decision-making process of the individual. *Anti-Semite and Jew* is one of the first instances in Sartre's oeuvre in which Sartre places his philosophy of freedom and ontology within the framework of contemporary social, political, and economic realities. Later works such as *Critique of Dialectical Reason* (1960) explore in greater detail the relationship between the free individual and the systemic forces that mitigate the choices he or she makes.

Anti-Semite and Jew echoes many of the themes Sartre introduced in *Being and Nothingness*. The anti-Semite endeavors to be a being-in-itself—he wants to escape from freedom, to become an anti-Semite in the way a fireplace is a fireplace. Becoming an anti-Semite is choice, and though this choice emanates from freedom, it ultimately annihilates that freedom. Both the anti-Semite and the inauthentic Jew represent identity formations that come of "bad faith," as identities symptomatic of the being-for-itself convincing itself it is no longer free, or no longer wants to be free, and is now a being-in-itself, an unconscious being that strives only to live up to the essence it has imagined for itself. In this, however, Sartre displays what some thought was a problematic anti-Semitic tendency, as he argued that the Jew, whether authentic or inauthentic, is alone in society in being eternally stuck in the present and alone in society in being wholly determined by his social context.

CRITIQUE OF DIALECTICAL REASON

Summary

The *Critique of Dialectical Reason*, published in 1960, is Sartre's greatest attempt at synthesizing his existentialist philosophy with sociological analysis. In the work, his previous focus on human freedom and responsibility is placed within a corresponding analysis of the specific structures of domination that humanity confronted in 1960. In the *Critique*, Sartre deconstructs the individual actions of capitalists and imperialists while dissecting the oppressive and suffocating institutions that uphold established political and economic structures.

Sartre states that he is a Marxist, in the sense that he believes in the aim of a classless society and the abolition of private property. However, he approaches the assumptions and dictums of Marxism with a critical eye. His implicit goal is not to show how existentialism is compatible with orthodox Marxism. Rather, in *Critique of Dialectical Reason* he offers a corrective to Marxism and demonstrates how his views on ontology and freedom can be synthesized with a new articulation of Marxist ideology.

Sartre affirms that his own dialectical philosophy shares much with its two most famous exponents—Hegel, its originator, and subsequently Marx. He shares a basic understanding with Hegel and Marx of the dialectic relationship between man the universe he inhabits. Simply put, Sartre echoes these thinkers in writing that man exists *mutually* with the world. Man affects the universe, and in turn, the universe affects man. Placed in a societal framework, the dialectic iterates that man both forms and is formed by the social, political, and economic forces that surround him. Sartre states that philosophy is born from this dialectic. The philosophy of "the moment" is simply the consciousness of the ascendant class, asserting its identity and seeking its freedom.

Regarding the Marxist philosophy of history, however, Sartre writes that he disagrees with the idea that the future is determined and that the project of man is prophesied by the history of man. He regards this idea as foolish, for as he emphasizes time and again in other works and reiterates here, man is condemned to freedom, and man is constantly becoming. Sartre affirms that the free individual certainly interacts dialectically with the world, with other individuals, and with the collective. Yet the constant and inherent complexity and transience of these relationships cannot be reduced to a simple dialectic, such as capital versus labor, that has one inevitable endpoint. This version of history is the traditional Marxist one, and Sartre has major misgivings about the determinism inherent in it.

Analysis

Although Sartre was certainly a Marxist, the *Critique of Dialectical Reason* details where his thought diverges from mainstream Marxism. Sartre questioned the more rationalist or positivist elements of Enlightenment thought, and, fittingly, he also has some misgivings about the Marxist view of history as essentially mechanistic and predictable. Sartre disagreed strongly with the idea that human consciousness is determined by material realities, such as a society's mode of production. He argues that consciousness emanates from man, the being-for-itself, and is not imposed on him by social or material realities. Consciousness is beyond matter and thus exists independently of a dialectic that views man as an object.

Sartre, as he evolved both as a philosopher and a political activist, came to focus much of his energy on changing the institutions and systems in the world that he felt were repressive for both individuals and society as a whole. During the 1960s, the Cold War rolled on, and the process of decolonization in the third world moved gingerly along. Sartre became an outspoken critic of imperialism in any form, most famously voicing his support for the Algerian resistance to French occupation. On this subject, Sartre wrote the forward to Franz Fanon's seminal anticolonial work, *The Wretched of the Earth*. In the context of the Cold War, Sartre maintained his support for the Soviet Union and developing countries, such as Cuba, that had chosen a socialist path.

Whatever inconsistencies may exist in his philosophical oeuvre, Sartre's commitment to the social and political battles he viewed as most important in his day was always impassioned and unwavering. As he expresses time and again in his philosophy, Sartre believed above all else in the innate freedom of humanity. *Critique of Dialectical Reason* is the work in which Sartre most thoroughly articulates how his philosophy, if at times abstract, is directed toward concrete change in the empirical, lived reality of individuals and societies.

Last week, despite having a new baby in the house, your brother-in-law Johnny asked your sister for a divorce. He called her from a pay phone in Dallas, saying, "It's not you, it's me. Look, I'm just not husband material. I'll end up disappointing you in the long run. That's what I always seem to do. You need someone stronger than me. We should break up now and spare ourselves any future pain." How would Sartre evaluate Johnny's actions?

Johnny presents his case in very absolute terms. "This is the way I am," he claims. "I'll never change, and I'll never improve." He implies that my sister can do nothing to affect his behavior or transform his character, so any attempt to do so would be pointless and futile. Johnny's fundamental argument is based on a conception of the self as static, stable, and unchanging. Sartre would argue that this attitude is an act of bad faith on Johnny's part and betrays an inauthentic conception of the self.

Sartre believed that fluidity and indeterminacy characterized the individual self. The being-for-itself has no essential nature, and its actions can never be accurately predicted or otherwise predetermined. The human being operates in absurdity, without the guiding influence of logical structures or systematic principles. This notion of a freewheeling and lawless existence is distressing, but it also creates the potential for true freedom. The existentialist has the terrible but exhilarating possibility of transcendence. According to Sartre, human beings bear a tremendous responsibility to this freedom.

Johnny claims to have a fixed, permanent nature and thus commits what Sartre would call an act of bad faith, or self-deception. Johnny thinks of himself as a being-in-itself, without the capacity to change or contradict his essential, inflexible nature. This attitude not only robs him of his freedom but releases him from the burden of responsibility. No one can expect Johnny to behave maturely and reasonably if his fundamental self is immature and selfish. This attitude shuts down any discussion of moral and ethical behavior, because it turns humans into unthinking, unreflecting objects without the power of choice.

Student Essay

Sartre would say that Johnny is living an inauthentic life if he truly believes he lacks the ability to change his pattern of behavior.

Although Sartre had faith in the essential freedom of the existential individual, he also understood that this individual lives under particular socioeconomic conditions. The transcendence of the self is always bounded and limited by numerous external forces, which Sartre calls *facticity*. The freedom of the individual and the pressures of facticity always work in concert to determine the current situation. Various social forces could obstruct a romantic relationship. Perhaps Johnny and my sister come from different economic classes or ethnic groups, and the disparity between them has proved too difficult to overcome. Johnny's speech, however, blames none of these external factors. Although he takes no real responsibility for his actions—in the sense that, by being passive, he's not really acting at all—Johnny admits that the inability to act lies within himself and not in the external world. He asserts that he has habitually made bad choices regarding relationships. His previous actions have a facticity to them: they are complete and cannot be changed. In Sartrean terms, the past relates to the future as the in-itself corresponds to the for-itself. The solidness of our past can feel overwhelming and immutable when compared to the haziness and indeterminacy of our present. Sometimes, accepting the past as a blueprint for the future seems easier than truly changing our course. However, no human is purely reducible to his facticity or his givens. Johnny may feel that his romantic history is something he cannot overcome, but Sartre would say that he can, and that he must. An appeal to the facticity of his past might mitigate Johnny's guilt, but he has still performed an act of bad faith.

INDEX

INDEX

and empiricism, 260
and the Enlightenment, 260
ethics, 272–273
free will and determinism, 271
Groundwork for the Metaphysic of Morals, 260
influence of, 261
judgments of taste, 273–274
morality, 271
Prolegomena to Any Future Metaphysics, 260
  analysis, 267–270
  summary, 265–267
student essay, 276–277
synthetic a priori knowledge, 263, 266–267
time and space as intuitions of the faculty of sensibility, 266–267
transcendental idealism, 262–263
Katharine of Aragon, 132
Kierkegaard, Peter, 324
Kierkegaard, Søren, 323–341
aesthetic as the first stage on life's way, 326–327
aesthetic life, 327–329
on anxiety, 326
birth of, 323
on boredom, 326
Changelessness of God, The, 325
Corsair, The, 325
death of, 325
on despair, 326, 339
early life of, 323–324
education, 324–325
Either/Or, 325, 330–334, 340–341
  analysis, 332–334
  summary, 330–332
ethical as the second stage on life's way, 327–328
on faith, 328–329
Fear and Trembling, 334–337, 341
  analysis, 336–337
  summary, 334–335
Practices in Christianity, 337
religious as third stage on life's way, 328–329
repetition and recollection, 329
Sickness Unto Death, The, 337–339
  analysis, 338–339
  summary, 337–338
student essay, 340–341

Knowledge by acquaintance, 412

L

Labor theory of value, 348–349, 358
Landolfo of Aquino, 109
Language game, 429–431
Language of psychology, 431–432
Laws, 81
Laws of Thought, 291
Laws (Plato), 10, 81
Learning, in Utopia, 141, 143
Leibniz, Gottfried Wilhelm, 95, 269
Letters Concerning Toleration (Locke), 194–195
Leviathan (Hobbes), 175–177
  analysis (chapters 1-9), 180–181
  analysis (chapters 10-14), 183–184
  analysis (chapters 17-31), 186–187
  analysis (parts III and IV), 188–189
  summary (chapters 1-9), 178–180
  summary (chapters 10-14), 181–183
  summary (chapters 17-31), 184–186
  summary (parts III and IV), 187–188
Location, 67–68
  as category, 48
Locke, John, 3, 147, 193–213, 224
  abstract generals, 201
  birth of, 193
  complex ideas, 201
  death of, 194
  degrees of knowledge, 203–204
  early life of, 193–194
  empirical theory of knowledge, 196–197
  Essay Concerning Human Understanding, An, 195, 199–208
    analysis, 205–208
  essences, 201–202
  existence of an external world, 204
  government work, 195
  on innate knowledge, 199–200
  on language, abuses, 202–203

INDEX

INDEX